Lecture Notes in Computer Science 8599

Commenced Publication in 1973
Founding and Former Series Editors:
Gerhard Goos, Juris Hartmanis, and Jan van Leeuwen

Miguel Nicolau   Krzysztof Krawiec
Malcolm I. Heywood   Mauro Castelli
Pablo García-Sánchez   Juan J. Merelo
Victor M. Rivas Santos   Kevin Sim (Eds.)

Genetic Programming

17th European Conference, EuroGP 2014
Granada, Spain, April 23-25, 2014
Revised Selected Papers

 Springer

Volume Editors

Miguel Nicolau, University College Dublin, Ireland
E-mail: miguel.nicolau@ucd.ie

Krzysztof Krawiec, Poznan University of Technology, Poznań, Poland
E-mail: krawiec@cs.put.poznan.pl

Malcolm I. Heywood, Dalhousie University, Halifax, NS, Canada
E-mail: mheywood@cs.dal.ca

Mauro Castelli, Universidade Nova de Lisboa, Portugal
E-mail: mcastelli@isegi.unl.pt

Pablo García-Sánchez, Universidad de Granada, Spain
E-mail: pablogarcia@ugr.es

Juan J. Merelo, Universidad de Granada, Spain
E-mail: jmerelo@geneura.ugr.es

Victor M. Rivas Santos, Universidad de Jaén, Spain
E-mail: vrivas@ujaen.es

Kevin Sim, Edinburgh Napier University, UK
E-mail: k.sim@napier.ac.uk

Cover illustration designed by Laura Pirovano.

ISSN 0302-9743   e-ISSN 1611-3349
ISBN 978-3-662-44302-6   e-ISBN 978-3-662-44303-3
DOI 10.1007/978-3-662-44303-3
Springer Heidelberg New York Dordrecht London

Library of Congress Control Number: 2014944310

LNCS Sublibrary: SL 1 – Theoretical Computer Science and General Issues

Typesetting: Camera-ready by author, data conversion by Scientific Publishing Services, Chennai, India

Printed on acid-free paper

Springer is part of Springer Science+Business Media (www.springer.com)

Preface

The 17th European Conference on Genetic Programming (EuroGP) took place during April 23 and 25, 2015. Granada, Spain, home to 'The Alhambra' UNESCO World Heritage Site provided the setting, with the Universidad de Granada, Departamento de Arquitectura y Tecnología de los Computadores representing the venue. EuroGP represents the only conference exclusively devoted to the evolutionary generation of computer programs and attracts scholars from all over the world. The maturity of the event is in part reflected by the fact that 'Google scholar' now lists EuroGP as one of the top 20 venues in Evolutionary Computation with an h5 index and median of 14 and 26 respectively.[1] Collectively, over 9000 articles now appear in the online GP bibliography maintained by William B. Langdon.[2]

The unique character of genetic programing has been recognized from its very beginning. EuroGP has had an essential impact on the success of the field, by serving as an important forum for expressing new ideas, meeting fellow researchers, and starting collaborations. Indeed, EuroGP represents the single largest venue at which genetic programing results are published. Many success stories have been witnessed by the now 17 editions of EuroGP. To date, genetic programing is essentially the only approach that has demonstrated the ability to automatically generate, repair, and improve computer code in a wide variety of problem areas. It is also one of the leading methodologies that can be used to 'automate' science, helping researchers to induce hidden complex models from observed phenomena. Furthermore, genetic programing has been applied to many problems of practical significance, and has produced human-competitive solutions.

EuroGP 2014 received 40 submissions from 20 different countries across 5 continents. The papers underwent a rigorous double-blind peer review process, each being reviewed by at least three members of the international Program Committee from 23 countries. The selection process resulted in this volume, with 15 papers accepted for oral presentation (37.5% acceptance rate) and 5 for poster presentation (50% global acceptance rate for talks and posters combined). The wide range of topics in this volume reflects the current state of research in the field. Thus, we see topics as diverse as search-based software engineering, image analysis, dynamical systems, evolutionary robotics and operational research to the foundations of search as characterized through semantic variation operators.

---

[1] http://scholar.google.com/citations?view_op=top_venues&hl=en&vq=eng_evolutionarycomputation

[2] http://www.cs.bham.ac.uk/~wbl/biblio/

Together with 4 other co-located evolutionary computation conferences (Evo-BIO 2014, EvoCOP 2014, EvoMusArt 2014, and EvoApplications 2014), EuroGP 2014 was part of the Evo* 2014 event. This meeting could not have taken place without the help of many people.

First to be thanked is the great community of researchers and practitioners who contributed to the conference by both submitting their work and reviewing others' as part of the Program Committee. Their hard work, in evolutionary terms, provided both variation and selection, without which progress in the field would not be possible!

The papers were submitted, reviewed and selected using the MyReview conference management software. We are sincerely grateful to Marc Schoenauer of Inria, France, for his great assistance in providing, hosting, and managing the software.

We would like to thank the local organising team: Juan Julián Merelo Guervós, Victor M. Rivas Santos, Pedro A. Castillo Valdivieso, María Isabel García Arenas, Antonio M. Mora García, Pablo García-Sánchez, Antonio Fernández Ares, and Javier Asensio. Moreover, this was the first year in which the proceedings were produced post conference. We are therefore very grateful to the local organizers for taking on the additional role of constructing the web site to host the camera ready papers for distribution to the participants during the event.

We thank Kevin Sim from the Institute for Informatics & Digital Information, Edinburgh Napier University for creating and maintaining the official Evo* 2014 website, and Pablo García-Sánchez (Universidad de Granada, Spain) and Mauro Castelli (Universidade Nova de Lisboa, Portugal) for being responsible for Evo* 2014 publicity.

We would also like to express our sincerest gratitude to our invited speakers, who gave the inspiring keynote talks: Professor Thomas Schmickl of the University of Karl-Franzens University, Graz, Austria, Professor Federico Moran of University Complutense Madrid, Spain, and Professor Susan Stepney of the University of York, UK.

We especially want to express our genuine gratitude to Jennifer Willies of the Institute for Informatics and Digital Innovation at Edinburgh Napier University, UK. Her dedicated and continued involvement in Evo* since 1998 has been and remains essential for building the image, status, and unique atmosphere of this series of events.

April 2014

Miguel Nicolau
Krzysztof Krawiec
Malcolm I. Heywood
Mauro Castelli
Pablo García-Sánchez
Juan J. Merelo
Victor M. Rivas Santos
Kevin Sim

Organization

Administrative details were handled by Jennifer Willies, Edinburgh Napier University, Institute for Informatics and Digital Innovation, Scotland, UK.

Organizing Committee

Program Co-chairs

Miguel Nicolau	University College Dublin, Ireland
Krzysztof Krawiec	Poznan University of Technology, Poland

Publication Chair

Malcolm I. Heywood	Dalhousie University, Canada

Publicity Chairs

Mauro Castelli	Universidade Nova de Lisboa, Portugal
Pablo García-Sánchez	Universidad de Granada, Spain

Local Chairs

J.J. Merelo	Universidad de Granada, Spain
Victor Manuel Rivas Santos	Universidad de Jaén, Spain

Webmaster

Kevin Sim	Edinburgh Napier University, UK

Program Committee

Alexandros Agapitos	University College Dublin, Ireland
Lee Altenberg	University of Hawaii at Manoa, USA
R. Muhammad Atif Azad	University of Limerick, Ireland
Wolfgang Banzhaf	Memorial University of Newfoundland, Canada
Mohamed Bahy Bader	University of Portsmouth, UK
Helio Barbosa	LNCC/UFJF, Brazil
Anthony Brabazon	University College Dublin, Ireland
Nicolas Bredeche	Université Pierre et Marie Curie, France
Stefano Cagnoni	University of Parma, Italy
Ernesto Costa	University of Coimbra, Portugal
Luis Da Costa	Université Paris-Sud XI, France
Antonio Della Cioppa	University of Salerno, Italy

Federico Divina	Pablo de Olavide University, Spain
Marc Ebner	Ernst-Moritz-Arndt Universität Greifswald, Germany
Aniko Ekart	Aston University, UK
Daryl Essam	University of New South Wales @ ADFA, Australia
Francisco Fernandez de Vega	Universidad de Extremadura, Spain
Gianluigi Folino	ICAR-CNR, Italy
James A. Foster	University of Idaho, USA
Christian Gagné	Université Laval, Québec, Canada
Steven Gustafson	GE Global Research, USA
Jin-Kao Hao	LERIA, University of Angers, France
Inman Harvey	University of Sussex, UK
Erik Hemberg	MIT, USA
Malcolm I. Heywood	Dalhousie University, Canada
Ting Hu	Dartmouth College, USA
David Jackson	University of Liverpool, UK
Colin Johnson	University of Kent, UK
Tatiana Kalganova	Brunel University, UK
Ahmed Kattan	Um Al Qura University, Saudi Arabia
Graham Kendall	University of Nottingham, UK
Michael Korns	Korns Associates, USA
Jan Koutnik	IDSIA, Switzerland
Krzysztof Krawiec	Poznan University of Technology, Poland
Jiri Kubalik	Czech Technical University in Prague, Czech Republic
William B. Langdon	University College London, UK
Kwong Sak Leung	The Chinese University of Hong Kong, China
John Levine	University of Strathclyde, UK
Evelyne Lutton	Inria, France
Penousal Machado	University of Coimbra, Portugal
Radek Matousek	Brno University of Technology, Czech Republic
James McDermott	University College Dublin, Ireland
Bob McKay	Seoul National University, Korea
Jorn Mehnen	Cranfield University, UK
Julian Miller	University of York, UK
Alberto Moraglio	University of Exeter, UK
Xuan Hoai Nguyen	Hanoi University, Vietnam
Miguel Nicolau	University College Dublin, Ireland
Julio Cesar Nievola	Pontificia Universidade Catolica do Parana, Brazil
Michael O'Neill	University College Dublin, Ireland
Una-May O'Reilly	MIT, USA
Fernando Otero	University of Kent, UK
Ender Ozcan	University of Nottingham, UK

Table of Contents

Oral Presentations

Posters

Higher Order Functions for Kernel Regression

Alexandros Agapitos[1], James McDermott[2], Michael O'Neill[1],
Ahmed Kattan[3], and Anthony Brabazon[2]

[1] School of Computer Science and Informatics, University College Dublin, Ireland
{alexandros.agapitos,m.oneill,anthony.brabazon}@ucd.ie
[2] School of Business, University College Dublin, Ireland
jmmcd@jmmcd.net
[3] Um Al Qura University, Dept. of Computer Science, Kingdom of Saudi Arabia
ajkattan@uqu.edu.sa

Abstract. Kernel regression is a well-established nonparametric method, in which the target value of a query point is estimated using a weighted average of the surrounding training examples. The weights are typically obtained by applying a distance-based kernel function, which presupposes the existence of a distance measure.This paper investigates the use of Genetic Programming for the evolution of task-specific distance measures as an alternative to Euclidean distance. Results on seven real-world datasets show that the generalisation performance of the proposed system is superior to that of Euclidean-based kernel regression and standard GP.

1 Introduction

One of the oldest and most commonly used nonparametric methods for function estimation is kernel regression [12]. It achieves flexibility in estimating a regression function $F(\mathbf{x})$ over the domain $\mathbb{R}^d$ by fitting a different, *local* model at each query point x_0. This is achieved by using only those observations close to x_0 in such a way that the resulting estimated function $F(\mathbf{x})$ is *smooth* in $\mathbb{R}^d$. The value of $F(x_0)$ is then computed as a weighted average of the function values observed at training inputs.

We note three substantial drawbacks of standard methods for kernel regression. First, they require an *a priori* well-defined distance metric on the input space, which may preclude their usage in datasets where such metrics are not meaningful. For example, the well-known Boston housing dataset [5] contains 13 input features representing completely disparate quantities such as population levels, crime rates, pupil-teacher ratios, etc. Similar difficulties can arise in cases of a mixture of qualitative, ordinal and numerical features. Secondly, a pre-defined distance metric may not be particularly relevant to the regression task at hand. The typical Euclidean distance is calculated on all features defining a point in $\mathbb{R}^d$. In a high-dimensional input space, the distance metric may become dominated by a large number of irrelevant features, as it ascribes to them identical weight to that of the most significant ones. The irrelevant features ideally should not contribute at all to the distance calculation. Thirdly, in

M. Nicolau et al. (Eds.): EuroGP 2014, LNCS 8599, pp. 1–12, 2014.

cases of input spaces of high-dimensionality, most neighbours of a point can be very far away, causing bias and degrading the performance of the kernel function. As a simple example [4] (Figure 1.22, page 36), consider a sphere of radius $r = 1$ in a space of D dimensions, and ask what is the fraction of a volume of the sphere that lies between radius $r = 1 - \epsilon$ and $r = 1$. It is shown that as D grows (i.e. $D > 20$), most of the volume of the sphere is concentrated in a thin shell near the surface. This causes most of the points in the feature space to be neighbours, and renders the determination of the kernel width problematic. An additional manifestation of the curse of the dimensionality for kernel regression is that it is impossible to maintain localness (low bias) and a sizeable sample in the neighbourhood (low variance) as D increases, without the training sample size increasing exponentially in D [12].

We propose a novel method to learn a problem-specific distance measure over an input space in which small distances between two vectors imply similar target values, and so we can exploit local interpolation-like techniques to allow us to make predictions of the target variables for new values of the input variables. We employ Genetic Programming (GP) [10] to learn such distance measures by searching the space of programs composed of general-purpose higher-order functions, which allow for implicit iteration over lists of feature values. Typical distance functions, such as Euclidean and other l_p distances, involve *iteration* over the multiple dimensions of the pair of input points. This feature is likely to be useful in new evolved distances also. Including the ability to iterate in our GP language makes it far more general than the constant-time numerical language typical of GP symbolic regression. Success or failure in our work therefore has implications for the broader project of evolutionary synthesis of general computer programs. It also raises the issue of halting, to be addressed by our choice of language.

The reader's guide to the rest of the paper is as follows. Section 2 formalises the method of kernel regression. Section 3 introduces the higher-order functions that will be used in the experiments. Section 4 presents the proposed method and details the experiment design. Section 5 analyses the empirical results, and finally Section 6 wraps up and sketches future research directions.

2   Kernel Regression

In the general function estimation problem, one is given a set of training examples $\{x_i, y_i\}$, $i = \{1, \ldots, N\}$, where y is the response variable and $\mathbf{x} \in \mathbb{R}^d$ is a vector of explanatory variables. The goal is to find a function $F^*(\mathbf{x})$ that maps $\mathbf{x}$ to y, such that over the joint distribution $P(\mathbf{x}, y)$ the expected value of some specified loss function $L(y, F(\mathbf{x}))$ is minimised:

$$F^*(\mathbf{x}) = \arg\min_{F(\mathbf{x})} \mathbb{E}_{x,y}[L(y, F(\mathbf{x}))] \tag{1}$$

Kernel regression or kernel smoothing [12] (page 192) uses the so called Nadaraya-Watson kernel-weighted average to fit a constant locally as follows:

$$F^*(x_0) = \frac{\sum_{i=1}^{N} K_\lambda(x_0, x_i) y_i}{\sum_{i=1}^{N} K_\lambda(x_0, x_i)} \tag{2}$$

with a *kernel* K_λ, which is typically a probability density function, defined as:

$$K_\lambda(x_0, x) = D\left(\frac{||x - x_0||}{\lambda}\right) \tag{3}$$

where $|| \cdot ||$ is the Euclidean norm, and λ is the smoothing parameter called the kernel *width*. The smoothing parameter λ determines the width of the local neighbourhood and is usually set by means of cross-validation. Large λ implies lower variance (averages over more observations) but higher bias. Constant values for λ tend to keep the bias of the estimate constant, while the variance is inversely proportionate to the local density.

The function $D(\cdot)$ is typically a positive real-valued function, which decays with increasing distance between x_0 and x. The optimal rate of decay depends on the noisiness and smoothness of the target function, the density of training examples, and the scale of the input features. A wide variety of kernel functions can be found in statistics, see [1].

The application of kernel regression to model a noisy sinusoidal function (green curve) is illustrated in Figure 1. The example uses the Epanechnikov kernel with λ set to 0.2. The fitted function (red curve) is continuous and quite smooth. As we move the target from left to right, points enter in the neighbourhood initially with weight zero, and then their contribution to the weighted average of Equation 2 slowly increases.

A general approach for constructing a task-specific distance metric in order to overcome some of the difficulties outlined in the introductory section is to use a *Mahalanobis* metric instead of the Euclidean norm in Equation 5, in which the distance between vectors x and x_0 is defined as:

$$d(x_0, x) = \sqrt{(x - x_0)^T \mathbf{A}(x - x_0)} \tag{4}$$

where $\mathbf{A}$ can be any symmetric positive semi-definite matrix (setting $\mathbf{A}$ to identity results in the standard Euclidean distance). $\mathbf{A}$ is then used to weight different features [12]. Entire coordinates can be downgraded or omitted by imposing appropriate restrictions on $\mathbf{A}$. For example, if $\mathbf{A}$ is diagonal, then we can increase or decrease the influence of individual features x_j by increasing or decreasing $\mathbf{A}_{jj}$. Various methods for adapting $\mathbf{A}$ in the Mahalanobis distance are presented in the studies of [6,7,8,11,13]. An additional method for adapting the feature weights in the calculation of Euclidean distance was originally developed for nearest-neighbour classification [3], and can be directly applied to kernel regression.

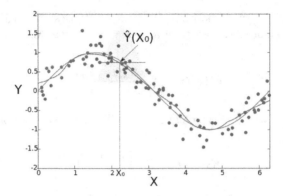

Fig. 1. Example of kernel smoothing. $\hat{Y}(x_0)$ is the fitted constant (calculated using Equation 2), and the red circles indicate those observations contributing to the fit at x_0. The solid yellow region indicates the weights assigned to observations. The green curve is the resulting kernel-weighted average using an Epanechnikov kernel with $\lambda = 0.2$. The figure is adapted from the one found in $http : //en.wikipedia.org/wiki/Kernel\_smoother$.

3   Higher Order Functions

This paper adopts a different approach to the work cited in the previous section for adapting the metric used in the kernel function. There, the underlying structure of the metric remains fixed. That is, the overall distance between two multi-dimensional input vectors is based on the sum of weighted squared pair-wise distances for each dimension, with the adaptation concerning only the weights. Herein, our aim is to simultaneously learn the underlying computation of similarity as well as the weighting of different features for a particular problem. He have hypothesised that the ability to iterate over the multiple dimensions of an input vector is essential to the evolution of similarity measures, thus we will allow GP to search the space of programs populated by high-level iteration constructs, named *higher-order* functions.

Higher-order functions are functions that take other functions as arguments or produce other functions as results. They are a powerful method of abstraction and re-use, and have been the subject of research in GP for evolving even-n-parity programs [14], music and architectural designs [9], and recursive sorting algorithms [2]. Higher-order functions can be used as general iteration schemata that are bound to a finite-sized list of elements. The iterative behaviour is encapsulated within the body of the function, bypassing the problem of non-halting programs that arises when GP operates on a search space of programs with unbounded iteration/recursion capabilities. Bellow we present the higher-order functions *Reduce*, *Mapcar*, and *Filter*.

Reduce(list, body). It is a function that uses a combining operation to recursively process the constituent elements of an argument list, building up a return value. It requires two expression-trees as arguments; the first being of type `list`, whereas the second being of type `double`. It returns a scalar value of type `double`. The *body* argument is repeatedly evaluated, once per element of the *list* argument. The result returned after each evaluation of the body is stored as the value of a local variable, and when the list is exhausted, the value of this local variable is returned as the value of `Reduce`.

Bellow is an example of a function that computes the sum of `double` elements of `listA`. `res_var_listX` is the result local variable that is returned once the argument list is exhausted. `elt_var_listX` is a local variable that is bound to the current element of the argument list throughout iteration.

```
(Reduce (listA)
    (+ res_var_listA elt_var_listA))
```

`Mapcar(list, body).` It is a higher-order function that applies a given operation to each element of the argument list, returning a list of results. It accepts two arguments, the first being of type `list`, and the second being of type `double`. It returns a list of elements of the same size as the argument list. As an example:

```
(Mapcar (listA)
    (* elt_var_listA  elt_var_listA))
```

returns a list of elements, where each element is the respective element of `listA` raised to the power of two.

`Filter(list, body).` This higher-order function applies the *body* expression-tree, which is a predicate expression (i.e. returns a boolean value) to each element of the *list* argument to return a list containing items that satisfy the predicate expression. The size of the returned list is less than or equal to the size of the argument list. For example:

```
(Filter (listA)
    (> elt_var_listA  0))
```

returns a list containing only the positive elements of `listA`.

4   Method

4.1   Wrapper Approach to the Evolution of Distance Measures

The proposed method for evolving a task-specific distance measure is based on a wrapper approach, in which kernel regression is wrapped around an evolved distance measure, with the mean squared error (MSE) that accrues from the regression serving as the fitness of the distance measure.

While kernel regression can be performed with many types of kernel functions, we hereafter focus our research on a particular instance of a logistic kernel that takes the following form:

$$K_\lambda(x_0, x) = D\left(evo(x_0, x)\right) \tag{5}$$

where width λ is absorbed in the evolved distance measure $evo(x_0, x)$, with

$$D(t) = \frac{1}{e^t + 2 + e^{-t}} \tag{6}$$

We decided on the use of the logistic kernel after some initial runs with a range a different kernel functions. Table 1 presents the strongly-typed representation language that was designed for the experiments. The signature of an evolved program is `double measure(list x, list x0)`. The function `zip` is a standard Lisp function that takes two lists and creates a list of pairs, i.e. `zip`($\{1, 2, 3\}$, $\{4, 5, 6\}$) returns $\{\{1, 4\}, \{2, 5\}, \{3, 6\}\}$. In our version, `zip` is defined to return its first argument if not both of its arguments are lists of `double` elements.

Table 1. Representation Language

Function set		
Function	**Argument(s) type**	**Return type**
Reduce	list, double	double
Mapcar	list, double	list
Filter	list, boolean	list
zip	list, list	list
add, sub, mul	double, double	double
exp, log, sqrt, sin	double	double
$|a - b|$, $(a - b)^2$	double, double	double
$\geq$, $<$	double, double	boolean
Terminal set		
Terminal	**Type**	
x_0, x	list	
local vars (used in higher-order funcs)	double	
random constants $\in [0.0, 1.0]$	double	
input features (in case of standard GP)	double	

4.2 Experiment Design

In this study we use seven real-world datasets obtained from the UCI Machine Learning repository [5], and the Dow Chemical dataset which was the subject of the Symbolic Regression EvoCompetitions event of the 2010 EvoStar conference [1]. Table 3 presents the details of the benchmarks. In all datasets, feature values were standardised to have zero mean and unit variance. Each dataset was randomly split into training and test sets with proportions of 70%-30%. Currently, no validation set is used to select the best-of-run individual.

We perform a comparison between standard Euclidean-based kernel regression using different kernels found in [1], the method of evolutionary-distance-based kernel regression ($KernelGP$) presented in Section 4.1, and standard GP ($StdGP$) that evolves a multi-variate model to predict a response variable. In the case of Euclidean-based kernel regression, width λ is set via 10-fold cross-validation performed on the training set. We cross-validated $2,000$ values for λ in the range of $\{0.01, \ldots, 20.0\}$ with a step-size of 0.01. Tables 2 and 4 show the setup of the evolutionary systems. Previous research has shown generalisation improvements accruing from the use of small, dynamically-sampled sets of

---

[1] `http://casnew.iti.upv.es/index.php/evocompetitions/105-symregcompetition`

training examples, thus for $KernelGP$ training is based on 20 cases drawn at random from the complete training set in each generation. For $StdGP$ we tried two different variations; $StdGP_{(N=20)}$ trains using 20 random cases dynamically drawn in every generation similarly to $KernelGP$, whereas $StdGP_{(N=all)}$ uses the complete training set.

Table 2. GP systems under comparison

Name	Primitives	Constraints	Max. depth	Fitness function
$KernelGP_1$	Reduce, zip, add, sub, mul, exp, log, sqrt, sin, $|a - b|$, $(a - b)^2$, x_0, x, local vars, constants	1) Reduce at the root 2) No nesting of Reduce	6	MSE of kernel regression
$KernelGP_2$	Reduce, Mapcar, Filter, zip, add, sub, mul, exp, log, sqrt, sin, $|a - b|$, $(a - b)^2$, x_0, x, local vars, constants	n/a	6	MSE of kernel regression
$StdGP$	add, sub, mul, exp, log, sqrt, sin, features, constants	n/a	10	MSE of evolved program

Since the iterations performed implicitly in the higher-order functions are bounded by the size of the argument lists, we do not have to worry about non-halting programs, however it is reasonable to anticipate programs with deep nesting of higher-order functions. Preliminary runs devoted to configure the parameters of the evolutionary systems suggested that in the case of $KernelGP_2$ configuration, a constraint on the depth of the expression-tree was not enough to keep the run-time within a reasonable frame. We thus decided to impose an *iteration-monitor* for fitness evaluation. This is simply a counter on the number of times a higher-order function is called within an expression-tree. When the limit of this monitor is exceeded, an individual is assigned a high error and its evaluation is abandoned. In these experiments we used the limit of $10,000$ higher-order function calls. To put this number into context, two nested `Reduce` functions would result in $3,249$ `Reduce` function calls in the case of the Dow Chemical dataset of dimensionality 57.

Table 3. Datasets

Dataset	Training set size	Test set size	Dimensionality
Dow Chemical	747	319	57
Concrete compressive strength	721	309	8
Energy efficiency (heating load)	538	230	8
Parkinsons (motor UPDRS)	4,113	1,762	16
Wine quality (red)	1,120	479	11
Yacht hydrodynamics	216	92	6
Boston housing (price)	355	151	13

In addition to performing regression, we analyse the fitness landscape. To this end, we perform a *perturbation analysis*, in which random walks (using subtree mutation) are taken from a fit individual, plotting the average *Canberra distance* (between targets and predictions) of consecutive neighbours versus the number of mutations. Given a model F and a training example $\{x_i, y_i\}$, the Canberra distance (CD) between prediction $F(x_i)$ and target y_i is given by $|F(x_i) - y_i|/(|F(x_i)| + |y_i|)$, which is implicitly normalised within the $[0.0, 1.0]$ interval. Its average is simply calculated on N examples in the respective training dataset. For this type of analysis, CD was preferred over MSE because it is bounded (a very bad individual can be clearly indicated), and it makes the results of different random walks and different datasets directly comparable.

Table 4. Setup shared by all GP systems

Evolutionary algorithm	elitist (k=1), generational, expression-tree representation
No. of generations	51
Population size	1,000
Tournament size	4
Tree creation	ramped half-and-half (depths of 2 to 4)
Subtree crossover	20% (90% inner-nodes, 10% leaf-nodes)
Subtree mutation	50% (max. depth of subtree: uniform randomly in [1, 4])
Point mutation	30% (probability of a node to be mutated: 10% or 30% or 40%)

5   Results Analysis

We performed 50 independent runs for each evolutionary system. Table 6 compares the test-set MSE. Each best-of-50-runs individual is determined as the one out of 50 final-generation elitists having the lowest training MSE, then its test-set MSE is shown in Table 6. Mean MSE is similarly calculated on 50 final-generation elitists. In every dataset, we used the best-of-50-runs individuals in order to compare the evolutionary methods against the deterministic, Euclidean-based kernel regression. Results suggest that the evolutionary-distance based kernel regression is outperforming the euclidean-based one in all datasets. We also note that the exponential kernels (Gaussian, Logistic) based on the Euclidean distance consistently performed the best.

Comparing Euclidean-based kernel regression against standard GP, we observe that $StdGP_{(N=20)}$ outperforms the former in 1 out of 7 datasets, with the opposite being the case in 4 datasets. On the other hand, $StdGP_{(N=all)}$ outperforms standard kernel regression in 4 out of 7 datasets. Interestingly, a comparison between the two different $StdGP$ setups suggests that the complex evolved models trained on all available data consistently generalised better than those trained on random data samples, a result that is inline with theoretical results in the ML field about matching the model complexity with the amount of training resources available. We identified pathologies (MSE $\geq 1,000$ and MSE $= \infty$) in final-generation individuals, and calculated the percentage of these individuals in 50 runs. We observe that the MSE loss function can lead to severe pathologies partly indicative of overfitting in case where complex models are trained on small-sized, even dynamically samples, sets of examples. In the case of $StgGP_{(N=all)}$ no pathologies were observed.

Table 5. Best-of-50-runs simplified distance measures using $KernelGP_1$ configuration

Boston housing	Parkinsons	Concrete
<pre>(Reduce
(zip
x0
x
)
(+
(sin
(sqrt
(exp
elt_var_x0
)
)
)
(+
(+
0.577
res_var
)
(absdiff
elt_var_x
elt_var_x0
)
)
)
)</pre>	<pre>(Reduce
(zip
x0
x
)
(-
(-
(+
(log
res_var
)
res_var
)
(absdiff
elt_var_x0
elt_var_x
)
)
(absdiff
elt_var_x0
elt_var_x
)
)
)</pre>	<pre>(Reduce
(zip
x0
x
)
(+
(sqrdiff
(-
-0.962
(absdiff
elt_var_x
elt_var_x0
)
)
(exp
(absdiff
elt_var_x0
elt_var_x
)
)
)
(*
res_var
0.524
)
)
)</pre>

It is interesting to note that despite the fact that $KernelGP$ uses the same training examples sampling configuration as $StdGP_{(N=20)}$, there were no pathologies in the final-generation models. The synergy between the evolved-distance-based kernel and the kernel-weighted average seems to have created a fitness landscape, where search was able to locate models with relatively smooth response surfaces – even in the case where search was guided by a kernel regression MSE estimate based on a limited-sized set of examples. There is a clear superiority in the out-of-sample performance of $KernelGP$ as opposed to $StdGP_{(N=20)}$. Compared against $StdGP_{(N=all)}$, $KernelGP$ generalises better, and in most problems the differences in out-of-sample performance are statistically significant.

Figure 5 presents the simplified best-of-50-runs evolved distances for the Boston, Parkinsons and Concrete datasets, using the $KernelGP_1$ configuration. The evolved solutions are quite neat and comprehensible. All of them are using the $|a-b|$ primitive (shown as absdiff in Table 5) operating on the returned list of pairs from the zip function. Also, they all rely on some kind of transformation of the result_var or element_var that is linearly combined with the output of $|a-b|$ to update the result_var is each iteration of Reduce.

Finally, Figure 2 presents the results of the perturbation analysis for two of the problems. The graphs for the rest of the problems are omitted, but exhibit the same trend. It is evident that higher-order functions craft a neighbourhood in which very bad individuals (avg. CD of approx. 1.0) can be reached using a single mutation step. This is the case in all problems, and it becomes particularly pronounced in the Energy dataset (Figures 2(c), 2(d)), where the performance of a fit individual can be severely degraded during the first step of the random walk. This indicates that while higher-order functions are a powerful addition to the GP paradigm, they can result in very difficult to search program spaces, where gradient quickly diminishes and gradient-based methods are left hopeless. We suspect that it was the implicit parallelism of the evolutionary algorithm that enabled search to counteract this issue to some degree, and allowed for the induction of good-performing individuals. Also, an observation that is consistent across all problems is that on average there is more gradient in the space of programs that is based on all three higher order functions, than there is in the space of programs composed of a single Reduce function serving as the root-node of an expression-tree. This can be seen by comparing Figure 2(a) (using Reduce at the root) and Figure 2(b) (using all three higher-order functions).

Table 6. Test-set MSE of different regression methods. λ values in parentheses for standard Euclidean-based kernel regression. Statistics for the evolutionary methods were calculated on 50 runs. Std. deviation in parentheses for mean. An asterisk * indicates that the difference in mean values between $KernelGP$ and $StdGP_{N=all}$ are statistically significant at the 5% level (two-tailed Student's t-test, 98 degrees of freedom).

	Boston	Concrete	Dow	Energy	Parkinsons	Wine	Yacht
Euclidean-based kernel regression							
Biweight	0.39 (2.82)	0.36 (2.13)	0.38 (5.61)	0.05 (1.46)	0.98 (0.23)	0.68 (3.10)	0.43 (2.07)
Cosine	0.34 (2.61)	0.38 (2.13)	0.40 (5.61)	0.05 (1.34)	0.98 (0.23)	0.69 (3.09)	0.44 (1.81)
Epanechnikov	0.35 (2.61)	0.39 (2.13)	0.40 (5.61)	0.05 (1.34)	0.98 (0.23)	0.69 (3.08)	0.44 (1.81)
Gaussian	0.27 (0.63)	0.33 (0.58)	0.26 (1.47)	0.05 (0.40)	0.97 (3.75)	0.66 (0.95)	0.22 (0.28)
Logistic	0.27 (0.19)	0.32 (0.17)	0.24 (0.30)	0.05 (0.13)	0.97 (2.08)	0.61 (0.37)	0.19 (0.05)
Triangular	0.41 (2.76)	0.37 (2.13)	0.39 (5.61)	0.05 (1.34)	0.98 (0.23)	0.68 (3.10)	0.41 (1.81)
Tricube	0.39 (2.82)	0.37 (2.30)	0.38 (5.61)	0.05 (1.49)	0.98 (0.23)	0.69 (3.10)	0.44 (2.07)
Triweight	0.38 (3.93)	0.38 (2.76)	0.36 (5.61)	0.05 (1.49)	0.98 (0.23)	0.67 (3.10)	0.40 (2.07)
Evolutionary-distance-based kernel regression							
$KernelGP_1$							
best-of-50	0.24	0.18	0.22	0.002	0.68	0.55	0.007
mean	0.37	*0.24	*0.31	*0.009	*0.89	*0.62	*0.01
	(0.14)	(0.04)	(0.08)	(0.007)	(0.25)	(0.07)	(0.007)
$KernelGP_2$							
best-of-50	0.26	0.19	0.22	0.003	0.90	0.61	0.007
mean	0.30 (0.06)	0.38 (0.14)	0.44 (0.20)	0.04 (0.07)	0.94 (0.05)	0.79 (0.22)	0.02 (0.04)
Standard GP							
$StdGP_{(N=20)}$							
best-of-50	0.31	0.36	0.60	0.05	0.97	0.72	0.12
mean	0.58 (0.51)	0.77 (1.11)	0.84 (0.18)	0.13 (0.04)	97.25 (577.4)	1.09 (0.47)	0.07 (0.09)
Pathologies:							
MSE $\geq$ 1,000	0%	0%	0%	0%	4%	0%	0%
MSE $= \infty$	0%	0%	2%	0%	6%	2%	0%
$StdGP_{(N=all)}$							
best-of-50	0.25	0.28	0.35	0.05	0.88	0.67	0.009
mean	0.45 (0.74)	0.38 (0.04)	0.54 (0.09)	0.08 (0.02)	0.95 (0.01)	0.72 (0.02)	0.06 (0.01)

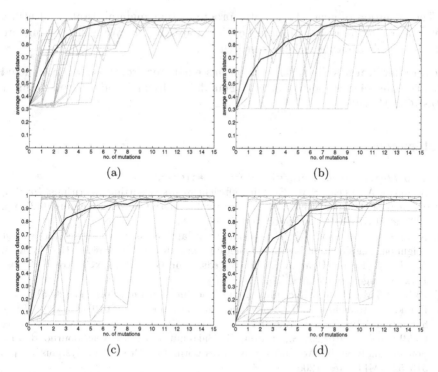

Fig. 2. Random walks. We start from a best-of-50-runs individual and perform 50 different random walks of length 15 – average shown in bold. (a) DowChem $KernelGP_1$; (b) DowChem $KernelGP_2$; (c) Energy $KernelGP_1$; (d) Energy $KernelGP_2$.

6 Conclusion and Future Work

The generalisation performance of interpolation-like function estimation methods can be significantly improved when the distance measure utilised in the kernel function is adapted to the data. We presented a successful, hybrid ML technique that combines kernel regression with the evolutionary learning of the distance measure used in the kernel function. As an additional advantage, the width of the kernel is absorbed in the evolved distance, thus there is no need to set this parameter via cross-validation.

There are a number of avenues for extending this research. First, the use of a validation set to designate a best-of-run individual is believed to further boost the out-of-sample performance of the system. In addition, we plan to perform experiments using the complete set of training examples. Secondly, we note that the configuration of $KernelGP_2$ is of greater generality that the one of $KernelGP_1$. However the performance of the former was somewhat dissatisfying in the sense that it did not outperform the latter. We suspect that this is due to an insufficient search effort devoted in $KernelGP_2$, and expect that a new experiment based on a more extended search will reveal the true potential of spaces populated by programs composed of these high-level iteration constructs.

The evolution of general computer programs that maintain state and utilise iteration/recursion is still an under-explored area in GP. We wish to stimulate interest in this exciting niche of research.

Acknowledgments. This publication has emanated from research conducted with the financial support of Science Foundation Ireland under Grant Number 08/SRC/FM1389.

References

1. http://en.wikipedia.org/wiki/Kernelstatistics
2. Agapitos, A., Lucas, S.M.: Evolving efficient recursive sorting algorithms. In: Proceedings of the 2006 IEEE Congress on Evolutionary Computation, July 6-21, pp. 9227–9234. IEEE Press, Vancouver (2006)
3. Agapitos, A., O'Neill, M., Brabazon, A.: Adaptive distance metrics for nearest neighbour classification based on genetic programming. In: Krawiec, K., Moraglio, A., Hu, T., Etaner-Uyar, A.Ş., Hu, B. (eds.) EuroGP 2013. LNCS, vol. 7831, pp. 1–12. Springer, Heidelberg (2013)
4. Bishop, C.M.: Pattern Recognition and Machine Learning. Springer (2006)
5. Frank, A., Asuncion, A.: UCI machine learning repository (2010), http://archive.ics.uci.edu/ml
6. Goldberger, J., Roweis, S., Hinton, G., Salakhutdinov, R.: Neighbourhood components analysis. In: Advances in Neural Information Processing Systems 17, pp. 513–520. MIT Press (2004)
7. Goutte, C., Larsen, J.: Adaptive metric kernel regression. Journal of VLSI Signal Processing (26), 155–167 (2000)
8. Huang, R., Sun, S.: Kernel regression with sparse metric learning. Journal of Intelligent and Fuzzy Systems 24(4), 775–787 (2013)
9. McDermott, J., Byrne, J., Swafford, J.M., O'Neill, M., Brabazon, A.: Higher-order functions in aesthetic EC encodings. In: 2010 IEEE World Congress on Computational Intelligence, July 18-23, pp. 2816–2823. IEEE Computation Intelligence Society, IEEE Press, Barcelona, Spain (2010)
10. Poli, R., Langdon, W.B., McPhee, N.F.: A Field Guide to Genetic Programming. Lulu Enterprises, UK Ltd. (2008)
11. Takeda, H., Farsiu, S., Milanfar, P.: Robust kernel regression for restoration and reconstruction of images from sparse, noisy data. In: Proceeding of the International Conference on Image Processing (ICIP), pp. 1257–1260 (2006)
12. Trevor, H., Robert, T., Jerome, F.: The Elements of Statistical Learning, 2nd edn. Springer (2009)
13. Weinberger, K.Q., Tesauro, G.: Metric learning for kernel regression. In: Eleventh International Conference on Artificial Intelligence and Statistics, pp. 608–615 (2007)
14. Yu, T.: Hierachical processing for evolving recursive and modular programs using higher order functions and lambda abstractions. Genetic Programming and Evolvable Machines 2(4), 345–380 (2001)

Flash: A GP-GPU Ensemble Learning System for Handling Large Datasets

Ignacio Arnaldo, Kalyan Veeramachaneni, and Una-May O'Reilly

MIT, Computer Science and Artificial Intelligence Laboratory, Cambridge, MA, USA
iarnaldo@mit.edu, {kalyan,unamay}@csail.mit.edu

Abstract. The Flash system runs ensemble-based Genetic Programming (GP) symbolic regression on a shared memory desktop. To significantly reduce the high time cost of the extensive model predictions required by symbolic regression, its fitness evaluations are tasked to the desktop's GPU. Successive GP "instances" are run on different data subsets and randomly chosen objective functions. Best models are collected after a fixed number of generations and then fused with an adaptive, output-space method. New instance launches are halted once learning is complete. We demonstrate that Flash's ensemble strategy not only makes GP more robust, but it also provides an informed online means of halting the learning process. Flash enables GP to learn from a dataset composed of 370K exemplars and 90 features, evolving a population of 1000 individuals over 100 generations in as few as 50 seconds.

Keywords: Genetic Programming, GPGPU computing, Ensembles.

1 Introduction

The fitness evaluation component of Genetic Programming (GP) symbolic regression (GPSR) dominates its cost because, at every generation, each model has to be evaluated on multiple fitness cases, i.e. the dataset. If the dataset does not saturate the memory of a single node, it can be replicated across nodes and the algorithm can be parallelized by splitting the population across them as *islands with migration*. On each node/island, "local" fitness evaluation is parallelized via multi-threading. If the dataset size exceeds single node memory capacity, *data-level* parallel approaches evolve models locally on each node with a subset of the data, then a *meta* model is built that fuses outputs from several of these models. Such ensemble strategies provide robustness to the learning process [8]. The *population-parallel* and *data-parallel* approaches are ideal if one has access to a cloud or cluster [18]. However some scenarios may prevent their adoption:

- Privacy and security policies around data may require that the machine learning and data mining be carried out locally.
- Large data transfers may be prohibitively expensive or require too extensive a prior setup.
- A scientist may wish to use GPSR as an exploratory tool, tightly integrated into a desktop workflow that requires timely delivery of models.

M. Nicolau et al. (Eds.): EuroGP 2014, LNCS 8599, pp. 13–24, 2014.

Flash serves this class of scenarios wherein desktop computing is necessary or desired but the dataset is larger than the desktop's memory capacity. It is a serial, desktop alternative to a cloud-based GPSR ensemble system. Rather than node-based learning in parallel on different subsets of data and different parameter sets, the Flash GP learner is invoked sequentially; each time with a different subset of data and a different set of parameters. Because it exploits General Purpose GPUs to reduce the time cost of model evaluation, it is able to replicate GPSR ensemble functionality within a single desktop and still obtain reduced learning times, despite datasets sizes that are larger than the desktop's memory capacity. Flash comprises:

- **GPU-optimized GPSR:** Flash exploits different fitness functions that are well suited to run on the GPU. In particular, it uses the correlation between target values and predictions to drive GPSR. Diverse models are combined with the algorithm Adaptive Regression by Mixing [20].
- **Incremental Learning:** Flash, as opposed to cloud-based GPSR ensembles in which all the GP instances are run in a single batch of a preset size, decides after each run whether to run an additional instance or to stop learning.
- **High speed GPSR with large datasets:** Flash implements fitness evaluation in CUDA for execution in a low-cost gaming card, namely a NVIDIA Geforce GTX 690. The card has two GPUs and allows concurrent kernel executions. Our implementation enables GP to learn from a dataset composed of 370K exemplars and 90 features, evolving a population of 1000 individuals during 100 generations in as less as 50 seconds.

We proceed as follows: Section 2 reviews existing GPU implementations of GP algorithms. Section 3 presents the GPU specialized fitness functions. Section 4 describes Flash's ensemble approach. Section 5 describes the experimental setup while Section 6 presents the results. Section 7 concludes.

2   Related Work: Accelerating GP with GPUs

The capability of GPUs to speed up Genetic Programming has not escaped the attention of researchers. Table 1 summarizes the experimental conditions of significant contributions. In a nutshell, there are two recurrent approaches: compiling the population at each generation and executing the resulting program or creating an optimized interpreter of GP individuals.

Population Compilation This approach has its roots in GP scenarios targeting the automatic generation of executable programs where the compilation step verifies the feasibility of candidate solutions. However it can be applied to GP problems in general for execution speed. Compiled expressions are expected to execute faster since compiled code is optimized (code reordering, removal of useless or redundant operations). This advantage must be balanced with the overhead of compilation however.

Interpretation An interpreter that is capable of evaluating the GP "language" of a given GP problem is implemented in the GPU. This approach waives compilation and its overhead. It exploits evaluation parallelism at the individual

Table 1. Experiment conditions of closely related work and reported speedup

Contribution	Pop. size	Test Cases	Approach	Speedup	As compared to
Harding-2007 [5]	100	65536	Pop. compilation	7351.06	Tree traversal
Chitty-2007 [3]		40000	Pop. compilation	29.98	CPU equivalent
Langdon-2008[9]	204800	1200	Interpreter	12.00	CPU equivalent
Banzhaf-2008 [1]		494021	Pop. compilation	7.40	CPU equivalent
Robilliard-2008 [16]	12500	2048	Interpreter	80.00	CPU equivalent
Wilson-2008 [19]	4000	251	Interpreter	2.51	Xbox CPU
Harding-2009 [7]	2048	10023300	Pop. compilation	55.00	Single GPU
Langdon-2009 [10]	262144	8192	Interpreter	34.00	CPU equivalent
Robilliard-2009 [17]	12500	100000	Interpreter	111.40	CPU equivalent
Lewis-2009 [12]	400	512	Interpreter	1259.57	CPU equivalent
Maitre-2010 [14]		1200	Interpreter	50.00	CPU equivalent
Langdon-2010 [11]	262144	8192	Interpreter	-	Never done in CPU
Maitre-2010b [13]	65536	65536	Interpreter	140.00	CPU equivalent
Harding-2011[6]		2000000	Interpreter	-	Never done in CPU

and fitness case level and suits GP scenarios with a small number of test cases. Because threads in charge of evaluating short expressions will be idle waiting for longer expressions to finish their execution, some resources are wasted.

Preliminary Analysis We compare the speedup obtained with the compilation and interpretation approaches against a standard tree traversal evaluation. We generate 5 random datasets composed of and 5,10,20,50, and 100 explanatory variables respectively and a million exemplars. For each of the five resulting datasets, we generate a population of 1000 individuals with a ramped half-and-half strategy. The time per population evaluation of these two approaches is shown in Figure 1. The comparative analysis shows that the interpreter approach obtains faster evaluations. As shown in Table 1b, the compilation time severely impacts the speedup obtained with the compilation approach. Therefore, we adopt the interpreter approach in our work.

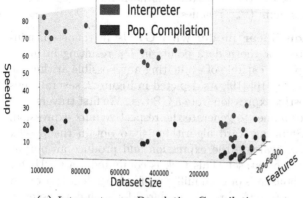

Step	% runtime
traversals	0.48%
code	0.30%
compile	86.90%
run	12.32%

(a) Interpreter vs. Population Compilation

(b) Population compilation profiling

Fig. 1. Speedup obtained with the CUDA interpreter (80×) and compiling (14×) approaches with different data dimensionality and size as compared to a standard CPU-based evaluation, and profiling of the compilation approach

3   The Core GP Learner

We now present the core GP learner that uses the GPU. Most of the steps in the GP learning algorithm, like other approaches are carried out in the CPU. Fitness function evaluation, which is biggest bottleneck and scales with the data size is carried out on a GPU. To support ensemble learning we developed a library of interpreter approach based fitness evaluation functions. We then allow the flexibility to a choose a fitness function by the ensemble learning system. We illustrate how we implement two fitness functions on GPU: Mean Squared Error and Pearson Correlation coefficient between model output and target values computed as follows:

$$MSE = \frac{1}{n}\sum_{i=1}^{n}(\hat{Y}_i - Y_i)^2 \qquad r = \frac{\sum_{i=1}^{n}(\hat{Y}_i - \overline{\hat{Y}})(Y_i - \overline{Y})}{\sqrt{\sum_{i=1}^{n}(\hat{Y}_i - \overline{\hat{Y}})^2}\sqrt{\sum_{i=1}^{n}(Y_i - \overline{Y})^2}}$$

where Y is the target vector and $\hat{Y}$ is the model output or predictions. These two functions are embedded in a multi-objective GP based on NSGA-II targeting both accuracy and Subtree Complexity. The fixed structure of NSGA-II allows to evaluate the population in fixed-sized batches, which is useful for GPU execution.

3.1   Mean Squared Error and Pearson Correlation on GPUs

The computation required to score a model is broken in several steps. Note that, in Genetic Programming-based Symbolic Regression, it is typical to set the target and prediction values in the same range (see Step 0 and Step 3) prior to the computation of the error. This approach is meant to focus the search process to capture the shape of the curve rather than its scale.

Step 0: Normalization of the target values In this step, performed before the start of the GP algorithm, the target vector Y is normalized according to the minimum (Y_{min}) and maximum (Y_{max}) values.

Step 1: Evaluation of non linear model with GPUs In this step, non-linear model $f(\bar{X})$ is evaluated for the n data points in D_T resulting in $y_{1...n}$. We implement a GPU interpreter capable of evaluating any possible arithmetic expression in postfix notation [9] [16] [19]. As depicted in Figure 2, several steps are required to obtain the postfix expression from a GP tree. We first traverse the tree in a depth-first in-order manner to generate the respective infix expression. We then apply Dijkstra's Shunting Yard algorithm [4] to obtain the postfix notation. The interpreter will evaluate the expression and produce an output value for each data point in the dataset. This task is computed via GPUs for datasets of size hundreds of thousands or even millions of independent test cases. In our GPU implementation, a CUDA thread is declared for each data point in the dataset. Thus multiple CUDA threads will execute the interpreter function shown in Figure 2 simultaneously on different data points, ensuring that all threads follow the exact same execution path. Note that conditional instructions such as *if* or *while* statements are pernicious for the performance of CUDA

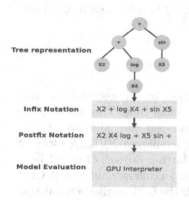

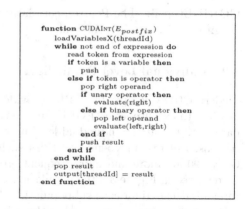

Fig. 2. GP Tree and corresponding infix, and postfix expressions (left) and pseudocode of the postfix interpreter (right)

programs only when they trigger a divergence in the execution of threads within a *warp* (see [15]). In such case, their execution is serialized. To benefit from coalesced memory accesses, we transpose the input matrix before storing it in global memory in such way that exemplars are displayed in columns while each line corresponds to an explanatory variable. This way, contiguous threads will access adjacent memory positions, thus reducing the number of expensive global memory accesses. At the end of this step we obtain the output of the model $\hat{Y}_{1...n}$ for all the n data points in D_T.

Step 2: retrieval of $\hat{Y}_{min}$ and $\hat{Y}_{max}$ A CUDA parallel reduction is employed to retrieve the maximum and minimum values of the model's output.

Step 3: normalization of the predictions $\hat{Y}$ We normalize the model's output according to minimum $(\hat{Y}_{min})$ and maximum $(\hat{Y}_{max})$ predictions.

The remaining steps are different for the computation of the Mean Squared Error (MSE) and the Pearson correlation coefficient (CORR):

MSE-Step 4: With both the target and prediction values in the same range, we compute the sum of the squared differences $\sum_1^n (\hat{Y}-Y)^2$ with a CUDA parallel reduction sum.
MSE-Step 5: The result of the sum is averaged over the number of exemplars of the dataset in CPU and assigned as fitness of the individual.

CORR-Step 4: We employ a CUDA parallel reduction sum to compute the mean of targets $\overline{Y}$ as well as the mean of the predictions $\overline{\hat{Y}}$

CORR-Step 5: Once again a CUDA parallel reduction sum is employed to compute the denominator $\sum_{i=1}^n (\hat{Y}_i-\overline{\hat{Y}})(Y_i-\overline{Y})$ and the numerator terms $\sqrt{\sum_{i=1}^n (\hat{Y}_i-\overline{\hat{Y}})^2}$ and $\sqrt{\sum_{i=1}^n (Y_i-\overline{Y})^2}$

CORR-Step 6: The Pearson correlation coefficient is computed in CPU and assigned as fitness of the individual.

3.2 Individual Level Parallelism

Modern CUDA compatible GPUs provide concurrent kernel execution, i.e. it is possible to execute several GPU functions at the same time. This allows us to parallelize GP at the individual level in a clean and easy way. Moreover, GPUs composed of two independent GPUs such as the employed NVIDIA GeForce GTX 690 are more and more frequent, granting further degrees of parallelism. As depicted in Figure 3a, the population is split into 4 different subsets. A CPU thread is declared for each subpopulation that calls the GPU evaluation function sequentially for each individual of the subset. The two first threads will employ the first GPU while the third and fourth threads employ the second GPU. The memory space of each of the two GPUs is independent, therefore data is copied to the Global Memory of both GPUs.

4 Flash - The GP-GPU Ensemble Learning System

Having designed a flexible core GP-GPU learner, we adopt an ensemble strategy in which several GP instances are run sequentially with different data subsets and parameters (such as fitness functions). In a step prior to the machine learning process, the targeted data D is split into training set D_T, cross-validation set D_{CV}, and test set D_{TEST}. GP instances learn from D_T while D_{CV} is employed to train the fused model. Finally, D_{TEST} is reserved to test the accuracy of the retrieved models. Figure 3b presents the Flash-GP approach: a subset of data is randomly selected and the objective function for the GP algorithm is picked randomly. The core GP learner is then executed with these parameters. After a fixed number of generations the best model is selected. The fusion module generates the fused model by training the weights within the "Adaptive Regression by Mixing" methodology using D_{CV}. A decision is made whether to continue the learning or not and the loop is repeated.

4.1 GP Instances

Factorization. As depicted in Figure 3b, each GP instance learns from a subsample of the exemplars and explanatory variables of D_T.
Exemplars: Each GP instance samples from the test cases of the training data D_T which will speed up model fitness evaluation and result in diverse model results across the sequential GP instances.
Explanatory Variables: Sampling from different explanatory variables reduces the dimensionality of the targeted dataset. On the other hand, the evolved models might exhibit low accuracy if the sampled variables can't sufficiently relate to the target values Y.

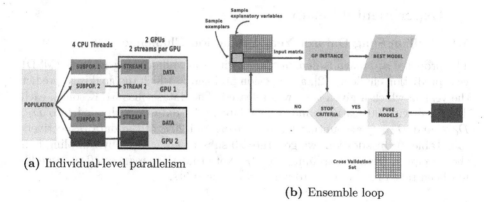

(a) Individual-level parallelism

(b) Ensemble loop

Fig. 3. The evaluation is parallelized at the individual level by exploiting concurrent kernel executions in two GPUs. Flash-GP: GP instances learn from different samples of the data and the retrieved models are fused in a later step.

Best Model per GP Instance. GP instances learn from the sampled data and are executed with a time or computational budget. At each generation, we store the model exhibiting the highest fitness value (MSE or correlation) with respect to D_T. The motivation to save the best model per generation is that models from advanced generations might overfit the data while some of the models obtained earlier might exhibit better generalization capability, i.e. a better accuracy with respect to unseen data. Once the GP run is finished, the stored models (best per generation) are evaluated against D_{CV} to obtain their MSE. The model exhibiting the lowest error with respect to the validation set is then selected as the best model of the run and will be used in the fusion process.

4.2 Generating a Fused Model

We employ the algorithm Adaptive Regression by Mixing (ARM) [20] that allows to fuse a set of models M according to an estimation of their accuracy. The fused model z obtained with ARM is a linear combination of the models $m \in M$. Given a test sample $\overline{X_j}$, the prediction $\hat{z}_j$ issued by the fused model is the weighted average of model predictions $\hat{z}_j = \sum_{m=1}^{o} W_m \hat{Y}_{mj}$. Thus, the fusion process consists of learning the weight W_m for each model. Let $r = |D_{CV}|$ be the size of the fusion training set, and $o = |M|$ be the number of models in the ensemble. Here, we assume that the errors for each model are normally distributed. We use the variance in these errors to identify the weights by executing the following steps:

Step 1: Split D_{CV} randomly into two equally sized subsets $D_{CV}^{(1)}$ and $D_{CV}^{(2)}$.

Step 2: Evaluate σ_m^2 which is the maximum likelihood estimate of the variance of the errors, $\overline{e}_m = \{\hat{Y}_{mj} - Y_j | \overline{X_j}, Y_j \in D_{CV}^{(1)}\}$. Compute the sum of squared errors on $D^{(2)}$, $\beta_m = \sum_{j=\frac{r}{2}+1}^{r} (\hat{Y}_{mj} - Y_j)^2$.

Step 3: Estimate the weights using: $W_m = \dfrac{(\sigma_m)^{-r/2} exp(-\sigma_m^{-2}\beta_m/2)}{\sum_{j=1}^{o}(\sigma_j)^{-r/2} exp(-\sigma_j^{-2}\beta_j/2)}$

Step 4: Repeat steps 1-3 for a fixed number of times. Average the weights from each iteration to get the final weights for the models.

5   Experimental Setup

5.1   Million Song Dataset Year Prediction Challenge

The proposed approach is demonstrated with the Million Song Dataset (MSD) year prediction challenge [2], a regression problem in which the goal is to predict the year in which a given song was released. The dataset has 515K songs, each described with 90 features and a year label. The dataset is divided into D_T, D_{CV}, and D_{TEST} accounting for 70%, 10%, and 20% of the data respectively (see Table 2). In addition, we generate 20 subsets $D_T^{f1}...D_T^{f20}$ by sampling half the exemplars from the training set D_T. Note that the *producer effect* issue [2] has been taken into account to perform all the splits.

5.2   Ensemble Configurations

We set up different configurations of Flash by selecting different objective functions and choosing whether or not to factor the data. We select from three objective combinations:

1. MSE: Mean Squared Error + Subtree Complexity
2. CORR: Pearson correlation coefficient + Subtree Complexity
3. MSE-CORR: MSE + Pearson correlation coefficient + Subtree Complexity

All the studied configurations are multi-objective and all use the Subtree Complexity measure to prevent bloating issues. We compare two data strategies:

1. The complete training set D_{TR} is considered in each of the GP instances of the ensemble
2. Data factoring: each GP instance of the ensemble randomly selects a set D_{TR}^{fi}, where $i \in [1; 20]$. Additionally, each instance randomly selects v explanatory variables of D_{TR}^{fi}, where $v \in \{5, 10, 20, 40, 60, 80, 90\}$. The f (as in *factoring*) suffix is appended to the name of the configuration when this data strategy is adopted.

The 6 resulting configurations: MSE, MSE$_f$, CORR, CORR$_f$, MSE-CORR, and MSE-CORR$_f$ are summarized in Table 3. The following settings are fixed in all the experiments. Each GP instance is run for 100 generations with a population of 1000 individuals. A time budget of an hour is imposed on the GP ensembles. Finally, the number of iterations of the ARM fusion process is set to 100. We perform 20 replicas of each of the ensemble configurations. Thus, in summary, we perform a total of: *6(configurations)×20(replicas)=120* ensemble runs. All the experiments are run on the same computer, equipped with an Intel Core-i7-3930K composed of 6 cores with hyper-threading running at 3.20GHz and a NVIDIA Geforce GTX 690 that counts two GPUs, each with 1536 CUDA cores. The GPU postifx interpreter (see Figure 2) is compiled with the *fast-math* flag.

6   Results

6.1   Prediction Error Analysis

A key question is whether the objective function designed to suit GPU usage and a strategy of learning with less data compromises quality. Our first merit of

Table 2. MSD splits

D	D_T	D_T^{fi}	D_{CV}	D_{TEST}
100%	70%	35%	10%	20%
515K	362K	181K	51K	102K

Table 3. Configuration of the compared ensembles

Configuration	Fitness Functions	Factor Data
MSE	MSE, Subtree Comp	no
MSE$_f$	MSE, Subtree Comp	yes
CORR	P. Corr, Subtree Comp	no
CORR$_f$	P. Corr, Subtree Comp	yes
MSE-CORR	MSE, P. Corr, Subtree Comp	no
MSE-CORR$_f$	MSE, P. Corr, Subtree Comp	yes

quality will be prediction error with respect to Mean Squared Error of the unseen data D_{TEST}. Figure 4a shows the boxplots generated with the MSE$_{TEST}$ errors corresponding to the 20 replicas of the runs. First, we observe that, independent of the objective functions, the data factoring strategy leads to a better accuracy. Second, we observe that the maximization of the Pearson correlation coefficient outperforms the standard MSE approach.

To statistically validate these observations, we perform a pairwise Anova test and multiple testing using the Tukey-Kramer or also known as Tukey's honestly significant difference (HSD) method for the prediction errors MSE$_{TEST}$ of the different ensemble configurations. The results are shown in Table 4 where each row presents a test result and the two entries $[x_l, x_u]$ represent the 95% confidence interval between true differences of the mean. Any time the confidence interval does not enclose 0 the difference is significant at $\alpha = 0.05$. The table verifies that factoring is a statistically superior configuration, regardless of objective function: MSE$_f$, CORR$_f$, and MSE-CORR$_f$ respectively outperform MSE, CORR, and MSE-CORR. The superior prediction accuracy of CORR$_f$ versus the remaining approaches is statistically significant.

6.2   Prediction Error vs. GP Instances

We study the impact of the number of GP instances forming the ensemble in the accuracy of the fused model. In Figure 5, we plot the average and standard deviation of the MSE$_{TEST}$ of the fused model when the number of GP instances increases. In all the studied cases, the prediction error of the fused model decreases when a higher number of GP runs are performed. However, a high variability can be observed in the cases where the factoring strategy is employed. It is due to the fact that a fraction of the GP instances learn from a

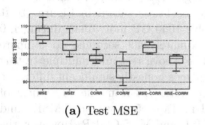

(a) Test MSE

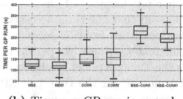

(b) Time per GP run in seconds

Fig. 4. Accuracy (a) and time per GP run in seconds (b) of the 6 ensemble configurations

Table 4. Pairwise MSE comparison with ANOVA test

	MSE	MSE$_f$	CORR	CORR$_f$	MSE-CORR
MSE	-				
MSE$_f$	[1.08;6.26]	-			
CORR	[6.02;11.20]	[2.35;7.53]	-		
CORR$_f$	[9.72;14.90]	[6.05;11.23]	[1.11;6.29]	-	
MSE-CORR	[2.59;7.77]	[-1.08;4.10]	[-6.02;-0.84]	[-9.72;-4.54]	-
MSE-CORR$_f$	[6.98;12.16]	[3.31;8.49]	[-1.64;3.55]	[-5.34;-0.16]	[1.80;6.98]

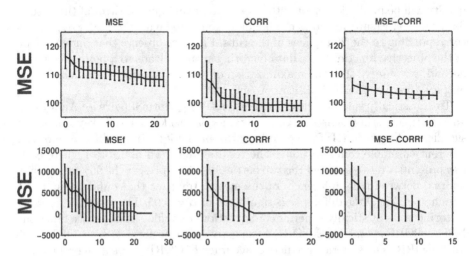

Fig. 5. Average MSE of the fused model with an increasing number of GP instances for the 6 different ensemble configurations

reduced set of non representative variables and achieve poor predictions. However, as more GP instances are considered, the average accuracy increases and the variability decreases. Therefore, ensemble approaches adopting the data factoring strategy need to consider a larger number of GP instances to minimize the variability in the prediction accuracy.

6.3   Runtime Analysis

We analyze whether the data factoring strategies lead to shorter runtimes. The time per GP instance of the compared approaches is shown in Figure 4b. It can be seen that the time necessary to evolve 1000 GP individuals during 100 generation varies from 50 seconds to approximately 400 seconds. To compare the different runtimes, we perform a pairwise Anova test and multiple testing using the Tukey-Kramer or also known as Tukey's honestly significant difference (HSD) method for the time per GP instance retrieved from the 20 replicas of the ensemble runs. The analysis presented in Table 5 shows that MSE$_f$ and MSE-CORR$_f$ are respectively faster than MSE and MSE-CORR. However, the runtime of the CORR and CORR$_f$ approaches is not statistically different.

Table 5. Pairwise time per GP instance comparison with ANOVA test

	MSE	MSE$_f$	CORR	CORR$_f$	MSE-CORR
MSE	-				
MSE$_f$	[6.77;22.33]	-			
CORR	[-23.98;-7.57]	[-38.33;-22.33]	-		
CORR$_f$	[-28.61;-12.04]	[-42.95;-26.79]	[-13.04;3.95]	-	
MSE-CORR	[-157.74;-138.17]	[-172.11;-152.89]	[-142.14;-122.22]	[-137.65;-117.61]	-
MSE-CORR$_f$	[-126.21;-107.09]	[-140.58;-121.82]	[-110.61;-91.14]	[-106.13;-86.52]	[20.20;42.40]

7 Conclusions and Future Work

We have presented a GPU-based implementation of a GP ensemble strategy where different GP instances are run sequentially on a single desktop, and the models retrieved from the different runs are fused with Adaptive Regression by Mixing. Our approach is demonstrated with the Million Song Dataset year prediction challenge, a symbolic regression problem that has 515K exemplars. The execution of the evaluation step in a dual-GPU with concurrent kernels allows GP instances with 1000 individuals to run for 100 generations in as few as 50 seconds. The experimental work shows that the implementation of a data reduction strategy in which each GP instance of the ensemble samples a subset of the exemplars and explanatory variables of the data outperforms the standard strategy that considers the whole dataset. It also shows that employing the Pearson correlation coefficient between predictions and targets to drive the search leads to a higher accuracy than the generally used Mean Squared Error metric.

Acknowledgments. The ALFA group gratefully recognizes the financial support of the Li Ka Shing Foundation and the G.E. Global Research Center. Any opinions, findings, and conclusions or recommendations expressed in this material are those of the authors and do not necessarily reflect the views of G.E.

References

1. Banzhaf, W., Harding, S., Langdon, W., Wilson, G.: Accelerating genetic programming through graphics processing units. In: Genetic Programming Theory and Practice VI. Genetic and Evolutionary Computation, pp. 1–19. Springer US (2009)
2. Bertin-Mahieux, T., Ellis, D.P., Whitman, B., Lamere, P.: The million song dataset. In: Proceedings of the 12th International Conference on Music Information Retrieval, ISMIR 2011 (2011)
3. Chitty, D.M.: A data parallel approach to genetic programming using programmable graphics hardware. In: Proceedings of the 9th Annual GECCO Conference, GECCO 2007, pp. 1566–1573. ACM, New York (2007)
4. Dijkstra, E.W.: Algol 60 translation. Supplement, Algol 60 Bulletin 10 (1960)
5. Harding, S., Banzhaf, W.: Fast genetic programming on GPUs. In: Ebner, M., O'Neill, M., Ekárt, A., Vanneschi, L., Esparcia-Alcázar, A.I. (eds.) EuroGP 2007. LNCS, vol. 4445, pp. 90–101. Springer, Heidelberg (2007)

6. Harding, S., Banzhaf, W.: Implementing cartesian genetic programming classifiers on graphics processing units using GPU.NET. In: Proceedings of the 13th GECCO Conference, GECCO 2011, pp. 463–470. ACM, New York (2011)
7. Harding, S.L., Banzhaf, W.: Distributed genetic programming on GPUs using CUDA. In: Hidalgo, I., Fernandez, F., Lanchares, J. (eds.) PABA Workshop, Raleigh, NC, USA, September 13, pp. 1–10 (2009)
8. Kotanchek, M., Smits, G., Vladislavleva, E.: Trustable symbolic regression models: using ensembles, interval arithmetic and pareto fronts to develop robust and trust-aware models. In: Riolo, R., Soule, T., Worzel, B. (eds.) Genetic Programming Theory and Practice V. Genetic and Evolutionary Computation Series, pp. 201–220. Springer US (2008)
9. Langdon, W.B., Banzhaf, W.: A SIMD interpreter for genetic programming on GPU graphics cards. In: O'Neill, M., Vanneschi, L., Gustafson, S., Esparcia Alcázar, A.I., De Falco, I., Della Cioppa, A., Tarantino, E. (eds.) EuroGP 2008. LNCS, vol. 4971, pp. 73–85. Springer, Heidelberg (2008)
10. Langdon, W.: A CUDA SIMT interpreter for genetic programming. Tech. Rep. TR-09-05, Department of Computer Science, Strand (June 2009) (revised)
11. Langdon, W.B.: A many threaded CUDA interpreter for genetic programming. In: Esparcia-Alcázar, A.I., Ekárt, A., Silva, S., Dignum, S., Uyar, A.Ş. (eds.) EuroGP 2010. LNCS, vol. 6021, pp. 146–158. Springer, Heidelberg (2010)
12. Lewis, T.E., Magoulas, G.D.: Strategies to minimise the total run time of cyclic graph based genetic programming with GPUs. In: Proceedings of the 11th GECCO Conference, GECCO 2009, pp. 1379–1386. ACM, New York (2009)
13. Maitre, O., Querry, S., Lachiche, N., Collet, P.: EASEA parallelization of tree-based Genetic Programming. In: 2010 IEEE Congress on Evolutionary Computation (CEC), pp. 1–8 (2010)
14. Maitre, O., Lachiche, N., Collet, P.: Fast evaluation of GP trees on GPGPU by optimizing hardware scheduling. In: Esparcia-Alcázar, A.I., Ekárt, A., Silva, S., Dignum, S., Uyar, A.Ş. (eds.) EuroGP 2010. LNCS, vol. 6021, pp. 301–312. Springer, Heidelberg (2010)
15. NVIDIA Corporation: NVIDIA CUDA C programming guide, version 3.2 (2010)
16. Robilliard, D., Marion-Poty, V., Fonlupt, C.: Population parallel GP on the G80 GPU. In: O'Neill, M., Vanneschi, L., Gustafson, S., Esparcia Alcázar, A.I., De Falco, I., Della Cioppa, A., Tarantino, E. (eds.) EuroGP 2008. LNCS, vol. 4971, pp. 98–109. Springer, Heidelberg (2008)
17. Robilliard, D., Marion-Poty, V., Fonlupt, C.: Genetic programming on graphics processing units. Genetic Programming and Evolvable Machines 10(4), 447–471 (2009)
18. Veeramachaneni, K., Derby, O., Sherry, D., O'Reilly, U.M.: Learning regression ensembles with genetic programming at scale. In: Proceeding of the Fifteenth GECCO Conference, GECCO 2013, pp. 1117–1124. ACM, New York (2013)
19. Wilson, G., Banzhaf, W.: Linear genetic programming GPGPU on Microsoft Xbox 360. In: IEEE Congress on Evolutionary Computation, pp. 378–385 (2008)
20. Yang, Y.: Adaptive regression by mixing. Journal of the American Statistical Association 96(454), 574–588 (2001)

Learning Dynamical Systems
Using Standard Symbolic Regression[*]

Sébastien Gaucel[1], Maarten Keijzer[2], Evelyne Lutton[1], and Alberto Tonda[1]

[1] INRA UMR 782 GMPA, 1 Av. Brétignières, 78850, Thiverval-Grignon, France
{sebastien.gaucel,evelyne.lutton,alberto.tonda}@grignon.inra.fr
[2] Pegasystems Inc., Amsterdam, Netherlands
maarten.keijzer@pega.com

Abstract. Symbolic regression has many successful applications in learning free-form regular equations from data. Trying to apply the same approach to differential equations is the logical next step: so far, however, results have not matched the quality obtained with regular equations, mainly due to additional constraints and dependencies between variables that make the problem extremely hard to tackle. In this paper we propose a new approach to dynamic systems learning. Symbolic regression is used to obtain a set of first-order Eulerian approximations of differential equations, and mathematical properties of the approximation are then exploited to reconstruct the original differential equations. Advantages of this technique include the de-coupling of systems of differential equations, that can now be learned independently; the possibility of exploiting established techniques for standard symbolic regression, after trivial operations on the original dataset; and the substantial reduction of computational effort, when compared to existing ad-hoc solutions for the same purpose. Experimental results show the efficacy of the proposed approach on an instance of the Lotka-Volterra model.

Keywords: Differential Equations, Dynamic Systems, Evolutionary Algorithms, Genetic Programming, Symbolic Regression.

1   Introduction

In recent years, Genetic Programming (GP) gained popularity as an effective optimization technique [1], and its capabilities of automatically uncovering hidden relationships in datasets and producing rules to control complex systems haves been proved in several real-world applications [2] [3].

Differential equations are mathematical equations for an unknown function of one or several variables that relates the values of the function itself and its derivatives of various orders: they play a prominent role in engineering, physics, economics, biology, and other disciplines.

The idea of using symbolic regression to learn differential equations is present since the beginnings of GP [4]: given the great interest towards this topic, several

---

[*] All authors contributed equally and their names are presented in alphabetical order.

M. Nicolau et al. (Eds.): EuroGP 2014, LNCS 8599, pp. 25–36, 2014.

research lines have followed. Babovic and Keijzer [5] propose a dimensionally-aware GP to learn dynamic systems in hydraulic engineering. Cao et al. [6] present a GP-based technique where an individual is a set of trees, representing a system of equations. Coefficients of the equations are optimized via a Genetic Algorithm, then the system is solved through a numerical integration method and the resulting equations are finally evaluated against training data. Iba [7] proposes an improvement over the previous approach, where coefficients are optimized through a least mean square technique, and a Runge-Kutta method of 4th order is used to build a solution. Bernardino and Barbos [8] use Grammar-Based Immune Programming to tackle the problem. It is important to notice that, while quite effective, all these concepts rely upon the use of ad-hoc individual construction, and significant computational costs to first solve the candidate equations and then compare them to experimental data.

We investigate a novel methodology for learning ordinary differential equations (ODE) through symbolic regression, whose original idea stems from an invited talk given by Maarten Keijzer during the GECCO conference in 2013 [9]. Given a system of ODEs, we show how the problem can be reduced to finding the first-order approximation of each ODE.We then apply the subsequent steps:

1. For each equation, standard symbolic regression is used to obtain a small group of candidate solutions that represent a trade-off between complexity and fitting;
2. A simple derivation procedure, following the properties of the first-order approximation of an ODE, is applied to each candidate solution, transforming them in ODEs;
3. Finally, corresponding equations are coupled in systems and examined with respect to dynamical behavior and fitting on the original data. The best system is returned to the user as the solution for the original problem.

Important advantages of our method are the possibility of learning differential equations using established symbolic regression techniques, instead of devising ad-hoc individual representations and fitness functions; the greatly reduced computational cost, since the most expensive procedures are performed *a posteriori* on a reduced set of candidate solutions; and the possibility of separately learning each differential equation in a target system, since the first-order approximation removes dependencies between variables.

Using the Lotka-Volterra model as a case study, we show the applicability of the proposed methodology through experimental validation. We find that the described approach is able to regularly find the correct structure of the original model, even in presence of noise. Results are discussed, and future works outlined.

The rest of the paper is structured as follows: Section 2 recalls a few necessary concepts related to symbolic regression and differential equations. The proposed approach is outlined in Section 3. The case study is presented in Section 4, while the experimental evaluation is described in Section 5. Results are discussed in Section 6, and finally Section 7 draws the conclusions and prospects future works.

2   Background

2.1   Genetic Programming and Symbolic Regression

Symbolic regression is an evolutionary technique able to extract free-form equations that correlate data from a given experimental dataset. The original idea is presented in [4]. Candidate solutions are encoded as trees, with terminal nodes corresponding to constants and variables of the problem, while intermediate nodes encode mathematical functions such as $\{+, -, *, /, ...\}$. The fitness function is usually proportional to the absolute or squared error between experimental data, with parsimony corrections to favor more compact solutions. An example of an individual for a symbolic regression problem is presented in Figure 1.

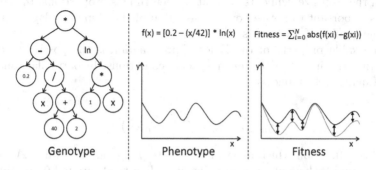

Fig. 1. A candidate solution in a typical symbolic regression problem. The internal representation (genotype) is a binary tree. The phenotype is the corresponding function, while the fitness to minimize is usually the absolute or squared error with respect to experimental points.

2.2   Differential Equations and First-Order Approximation

In order to clarify the scope of our work, we briefly summarize a few basic concepts related to differential equations that will be extensively used in the following. A differential equation is defined as *an equation containing the derivatives of one or more dependent variables, with respect to one of more independent variables* [10]. We will focus on *ordinary differential equations* (ODE), that contain derivatives as a function of a single variable (e.g. the time). A classical example of a differential equation is the first-order ordinary differential equation :

$$y'(t) = f(t, y(t)) \qquad y(t_0) = y_0 \tag{1}$$

where $y(t)$ is a function and y_0 is an initial condition.

The *(Explicit) Euler method* [11] is a first-order numerical procedure for solving ordinary differential equations with a given initial value: it is the most basic explicit method for numerical integration of ordinary differential equations. With reference to Equation 1, we use the finite difference formula to approximate $y'(t)$:

$$y'(t_n) = \lim_{\Delta_t \to 0} \frac{y(t_n + \Delta t) - y(t_n)}{\Delta_t} \simeq \frac{y(t_n + \Delta t) - y(t_n)}{\Delta_t} \tag{2}$$

Choosing a value Δt for the size of every step and setting $t_n = t_0 + n \cdot \Delta t$, one step of the Euler method from t_n to $t_{n+\Delta t} = t_n + \Delta t$ is:

$$y_{n+\Delta t} = y_n + \Delta t \cdot f(t_n, y_n) \tag{3}$$

where the value of y_n is an approximation of the solution to the ODE at time t_n, so that $y_n \approx y(t_n)$. The error per step of this method is proportional to the square of the step size, while its error at a given time is proportional to the step size. It is important to notice how the selection of the step size plays a crucial role in the quality of the results.

A remarkable property of the Euler approximation is the possibility of reconstructing the initial ODE, under specific conditions. In particular, one can rewrite Equation 3 as follows:

$$y_{n+\Delta t} - y_n = F(t_n, y_n, \Delta_t) \tag{4}$$

where F is a function which allows to evaluate $y_{n+\Delta t}$ for any value Δ_t. From Equation 4 and looking at the derivative according to Δ_t around 0, we obtain

$$\lim_{\Delta_t \to 0} \frac{y_{n+\Delta t} - y_n}{\Delta_t} = \lim_{\Delta_t \to 0} \frac{F(t_n, y_n, \Delta_t) - F(t_n, y_n, 0)}{\Delta_t} \tag{5}$$

which can be rewritten as

$$f(t, y(t)) = y'(t) = \left. \frac{\partial F(t_n, y_n, \Delta_t)}{\partial \Delta_t} \right|_{\Delta_t = 0} \tag{6}$$

going back to Equation 1.

In a practical scenario, Equation 4 can be used to iteratively build the approximate solution of Equation 1. At the opposite, assuming that an analytical form of the approximate solution of Equation 1 is available, Equation 6 can be used to obtain function f.

3   Proposed Approach

From Equation 6, we see how it is possible to return to the original ODE starting from the first-order approximation given in Equation 4. It is sufficient to find the classical function F in Equation 4.

In order to find F, additional data must be computed. Given a standard dataset with values of y for different values of time t, we need to add information to each line y_n, t_n, by computing the values of Δt and $y_n + 1$: in fact, in a real-world dataset, it is not given that $\Delta t = t_{n+1} - t_n$ will be constant for every n. Nevertheless, the procedure is trivial: an example is reported in Table 1. Once the new data are obtained, symbolic regression can be straightforwardly applied to the new dataset, to learn F.

Table 1. An example on how the values of the additional variables (**right**) can be easily produced starting from the original dataset (**left**). In this case, for each line, we computed the values of Δt and F to the next point, only.

t	y	Δt	$F = y_{n+\Delta t} - y_n$
0	20	0	0
0	20	1.8	-3.9
1.8	16.1	0	0
1.8	16.1	1.7	-2.9
3.5	13.2	0	0
3.5	13.2	1.9	-2.3
5.4	10.9	0	0
5.4	10.9	2.0	-2.1
...	...	...	...

t	y
0	20
1.8	16.1
3.5	13.2
5.4	10.9
7.4	8.8
...	...

One of the known issues of symbolic regression and GP in general is the so-called *overfitting*: solutions that closely approximate training data often exploit exclusive features of the dataset, for example by including terms that model the noise as well. This leads to poor performances on validation sets. Overfitting is sometimes associated with *bloating*, that is, the tendency of GP algorithms to produce bigger and bigger solutions as the evolution goes on. Connections between overfitting and bloating are still being investigated [12] [13], but empirical evidence shows how it can be beneficial to add parsimony measurements in the fitness function or preserve solutions of different complexity, in order to contain the phenomenon.

While overfitting is always undesired, it is particularly deleterious for the proposed approach: even if the F found through symbolic regression performed reasonably well on validation data, when using our procedure to go back to the original ODE, terms with a limited influence on F could create degenerate solutions. For this reason, instead of just using the best solution obtained at the end of the process, we prefer to have a set of candidate equations, each one a different compromise on a Pareto front between complexity and fitting on data.

Dynamic systems are usually represented by a set of ODEs and our approach allows the user to run a symbolic regression algorithm independently on each equation: however, since we prefer to work with a set of candidate solutions for each equation, we need an extra step to choose the best combination to represent the original system. Thus, we apply the procedure described in Equation 6 to every candidate solution of each set; we generate a set of n-uples, where n is the number of equations in the original system, by permuting solutions in all sets; we discard degenerate n-uples, showing a behavior dissimilar from the original data; and finally we choose the n-uple with the least absolute error with regards to the training data. The whole procedure is summarized in Figure 2.

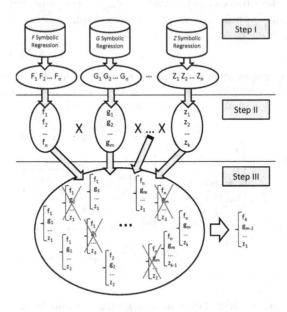

Fig. 2. Summary of the proposed approach. In **Step I**, standard symbolic regression is executed independently on each equation of the original dynamic system: each run returns a set of candidate solutions of variable size, representing different compromises between complexity and fitting on training data. During **Step II**, the obtained sets are transformed into sets of ODEs, following our methodology, and then permuted. Finally, in **Step III**, the resulting set of systems of ODEs is pruned of degenerate equations, the remaining candidate solutions are sorted by fitting on the original data, and the best solution is returned to the user.

4   Case Study

In order to attest the viability of our approach, we choose the Lotka-Volterra model [14] as a case study. This model, also known as *predator-prey equations*, is a system composed of two first-order, non-linear, differential equations frequently used to describe the dynamics of biological systems in which two species interact, one as a predator and the other as prey. The equations have been extensively used in biology and other fields, such as economic theory [15]. Their form is:

$$\begin{cases} \frac{dx}{dt} = x(\alpha - \beta y) \\ \frac{dy}{dt} = -y(\gamma - \delta x) \end{cases} \tag{7}$$

where x is the number of prey, y is the number of predators, t represents time, $\frac{dx}{dt}$ and $\frac{dy}{dt}$ represent the growth rates of the two populations over time. α, β, γ and δ are parameters that describe the interaction between the two species.

We focus on a particular configuration of the Lotka-Volterra model, where the parameters' values have been chosen so that no population goes extinct, leading to periodic solutions: $\alpha = 0.04$, $\beta = 0.0005$, $\gamma = 0.2$ and $\delta = 0.004$. Initial populations were taken as $x_0 = y_0 = 20$. A plot of the chosen configuration is reported in Figure 3.

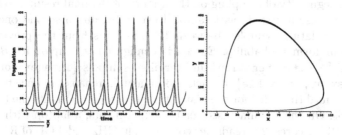

Fig. 3. Plots of the Lotka-Volterra model with parameters used in the experiments. On the left, the variation of the two population with respect to time (x in black, y in blue/light grey). On the right, the state plane with x on the horizontal axis and y on the vertical axis.

Following Equation 4, we are then interested in finding the two functions F and G, first-order approximations of the first and second differential equation of the Lotka-Volterra model, respectively:

$$x_{n+\Delta t} - x_n = F(\Delta t, x_n, y_n) \tag{8}$$
$$y_{n+\Delta t} - y_n = G(\Delta t, x_n, y_n) \tag{9}$$

A major feature of the proposed approach is the ability to learn the two functions in two separate and independent runs of the symbolic regression algorithm. Indeed, the reciprocal dependency of the Lotka-Volterra system has been removed.

5   Experimental Results

Since one of the main advantages of the proposed approach is the possibility of exploiting existing tools for standard symbolic regression, for our study we choose *Eureqa Formulize*[1] [1], considered a state-of-the-art software in the field. Eureqa has one feature of particular interest for our purpose: instead of returning a single solution per run, it presents the user a group of solutions that represent a Pareto front for the objectives of fitting and complexity: see Figure 5 for an

---

[1] http://formulize.nutonian.com/

example. In Eureqa, each symbol that can appear in a GP tree is associated with a weight, and the complexity of a candidate solution is simply the sum of all weights of terms appearing in it; fitting is computed with respect to the squared error with regards to the training data. It must be noted that, in principle, any GP-based technique able to preserve individuals of different complexity in the final population could be used for our methodology.

Each dataset is modified following the procedure described in Section 3: we use 200 points for the training set. We are interested in exploring the influence of noise and regularity of sampling on the quality of the final results, so for each experiment we use a first dataset sampled every 2 s, and a second one, where every point of data is sampled between 1.5 and 2.5 s from the previous one, following a uniform probability. Eureqa is configured to employ its *Basic* set of functions {+,-,*,/,negation} and terminal symbols {integer constant, float constant, variable}. In each experiment Eureqa is run once to stagnation, that is, until the index for the maturity of the population hits the threshold value of 90%. On the machine used for the experiments, a laptop with an Intel i5-2430M CPU (2 cores, 2 threads per core) at 2.40 GHz and 4 GB of RAM, running to stagnation takes 15-20 minutes, and around 10^{10} total fitness evaluations. After each run, Eureqa typically returns about 20 solutions on its Pareto front. In many real-world scenarios, it is almost impossible to make assumptions on the type of noise affecting the measurements, so we chose to try our approach in different conditions. The following experiments consider the same dataset, first noise-free, then with absolute and relative noise of different magnitude added to the original data.

5.1   Noise-Free Data

In the simplest scenario, we use datasets with no noise added. The first run, with data regularly sampled, returns 20 candidate solutions for F and 20 candidate solutions for G. Each equation is transformed into an ODE, following our proposed approach. The resulting 400 systems are then pruned of degenerate solutions, that is, solutions that converge towards a point in the x, y plane (see Figure 4 for an example). The remaining systems of ODEs are finally sorted by fitting on the original unmodified training data. The same procedure is followed for the dataset with irregular sampling. This time, 21 candidate solutions are produced for F and 25 for G. The best ODE systems are:

$$\begin{cases} \frac{dx}{dt} = 0.04114x - 0.0004946xy \\ \frac{dy}{dt} = 0.00367xy - 0.1861y \end{cases} \quad \begin{cases} \frac{dx}{dt} = 0.04116x - 0.0004924xy \\ \frac{dy}{dt} = 0.003599xy - 0.1826y \end{cases} \tag{10}$$

with the result for regular sampling on the left, and the result for irregular sampling on the right. Both show the same form of the original Lotka-Volterra model, and a remarkable approximation of the parameters' values. As a comparison, in Figure 4 the two systems found with the proposed approach are compared to the systems obtained by simply coupling the best fitting-wise candidate solutions produced in each run.

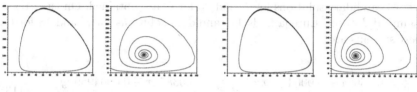

(a) Regular sampling, noise-free   (b) Irregular sampling, noise-free

Fig. 4. Side-by-side comparison on the noise-free dataset, of the best system found through the proposed approach (**left**), and the system obtained by pairing the two fitting-wise best solutions of each run (**right**). It is easy to notice how simply pairing the best candidate solutions leads to degenerate forms or to a lowest fitting on the original training data.

5.2 Absolute Noise

In a second trial, random noise (selected from the interval $(-5, 5)$ with uniform probability) is added to the x and y outputs of the model. On the regularly sampled dataset, Eureqa finds 17 candidate solutions for F and 20 for G. On the irregularly sampled dataset, 13 solutions for F and 19 for G are obtained. The best resulting systems are:

$$\begin{cases} \frac{dx}{dt} = 0.03992x - 0.0005548xy \\ \frac{dy}{dt} = 0.003525xy - 0.1916y \end{cases} \quad \begin{cases} \frac{dx}{dt} = 0.03946x - 0.0005354xy \\ \frac{dy}{dt} = 0.003662xy - 0.1948y \end{cases} \quad (11)$$

with the result for regular sampling on the left, and the result for irregular sampling on the right.

5.3 Noise 5%

In the third experimental run we add random noise proportional to the output value, ranging from -5% to +5% with uniform probability. On the regularly sampled dataset, Eureqa returns 16 candidate solutions for F and 15 for G. On the irregularly sampled dataset, we obtain 16 candidate solutions for F and 16 for G. The best resulting systems are:

$$\begin{cases} \frac{dx}{dt} = 0.03947x - 0.0004883xy \\ \frac{dy}{dt} = 0.003706xy - 0.1902y \end{cases} \quad \begin{cases} \frac{dx}{dt} = 0.03743x - 0.0004522xy \\ \frac{dy}{dt} = 0.003707xy - 0.1916y \end{cases} \quad (12)$$

with the result for regular sampling on the left, and the result for irregular sampling on the right.

5.4 Noise 10%

In the last experiment, we add random noise proportional to the output value, ranging from -10% to +10% with uniform probability. On the regularly sampled dataset, 23 candidate solutions for F and 20 for G are obtained. On the irregularly sampled dataset, Eureqa finds 17 candidate solutions for F and 18 for G. The best systems are:

$$\begin{cases} \frac{dx}{dt} = 0.0362x - 0.0004797xy \\ \frac{dy}{dt} = 0.003306xy - 0.1841y \end{cases} \quad \begin{cases} \frac{dx}{dt} = 0.03874x - 0.0004959xy \\ \frac{dy}{dt} = 0.003587xy - 0.1898y \end{cases} \quad (13)$$

with the result for regular sampling on the left, and the result for irregular sampling on the right.

6   Results Discussion

The proposed approach is able to find the correct model for the Lotka-Volterra function during each run, even if the parameters (α, β, γ, δ) might slightly differ, especially when dealing with noise. Remarkably, the irregularity of the sampling for the training set does not seem to influence the final outcome; while the presence of noise predictably returns results of lower quality.

From the experimental evaluation, we can see how Eureqa consistently returns a set of candidate solutions in the order of 10^1: since there are only two differential equations in the model, the search space for coupling the candidate solutions and assessing the results in the second step of our process explores a search space of 10^2. However, when dealing with huge systems of differential equations, the

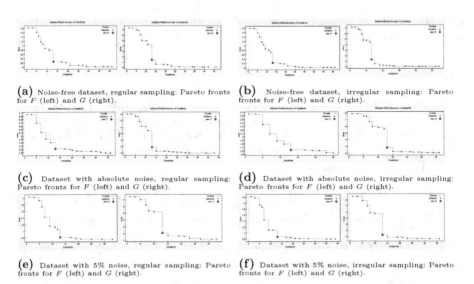

(a) Noise-free dataset, regular sampling: Pareto fronts for F (left) and G (right).

(b) Noise-free dataset, irregular sampling: Pareto fronts for F (left) and G (right).

(c) Dataset with absolute noise, regular sampling: Pareto fronts for F (left) and G (right).

(d) Dataset with absolute noise, irregular sampling: Pareto fronts for F (left) and G (right).

(e) Dataset with 5% noise, regular sampling: Pareto fronts for F (left) and G (right).

(f) Dataset with 5% noise, irregular sampling: Pareto fronts for F (left) and G (right).

Fig. 5. Pareto fronts of the solutions found by Eureqa during some of the experiments. The individual with the correct form of the Lotka-Volterra function is highlighted in red, and it is noticeable how it almost always lies in the middle of the Pareto front, often showing the biggest improvement over the previous step.

complexity quickly explodes: if the GP routinely returns n solutions, the search space of possible systems of m equations would become $O(n^m)$. Thus, it would be beneficial to reduce the number of viable equations in each set before the coupling process. For example, all equations that, after the derivation process from Equation 6, are reduced to a constant, can be dismissed. This subset, however, includes only 1-2 candidate solutions per set: other methods to prune the Pareto front from uninteresting models should be explored. From the experimental results, we observe how most of the exact forms for the Lotka-Volterra equations always lie in the middle part of the Pareto front fitting/complexity provided by Eureqa (see Figure 5). It would be interesting to investigate whether this property can be generalized to all problems: in that case, the extremes of the Pareto front could be excluded; also, from the Pareto fronts, it looks that often the correct solution shows the biggest improvement with regards to the previous one. These considerations could be included in a heuristic coupling to reduce the number of associations.

7 Conclusions and Future Works

In this paper, we presented a GP-based methodology to learn ordinary differential equations starting from experimental data. The basic idea is reducing the problem to finding Euler's first-order approximation of an ODE, that is, a regular equation. Once the starting dataset is modified accordingly, we can apply a standard symbolic regression technique, obtaining a group of candidate solutions that represent a trade-off between complexity and fitting to data. Through an inverse procedure to reconstruct an ODE starting from its first-order approximation, used on the whole group of candidate solutions, we acquire a group of ODEs. Finally, by coupling the ODEs obtained, discarding degenerate solutions, and sorting the remaining ones by fitting on the training data, we are able to find a system of ODEs that solves the initial problem.

From the preliminary experiments, it is clear that the coupling step might lead to a combinatorial explosion for the systems to evaluate. Future works will explore an automated coupling of candidate solutions, using theoretical and heuristic measurements to return the best set of solutions. We are currently working on the application of the proposed methodology to a real-world problem for the modelling of processes in the food industry.

Acknowledgments. The authors would like to thank Luuk van Dijk for providing the original idea underlying this work.

References

1. Schmidt, M., Lipson, H.: Distilling free-form natural laws from experimental data. Science 324(5923), 81–85 (2009)
2. Pickardt, C., Branke, J., Hildebrandt, T., Heger, J., Scholz-Reiter, B.: Generating dispatching rules for semiconductor manufacturing to minimize weighted tardiness. In: Proceedings of the 2010 Winter Simulation Conference (WSC), pp. 2504–2515. IEEE (2010)

3. Soule, T., Heckendorn, R.B.: A practical platform for on-line genetic programming for robotics. In: Genetic Programming Theory and Practice X, pp. 15–29. Springer (2013)
4. Koza, J.R.: Genetic Programming: On the programming of computers by means of natural selection, vol. 1. MIT Press (1992)
5. Babovic, V., Keijzer, M., Aguilera, D.R., Harrington, J.: An evolutionary approach to knowledge induction: Genetic programming in hydraulic engineering. In: Proceedings of the World Water and Environmental Resources Congress, vol. 111, p. 64 (2001)
6. Cao, H., Kang, L., Chen, Y., Yu, J.: Evolutionary modeling of systems of ordinary differential equations with genetic programming. Genetic Programming and Evolvable Machines 1(4), 309–337 (2000)
7. Iba, H.: Inference of differential equation models by genetic programming. Information Sciences 178(23), 4453–4468 (2008)
8. Bernardino, H.S., Barbosa, H.J.C.: Inferring systems of ordinary differential equations via grammar-based immune programming. In: Liò, P., Nicosia, G., Stibor, T. (eds.) ICARIS 2011. LNCS, vol. 6825, pp. 198–211. Springer, Heidelberg (2011)
9. Keijzer, M.: Inducing differential/flow equations. Invited talk to the GECCO Conference (July 2013)
10. Zill, D.G.: A First Course in Differential Equations: With Modeling Applications. Cengage Learning (2008)
11. Euler, L.: Institutionum calculi integralis. Imp. Acad. imp. Saènt, vol. 1 (1768)
12. Vanneschi, L., Castelli, M., Silva, S.: Measuring bloat, overfitting and functional complexity in genetic programming. In: Proceedings of the 12th Annual Conference on Genetic and Evolutionary Computation, pp. 877–884. ACM (2010)
13. O'Neill, M., Vanneschi, L., Gustafson, S., Banzhaf, W.: Open issues in genetic programming. Genetic Programming and Evolvable Machines 11(3-4), 339–363 (2010)
14. Lotka, A.J.: Contribution to the theory of periodic reactions. The Journal of Physical Chemistry 14(3), 271–274 (1910)
15. Goodwin, R.M.: A growth cycle. In: Socialism, Capitalism and Economic Growth, pp. 54–58 (1967)

Semantic Crossover
Based on the Partial Derivative Error

Mario Graff[1], Ariel Graff-Guerrero[2], and Jaime Cerda-Jacobo[1]

[1] Division de Estudios de Posgrado
Facultad de Ingenieria Eléctrica
Universidad Michoacana de San Nicolás de Hidalgo, México
mgraffg@dep.fie.umich.mx, jcerda@umich.mx
[2] PET Centre, Centre for Addiction and Mental Health, Toronto, ON, Canada
Ariel_graff@yahoo.com.mx

Abstract. There is great interest for the development of semantic genetic operators to improve the performance of genetic programming. Semantic genetic operators have traditionally been developed employing experimentally or theoretically-based approaches. Our current work proposes a novel semantic crossover developed amid the two traditional approaches. Our proposed semantic crossover operator is based on the use of the derivative of the error propagated through the tree. This process decides the crossing point of the second parent. The results show that our procedure improves the performance of genetic programming on rational symbolic regression problems.

Keywords: Semantic Crossover, Symbolic Regression.

1 Introduction

Semantic genetic operators have been proposed to improve the performance of genetic programming. Semantic operators use the information of the phenotype to create new individuals. There are two approaches to develop semantic operators, the first is experimentally-based, and the second is theoretically-based.

The experimentally-based approach produces a semantic crossover based on either the fitness function or the behaviour of the trees. Blickle et al. [1] propose to select as crossing points only those nodes that have an impact in the fitness function, this is implemented using a flag on the nodes, that is set during the evaluation of the tree. Nguyen et al. [2, 3] produce offspring that are semantically different from its parents; this difference is measured by evaluating the individuals in a set of random inputs.

On the other hand, following a theoretically-based approach, Beadle et al. [4, 5] propose a semantic operator that only accepts an offspring if it is semantically non-equivalent to its parents. The non-equivalent property is verified by using a reduced ordered binary decisions diagram, which is also employed to develop a semantically different initial population (see [6]). In addition, Krawiec et al. [7] develop an approximation of a geometric semantic crossover that is important

M. Nicolau et al. (Eds.): EuroGP 2014, LNCS 8599, pp. 37–47, 2014.
© Springer-Verlag Berlin Heidelberg 2014

because has the potential to convert the landscape into a cone. Furthermore, Moraglio *et al.* [8] have shown the feasibility of creating a geometric semantic crossover and mutation. The procedure proposed by Moraglio *et al.* to generate the offspring is clean and easy to implement; however, it has the drawback that the constructed offspring is always bigger than the sum of the lengths of its parents which imposes a limitation for applicability. Nonetheless, Vanneschi *et al.* [9] overcome this original limitation allowing the algorithm to be executed with the traditional parameters used in GP.

Our current contribution proposes a semantic crossover for tree-based genetic programming (GP) that is in-between the experimentally-based and the theoretically-based approaches. The proposed semantic crossover is based on the derivative of the error, i.e., the derivative of the fitness function $f(p)$. In symbolic regression problems, it is common to compute the fitness function as: $f(p) = \sum_{(x,y) \in \mathcal{T}} (y - p(x))^2$, where $\mathcal{T} = \{(x_i, y_i) : i = 1 \ldots N\}$ is the training set, and $p(x)$ represents the output of the individual p on input x.

The semantic crossover proposed here works by:

1. Computing $\frac{\partial f}{\partial v}$ equivalently to what backpropagation algorithm [10] does to update the weights of an Artificial Neural Network.[1] However, in our procedure, v is a node randomly selected from the first parent, whereas in backpropagation v is always a constants, i.e., a weight.
2. The result of $\frac{\partial f}{\partial v}$ is used to select the crossing point of the second parent.
3. The two points are used to perform a traditional subtree crossover.

The results illustrate, that GP enhanced with the proposed semantic crossover statistically outperforms a GP with traditional crossover on 1,100 rational functions used as testbed.

The current paper is organized as follows. Section 2 presents our novel semantic crossover. Section 3 describes the procedure used to generate the symbolic regression problems and the GP systems used to illustrate the effectiveness of our approach. Section 4, conclusions and future directions are presented.

2   Semantic Crossover Based on Partial Derivative Error

The semantic crossover proposed is computed as follows: a) let v be a node randomly selected from the first parent; b) given v, $\frac{\partial f}{\partial v}$ is computed; c) a node u is selected from the second parent using the information of the partial derivative with respect to v; and d) finally, it is performed a subtree crossover using as crossing points v and u. The rest of the section contains a detailed description of this procedure. Subsection 2.1 shows the procedure used to compute $\frac{\partial f}{\partial v}$, i.e., it presents the backpropagation algorithm implemented in a tree structure; and Subsection 2.2 describes the process to select u.

---

[1] The use of backpropagation in GP has been previously proposed in [11–14].

2.1   Backpropagation

The first step, in order to describe the semantic crossover proposed, is to show the process used to compute $\frac{\partial f}{\partial v}$. As we mentioned, the backpropagation algorithm can be used to obtain $\frac{\partial f}{\partial v}$. Backpropagation can be easily explained using the ideas presented on [10]. R. Rojas used a graphical representation to explain it and this representation can be easily codified in a tree-based GP.

Let us describe backpropagation by computing the chain rule, i.e., $\frac{\partial g(h(x))}{\partial x}$. The first step is to compute $g(h(x))$, see upper part of Figure 1 and, note, that each inner node is split in two part; the right part corresponds to the node's output and the left part stores the output of the operation shown in each node. The flow of information is indicated by the arrows. The second and, final step, is to traverse the tree backwards, see lower part of Figure 1. This backward step is performed by supplying a constant to the root, in this case 1 and then multiplying this constant by the value stored on the left side of each node. This process recursively continues until a leaf is reached. It is observed, in the lower part of the figure, that $\frac{\partial g(h(x))}{\partial x}$ is obtained at the end of this process.

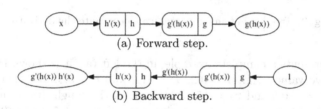

(a) Forward step.

(b) Backward step.

Fig. 1. Computing the derivative in a graph

Continuing with the description of backpropagation, let us suppose that a leaf node is a constant w, then, the process mentioned above computes $\frac{\partial f}{\partial w}$. This can be used to update w following the rule $w = w - \nu \frac{\partial f}{\partial w}$, where ν is the learning factor. This update can be performed per training case, or for the whole training set, the former is known as *incremental learning* and the later is *batch learning*. In batch learning w is updated using the rule $w = w - \nu \sum_{i=1}^{|T|} \frac{\partial f_i}{\partial w}$, where f_i be the error in the ith case of the training set. In addition to this, the resilient backpropagation (RPROP) [15] can be implemented using only the sign and a different ν for the increase and decrease values, i.e., $w = w - \nu_x \cdot \text{sign}(\sum_i^{|T|} \frac{\partial f_i}{\partial w})$, where x stands for decrease or increase learning rate.

In order to have a complete picture of how the process, Figure 2 presents an example. In the left of the figure (a), it is illustrated a function represented as a tree. In the right (b), we have the same tree is presented with the additional information required to compute the derivatives. Note that two slots are needed for the functions having two arguments. For example, in the product the first part stores the second input, given that $\frac{\partial x \cdot y}{\partial x} = y$ and the second part contains the first input. We have illustrated that the sum nodes store ones which is the partial derivative with respect to each input. However, there is not need to store information on the sum nodes and has been included only to ensure a clear description of the example.

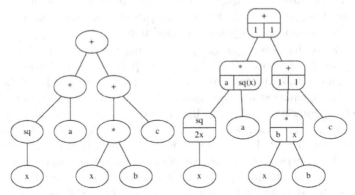

(a) Tradition tree on GP repre- (b) Tree with additional storage
senting $y(x) = ax^2 + bx + c$.   to save the derivatives.

Fig. 2. Tree having an extra storage to compute the derivative

Figure 3 presents a complete example, in the left (a), it is shown that all the constants have values, e.g., $a = 0.2$, $b = -1.2$ and $c = 0.3$, and that there are two inputs $x_1 = -0.5$ and $x_2 = 0.5$. Furthermore, the sought function is $y(x) = 0.5x^2 - 2.25x + 0.6$ which leads to a training set $\mathcal{F} = \{(-0.5, 1.85), (0.5, -0.4)\}$. Under these circumstances the tree's output is $(0.95, -0.25)$. In the evaluation process, i.e., the forward step, all the partial derivatives are computed and stored in their respective nodes; this is shown in the lower part of each node (left of the figure). The backward step requires to feed the node with a value, this value is the derivative of the error, which depends on the function used to compute the error. Let $f(p) = (y - p)^2$ be the error function, then its derivative with respect to p is $-2(y-p)$. Given that $y = (1.85, -0.4)$ is the desired output and $p = (0.95, -0.25)$ is the tree's output, hence the value fed is $-2(y - p) = (-1.8, 0.3)$. This value is propagated through the tree until a constant is reached. Finally, this constant is updated using the sign of all the values reach to that specific node. The constants are decreased or increased depending on whether the sign is positive or negative, respectively. In the case the value received by a constant is zero, then that constant is not updated.

2.2 Selecting the Crossing Points

So far, we have described the backpropagation algorithm implemented in a tree. This algorithm is recursive and in the backward step it stops when a leaf is reached; however, nothing forbids to stop it at any particular node. Let us suppose that the procedure is stopped at node v (v is randomly selected from the

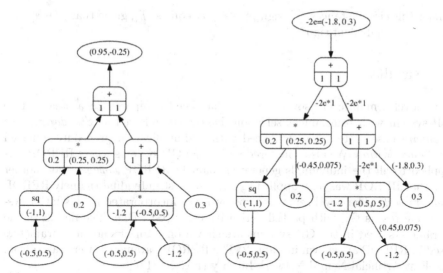

(a) Individual evaluated on $x = -0.5$ and (b) Error propagation on the two fitness $x = 0.5$. The root node is the result of the cases. The root contains the error between $y(x)$ and the individual's output.

Fig. 3. Example of the use of back-propagation in a tree, when the sought function is $y(x) = 0.5x^2 - 2.25x + 0.6$. The sum of the error on constant 0.2 is -0.375, on constant -1.2 is 1.05 and on 0.3 is -1.5, indicating that the value of the constants must be incremented, decremented and incremented, respectively.

first parent), then, at this point, it is obtained $\frac{\partial f}{\partial v}$, which indicates whether the values returned by v must be either decreased or increased depending on whether $\frac{\partial f}{\partial v} > 0$ or $\frac{\partial f}{\partial v} < 0$, respectively.

In order to select the crossing point of the second parent, the following procedure is performed. Let e be $\text{sign}(\frac{\partial f}{\partial v})$, e_i corresponds the sign of the partial derivative error in the ith training case and v correspond to the crossing point of the first parent. In a tree-based GP v can be seen as a complete tree, i.e., one can remove v from the parent and treat it as new individual. In this context let p^v be the output of v when it is evaluated with the inputs of $\mathcal{T}$ and p_i^v represents the output of v in the ith training case. Equivalently, for the second parent, we can compute the output of all the nodes, let s^j represent the output of node j of the second parent. Using e, p and s, we can find the crossing point of the second parent, i.e., u, as:

$$u = \arg\max_j \sum_i \text{sign}(p_i^v - s_i^j) \cdot e_i. \tag{1}$$

In order to clarify Equation (1), let us analyse the two possible scenarios found in the maximum of Equation (1). Firstly, in the case $e_i > 0$, then s_i^u is higher than p_i^v consequently $p_i^v - s_i^m$ is positive. On the other hand, $e_i < 0$ implies that $p_i^n - s^m$ is negative; however, $e_i < 0$ is also negative and the result is positive.

Under this circumstances, $\sum_i \text{sign}(p_i^v - s_i^u) \cdot e_i$ equals $|\mathcal{T}|$, given that $p_i^v - s_i^u$ and e_i have an equivalent sign.

3 Results

Our novel semantic crossover operator has been compared to a steady-state GP system with tournament selection, henceforth referred as *Standard*[2]. This *Standard* base system was enhanced with a simplification procedure, referred as, *Simplification*. We also compared additional GP systems where RPROP was applied to all the individuals generated (namely RPROP *always*) and another one that RPROP was only applied to any new best individual (namely RPROP *only on best*). The novel semantic crossover was incorporated in this latter system referred as GP with partial derivative error (GPPDE). The details of the parameters used in the GP systems are shown on Table 1 and the parameters used in RPROP are shown in Table 2. The RPROP parameters were taken from the Fast Artificial Neural Network Library (FANN) [17]

In our implementation, each epoch spent in RPROP was counted as an individual generated and the maximum number of generated individuals was $50,000$. In addition, only an individual that has been optimized with RPROP was kept only if the individual was better than the original.

Table 1. Genetic Programming Parameters

Parameter	Value
Function Set	$\mathcal{F} = \{+, -, \times, /\}$
Terminal set ($\mathbb{T}$)	$\mathbb{T} = \{x, \Re\}$
Random constants (i.e., $\Re$)	100 real value constants $\in [-10, 10]$
Max length	262143
Crossover rate	90%
Mutation rate	10%
Population size	1000
Number of Generations	50
Mutation depth	random $\in [1, 5]$
Tournament size	2
Max. number of epochs without improvement	5

The simplification mechanism was used in all the GP systems except the Standard GP. This simplification was applied to all the elements of the initial population and to every new offspring. This procedure was very simple, it only incorporated rules to reduce the tree in the following cases, where s stands for any subtree, $\Re$ is a constant and *op* represents any operation.

---

[2] This is very similar to TinyGP [16], it is only modified to allow the evolution of constants for each individual in the population.

Table 2. RPROP's parameters

Parameter	Value
Increase Factor	1.2
Decrease Factor	0.5
Delta min	0.0
Delta max	50.0
Init previous step value	0.0001

- Replace $(op\ \Re\ \Re)$ with the result of that operation.
- Replace $(+\ s\ 0)$ with s.
- Replace $(-\ s\ s)$ with 0.
- Replace $(*\ s\ 0)$ with 0.
- Replace $(*\ s\ 1)$ with s.
- Replace $(/\ 0\ s)$ with 0.
- Replace $(/\ s\ s)$ with 1.
- Replace $(op\ op^{-1}\ s)$ with s.

Figure 4 shows an example of the simplification mechanism. For example, the subtree $(*-3.01.2)$ is replaced by the constant -3.6 and the whole left subtree is replaced by 1.0. The rules were applied recursively and as consequence it might be a case in which an entire tree could be substituted by a constant.

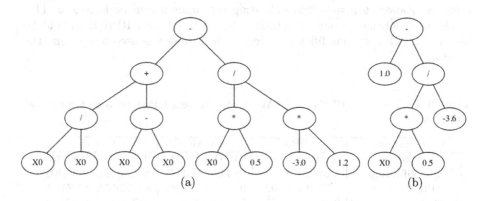

(a)   (b)

Fig. 4. Simplifying a tree, a) shows the original tree, and b) presents the tree after the simplification

The problem employed as benchmark, was a continuous symbolic regression problem on rational functions. We created 1,100 different rational functions using the following procedure. Two polynomials, $W(x)$ and $Q(x)$, were built by randomly choosing the degree of each in the range 2 to 8, and then choosing random real coefficients in the interval $[-10, 10]$ for the powers of x up to the chosen degree. A rational function in our training set is then given by $y(x) = \frac{W(x)}{Q(x)}$. Each of the rational functions in the set was then sampled at 21 points uniformly distributed in the interval $[-1, 1]$. This resulted in a target vector $\mathbf{y} \in \Re^{21}$. The aforementioned procedure was previously used in [18] to test their approach.

For each $\mathbf{y}$ vector 30 independent runs were performed recording the output of the best individual found, namely $\mathbf{p}$. With this value, it was computed $|\mathcal{T}|^{-1} \sum_i^{|\mathcal{T}|} \sqrt{(|\hat{\mathbf{y}}_i - \hat{\mathbf{p}}_i|)}$, where $\hat{\mathbf{y}} = \frac{\mathbf{y}-\mu}{\sigma}$ and $\hat{\mathbf{p}} = \frac{\mathbf{p}-\mu}{\sigma}$, μ is the mean of $\mathbf{y}$ and σ is the standard deviation of $\mathbf{y}$. Finally, this value was recorded for each of the 30 independent runs and the performance was the average of these values defined as nBRF. Another measure of performance was used which is a normalize version of the mean absolute error (nMAE), i.e., $|\mathcal{T}|^{-1} \sum_i^{|\mathcal{T}|} |\hat{\mathbf{y}}_i - \hat{\mathbf{p}}_i|$, where $\hat{\mathbf{y}} = m\mathbf{y} + b$ and $\hat{\mathbf{p}} = m\mathbf{p} + b$. In this case, m and b were $[0, 1]$, zero stands for the minimum value of $\mathbf{y}$ and one for the maximum.

Table 3 presents the performance of the different GP systems. It includes the performance of the standard GP, GP with the simplification procedure, GP with RPROP applied to all the individuals (RPROP always), GP with RPROP applied to every new best (RPROP only on best). GPPDE showed the best performance in the two performance measures. In order to test whether the differences in performance were statistically significant, a Wilcoxon signed-rank test [19] were performed, the p values were well below 0.01 indicating that the performance of GPPDE was better than the second best with a confidence of 99%.

A particular result of note was the nMAE's performance of the GP with simplification. The comparison of the performance using a Wilcoxon signed-rank test showed a $p = 0.2948$ indicating not difference in performance. This result was contrary to our expectations because GP with RPROP should be better than GP with simplification because the former was used to optimize the constants.

Table 3. Performance (BRF and nMAE) of the different GP systems on the rational functions

GP systems	nBRF	nMAE	Length
Standard	0.2492 ± 0.0857	0.0741 ± 0.0486	958.6116 ± 178.0225
Simplification	0.2450 ± 0.0853	0.0719 ± 0.0475	990.1021 ± 193.6305
RPROP always	0.5370 ± 0.1027	0.3063 ± 0.1042	$\mathbf{61.8987 \pm 11.7165}$
RPROP only on best	0.2394 ± 0.0852	0.0719 ± 0.0480	647.3761 ± 154.5169
GPPDE	$\mathbf{0.1320 \pm 0.0535}$	$\mathbf{0.0251 \pm 0.0263}$	6077.9015 ± 2178.9033

GPPDE showed the best performance; however, the average length of the trees was considerable longer than those obtained with others GP systems. GP-PDE generates trees that were on average more than 6 times longer than those obtained with Simplification GP. On the other hand, when RPROP was applied to all the generated individuals, the trees were short and this might be the cause for the poor performance observed. The results indicate that RPROP should be used more carefully in order to allow more exploration of the search space, or used a larger number of generations.

In order to complement the information presented in Table 3, the number of times each algorithm presented the best performance was counted, the performance measure used was nMAE. This procedure showed that Simplification GP presented the best performance in 5 of the 1,100 problems and GPPDE has the best performance in 1095 of the 1,100 problems.

Figure 5 presents the average output of Simplification GP and GPPDE on one of the five problems in which GPPDE did not exhibit the best performance. In this problem, Simplification GP had 0.0362 and GPPDE has 0.0464, these two values were computed using nMAE. GPPDE did not reach the peaks as closely as Simplification GP, although the behaviour of these two systems on this problem was qualitatively equivalent.

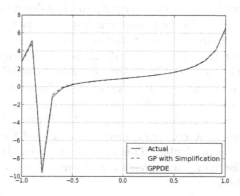

Fig. 5. Average output of GP with simplification and GPPDE on a problem where GPPDE does not have the best performance

The performance (nBRF) presented on Table 3 can be compared with the performance of the different GP algorithms previously presented by Graff and Poli [18]. The systems presented by Graff and Poli [18] include: generational GP systems with roulette and tournament selection, steady-state GP systems with tournament selection, generational gene expression programming (GEP) with roulette and tournament selection, steady-state GEP with tournament selection and different versions of stochastic iterated hill climber (SIHC). In total there are 20 different GP systems. First our standard GP system correspond to the steady-state GP system with tournament selection and 100% crossover. Our implementation has a performance of 0.2492 and the performance previously presented by our group [18] was 0.2535. These two values seems to be comparable and the difference might be due to the random number generators or any other minor modification.

The GPPDE showed the best performance overall the systems tested. Our previous work [18] showed that SIHC system with subtree mutation and 25000 as the maximum number of mutations showed a performance of 0.2021 which is considerable higher than the performance obtained by GPPDE (0.0464). Unfortunately, it is not available the lengths of the tree generated by SIHC and consequently the full performance cannot be compared.

4   Conclusions

Our work presents the development of a novel semantic crossover operator that is based on the derivative of the errors. The results showed that choosing the crossover point of the second parent according to Equation 1 improves considerably the learning abilities of the GP systems. GPPDE showed the best performance in almost all the problems tested (1095 out of 1100), and it also obtained on average the best performance in comparison to the systems presented here, and, also, to the 20 systems previously presented by our group [18].

The improvement presented needs plenty of computations performed on the trees. That is, one needs to keep the output, and the derivative of the output, for every node of every tree in the population. This may be a drawback because the technique may be limited to small populations and/or small trees. However, the full potential that this amount of information can provide has not been properly explored. For example, in order to evaluate an offspring, it is only needed to recalculate the nodes whose values have been changed, this would make the algorithm faster. On the other hand, one can measure the fitness of each node, and take decisions dynamically based on the fitness. Another limitation with the proposed semantic crossover operator is that all the functions in the function set need to be derivable. This may be a major drawback for some problems; however, for symbolic regression problems it seems reasonable to use only derivable functions.

Acknowledgments. This project would not be possible without the use of the CAMH Specialized Computing Cluster (SCC).

We would like to anonymous reviewers for their fair and useful comments and ideas. The paper has been considerably strengthened thanks to their feedback.

References

1. Blickle, T., Thiele, L.: Genetic programming and redundancy. Choice 1000, 2 (1994)
2. Nguyen, Q.U., Nguyen, X.H., O'Neill, M.: Semantic aware crossover for genetic programming: The case for real-valued function regression. In: Vanneschi, L., Gustafson, S., Moraglio, A., De Falco, I., Ebner, M. (eds.) EuroGP 2009. LNCS, vol. 5481, pp. 292–302. Springer, Heidelberg (2009)
3. Uy, N.Q., Hoai, N.X., ONeill, M., McKay, R.I., Galvn-López, E.: Semantically-based crossover in genetic programming: application to real-valued symbolic regression. Genetic Programming and Evolvable Machines 12(2), 91–119 (2010)
4. Beadle, L., Johnson, C.: Semantically driven crossover in genetic programming. In: IEEE Congress on Evolutionary Computation, CEC 2008 (IEEE World Congress on Computational Intelligence), pp. 111–116 (2008)
5. Beadle, L., Johnson, C.: Semantically driven mutation in genetic programming. In: IEEE Congress on Evolutionary Computation, CEC 2009, pp. 1336–1342 (2009)

6. Beadle, L., Johnson, C.G.: Semantic analysis of program initialisation in genetic programming. Genetic Programming and Evolvable Machines 10(3), 307–337 (2009)
7. Krawiec, K., Lichocki, P.: Approximating geometric crossover in semantic space. In: Proceedings of the 11th Annual Conference on Genetic and Evolutionary Computation, GECCO 2009, pp. 987–994. ACM, New York (2009)
8. Moraglio, A., Krawiec, K., Johnson, C.G.: Geometric semantic genetic programming. In: Coello, C.A.C., Cutello, V., Deb, K., Forrest, S., Nicosia, G., Pavone, M. (eds.) PPSN 2012, Part I. LNCS, vol. 7491, pp. 21–31. Springer, Heidelberg (2012)
9. Vanneschi, L., Castelli, M., Manzoni, L., Silva, S.: A new implementation of geometric semantic GP and its application to problems in pharmacokinetics. In: Krawiec, K., Moraglio, A., Hu, T., Etaner-Uyar, A.Ş., Hu, B. (eds.) EuroGP 2013. LNCS, vol. 7831, pp. 205–216. Springer, Heidelberg (2013)
10. Rojas, R.: Neural Networks: A Systematic Introduction, 1st edn. Springer (July 1996)
11. Topchy, A., Punch, W.F.: Faster genetic programming based on local gradient search of numeric leaf values. In: Proceedings of the Genetic and Evolutionary Computation Conference (GECCO 2001), pp. 155–162 (2001)
12. Smart, W., Zhang, M.: Continuously evolving programs in genetic programming using gradient descent. In: Proceedings of 2004 Asia-Pacific Workshop on Genetic Programming (2004)
13. Zhang, M., Smart, W.: Genetic programming with gradient descent search for multiclass object classification. In: Keijzer, M., O'Reilly, U.-M., Lucas, S., Costa, E., Soule, T. (eds.) EuroGP 2004. LNCS, vol. 3003, pp. 399–408. Springer, Heidelberg (2004)
14. Graff, M., Pena, R., Medina, A.: Wind speed forecasting using genetic programming. In: 2013 IEEE Congress on Evolutionary Computation (CEC), pp. 408–415 (2013)
15. Igel, C., Hüsken, M.: Empirical evaluation of the improved rprop learning algorithms. Neurocomputing 50, 105–123 (2003)
16. Poli, R.: TinyGP. See Genetic and Evolutionary Computation Conference (GECCO 2004) (June 2004), competition at
http://cswww.essex.ac.uk/staff/sml/gecco/TinyGP.html
17. Nissen, S.: Implementation of a fast artificial neural network library (fann). Technical report, Department of Computer Science University of Copenhagen, DIKU (2003), http://fann.sf.net
18. Graff, M., Poli, R.: Practical performance models of algorithms in evolutionary program induction and other domains. Artificial Intelligence 174(15), 1254–1276 (2010)
19. Wilcoxon, F.: Individual comparisons by ranking methods. Biometrics Bulletin 1(6), 80 (1945)

A Multi-dimensional Genetic Programming Approach for Multi-class Classification Problems

Vijay Ingalalli[1,2,3], Sara Silva[1,4,5], Mauro Castelli[6], and Leonardo Vanneschi[6]

[1] INESC-ID, Lisbon, Portugal
[2] LIRMM, Montpellier, France
[3] IRSTEA, Montpellier, France
[4] LabMAg, FCUL, University of Lisbon, 1749-016 Lisbon, Portugal
[5] CISUC, Universidade de Coimbra, 3030-290 Coimbra, Portugal
[6] ISEGI, Universidade Nova de Lisboa, 1070-312 Lisbon, Portugal
{vijay.ingalalli,castelli.mauro}@gmail.com, sara@fc.ul.pt,
lvannesc@gmail.com

Abstract. Classification problems are of profound interest for the machine learning community as well as to an array of application fields. However, multi-class classification problems can be very complex, in particular when the number of classes is high. Although very successful in so many applications, GP was never regarded as a good method to perform multi-class classification. In this work, we present a novel algorithm for tree based GP, that incorporates some ideas on the representation of the solution space in higher dimensions. This idea lays some foundations on addressing multi-class classification problems using GP, which may lead to further research in this direction. We test the new approach on a large set of benchmark problems from several different sources, and observe its competitiveness against the most successful state-of-the-art classifiers.

1 Introduction

In the last two decades, Genetic Programming (GP) [1] has established itself as a solid research field, not only because of the numerous practical successes that have been reported in many different application domains [2], but also due to the strengthening of the theoretical foundations [3], and the several attempts to bridge theory and practice [4]. Nevertheless, various references report on the poor performance of GP in multi-class classification (intended here, as opposite to binary classification, as the supervised learning task of partitioning data into a number of classes larger than two) when compared to other state-of-the-art classifiers (see for instance [5]).

With the objective of attenuating this possible weakness of GP, in this paper we propose a new GP framework called Multi-dimensional Multi-class Genetic Programming (M_2GP). Several ideas have inspired the definition of this framework. First of all, we hypothesize that single expressions, being represented as trees or any other existing flavors of GP, are not an informative enough representation to effectively solve multi-class classification tasks. For this reason M_2GP uses a multi-expression representation of individuals. Although the idea is not new [6], we present it in a different light by integrating multiple expressions into a single tree. This makes the representation more

M. Nicolau et al. (Eds.): EuroGP 2014, LNCS 8599, pp. 48–60, 2014.

compact and allows us to implement M_2GP with very few modifications to standard GP. Secondly, we do not prefix any explicit connection between the different expressions represented in an individual and the classes. This relationship is free to evolve and allows a higher effectiveness of the algorithm. Thirdly, we present a new algorithm that tends to cluster the numeric values returned by the expressions belonging to a class, minimizing their dispersion. Also this not being a new idea [7,8], M_2GP presents it under a new light by introducing a new fitness function. Finally, M_2GP returns an enriched data model, including not only the set of expressions that compose the best individual, but also other information that is useful for the evaluation of new data.

The paper is structured as follows: Section 2 discusses some previous work in multi-class classification with GP. Section 3 introduces M_2GP, motivating the choices that led us to the definition of the proposed algorithm. Section 4 presents the M_2GP algorithm. Section 5 contains our experimental study, where the test problems are presented, the experimental settings are specified and the results are shown and discussed. Finally, Section 6 concludes the paper and suggests possible future research.

2 Related Work

In this section, we outline several methods that have been proposed in order to tackle multi-class classification problems using GP. The section only presents a restricted subset of the most important and recent contributions in this area. For a more complete survey on this topic the reader is referred to [9].

Several works [10,11,12,13,14] in this area are based on a common and straightforward approach that consists in evolving a single rule in each GP run. In particular, c runs are performed for a c-class classification problem. In this way, the final classifier has a single rule for each class. All these works evolve multiple comprehensible IF-THEN classification rules.

However, the focus of this short literature review is on another common approach, which consists in evolving a discriminant function. In this case the two main approaches are (1) range selection methods and (2) binary decomposition methods. Range selection methods are applicable to GP classifiers that output numerical values. The method works by declaring $c - 1$ thresholds for c-class classification problems. To select optimal thresholds, several mechanisms have been proposed, including static thresholds selection [15,7], dynamic thresholds [8,16] and slotted thresholds [8]. In binary decomposition methods, one classifier is trained to recognize samples belonging to a particular class and reject all other samples. This results in c classifiers for a c-class classification problem. A well-known drawback of this approach is related to the fact that the multiple classifiers may result in conflicts, whose number usually grows up proportionally to the number of classes. Hence, this approach produces an increased classification error as the number of classes gets larger. Binary decomposition methods have been explored in [17,18,19]. The two approaches for multi-class classification, constructing a single classification function or c binary classifiers, are compared in [20], by considering a hand-written digit recognition problem. As reported in [9], when a single function is evolved, able to discriminate all the classes, the function directly outputs the numeric value of the predicted class, since each class is an integer digit. In both cases, the fitness function is based on classification accuracy.

In [6] the authors proposed a GP-based approach to multi-class classification in which each individual is a multi-tree structure made of c trees, where c is the number of classes. Each of these c trees $(T_1, \cdots, T_c)$ encodes a threshold function for a particular class. The system considers that a data instance x belonging to class i is correctly classified if $T_i(x) \geq 0$ and $T_j(x) < 0$, for all $j \neq i$. The fitness function is computed as the classification accuracy. A similar system evolving a multiple-threshold discriminant function is described in [21], where a fitness function based on the sum of squared errors is employed.

One of the most recent contributions of GP for multi-class classification is found in [22]. In this work, the authors propose a two-stage strategy for multi-class classification problems, which is an improvement of a traditional binary decomposition method.

3   Formulation of Multi-dimensional GP

This section introduces the novel ideas we have explored and adopted to tackle the problem of efficient classification of multi-class data sets. Although this work focuses on tree based GP [1], it can be generalized for other types of GP.

Solution Tree. For classification tasks, tree based GP generally uses parse trees for representing the individuals, where the root node and all other non-terminal nodes belong to a set $\mathcal{O}$ of predefined operations (e.g., $\mathcal{O} = \{+, -, *, /\}$), and the terminal nodes/leaves belong to the given attribute set $\mathcal{A}$ for the given data set. At the end of the search process, the solution is available at the root of the best tree, which is a readily interpretable function that is used for the task of classification.

In our approach, we slightly modify the representation of each parse tree by adding a root node (r) of arity d ($d \geq 1$), as shown in Figure 1. Thus, the root node (r) shall have d branches, $T_1, \ldots, T_d$, each one of them being a normal GP tree, created according to the regular settings discussed in Section 5.2. Once the evolution terminates, GP individuals can still be evaluated at the root node (r), as before; but instead of one solution, we obtain d different solutions, which we use/explore later to perform the task of classification. For any data set, the value of d is independent of any parameters (e.g., the number of classes/attributes) and we will discuss its choice in Section 5.2. The genetic operators (e.g., mutation, crossover) are used normally, with the only restriction that the mutation and crossover points must be chosen below the root node (r). In this way, all the GP individuals will be rooted in (r) during the whole evolution.

Solution Space. Let $\mathbf{X} = \{\mathbf{x}_1, \mathbf{x}_2, \ldots, \mathbf{x}_n\}$ be the training data with n number of samples and $|\mathcal{A}|$ number of attributes. Each sample $\mathbf{x}_i$ corresponds to any class value

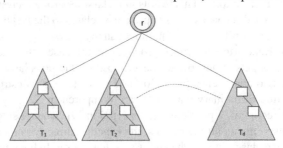

Fig. 1. Representation of a solution tree

$E_i \in C$, where C is the unique set of all the classes. In the usual single tree representation, where we obtain a single function f at the root node, solutions can be mapped in a space (that we call solution space from now on) of 1-dimension, because the output is a scalar numeric value. It is normally in this mono-dimensional solution space that GP is required to perform the task of classification. However, now that individuals are represented by d different functions $\mathcal{F} = \{f_1, f_2, \ldots, f_d\}$, they can be mapped in a d-dimensional solution space. Thus, any individual represented by a tree with a d-arity root node ⓡ, can be represented in a d-dimensional space.

4 Algorithm

With the formulation of multi-dimensional GP, we now propose the algorithm called Multi-dimensional Multi-class GP (M_2GP).

Algorithm 1. M_2GP - Training Module

---
1 INPUT: $\mathbf{X}, \mathbf{E}, d$
2 **for** $g \in 1 \ldots \mathcal{G}$ **do**
3   GENERATE: $\mathcal{F} = \{f_1, f_2, \ldots, f_d\}$ - set of d solutions
4   EVALUATE: $\mathbf{Z_s} = Eval(f_s(\mathbf{X}))$ for all $s \in 1, \ldots, d$
5   CLUSTER: $\mathbf{Z^k} \in \mathbf{Z}$ for all $k \in 1, \ldots, |C|$
6   **for** $k \in 1 \ldots |C|$ **do**
7          $C^k = covar(\mathbf{Z^k})$, a $d \times d$ co-variance matrix   % C^k must be non-singular %
8          $\mathcal{M}^k = centroid(\mathbf{Z^k})$, a $1 \times d$ centroid vector
9          $\mathcal{D}_i^k = \sqrt{(Z_i - \mathcal{M}^k) \cdot (C^k)^{-1} \cdot (Z_i - \mathcal{M}^k)^T}, \forall i = 1, 2, \ldots, n$ % Mahalanobis distance %
10   % where n is the number of samples in the training set %
11     $\forall i = 1, 2, \ldots, n : \ Pred_i = h$ such that $\mathcal{D}_i^h = min(\mathcal{D}_i^1, \mathcal{D}_i^2, \ldots, \mathcal{D}_i^{|C|})$
12     $\forall i = 1, 2, \ldots, n : \ Matched_i = 1$ if $Pred_i = E_i$
13   MAXIMIZE: $\frac{1}{n} \sum_{i \in n} Matched_i$;   % fitness function %
14 RETURN: $\mathcal{F}, C, \mathcal{M}$

Training Phase. The training module is run for $\mathcal{G}$ generations as described by Algorithm 1. The goal of M_2GP is to maximize the percentage of correctly classified samples, i.e., the classification accuracy (line 13). As M_2GP iterates over the generations, solutions with better training accuracy should be generated. In every generation, a population of new sets of functions $\mathcal{F}$ is generated. The training data is evaluated by every function solution to obtain the mapped data $\mathbf{Z} = \mathcal{F}(\mathbf{X})$, where $\mathbf{Z}$ represents the mapped data in the d-dimensional solution space. Since we are using the training data, and we know the class value for each mapped sample, we cluster/group the mapped samples $\mathbf{Z}$ according to their corresponding class values (line 5). Then we calculate the distance $\mathcal{D}_i$ between every mapped training sample Z_i and the centroid of the clustered mapped data $\mathbf{Z^k}$ for each class $k \in |C|$ (line 6-9).[1] Any mapped sample is predicted to belong to class k if it has the minimum Mahalanobis distance measured against the centroid of

---

[1] To calculate the Mahalanobis distance, one needs to calculate the inverse of co-variance matrix C^k, and hence C^k should be non-singular.

Algorithm 2. M_2GP - Classification Module

---

1 INPUT: $\mathbf{U}, \mathcal{F}, \mathcal{C}, \mathcal{M}, d$

2 OUTPUT: **Pred** - Predicted classes

3 EVALUATE: $\mathbf{Z_s} = Eval(f_s(\mathbf{U})), \forall s = 1, 2, ..., d$

4 **for** $k \in 1 \ldots |C|$ **do**

5     $\mathcal{D}_i^k = \sqrt{(Z_i - \mathcal{M}^k) \cdot (C^k)^{-1} \cdot (Z_i - \mathcal{M}^k)^T}, \forall i = 1, 2, ..., n$ % Mahalanobis distance %

6   % where n is the number of samples in the test set %

7 RETURN: $Pred_i = h$ such that $\mathcal{D}_i^h = min(\mathcal{D}_i^1, \mathcal{D}_i^2, ..., \mathcal{D}_i^{|C|}), \forall i = 1, 2, ..., n$;

---

the kth $|C|$-clustered mapped data $\mathbf{Z}$ (line 11), which is then used to maximize the fitness function. The importance/usefulness of the Mahalanobis distance, and the choice of dimension d - an important input for M_2GP - will be discussed in Section 5.2. After training for $\mathcal{G}$ generations, we return a classification model $\mathcal{S} = \{\mathcal{F}, \mathcal{C}, \mathcal{M}\}$, comprising of 3 components: $\mathcal{F}$ - a set of d solutions, $\mathcal{C}$ - a set of $|C|$ co-variance matrices of size $d \times d$, and $\mathcal{M}$ - a set of $|C|$ centroid vectors of size $1 \times d$.

Testing phase. To verify the performance of the classification model and to check its generalization ability, we use the evolved model $\mathcal{S}$ to predict the classes for the test data set $\mathbf{U}$. Algorithm 2 describes the procedure to classify the test data set $\mathbf{U}$.

5 Experimental Analysis

5.1 Data Sets

We have used a variety of data sets to test the performance of M_2GP. Table 1 lists the pool of data sets that encompass both real world and synthetic data, having integer and real data types, with varying number of attributes, classes and samples. The 'Heart' (HRT), 'Segment' (SEG), 'Vowel' (VOW), 'Yeast' (YST) and 'movement-libras' (M-L) data sets can be found at KEEL[2] [23], whereas the 'Waveform' (WAV) data set is available at [24]. 'IM-3' and 'IM-10' are the landsat satellite data sets that were used in [25]. All the data sets we have used have no missing values. We have partitioned each data set with the training and test data ratio of 70:30. In order to maintain consistency in the results and perform fair comparisons, we have generated 30 different random partitions for each data set, to be used henceforth.

Table 1. Data sets used for the experimental analysis

Data Set	HRT	IM-3	WAV	SEG	IM-10	YST	VOW	M-L
No. of classes	2	3	3	7	10	10	11	15
No. of attributes	13	6	40	19	6	8	13	90
No. of samples	270	322	5,000	2,310	6,798	1484	990	360

---

[2] KEEL - dataset repository, http://keel.es/datasets.php

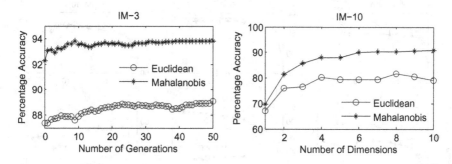

Fig. 2. Percentage accuracy for Euclidean and Mahalanobis distance. For IM-3, dimension $d=1$; for IM-10, number of generations $g=50$.

5.2 Experiments with GP Classifiers

Tools and Settings. We have used a modified version of GPLAB[3] [26], version 3 (latest) to conduct all the GP experiments. The GPLAB settings, subject to minimum tuning, are listed next. The remaining GPLAB settings were the ones set by default on the software. Generations = 50 (for analysis) and 100 (for final results - Table 4); Population size = 500 individuals; Crossover / Mutation Rate = 0.9 / 0.1; Function set ($\mathcal{O}$) = {+,-,*,/ (division protected as in [1])}; Terminal set = one variable for each attribute in the data set, plus ephemeral random constants (as in [1]), randomly generated with uniform probability from the interval $[0, 1]$; Tree Initialization: Ramped Half-and-Half with the ratio of 75:25 between the Full and Grow methods.

Importance of Distance Measure. Since one of the crucial steps in M_2GP is to calculate the distance between the sample and the centroid of each class clusters, we have compared two distance measures - Euclidean and Mahalanobis. Figure 2 shows examples of the performance of both distance measures for the data sets IM-3 and IM-10. For IM-3, we plot the mean of 30 different runs for $d = 1$ (which is equivalent to standard GP in terms of solution representation), in order to prevent the effect of using higher dimensions. For IM-10, we plot the mean of 3 different runs for each number of dimensions from 1 to $|C|$. The results were highly consistent, with very low dispersion among the different runs. From these plots we claim that the distance measure indeed plays a significant role in the performance of M_2GP, especially in the higher dimensional solution spaces. Unlike the Euclidean distance, the Mahalanobis distance not only is able to capture the physical distance between the test sample and the class clustered data sets, but also considers the statistical correlation between them, thereby reasserting the work of [27].

Effect of Augmenting Dimensions. As already explained in Algorithm 1, we are representing the mapped input sample $\mathbf{Z}$ (evaluated with the help of d-function solutions) in a d-dimensional solution space. Now, with the help of various data sets, we analyze

---

[3] GPLAB – A Genetic Programming Toolbox for MATLAB,
http://gplab.sourceforge.net/

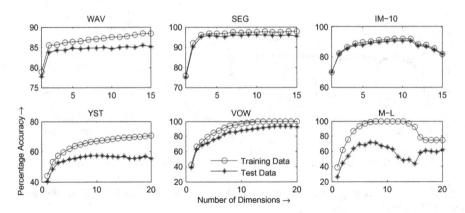

Fig. 3. Variation of accuracy values with increasing number of dimensions for various data sets

the effect of increasing the number of dimensions d. Figure 3 shows plots of accuracy (final values after 50 generations) against the increasing number of dimensions. The plots show the mean values obtained in 10 different runs, randomly chosen from the set of 30 different partitions. Looking at the training lines, we observe two distinct phases as we add dimensions in M_2GP, that we call progressive learning and regressive learning. In the progressive learning phase, the training accuracy improves with increasing dimensions. Progressive learning can be observed in the lower dimensions for all the data sets. If we observe the test lines in the progressive learning phase, we can infer that the classifiers perform the best during this phase, also in terms of generalization. WAV, SEG, YST and VOW enjoy this progressive phase almost until the end of their respective plots. For other data sets, this phase is followed by a regressive learning phase where accuracy degrades with increasing dimensions, as clearly visible in IM-10 and M-L. We hypothesize that a strong regressive learning would be observed for all data sets at much higher dimensions, depending on the complexity of the data set - which in turn depends on n, $\mathcal{A}$ and C. Additionally, it is interesting to observe that the beginning of the regressive phase is always greater than the number of classes for that particular data set, except in the case of M-L. We are regarding M-L as a special category of data set, since it is the only one where $n \ll |\mathcal{A}| \cdot |C|$, owing to its small sample size. It is also the only data set where the test accuracy decreases substantially during the progressive phase, suggesting strong overfitting. We regard M-L as a challenging data set, in particular when it comes to choosing the best dimension to use.

Choice of Dimension d. In Figure 4, we can observe the evolution of the accuracy on both training and test data, for a selected number of dimensions ($d = 1, 2, 12, 13$) on the IM-10 data set. Looking at the training plot we observe that the accuracy curves of different dimensions remain almost parallel to each other, from the initial generation to the final generation, even when the switch between progressive and regressive phase happens (from $d=12$ to $d=13$). This pattern suggests that, if we look at the accuracy values obtained in the initial generation for various dimensions, we will be able to predict which value of d will achieve the best accuracy in the final generation. Indeed, there

Table 2. Automatically chosen dimension d

	IM-3 C=3	WAV C=3	SEG C=7	IM-10 C=10	YST C=10	VOW C=11	M-L C=15
Mean	3.47	5.50	4.53	7.23	6.10	9.27	10.37
Std.Dev.	1.07	2.26	1.17	1.52	2.98	2.90	1.30

exists a very strong correlation of 0.95 ± 0.04 between the initial and the final accuracy values on the training data, when measured for all the data sets from Figure 3, considering their respective set of d values. This helps us choose an appropriate dimension for a particular data set, just by looking at the accuracy values obtained in the initial generation. If we look at the test plots, similar patterns are observed, provided that M_2GP is good with generalization for all d. However this may not be the case, as already observed for M-L in Figure 3. Nevertheless, leaving room for improvement in the future (see Section 6) we adopt a simple procedure to automatically choose the dimension d, described next.

For any given data set, we adopt the best d of the progressive phase. To do this, we keep increasing the number of dimensions as long as the accuracy obtained with the initial generation keeps improving, and adopt as d the value used right before the first degradation occurs. For each problem, the choice of d may be different for different runs. We remark that M_2GP performs best when $d = 1$ for the binary classification data set, and for the remaining data sets we have recorded the chosen d for the 30 runs and obtained the values in Table 2. To validate the appropriateness of these choices, we present in Figure 5 the results on the test set of 30 runs using the automatically chosen d (a-d in the figure) side by side with the results obtained with $d = 1$ and with $d = |C|$ (respectively 1-d and c-d in the figure).

Looking at Figure 5, firstly we observe that in most data sets M_2GP largely improves its performance from 1-d to c-d or a-d. However, deciding the winner between c-d and a-d is not trivial, since their relative performance varies depending on the data set. Choosing $d = |C|$ usually results in a d higher than choosing d automatically (see Table 2), however this does not necessarily translate into a better accuracy. The M-L data

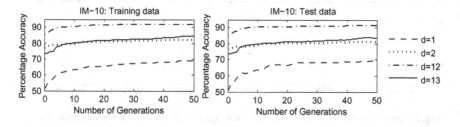

Fig. 4. Witnessing the correlation between the accuracy of the initial solutions and the accuracy of the evolved solutions

Table 3. Mean solution size for 1-d, c-d and a-d

	IM-3	WAV	SEG	IM-10	YST	VOW	M-L
1-d	29.37	107.66	70.57	84.10	56.93	46.23	28.53
c-d	37.03	80.67	39.60	90.27	189.23	40.57	291.06
a-d	24.30	131.97	42.87	123.30	152.06	47.66	42.83

set is the most obvious case where $d = |C|$ is not a good choice when compared to the automatically chosen d. We recall from Figure 3 that on this data set the procedure to automatically choose d does not even do a good job, since the test accuracy starts degrading early in the progressive phase. Still, it is much better than using $d = |C|$. All in all, at least in terms of accuracy, it seems fairly reliable to always use the automatically chosen d.

Size of the Individuals. Here we observe the effect of increasing the number of dimensions on the size of the individuals, i.e. the number of nodes of its tree, including any possible amount of redundant code. Table 3 reports the mean size of 30 different final solutions for each data set and each choice of d (excluding HRT that always uses d=1). We can observe that the increase in solution size from 1-d to c-d or a-d is not so prominent, and in many cases the size is indeed reduced. Therefore, also in terms of solution size the automatically chosen d seems to be a fair choice.

Comparison among GP Classifiers. With the goal of comparing the performance of M$_2$GP (using the automatically chosen d) with the performance of other GP systems, we chose the 'range selection method with static threshold selection' mentioned in Section 2 [8,16] as the benchmark for comparison, since it is a fairly standard way of performing multi-class classification with GP. However, in data sets with a higher number of classes we immediately observed the often reported inadequacy of this standard GP method to perform multi-class classification. It was losing the race too quickly, so we abandoned any further comparison. Just to provide some numbers, on the WAV and SEG data sets M$_2$GP improved the accuracy upon the standard method in approximately 25 and 55 percentual points, respectively.

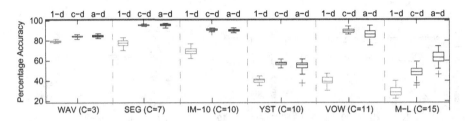

Fig. 5. Percentage accuracy of M$_2$GP for 3 settings of choosing d, for various data sets

5.3 Comparison with Various Classifiers

We now compare M_2GP with a number of classifiers available in Weka[4], version 3.6.10 (latest). Random Forests (RF) and Decision Trees (J48) are tree based classifiers; Random Subspace (RS) and Multi-Class Classifier (MCC) are meta classifiers; Multi-Layer Perceptron (MLP) and Support Vector Machines (SVM) are function based classifiers. For M_2GP, we set the number of generations to 100; we set dimension $d = 1$ for the binary class data set (HRT), and for the multi-class data sets we choose d automatically during the process of initialization, as already explained. For the rest of the classifiers, we use default settings from Weka. SVM uses the "one-against-one" approach to multi-

Table 4. Comparison among various classifiers. Median accuracy value and Best accuracy value on the test data set for 30 runs are reported. For each problem, the best values among the classifiers are in bold (if more than one, it means there is no statistically significant difference between their medians) and the worst values are in italics (the same). For each problem, a highlighted value means the classifier is significantly better than M_2GP values, while an underlined value means the classifier is significantly worse than M_2GP.

→ Data Set ↓ Classifiers		HRT C=2	IM-3 C=3	WAV C=3	SEG C=7	IM-10 C=10	YST C=10	VOW C=11	M-L C=15
SVM	Median	*55.556*	93.814	**86.3**	*55.844*	90.363	*41.124*	81.818	*14.352*
	Best	*65.432*	97.938	88.067	*61.616*	92.055	46.067	85.859	24.074
J48	Median	79.630	93.814	*74.800*	96.104	94.654	55.169	75.926	63.426
	Best	85.185	**98.969**	*78*	97.691	95.537	57.977	83.838	75.000
RF	Median	80.247	94.845	81.500	**97.258**	**96.861**	57.528	**89.394**	71.759
	Best	87.654	**98.969**	83.067	**98.557**	**97.744**	61.124	93.266	76.852
RS	Median	**81.481**	92.784	82.200	95.960	93.919	56.629	82.828	65.741
	Best	90.124	*97.938*	84.400	97.403	95.096	60.674	88.216	74.074
MLP	Median	80.247	95.876	83.333	96.320	90.216	57.977	82.492	**75.926**
	Best	87.654	*97.938*	85.200	97.403	91.319	**62.921**	87.542	**84.259**
MCC	Median	**83.951**	95.361	**86.800**	92.424	*81.829*	57.977	*57.576*	60.648
	Best	**90.124**	*97.938*	**88.267**	94.228	*83.865*	62.247	*65.657*	72.222
M_2GP	Median	82.099	94.845	84.867	95.599	90.191	53.82	85.859	62.963
	Best	88.889	**98.969**	86.467	97.403	92.545	60.225	**94.613**	74.074

class classification, which has comparable performance to "one-against-all" while requiring less training time [28]. Table 4 contains the median and the best accuracy values of the 30 different runs for the test data sets. We have used the same set of 30 different partitions to perform 30 different runs with all the classifiers listed in Table 4. To test for statistical significance of the results, the non-parametric Kruskal-Wallis with Bonferroni correction has been used under the alternative hypothesis that the accuracy values of the different classifiers do not have equal medians.

Table 4 has many things to reveal. First of all, on the IM-3 data set all the classifiers obtained median accuracy values that are not statistically different from each other.

---

[4] Weka – Waikato Environment for Knowledge Analysis,
http://www.cs.waikato.ac.nz/ml/weka/

In terms of best accuracy, on this data set M_2GP was one of the classifiers achieving the best value (in bold). Also in the VOW data set M_2GP achieved the best accuracy. Regarding the median accuracy values, M_2GP was one of the best classifiers on HRT (in bold), and never one of the worst classifiers on any of the data sets (in italics). On data sets WAV, YST and VOW, only the best classifiers were able to outperform M_2GP (highlighted values), whereas M_2GP was able to outperform many other classifiers (underlined values), at least one on each data set except IM-3. Recall that on the M-L data set M_2GP was not able to choose the ideal d, otherwise it would probably outperform more classifiers. Regarding the comparison with the other function based classifiers (MLP and SVM), M_2GP was clearly superior to SVM in almost all problems, and fairly competitive with MLP, which together with MCC was one of the best classifiers. RF was, however, the clear winner, in particular on the data sets with a higher number of classes.

6 Conclusions and Future Directions

We have proposed a novel approach for representing solutions, both in terms of solution tree and solution space, to address multi-class classification problems with GP. At the core, we have experimentally analyzed the effect of increasing the number of dimensions used to represent the solution space, and we have proposed a simple yet effective and relatively cheap way of choosing an appropriate dimension.

From the idea of multi-dimensional solution representation, we have proposed an efficient classification algorithm - M_2GP - and compared its performance with many of the best state-of-the-art methods for multi-class classification. We have shown that M_2GP offers competitive results on a large variety of data sets. We have also realized that being able to improve the choice of the number of dimensions would allow us to improve the competitiveness of M_2GP even further.

Naturally, we will focus our future work on better choosing the number of dimensions of the solution space. In fact, we will explore the idea that the number of dimensions does not have to be a parameter of M_2GP, and instead can be implicitly evolved together with the solution itself. The issue of overfitting should be taken into account in these future studies, and we also want to perform detailed analyses of diversity and bloat, with a strong focus on the interpretability of the M_2GP solutions.

Although still in its infancy, this new approach has already been able to elevate GP to a competitive method for multi-class classification, and we believe it represents the first step towards a general framework for multi-class classification with GP.

Acknowledgments. The authors acknowledge projects EnviGP (PTDC/EIA-CCO/ 103363/ 2008) and MaSSGP (PTDC/EEI-CTP/2975/2012), FCT, Portugal.

References

1. Koza, J.R.: Genetic Programming: On the programming of computers by means of natural selection, vol. 1. MIT Press (1992)
2. Poli, R., Langdon, W.B., Mcphee, N.F.: A field guide to genetic programming (March 2008)
3. Langdon, W., Poli, R.: Foundations of Genetic Programming. Springer (2002)

4. Special issue on bridging the gap between theory and practice in evolutionary algorithms research. Evolutionary Computation 15(4) (2007)
5. Castelli, M., Silva, S., Vanneschi, L., Cabral, A., Vasconcelos, M.J., Catarino, L., Carreiras, J.M.B.: Land cover/Land use multiclass classification using GP with geometric semantic operators. In: Esparcia-Alcázar, A.I. (ed.) EvoApplications 2013. LNCS, vol. 7835, pp. 334–343. Springer, Heidelberg (2013)
6. Muni, D., Pal, N., Das, J.: A novel approach to design classifiers using genetic programming. IEEE Transactions on Evolutionary Computation 8(2), 183–196 (2004)
7. Zhang, M., Ciesielski, V.: Genetic programming for multiple class object detection. In: Foo, N.Y. (ed.) AI 1999. LNCS (LNAI), vol. 1747, pp. 180–192. Springer, Heidelberg (1999)
8. Zhang, M., Smart, W.: Multiclass object classification using genetic programming. In: Raidl, G.R., et al. (eds.) EvoWorkshops 2004. LNCS, vol. 3005, pp. 369–378. Springer, Heidelberg (2004)
9. Espejo, P., Ventura, S., Herrera, F.: A survey on the application of genetic programming to classification. IEEE Transactions on Systems, Man, and Cybernetics, Part C: Applications and Reviews 40(2), 121–144 (2010)
10. Bojarczuk, C.C., Lopes, H.S., Freitas, A.A.: Genetic programming for knowledge discovery in chest-pain diagnosis. IEEE Engineering in Medicine and Biology Magazine 19(4), 38–44 (2000)
11. Sakprasat, S., Sinclair, M.: Classification rule mining for automatic credit approval using genetic programming. In: IEEE Congress on Evolutionary Computation, CEC 2007, pp. 548–555 (2007)
12. Shen, S., Sandham, W., Granat, M., Dempsey, M.F., Patterson, J.: A new approach to brain tumour diagnosis using fuzzy logic based genetic programming. In: Proceedings of the 25th Annual International Conference of the IEEE Engineering in Medicine and Biology Society, vol. 1, pp. 870–873 (2003)
13. Falco, I.D., Cioppa, A.D., Tarantino, E.: Discovering interesting classification rules with genetic programming. Applied Soft Computing 1(4), 257–269 (2002)
14. Tan, K.C., Tay, A., Lee, T., Heng, C.M.: Mining multiple comprehensible classification rules using genetic programming. In: Proceedings of the 2002 Congress on Evolutionary Computation, CEC 2002, vol. 2, pp. 1302–1307 (2002)
15. Tackett, W.A.: Genetic programming for feature discovery and image discrimination. In: Proceedings of the 5th International Conference on Genetic Algorithms, pp. 303–311. Morgan Kaufmann Publishers Inc., San Francisco (1993)
16. Li, X.M., Wang, M., Cui, L.J., Huang, D.M.: A new classification arithmetic for multi-image classification in genetic programming. In: 2007 International Conference on Machine Learning and Cybernetics, vol. 3, pp. 1683–1687 (2007)
17. Kishore, J.K., Patnaik, L., Mani, V., Agrawal, V.K.: Application of genetic programming for multicategory pattern classification. IEEE Transactions on Evolutionary Computation 4(3), 242–258 (2000)
18. Silva, S., Tseng, Y.-T.: Classification of seafloor habitats using genetic programming. In: Giacobini, M., et al. (eds.) EvoWorkshops 2008. LNCS, vol. 4974, pp. 315–324. Springer, Heidelberg (2008)
19. Lin, J.Y., Ke, H.R., Chien, B.C., Yang, W.P.: Classifier design with feature selection and feature extraction using layered genetic programming. Expert Systems With Applications 34(2), 1384–1393 (2008)
20. Teredesai, A., Govindaraju, V.: Issues in evolving gp based classifiers for a pattern recognition task. In: Congress on Evolutionary Computation, CEC 2004, vol. 1, pp. 509–515 (2004)
21. Winkler, S., Affenzeller, M., Wagner, S.: Advanced genetic programming based machine learning. Journal of Mathematical Modelling and Algorithms 6(3), 455–480 (2007)

22. Jabeen, H., Baig, A.R.: Two-stage learning for multi-class classification using genetic programming. Neurocomputing 116, 311–316 (2013)
23. Alcala-Fdez, J., Fernandez, A., Luengo, J., Derrac, J., Garcia, S., Sanchez, L., Herrera, F.: Keel data-mining software tool: Data set repository, integration of algorithms and experimental analysis framework. Journal of Multiple-Valued Logic and Soft Computing 17(2-3), 255–287 (2011)
24. Bache, K., Lichman, M.: (uci) machine learning repository, university of California, Irvine, school of information and computer sciences (2013),
    http://archive.ics.uci.edu/ml
25. U.S. geological survey (usgs) earth resources observation systems (eros) data center (edc),
    http://glovis.usgs.gov/
26. Silva, S., Almeida, J.: GPLAB - A Genetic Programming Toolbox for MATLAB. In: Proc. of the Nordic MATLAB Conference, NMC 2003, pp. 273–278 (2005)
27. Xiang, S., Nie, F., Zhang, C.: Learning a mahalanobis distance metric for data clustering and classification. Pattern Recognition 41(2), 3600–3612 (2008)
28. Hsu, C.W., Lin, C.J.: A comparison of methods for multi-class support vector machines. IEEE Transactions on Neural Networks 13(2), 415–425 (2002)

Generalisation Enhancement via Input Space Transformation: A GP Approach

Ahmed Kattan[1], Michael Kampouridis[2], and Alexandros Agapitos[3]

[1] Um Al Qura University, AI Real-World Applications Lab, Department of Computer Science,
Kingdom of Saudi Arabia
ajkattan@uqu.edu.sa
[2] University of Kent, School of Computing, UK
M.Kampouridis@kent.ac.uk
[3] Complex and Adaptive Systems Laboratory, School of Computer Science and Informatics,
University College Dublin, Ireland
alexandros.agapitos@ucd.ie

Abstract. This paper proposes a new approach to improve generalisation of standard regression techniques when there are hundreds or thousands of input variables. The input space X is composed of observational data of the form $(x_i, y(x_i)), i = 1...n$ where each x_i denotes a k-dimensional input vector of design variables and y is the response. Genetic Programming (GP) is used to transform the original input space X into a new input space $Z = (z_i, y(z_i))$ that has smaller input vector and is easier to be mapped into its corresponding responses. GP is designed to evolve a function that receives the original input vector from each x_i in the original input space as input and return a new vector z_i as an output. Each element in the newly evolved z_i vector is generated from an evolved mathematical formula that extracts statistical features from the original input space. To achieve this, we designed GP trees to produce multiple outputs. Empirical evaluation of 20 different problems revealed that the new approach is able to significantly reduce the dimensionality of the original input space and improve the performance of standard approximation models such as Kriging, Radial Basis Functions Networks, and Linear Regression, and GP (as a regression techniques). In addition, results demonstrate that the new approach is better than standard dimensionality reduction techniques such as Principle Component Analysis (PCA). Moreover, the results show that the proposed approach is able to improve the performance of standard Linear Regression and make it competitive to other stochastic regression techniques.

Keywords: Genetic Programming, Symbolic Regression, Approximation Models, Surrogate, Dimensionality Reduction.

1   Introduction

Science and engineering design problems oftentimes require the construction of a model $\hat{f}$ (referred to as meta-model, response surface model, or surrogate) that emulates the response of some black-box f which comes from some process. These black-box problems, i.e., whose problem class is unknown, are possibly mathematically ill-behaved

M. Nicolau et al. (Eds.): EuroGP 2014, LNCS 8599, pp. 61–74, 2014.
© Springer-Verlag Berlin Heidelberg 2014

(e.g., discontinuous, non-linear, non-convex). Generally, the model $f(x)$ represents some continuous quality or performance measure of a process defined by k-vector design variables $x \in X \subset \mathbf{R}^k$. In the remainder of this paper we will refer to X as the *input space*. Normally, the only insight available about the model $f(x)$ is through some discrete samples $(x_i, y(x_i)), i = 1...n$ where each x_i denotes a k-dimensional input vector of design variables and y is the response. The task here is to construct an approximation model $\hat{f}(x)$ to map any unseen $x \in X$ to its response with a reasonable accuracy.

It should be noted that reliable approximation models in the field of Machine Learning (ML) revolve around the fundamental property of generalisation. This ensures that the induced model is a concise approximation of a data-generating process and performs correctly when presented with data that has not been utilised during the learning process. To this end, it is desirable to avoid complexity of approximation models to maintain good generalisation. Thus, it is intuitively obvious that a higher number of design variables in a modelling problem will increase the complexity of objective function measuring locations of sampled variables in the input space and subsequently effect the generalisation ability. Moreover, the high number of design variables often requires more samples to build a reasonable accurate approximation model and, thus, increases the learner's complexity and may reduce its generalisation. This problem is referred to as *curse of dimensionality* [3]. To this end, many data-centric approximation methodologies in the ML literature that have been used to construct approximation models yield poor performance when the number of design variables is high.

One way to mitigate the curse of dimensionality problem is by reducing the number of design variables using some dimensionality reduction technique such as Principle Component Analysis (PCA) or Factor Analysis (FA) (e.g., see [8]). However, variables reduction is reasonable only when the significant variables are just a fraction of the overall set of variables. Variable reduction, some times, can increase the difficulty of the problem in cases where all variables have similar influence on the model response. Another way to deal with the curse of dimensionality is to construct a new input space that can be mapped to the original input space and is easer to approximate [13].

This paper proposes a model to improve the generalisation performance of standard regression models when the number of design variables is high. The main idea is to use Genetic Programming (GP) [11] to evolve a transformation function that transforms the original input space X into a new input space Z that has smaller number of variables and is easier to approximate to their corresponding responses. To this end, GP individuals (represented as trees) receives the design variables from the original input space as inputs and return a vector of outputs.[1] The evolution of the transformation function is guided by a fitness measure that drives search toward performance improvement of standard approximation models. For this task, GP is supplied with a function set that allows the extraction of statistical features from the original input space (details in Section 3).

The contribution of this paper is twofold. First, we show that it is possible to improve the generalisation of approximation models just by transforming the input space without

---

[1] We used a design similar to *modi GP* proposed by Zhang et. al. in [14] to allow GP trees produce multiple outputs.

changing anything in the approximation models themselves or in their objective functions. Second, we show that our approach can boost the performance of a simple linear regression and make it competitive to other state-of-the-art approximation techniques.

The reader's guide to the rest of the paper is as follows. Section 2 presents related work from the literature. Section 3 presents the proposed approach in details followed by experimental results and their analysis in Section 4. Finally, this paper concludes in Section 5.

2   Related Works

Dimensionality reduction techniques to mitigate the curse of dimensionality problem is a well explored topic. Many techniques have been developed and used with feature selection and classification problems (e.g., [12], [2]). However, the idea of reducing the number of design variables in the regression problems to improve generalisation of standard ML approaches is relatively little explored thus far. In this section we focus the review on dimensionality reduction approaches for models approximation since these are directly relevant to the work reported in this paper.

Sobester and Nair in [13] presented a GP approach for generating functions in closed analytic form that map the input space of a complex function approximation problem into one where the output is more amenable to linear regression. To achieve this, the authors used a co-evolutionary approach where multiple populations are evolved in parallel. However, the authors claimed that their results are not conclusive and they are merely serve as proof of concept. In addition, the new transformed input vector z has the same dimensionality as the original vector.

In [8] the authors proposed a technique based on latent variables, non-linear sensitivity analysis, and GP to manage approximation problems when the number of input variables is high. The proposed technique was tested with 340 input variable problems. The proposed approach was designed to consider problems where all input variables have similar influence on the model's output. Thus, standard variable pruning techniques are not applicable.

McConaghy [9] presented a deterministic technique, referred to as Fast Function Extraction (FFX), for solving a symbolic regression problem that achieves higher approximation accuracy than standard GP and several state-of-the-art regression techniques. Later, Icke and Bongard [5] hybridised FFX and GP to create an improved learner for symbolic regression problems. In this work, the authors showed that a hybrid deterministic/GP for symbolic regression outperforms GP alone and several state-of-the-art deterministic regression techniques alone on a set of multivariate polynomial symbolic regression tasks. The proposed approach was tested to approximate data-sets of different dimensionality, ranging from 1 to 25 dimensions.

As it can be seen, most of previous work tried to mitigate the curse of dimensionality problem by transforming the input space into a new input space. In this paper we show that it is possible to mitigate the curse of dimensionality problem and improve the generalisation of approximation models just by transforming the input space into new space that holds similar features. Unlike other works, our approach builds a transformation function for the input space based on its statistical features. This allows the

Table 1. GP Function set

Function	Arity	Input	Output
+, -, /, *	2	Real Number	Real Number
Mean, Median, StD, Variance, Average Div, Min, Max	1	Randomly selected variables from each x_i	Real Number
Constants 1-6	0	N/A	Real Number

*StD is Standard Deviation, and *Average Div* is Average Deviation.

transformation function to significantly reduce the number of design variables and relax the learners' performance.

3   Proposed Approach

The proposed approach uses GP as the main engine to transform the original input space into a new one. GP individuals are designed to receive the training samples from X as inputs and return a transformed samples as an output. This can be represented formally as follows: let the original input space be denoted as $X \subset \mathbf{R}^k$ where k is the dimensionality of the input samples. Normally, the input space is represented with a set of n discrete and possibly sparse samples $X = \{x_0, x_1, ..., x_n\}$. The aim is to evolve a transformation function $T(X) \Rightarrow Z$ where $Z \subset \mathbf{R}^q$ and $q < k$. The set $Z = \{z_0, ..., z_n\}$ where each z_i represent the x_i after being transformed from $X \Rightarrow Z$. The newly evolved Z set has to be easier to approximate and support the learner's generalisation. To this end, GP starts by randomly initialising a population of trees using ramped half-and-half approach [11]. We supplied GP with a function set, as illustrated in Table 1, to extract statistical features from the design variables of each sample in original input space. For each tree in the GP population, each node that holds a statistical function will be associated with a randomly selected sub-set of variables (up to k variables). For example, say $k = 10$, a tree could calculate the *Mean* function for variables $\{1, 2, 5, 6, 7\}$ while another tree (or even another node in the same tree) could calculate the *Mean* function for variables $\{9, 10\}$. We let the system picks up uniformly the number d of variables in $[1, k]$, and then uniformly choose the d variables among all variables. Once the system allocates a randomly selected sub-set of design variables to a node that holds a statistical function, it maintains the same sub-set for that node during its life cycle. Thus, all nodes that hold statistical functions maintain their selected sub-sets of variables after crossover or reproduction.

The next sub-section will explain the design used for GP trees to allow them to produce multiple outputs.

3.1   Trees Return Multiple Outputs

Standard GP tree representation proposed by Koza [7] utilises the evolved functions to perform a many-to-one mapping from inputs to an output. However, some problems, such as the one presented in this paper, raise a need to evolve functions that perform a many-to-many mapping between inputs and outputs. The idea of evolving trees with multiple outputs has been proposed by Zhang et. al. in [14]. In this work the authors proposed a new representation called *modi* trees to produce multiple outputs. Here, our design is inspired by modi trees, however, the difference is that modi was presented to evolve a fixed size vector of outputs while our approach can evolve a vector of any size. Similar to modi, our tree design consists of two main types of nodes: *(a)* **standards nodes** that pass their outputs to their parents, and *(b)* **outputs nodes** that append their output to a vector associated with the tree. As illustrated in Figure 1, for each tree, we let the system randomly selects some nodes and label them as output nodes. Thus, the size of the output vector of each tree is equal to the number of its output nodes. Also, once the system labels a node in any tree as an output node, it maintains its type during its life cycle (i.e., after crossover or reproduction). When evaluating trees, the system ensures to maintain the same traverse order, thus, the same tree will always produce the same output vector.

Using this representation allows the outputs of the evolved z_i vectors to be generated from different sub-trees or leaf nodes. Hence, any element in the generated output vector can be the result of a simple statistical feature for a sub-set of the design variables or the result of a linear function that combines several statistical features.

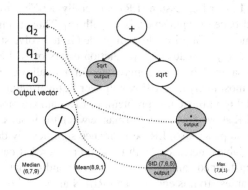

Fig. 1. GP tree representation to produce multiple outputs inspired by modi

3.2 Fitness Measure

As mentioned previously, the aim of the transformation function is to improve the generalisability of standard learners (or model approximation techniques). This is a challenging problem because the fitness measure needs to be aware of the generalisation level induced by the transformed space. In addition, the evolved transformation function has to be applicable to several learners without making any prior assumptions about which learner will be used to solve the approximation problem. One simple way to test the quality of the transformation function is to use the transformed input samples to train a single learner, e.g., Radial Basis Function Networks (RBFN), and then test this learner with unseen data (i.e., validation set). Although the simplicity of this idea is intuitively appealing, one problem would lie in the selection of the learner that will be used as fitness measure. As demonstrated in preliminary experiments, GP tunes the input space quickly in such a way to allow the learner to over-fit samples of the transformed input space. Thus, the learner loses its generalisation property. In fact, when we used prediction errors of RBFN as fitness measure, in preliminary experiments, we found that GP evolves a transformation functions that allows RBFN to over-fit the training set easily. Hence, the fitness value keeps improving, which gives an indication that RBFN is doing well on the transformed input space. However, when testing the RBFN on a transformed validation set results show very poor performance.

To avoid pathologies of this kind, another idea to evaluate the quality of the evolved transformation functions is to use multiple learners and solve the problem as multi-objectives optimisation, where the system is trying to reduce the prediction error of all learners simultaneously. Then the best evolved transformation function, at each generation, is evaluated against a validation set. In preliminary experiments, we found that this idea worked well to some extent, however, its main drawback is emphasised in the large computational cost required to train each learner using the transformed samples induced by each individual in the GP population. Hence, we reduced the number of learners (used as a fitness measure) gradually and explored different permutations of learners to balance between computational cost and solutions' quality.

After several experiments, based on trial and error, we used two learners as a fitness measure; RBFN and Linear Regression (LR). Generally, RBFN shows its best performance when the landscape of input space is smooth [6]. Thus, using prediction errors of RBFN as fitness measure, in principle, will guide GP to evolve smooth transformed input space in such a way to reduce the prediction errors of RBFN. However, if the transformed training samples became congregated in a small area at the transformed input space then it is most likely that RBFN will over-fit the training samples. Here, we also use the LR model to mitigate this problem. In LR, data are modelled using linear predictor functions. LR shows its best performance when the input samples are linearly correlated with their outputs. Also, LR performance significantly decreases when the number of design variables increases. With these properties, LR can encourage GP to linearly align the transformed samples to their corresponding outputs and reduce the number of input variables. To this end, LR and RBFN are selected to guide the fitness measure of GP. In addition, they both are relatively fast algorithms which will result in a reasonable computational cost when evaluating GP individuals. More formally, the fitness measure can be denoted as follows:

$$Fitness = \frac{\sum_{i=0}^{n} |LR(z_i) - y_i|}{n} + \frac{\sum_{i=0}^{n} |RBFN(z_i) - y_i|}{n} \qquad (1)$$

where $LR(z_i)$ and $RBFN(z_i)$ represent the predictions of LR and RBFN given the transformed point z_i. The n is the number of the transformed input samples and y_i is the ith output.

GP evolves individuals as described in Section 3.1 where each individual produces a $z_i \in Z$ output vector for each input sample $x_i \in X$. Remember that we assume each x_i denotes a k-dimensional input vector of design variables. The set $Z = \{z_0, ..., z_i\}$ is used to train RBFN and LR using 2-fold cross-validation technique. The prediction error is calculated as described in Equation 1 to rank individuals. The best individual of each generation is further tested with an unseen transformed validation set. The best individual across the whole run (that produced the best performance on the validation set) is used as the final transformation function that can be used to transform the input space.

4 Experiments and Analysis

4.1 Experimental Settings

A set of experiments have been conducted to evaluate the proposed approach. We tested the effects of the transformation function on four regression models, namely, RBFN, Kriging, LR, and GP (used as a regression model). These models were selected because they are some of the most important techniques in the literature. In addition, to compare the proposed approach against standard dimensionality reduction technique we included Principle Component Analysis (PCA) [1] in the experiments.

Experiments included the following 5 benchmark functions; *Rastrigin, Schwefel, Michalewicz, Sphere,* and *Dixon & Price* [10]. For each test function, we trained all approximation models to approximate the given function when the number of variables is 100, 500, 700 and 1000. The total number of test problems is 20 (i.e., 5 test functions ×4 different variables sizes). For all test problems, we randomly generated three dis-joint sets; a training set of 100 points, a validation set of 50 points, and a testing set of 150 points from the interval $[-5, 5]$. All techniques have been compared based on the average of absolute errors on the testing set.

For each function-variables combination, each approximation model has been tested three times; without and with PCA and our proposed approach (we will call it the Z set). In the experiments, some models are deterministic so we tested them only once with each problem. These, in particular, are RBFN, Kriging, and LR, with and without PCA. However, because the generation of the transformation function is based on an evolutionary process, we evolved 30 different transformation functions and tested them with each approximation model for each problem and reported the *mean, median, best,* and *standard deviation*. To evolve the transformation function, we used generational GP with the following settings; population size is 100, number of generations 100, maximum allowed size for trees is 300 nodes, elitism rate 0.01, crossover and mutation rates 0.7 and 0.3, respectively.

For the GP engine that has been used to solve the approximation problems, we used the same settings described previously. To assure fair comparison, we tested standard GP with and without PCA in 30 different runs and reported the same results.

4.2 Results

Tables 2, 3, and 4 summarise the results of 1200 GP runs and 60 RBFN, Kriging, and LR runs. In Table 2, it is clear that the Z set has improved all approximation techniques to obtain the best error in all four variables sizes (denoted by **bold** fonts in any column with a title starting with "Z set"). In addition, the Z set improved the GP performance in terms of mean in 7 out of 8 test cases and in terms of median in 5 cases (see again the numbers in **bold** fonts in the column entitled "Z set+SGP"). We also, noted that the Z set improved the performance of LR significantly by several orders of magnitude. In fact, LR obtained the best overall approximation for 6 out of 8 cases (denoted by underlined fonts). These are remarkable results given that LR simply uses a linear function to make predictions. The results suggest that the evolved transformation function has aligned the transformed input variables to be linearly correlated with their outputs.

Similarly, in Table 3, the Z set has improved all approximation techniques in terms of best results. Also, the Z set improved the GP performance in terms of mean in 7 out of 8 test cases and in terms of median in 4 cases. The LR obtained the best overall approximation for 6 out of 8 cases. Finally, in Table 4 results follow the same pattern[2]. The Z set again leads to consistently improved results in terms of best values. It also improved the mean and median results in all 4 cases. Lastly, the combination of the Z set with LR was again the champion, having the best overall approximation in all 4 cases.

To further verify the significance of the non-deterministic results on the GP, we used the non-parametric Friedman test to rank the three algorithms tested, namely SGP, Z set+SGP, and PCA+SGP. As we can observe from Table 5, the SGP approximation that uses the Z set was ranked first in 16 out of the 20 test cases; in addition, Holm's post-hoc test [4] showed that 12 out of these 16 first ranking were statistically significant at 5% or 10% level. It should also be noted that none of the other two algorithms (SGP, PCA+SGP) has managed to be ranked first at a statistical significance level of 5%. This once again demonstrates the improvement brought by the Z set to GP with these benchmark functions.

Overall, results show that the transformed input space has managed to improve the generalisation of all approximation techniques in the comparison. Thus, when the evolved Z set is applied, we can expect to have an improvement in the approximation error. In addition, results also show that our approach is better than a standard dimensionality reduction technique, such as PCA. Moreover, the transformed input space has significantly improved the LR in most of the test cases and make it competitive to other stochastic approximation techniques. In fact, LR has outperformed all of its competitors in most of the cases and it is not too far behind when it loses the comparison.

To have a closer look at LR improvement with the Z set, Figure 3 depicts the approximation of Sphere function (i.e., function 4), with 2 variables, of all models included in the comparison. It is interesting to visually see that LR can accurately approximate a non-linear function only by transforming the input space. In addition to this, the LR with the Z set approximation had the lowest error (0.0445021) among all 12 algorithms.

Despite the good improvements obtained by using the Z set, it is fair to report that the main disadvantage of the proposed approach that it requires extra computational cost and time to transform the input space. Also, in some cases the improvements are not significant and, thus, can not justify the extra costs. However, as demonstrated by the results, in some cases the margins of improvement can be several orders of magnitude (e.g., Functions 3 and 4) which justifies the extra computational costs in return of higher

---

[2] Due to space limitation we did not report the results of the RBFN (with and without PCA and the Z set) in Table 4. However, in our experiments we found that the Z set has also improved RBFN.

Table 2. Summary results for functions 1 and 2

Dimensions		SGP	Z set+SGP	PCA+SGP	RBFN	Z set+RBFN	PCA+RBFN	Kriging	Z set+Kriging	PCA+Kriging	LR	Z set+LR	PCA+LR
Function 1 (Rastrigin) Dimensions 100													
	Mean	7524868.16	**73.67**	159.83	82.19	90.10	82.48	73.68	73.67	73.68	72740.90	76.55	
	Best	75.37	**73.52**	73.65		**73.72**		73.52	73.52			**59.76**	
	Median	90.81	**73.68**	91.29		88.68		73.68	73.68			70.81	
Function 1 (Rastrigin) Dimensions 500													
	Mean	1001.54	**209.01**	916.14	185.74	210.75	185.82	180.56	184.92	180.56	1.54E+07	22618.21	
	Best	174.04	**130.82**	169.12		**162.89**		180.56	**176.93**			**148.69**	
	Median	213.37	**182.00**	215.46		209.07		180.56	180.56			167.80	
Function 1 (Rastrigin) Dimensions 700													
	Mean	2666.25	3824.53	572.18	216.14	269.65	216.15	207.39	207.42	207.39	4.07E+07	102342.89	
	Best	220.82	**174.74**	208.36		**211.43**		207.39	**206.43**			**176.47**	
	Median	256.34	252.04	**240.69**		262.31		207.39	207.39			226.80	
Function 1 (Rastrigin) Dimensions 1000													
	Mean	2624.30	2892.22	**411.94**	224.87	276.75	224.90	226.37	241.54	226.37	3.42E+08	135462.40	
	Best	227.57	**195.21**	232.02		**213.65**		**226.37**	**226.37**	**226.37**		**184.20**	
	Median	305.58	285.32	**273.02**		256.83		226.37	226.37			243.05	
Function 2 (Schwefel) Dimensions 100													
	Mean	13072.65	**4152.98**	9204.97	4116.45	2927.30	4100.54	3442.97	21681.90	3442.97	4.43E+06	2384.71	1.04E+06
	Best	3483.68	**2083.80**	3471.49		**2408.64**		3442.97	3413.25			**1808.15**	
	Median	4198.08	**2832.10**	4029.32		2880.16		3442.97	3460.26			2325.13	
Function 2 (Schwefel) Dimensions 500													
	Mean	1184267.92	**123639.32**	1378451.65	39841.60	36678.20	39844.80	38258.00	75874.60	38258.00	1.74E+08	28633.29	3.74E+08
	Best	38126.30	**22711.60**	37872.80		**26812.60**		38258.00	37875.30			**22197.20**	
	Median	52331.65	**36961.20**	48515.85		36363.70		38258.00	38275.65			27407.05	
Function 2 (Schwefel) Dimensions 700													
	Mean	18921991.63	**214283.00**	1913215.34	65553.50	51673.54	65583.20	64037.20	244632.34	2673180.00	5.70E+08	3700214.70	1.66E+09
	Best	65713.60	**31523.20**	67554.90		**37176.90**		64037.20	63658.60			**30852.70**	
	Median	89011.40	**61952.60**	83371.25		48647.55		64037.20	64182.30			39201.25	
Function 2 (Schwefel) Dimensions 1000													
	Mean	7444259.17	**1186439.44**	12553754.33	119038.00	105327.99	119056.00	117484.00	36850225.77	117484.00	1.21E+10	24271339.30	2.40E+09
	Best	116543.00	**68884.00**	115053.00		**69365.30**		117484.00	116987.00			**61209.80**	
	Median	4078830.00	181929.00	**139770.50**		97153.70		117484.00	117484.00			72801.55	

* **Bold** numbers are the lowest in each group and underlined numbers are the lowest in all groups.

Table 3. Summary results for functions 3 and 4

	SGP	Z.set+SGP	PCA+SGP	RBFN	Z.set+RBFN	PCA+RBFN	Kriging	Z.set+Kriging	PCA+Kriging	LR	Z.set+LR	PCA+LR
Function 3 (Michalewicz) Dimensions 100												
Mean	1.07E+04	**5.26E-06**	3.99E+03	15.74	6.07	15.72	20.74	184.12	20.74	9.47E+05	3.46	6.28E+05
Best	19.18	**2.89**	20.61		**2.65**			20.62			**1.39**	
Median	28.66	43.72	**24.89**		5.04			25.32			2.05	
Function 3 (Michalewicz) Dimensions 500												
Mean	1.89E+04	2.20E+05	**1.52E-04**	48.55	5877433.82	48.58	49.40	5.88E+06	49.40	4.89E+08	10.42	9.00E+07
Best	48.89	**9.15**	48.79		49.33			49.33			**4.13**	
Median	55.99	62.00	**54.78**		110.23			110.23			7.46	
Function 3 (Michalewicz) Dimensions 700												
Mean	8.71E+04	**2.58E+04**	5.60E+04	50.91	16.42	50.89	52.43	1.91E+07	52.43	1.04E+08	9.35	2.54E+08
Best	52.41	**9.12**	52.11		**7.04**			49.23			**4.73**	
Median	133.01	1625.70	**62.03**		14.93			168.26			7.48	
Function 3 (Michalewicz) Dimensions 1000												
Mean	1.34E+05	**1.05E+05**	6.04E+04	67.61	32.20	67.64	69.13	2.00E+08	3897.60	1.59E+08	6.50E+04	4.20E+08
Best	69.84	**9.11**	69.65		**9.87**			68.92			**6.80**	
Median	296.60	235.04	**79.51**		23.20			98.99			14.07	
Function 4 (Sphere) Dimensions 100												
Mean	61.06	**22.79**	61.58	55.65	11.28	56.51	48.98	1.56E+08	48.98	3.10E+04	11.17	3.10E+04
Best	49.79	**9.57**	48.67		**0.02**			48.09			**6.29**	
Median	58.41	**16.07**	54.63		12.52			94.32			10.26	
Function 4 (Sphere) Dimensions 500												
Mean	503.80	**132.65**	172.44	146.93	27.80	147.12	146.31	1.31E+04	146.31	1.71E+07	18.74	1.44E+06
Best	144.81	**11.74**	145.18		**0.21**			145.52			**8.84**	
Median	157.77	**71.33**	154.52		29.12			146.58			19.70	
Function 4 (Sphere) Dimensions 700												
Mean	653.16	**73.12**	256.48	148.94	32.56	148.99	147.31	4.41E+10	8139.38	1.46E+06	16.56	2.63E+06
Best	142.39	**13.00**	144.92		**8.56**			143.35			**7.08**	
Median	178.88	**50.89**	160.93		27.89			5718.59			15.57	
Function 4 (Sphere) Dimensions 500												
Mean	2420.14	**83.71**	572.57	176.93	34.72	176.93	177.25	2.48E+10	177.25	4.50E+07	18.32	1.53E+07
Best	172.42	**9.74**	180.50		**9.08**			175.56			**6.83**	
Median	233.90	**71.13**	219.29		32.72			1.33E+04			18.99	

* **Bold** numbers are the lowest in each group and underlined numbers are the lowest in all groups.

Table 4. Summary results for function 5 Function 5 (Dixson& Price)

	SGP	Z set+SGP	PCA+SGP	Kriging	Z set+ Kriging	PCA+ Kriging	LR	Z set+ LR	PCA+ LR
Dimensions 100									
Mean	4.9E+07	**7.4E+05**	2.9E+06		1.2E+05			2.2E+05	
Best	5.3E+05	**3.3E+05**	5.3E+05	4.3E+05	**2.6E+05**	4.3E+05	2.0E+07	<u>**1.8E+05**</u>	4.2E+06
Median	6.0E+05	**5.0E+05**	6.2E+05		2.3E+05			2.16E+05	
Dimensions 500									
Mean	5.8E+07	**2.8E+07**	3.9E+07		2.9E+06			2.4E+06	
Best	6.1E+06	**3.7E+06**	6.3E+06	3.72E+06	**2.3E+06**	3.7E+06	2.4E+10	<u>**2.1E+06**</u>	1.7E+10
Median	7.2E+06	**6.3E+06**	7.1E+06		2.9E+06			2.3E+06	
Dimensions 700									
Mean	4.7E+07	**4.3E+07**	6.3E+07		5.3E+06			9.1E+06	
Best	1.0E+07	**6.2E+06**	1.0E+07	6.5E+06	**4.1E+06**	6.5E+06	2.6E+10	<u>**3.65E+06**</u>	7.41E+10
Median	1.21E+07	**9.1E+06**	1.4E+07		5.0E+06			4.07E+06	
Dimensions 1000									
Mean	3.6E+08	**1.1E+08**	2.1E+08		9.7E+06			7.10E+06	
Best	1.7E+07	**1.0E+07**	1.7E+07	9.7E+06	**7.0E+06**	9.7E+06	1.2E+12	<u>**6.0E+06**</u>	1.2E+11
Median	1.8E+08	**1.7E+07**	3.4E+07		9.5E+06			6.87E+06	

* **Bold** numbers are the lowest in each group and <u>underlined</u> numbers are the lowest in all groups.

accuracy. Lastly, it is also worth noting that the results seem to worsen as the number of dimensions increases.

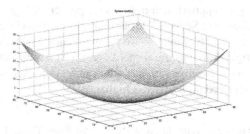

Fig. 2. The original Function 4 (Sphere function)

One last contribution of our work is the significant dimensionality reduction. Table 6 illustrates these reductions in each test problem. As can be seen, the proposed approach has generated a new input that has more than 50% smaller number of design variables. We believe the great amount of reduction is largely attributed to the fact that the new input space is based on statistical features extracted from the original space. Thus, in a sense, each design variable in the new transformed space is a result of several variables from the original space. To this end, both input spaces (the original and transformed) have similar statistical features.

However, an observation one could make is that the number of dimensions in the new input space does not seem to be correlated with the number of dimensions from the original input space; in fact, while the mean number of variables varies from 10.27 (F4) to 23.30 when Dimensions = 100, this mean range only slightly increases for Dimensions = 1000 (11.83 (F4) to 31.20 (F1)). This is very interesting and it could be an

Table 5. Friedman statistical significance test. Values that are in **bold** font denote that the respective algorithm's ranking is statistically better than one other algorithm (at 5% significance level). Values that are both in **bold** font and underlined denote that the algorithm has a statistically better ranking than both of the other two algorithms (at 5% significance level). Lastly, when a value has a star (*) next to it, this means that the respective algorithm has a statistically significant ranking at 10% level.

Function		F1	F2	F3	F4	F5
Dimension	Algorithm	Ranking				
100	SGP	2.3	2.56	2.13	2.6	2.16
	Z set+SGP	**1.63***	**1.23**	2	**1.06**	**1.36**
	GP+PCA	2.06	2.2	1.86	2.33	2.46
500	SGP	2.2	2.2	2.16	2.53	2.16
	Z set+SGP	**<u>1.53</u>**	1.73	1.76	**1.2**	1.7
	GP+PCA	2.26	2.06	2.06	2.26	2.13
700	SGP	2.23	2.23	2.06	2.4	2.20
	Z set+SGP	2	**1.33**	1.93	**1.2**	**1.40**
	GP+PCA	1.76	2.43	2	2.4	2.40
1000	SGP	2.23	2.18	2.36	2.46	2.40
	Z set+SGP	2.03	1.96	1.8*	**<u>1.1</u>**	**<u>1.43</u>**
	GP+PCA	1.73	1.85	1.83	2.43	2.16

explanation as to why the approximation results are poorer for higher number of dimensions. As explained earlier in Section 3.1, our multiple-outputs GP approach can evolve an output vector of any size. However, as we see in practice this size is not proportionate to the size of the original dimension of the X vector. It would thus be worth investigating in a future work if approximation results can be improved when the number of variables in the transformed input space is higher.

Table 6. Summary of dimensions produced by the evolved Z set. The table summaries the mean results of 30 independent runs for each test problem.

Dimensions	F1	F2	F3	F4	F5
100	14.97	14.27	12.27	10.27	23.30
500	21.97	14.43	14.37	12.77	25.20
700	33.67	17.30	12.73	11.23	25.30
1000	31.20	26.63	16.60	11.83	23.26

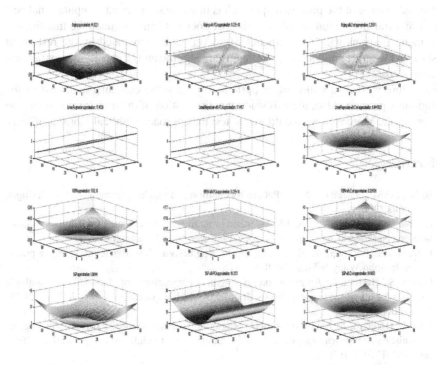

Fig. 3. Approximation of Sphere function (Function 4) with 2 variables. Each model (Kriging-1st row, Linear Regression-2nd row, RBFN-3rd row, SGP-4th row) was tested without (left) and with PCA (middle) and the Z set (right).

5   Conclusions

To summarise, this paper proposed a new approach to improve generalisation of standard regression techniques when dealing with hundreds or thousands of input variables. We used GP to transform the original input space X into a new input space $Z = (z_i, y(z_i))$, where Z has a smaller input vector and is thus easier to be mapped. We tested the effectiveness of our proposed approach over 5 different functions and over 4 different dimensionality sizes. Results over the above 20 problems showed that our approach leads to a remarkable dimensionality reduction of the original input space, thus making the problem at hand a less complex one. Furthermore, the transformed input space was able to lead to consistently improved performance of the standard approximation models tested in this paper, i.e. Kriging, RBFN, Linear Regression and GP. Moreover, our findings also demonstrated that our approach consistently outperforms a standard dimensionality reduction technique, such as the Principle Component Analysis. Lastly, another important result was that our proposed approach was able to significantly improve the performance of the standard Linear Regression, and actually make it the best performing technique in the majority of the cases tested in this paper.

A disadvantage of the proposed approach is that it requires extra computational cost to evolve a transformation function. This cost does not bring a guarantee that the improvements margins will be significant. However, as demonstrated by the results, in most cases the approximation improvements are significant thus justify the extra computational cost.

For future work, we will explore options to reduce the computational cost of the evolutionary process. Also, we will study the distribution of the transformed inputs on the new space. Moreover, we would like to test the approach with real-world problems.

References

1. Bishop, C.M., Nasrabadi, N.M.: Pattern recognition and machine learning, vol. 1. Springer, New York (2006)
2. Estébanez, C., Aler, R., Valls, J.M.: Genetic programming based data projections for classification tasks. World Academy of Science, Engineering and Technology (2005)
3. Forrester, A., Sóbester, A., Keane, A.: Engineering design via surrogate modelling: a practical guide. John Wiley & Sons (2008)
4. García, S., Herrera, F.: An extension on statistical comparisons of classifiers over multiple data sets for all pairwise comparisons. Journal of Machine Learning Research 9(66), 2677–2694 (2008)
5. Icke, I., Bongard, J.: Improving genetic programming based symbolic regression using deterministic machine learning. In: 2013 IEEE Congress on Evolutionary Computation (CEC), pp. 1763–1770 (2013)
6. Kattan, A., Galvan, E.: Evolving radial basis function networks via gp for estimating fitness values using surrogate models. In: 2012 IEEE Congress on Evolutionary Computation (CEC), pp. 1–7 (2012)
7. Koza, J.R.: Genetic Programming: On the programming of computers by means of natural selection, vol. 1. MIT Press (1992)
8. McConaghy, T.: Latent variable symbolic regression for high-dimensional inputs. In: Genetic Programming Theory and Practice VII, pp. 103–118. Springer (2010)
9. McConaghy, T.: Ffx: Fast, scalable, deterministic symbolic regression technology. In: Genetic Programming Theory and Practice IX, pp. 235–260. Springer (2011)
10. Molga, M., Smutnick, C.: Test functions for optimization needs (2005)
11. Poli, R., Langdon, W.W.B., McPhee, N.F., Koza, J.R.: A field guide to genetic programming. Lulu.com (2008)
12. Smits, G., Kordon, A., Vladislavleva, K., Jordaan, E., Kotanchek, M.: Variable selection in industrial datasets using pareto genetic programming. In: Yu, T., Riolo, R.L., Worzel, B. (eds.) Genetic Programming Theory and Practice III, Genetic Programming, May 12-14, vol. 9, ch. 6, pp. 79–92. Springer, Ann Arbor (2005)
13. Sobester, A., Nair, P., Keane, A.: Evolving intervening variables for response surface approximations. In: Proceedings of the 10th AIAA/ISSMO Multi-disciplinary Analysis and Optimization Conference, pp. 1–12. American Institute of Aeronautics and Astronautics (2004), http://eprints.soton.ac.uk/22962/, aIAA 2004-4379
14. Zhang, Y., Zhang, M.: A multiple-output program tree structure in genetic programming. In: Mckay, R.I., Cho, S.B. (eds.) Proceedings of the Second Asian-Pacific Workshop on Genetic Programming, Cairns, Australia, December 6-7, p. 12 (2004), http://www.mcs.vuw.ac.nz/~mengjie/papers/yun-meng-apwgp04.pdf

On Diversity, Teaming, and Hierarchical Policies: Observations from the Keepaway Soccer Task

Stephen Kelly and Malcolm I. Heywood

Dalhousie University, Halifax, NS, Canada
{skelly,mheywood}@cs.dal.ca

Abstract. The 3-versus-2 Keepaway soccer task represents a widely used benchmark appropriate for evaluating approaches to reinforcement learning, multi-agent systems, and evolutionary robotics. To date most research on this task has been described in terms of developments to reinforcement learning with function approximation or frameworks for neuro-evolution. This work performs an initial study using a recently proposed algorithm for evolving teams of programs hierarchically using two phases of evolution: one to build a library of candidate meta policies and a second to learn how to deploy the library consistently. Particular attention is paid to diversity maintenance, where this has been demonstrated as a critical component in neuro-evolutionary approaches. A new formulation is proposed for fitness sharing appropriate to the Keepaway task. The resulting policies are observed to benefit from the use of diversity and perform significantly better than previously reported. Moreover, champion individuals evolved and selected under one field size generalize to multiple field sizes without any additional training.

Keywords: Policy search, Keepaway soccer, Symbiosis, Fitness sharing, Diversity maintenance.

1 Introduction

Keepaway soccer was conceived as a simplification of the full RoboCup simulated soccer task in which the objective is for K 'keepers' to maintain possession of the ball for as long as possible from $K - 1$ 'takers' [1, 2]. The takers assume a pre-specified policy whereas the keepers need to learn an appropriate policy. Keepaway is implemented using the same RoboCup simulator as used for the full game of soccer, but with additional constraints on the rules, boundary of the field, and number of players. The Keepaway task is known to be non-Markovian and has a wide range of results from reinforcement learning and neuro-evolution (Section 2). However, to date, there has been little interest in applying genetic programming (GP) to this task. The goal of this work is to make an initial assessment of the capability of GP and the role of diversity maintenance in identifying effective keeper policies under this domain. Previous results using neuro-evolution have made use of genotypic diversity measures [3, 4]. While genotypic diversity metrics have been proposed for canonical forms of GP (e.g.,

M. Nicolau et al. (Eds.): EuroGP 2014, LNCS 8599, pp. 75–86, 2014.

[5]), their design is not necessarily obvious for the case of GP that supports task decomposition through teaming. Thus, in this work we introduce a novel formulation for phenotypic fitness sharing and empirically evaluate its effect on hierarchical GP under the Keepaway task.

The GP framework assumed in this work takes the form of symbiotic bid-based GP (hereafter SBB), where this has previously been illustrated under various reinforcement learning tasks e.g., Rubik cube [6], Pin-ball [7] and Ac-robot handstand [8]. In SBB, a control policy is defined by a team of simple programs that are coevolved, each specializing on a subcomponent of the task. Adopting a teaming approach to policy search implies that it is possible to start from simple policies at initialization and incrementally introduce more complexity as the task warrants. The utility of task decomposition in general has been demonstrated under supervised [9] and reinforcement learning [10]. Previous results with SBB have also indicated that if an initial run does not identify suitably general policies, then the contents of the initial population can be 'cashed' and referred to as a library of 'meta actions' [6–8]. Individuals evolved in a second independent run learn the context for deploying the previously evolved policies. That is to say, SBB supports a mechanism through which hierarchical policies may be incrementally constructed.

In this work, we are specifically interested in the role of diversity maintenance in the development of such hierarchical policies. The underlying assumption is that such diversity is necessary during the development of the initial population of SBB individuals (meta actions), but not necessary when constructing policies from meta actions. More generally, the need for diversity and modularity is frequently acknowledged, particularly in environments with dynamic properties [11, 12]. Thus, under the guise of ensemble methods as applied to streaming data tasks, diversity is seen to provide faster reaction times to a change, but does not necessarily facilitate faster convergence to the new concept [13]. Under a neuro-evolutionary setting in which solutions to the iterated prisoner's dilemma are coevolved, diversity is shown to support the development of a broader range of policies across the population as a whole, but it is difficult to integrate this diversity into a single individual [14]. Finally, the field of evolutionary robotics frequently reports better performance when reward is given for both novel solutions as well as optimizing fitness [15, 16]. However, it is also clear that defining an appropriate diversity metric is as an open ended activity.

In addition to investigating the role of diversity, we are also interested in discovering how a GP approach compares to the current state of the art under the most widely considered $K = 3$ (3-versus-2) configuration of the Keepaway task. As will be established in Section 2, progress on the Keepaway task has been dominated by reinforcement learning and neuro-evolutionary methods.

2   Related Work

As noted in the introduction, the Keepaway task represents a benchmark for both multi-agent and reinforcement learning / policy search in general [1–4].

Given that a decision maker is necessary for each keeper, reinforcement learning approaches have adopted a heterogeneous assignment of learners to keepers, where this is a function of the overhead in attempting to update a single function approximator w.r.t. multiple keepers [4]. Conversely, (evolutionary) policy search generally assumes a homogeneous assignment, where this is a reflection of the lack of specialization required in the keeper policies [17].

The original development of Keepaway defines the task of the decision maker in terms of a pre-specified decision tree in which, should another keeper be in possession of the ball, the free keepers assumes a "get open" behaviour. Otherwise if the keeper is not in possession of the ball but can get there faster than any other teammate, then the keeper approaches the ball. The task of the learning algorithm is to discover the appropriate strategy for the case of a keeper in possession of the ball [1, 2]. When in possession of the ball there are a total of K atomic actions, a; or $a \in$ {HoldBall, Pass2ThenReceive, ..., Pass$k$ThenReceive}; where the Pass$k$ThenReceive action defines which keeper to pass the ball to, with k indexing the nearest ($k = 2$) to most distant ($k = K$) keeper. This is the most common formulation of the keepaway task, and will be assumed in the work here.

Under reinforcement learning, the first obstacle to be addressed was how to formulate the task such that credit assignment mechanisms such as SMDP Sarsa(λ) could be applied [1, 2]. With this achieved, most emphasis has been on the type of function approximation used to model Q-values. Thus, function approximation based on tile coding [1, 2] has been superseded by the use of Radial Basis Functions [4] or kernel methods [18].

Several approaches to neuro-evolution have been applied to the Keepaway task, including NEAT [4, 19], EANT [3] and HyperNEAT [20]. All schemes make extensive use of genotypic diversity for maintaining multiple species during a run. These studies also adopt the result reporting framework established under the reinforcement learning approaches cited above, making comparison between different algorithms possible. The same approach is assumed here.

In the case of GP, we note that a layered learning approach has been adopted in the past to facilitate the incremental evolution of tree structured GP, with and without ADFs [21, 22]. However, these results are reported for a different soccer simulator (TeamBots) and hence different atomic actions. Layered learning assumes that the task undergoes some prior decomposition with training performed relative to the simpler tasks first. It was also necessary to enforce a prior discretization of the state variables (i.e., a simplification of the task) and limit the number of takers to 1 i.e., 3-versus-1 keepaway.

3   Hierarchical Symbiotic Policy Search

Frameworks for evolving teams of programs represent an alternative approach for deriving modular solutions under GP. Bremeier and Banzhaf assumed a representation in which a fixed number of programs were grouped (per team) and evaluated collectively, with variation operators switching programs between teams as well as modifying individual programs [23]. Thompson and Soule also assumed fixed sized teams, but introduced orthogonal selection operators i.e., building teams from the perspective of the program or team [24]. SBB explicitly supports 'incremental complexification' through the use of a symbiotic framework for coevolving team membership (host) and programs (symbionts) cooperatively [9]. Thus, host individuals define a team (host membership) by indexing some subset of the available symbionts (programs). Assuming a variable length representation for the hosts implies that the size of a team is free to evolve. Symbiosis appears because host and symbiont individuals exist in independent populations with fitness only evaluated at the host population.[1]

3.1 Symbiont

Symbiont programs take the form of bid-based GP [25]. Each symbiont represents a tuple consisting of a task specific discrete action, a, and a program, p. Without loss of generality, we assume a linear GP representation [26]. The role of a program is to define a bidding strategy. Thus, consider the case of a host consisting of two symbionts $\langle a_1, p_1 \rangle$ and $\langle a_2, p_2 \rangle$. Given a set of state variables describing the current state of the task domain, each symbiont associated with the host executes its program. The symbiont with largest output, say p_2, 'wins' the right to suggest its action at the current time step, or a_2 in the case of this example. Evaluation for the current host continues until an episodic end state is encountered i.e., for each new state of the task, the symbiont programs are executed and the winning symbiont suggests its action, in each case potentially updating the state of the task.

3.2 Variation Operators

Variation operators are asexual and take the form of a set of mutation operators applied to a host *after* it is cloned. Two mutation operators are used: remove symbiont from the host, add a symbiont to the host. In addition, a third operator can initiate the creation of a new symbiont. In this case a symbiont that is currently a member of the host is cloned and the cloned symbiont's action and / or program is modified (inserting / deleting instructions). For further details of the variation operators see [9].

3.3 Selection Operator

Evolution is conducted under a breeding metaphor, thus post fitness evaluation, the worst performing H_{gap} individuals are deleted. Any symbionts that are not part at least one remaining team are assumed to be ineffective and therefore also deleted. No attempt is made to derive symbiont fitness through, say, the average of the host fitness in which it is a member. In effect we are assuming multi-level selection in which an organism is only evaluated as a whole as opposed to the

---

[1] Hereafter host / team and symbiont / program will be used interchangeably.

sum of its parts [27]. One implication of this process is that the host population is a fixed size, whereas the symbiont population 'floats' under the action of the selection and variation operators.

3.4 Constructing Hierarchical Policies

Evolution will be performed in two distinct phases. During phase 1 symbionts assume atomic actions taken from the task domain. This lasts for a fixed number of generations and establishes a population of meta actions for use as actions by the second phase of evolution. The goal of phase 2 is to discover under what conditions to switch between different meta actions as identified during phase 1. No further modification of individuals from phase 1 tasks place. As per phase 1, evaluating a host from phase 2 (h_i^2) results in the identification of a winning symbiont (Section 3.1). However, at this point the action is a previously evolved host, h_j^1, as discovered during phase 1 i.e., a meta action. Thus, host h_j^1 is now executed for the current state variables, with the winning symbiont this time selecting an atomic action which is used to update the state of the game. Further details regarding the evolution of hierarchical policies is available from [6–8].

3.5 Fitness and Diversity

In the specific case of the 3-versus-2 Keepaway task, the soccer simulator defines the location of keepers and takers such that each keeper is stochastically initialized in one of the three corners of a square field and all takers are initialized in the fourth corner. The corners associated with keepers and takers do not vary, but the precise initial location does. Likewise, the ball is initialized 'near' one of the keepers, but this also varies. Unlike most episodic tasks, this means that it is not possible to precisely control the initial configuration of the task. Hence, during fitness evaluation, each host plays multiple games, but it is not possible to replicate the initial conditions, or for that matter other stochastic events that potentially occur during a game i.e., the soccer simulator adds noise to actions and state variables. Each host will play P games per generation, thus fitness of a host is merely the average total duration for a game as measured by the simulator over *at least* P games. We naturally hope this averaging smooths out some of the variation that is not explicitly due to the host's policy.

In terms of diversity maintenance, previous researchers have assumed linear combinations of fitness and novelty (e.g., [15]), Pareto multi-objective formulations (e.g., [16]), or fitness sharing based on genotypic diversity (e.g., [3, 19]). Each method varies with respect to the number of user-specified parameters and their sensitivity. Furthermore, a function for measuring genotypic or phenotypic distance between policies is typically required, where this can be task-specific or generic. In the following we will adopt a phenotypic fitness sharing methodology that incorporates a task-specific distance metric to select the most 'similar' game as played by other hosts. This is a significant departure from earlier formulations for diversity (e.g., [6–8]). The motivation for this approach stems from the observation that start states in the keepaway task are stochastic and both sensor readings and actuators are noisy. Thus, a policy's phenotype cannot be characterized solely by the reward received relative to a particular initial task configuration. Instead, the property captured by fitness sharing will summarize the configuration of the *failure state*. Thus, we reward diversity in failure, where this is taken as an indicator of policy behaviour. With this in mind, the following approach is taken to fitness sharing.

Let each host maintain a history of the end state and reward for the most recent P_{hist} games. State variables in keepaway are ego-centric, hence translation and rotation independent. This reduces the number of trivial differences that might appear in the end state of a game. Thus, for each of the last P_{hist} games we record the ego-centric state variables relative to the keeper initialized in the upper-left corner of the field. Our use of homogeneous keepers is taken to imply that a single keeper perspective is sufficient to characterize team behaviour. Each host plays P games per generation, overwriting the P oldest entries in that host's history. The actual size of a host's historical record will therefore range between P and P_{hist} depending on age. A host's shared fitness score, s_i, discounts the reward for each historical game as follows:

$$s_i = \frac{1}{h_{hist}} \sum_{j \in h_{hist}} \left(\frac{G(h_i, e_j)}{\sum_{k \neq i} (1 - dist(e_j, e_{hist})) G(h_k, e_{hist})} \right) \tag{1}$$

where $G(h_i, e_j)$ is the reward host i received for game j, the denominator summation $\sum_{k \neq i}$ is over all other hosts in the same population, e_{hist} is the game failure state from the historical record of host k that most closely matches e_j, with the corresponding reward $G(h_k, e_{hist})$, and $dist(e_j, e_{hist})$ is a Euclidean distance metric, normalized to the unit interval, with 1 denoting least similarity. h_{hist} represents all games currently stored in the historical record for host i.

In short, Eqn. (1) re-weights the reward that host i receives on game j relative to the historical record available for other hosts on the game they played with the most similar *failure state*. We also limit the estimation of final game state to that of the keeper positions alone. Hence, under the 3-versus-2 Keepaway task a total of 5 state variables are used to characterize the final state of a game. Given that evolution is applied in two distinct phases in order to construct explicitly hierarchical SBB policies (Section 3.4), fitness sharing is only applied during the first phase. In phase 2 the objective is explicitly exploitive, hence no fitness sharing will be deployed.

4   Results

As a guide to parameterizing SBB we note from Whiteson *et al.* [4], that NEAT utilized 6,000 evaluations per generation with 50 to 60 generations (the latter was not explicitly reported), implying that between 300,000 to 360,000 evaluations were performed per run. Under the SBB parameterization from Table 1, the corresponding total evaluation count is defined as: $t_{max} \times H \times P = 200,000$. However, there are two phases of evolution in order to construct hierarchical policies (Section 3.4), thus 400,000 evaluations in total. The publicly available code distribution provided the initial implementation for SBB[2], from which the necessary modifications were made to provide the new formulation for fitness sharing and interface to the Robocup Soccer Server[3]. Supporting code from the designers of the keepaway task[4], provides a full implementation of the keepaway environment. This work uses version 1.15.1 and 0.6 of the soccer server and keepaway code respectively.

Table 1. SBB Parameterization per phase of evolution (Section 3.4). t_{max} is the total generation limit; ω_{max} is the maximum number of symbionts a host may support under a variable length representation; H is the host population size; P is the number of games played by each host per generation; P_{hist} is the maximum number of games stored in each host's historical record; H_{gap} is the number of individuals replaced during breeding in the host population; p_{xx} denote the frequency with which different search operators are applied; $numRegisters$ and $maxProgSize$ represent the number of registers and maximum instruction count for (symbiont) programs.

Host (teams)				Symbiont (programs)	
Parameter	Value	Parameter	Value	Parameter	Value
t_{max}	250	ω_{max}	15	$numRegisters$	8
H	80	H_{gap}	40	$maxProgSize$	48
P	10	P_{hist}	100	p_{delete}, p_{add}	0.5
p_{md}	0.7	p_{ma}	0.7	p_{mutate}, p_{swap}	1.0
p_{mm}	0.2	p_{mn}	0.1		

As per established practice on the Keepaway task, reporting of performance will be conducted *throughout* the evolutionary cycle. Thus, at every 125 generations we let each host play 100 games and then have the champion host play 1,000 games. No fitness sharing is deployed during champion identification. A total of 12 independent runs are performed. Results from previous research are summarized in Table 2, where these are generally the result of 5 independent runs. Two experiments will be performed: hierarchical SBB without fitness sharing versus hierarchical SBB with fitness sharing (during phase 1 of constructing the hierarchy). In all cases a field size of 20 × 20 meters is assumed.

Figure 1 reports test performance of the champion individual at three points through each of the two phases necessary to develop the hierarchical SBB policy. Generation 1 corresponds to the champion individual at initialization. Generation 125 and 250 correspond to the performance of the champion individual half way and at the final generation. As there are two distinct phases of evolution

---

[2] http://web.cs.dal.ca/~mheywood/Code/SBB/
[3] http://sourceforge.net/apps/mediawiki/sserver
[4] http://www.cs.utexas.edu/~AustinVilla/sim/keepaway/

the generation count cycles from 1 to 250 twice. The 'simulation hours' reflects the total accumulated number of hours of simulated play on the soccer server.

Table 2. Summary of keeper possession times for 3-versus-2 Keepaway. Averages reflect 1,000 test games for a champion policy. Simulated hours represents the total number of simulation hours necessary to return the champion policy.

Algorithm	Avg. keeper possession time	Simulated hrs. (of play)
HyperNEAT [20]	15.4 sec	unknown
EANT [3]	14.9 sec	≈ 200
NEAT [4, 19]	14.1 sec	≈ 800
Sarsa with RBF [4, 19]	12.5 sec	≈ 50

Comparing the average values reported for test performance during the hierarchical SBB runs in Figure 1 with the previously reported best test performance (Table 2) it is apparent that both forms of SBB provide significant improvements by the end of the first phase of evolution. This is achieved with 286 (with diversity) to 650 (no diversity) simulation hours, which is comparable or better than either of the neuro-evolutionary methods. The second phase of evolution, in which the second level of the hierarchical policy is built, emphasizes consistency (fitness sharing is disabled). This focuses the performance of champion individuals such that there is less variation between different runs. Additional experiments with fitness sharing applied during both phases of evolution did not reach this level of performance or consistency.

A further post training test of generalization is performed as follows. At the last generation, the champion individual is identified (as reported in the last column of Figure 1). Such a champion has been evolved and selected with respect to a field size of 20 × 20 meters. This *same* champion individual is then deployed on three other field sizes *without* any additional modification, Figure 2. Naturally, the task becomes easier on larger field sizes. Such an experiment was previously performed relative to Sarsa under a tile coded representation [1]. In the case of the Sarsa–tile coding result, performance was very sensitive to the configuration on which training was performed e.g., even when trained on a more difficult field size, performance on the easier field size was worse. Conversely, both SBB configurations perform better on the easier field sizes and exceed any of the default behaviours under the most difficult field size. Similar general trends were reported for HyperNEAT, albeit with a much lower overall level of performance [20]. It is also clear that for each field size, SBB with diversity provides improved generalization e.g., the difference between mean game times for each field size is: 1.1, 2.5, 5.6, 0.5 seconds respectively. In comparison, note that a total of 1.3 seconds of game time separates the ranking of all three neuro-evolutionary methods applied to the 3-versus-2 Keepaway task (Table 2).

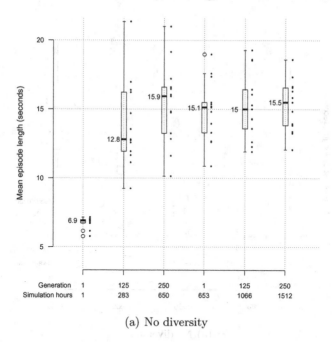

(a) No diversity

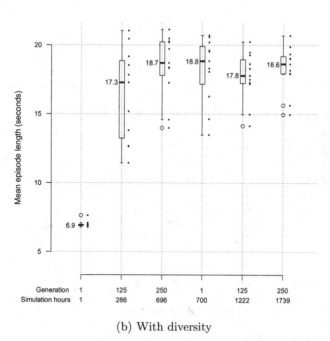

(b) With diversity

Fig. 1. Average performance of champion policy against 1,000 test games. Two level hierarchical policy with 250 generations per level. Box plot reflects the quartile distribution and scatter plot the actual performance points from 12 runs. Numerical value reports the median of the 12 runs.

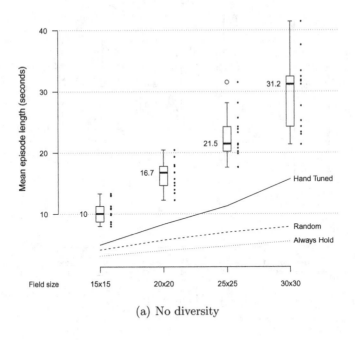

(a) No diversity

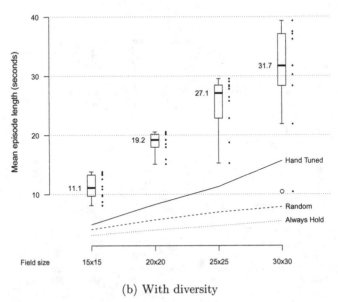

(b) With diversity

Fig. 2. Generalization of champion policy against multiple field sizes. Champions *evolved* and *identified* w.r.t. 20×20 meter field. 'Hand tuned', 'Random' and 'Always hold' represent baseline policies provided in the Keepaway code base [2].

5 Conclusion

The most popular form of the Keepaway soccer task (3-versus-2) has been revisited using a recently proposed scheme for evolving teams of programs hierarchically [6–8]. To do so, particular attention was applied to the definition of diversity maintenance. Specifically, a fitness sharing formulation was proposed, where this avoids the need to specify the relative weight of diversity to fitness. Including diversity results in the discovery of policies with an additional ≈ 3 seconds of play w.r.t. the field size for which evolution is performed and an additional 0.5 to 2.5 seconds of play when testing the same policy against games held on different field sizes. Moreover, when diversity is included, the policies provide games that last ≈ 3 seconds longer than previously published results.

Future research will investigate task-independent phenotypic *and* genotypic diversity measures as well as consider other formulations of the task domain, such as the more difficult 4-versus-3 configuration. Other properties of interest could include varying the players' field of view from 360 deg to more limited ranges or the ultimate objective of evolving entire soccer teams.

Acknowledgments. The authors gratefully acknowledge funding provided by the NSERC Discovery grant program (Canada).

References

1. Stone, P., Sutton, R.S.: Scaling reinforcement learning toward robocup soccer. In: The Eighteenth International Conference on Machine Learning, pp. 537–544 (2001)
2. Stone, P., Sutton, R.S., Kuhlmann, G.: Reinforcement learning for RoboCup soccer keepaway. Adaptive Behavior 13(3), 165–188 (2005)
3. Metzen, J.H., Edgington, M., Kassahun, Y., Kirchner, F.: Analysis of an evolutionary reinforcement learning method in a multiagent domain. In: Proceedings of the International Joint Conference on Autonomous Agents and Multiagent Systems, pp. 291–298 (2008)
4. Whiteson, S., Taylor, M.E., Stone, P.: Critical factors in the empirical performance of temporal difference and evolutionary methods for reinforcement learning. Autonomous Agents and Multi-Agent Systems 21(1), 1–35 (2009)
5. Burke, E.K., Gustafson, S., Kendall, G.: Diversity in genetic programming: An analysis of measures and correlation with fitness. IEEE Transactions on Evolutionary Computation 8(1), 47–62 (2004)
6. Lichodzijewski, P., Heywood, M.I.: The Rubik cube and GP temporal sequence learning: an initial study. In: Genetic Programming Theory and Practice VIII, pp. 35–54. Springer (2011)
7. Kelly, S., Lichodzijewski, P., Heywood, M.I.: On run time libraries and hierarchical symbiosis. In: IEEE Congress on Evolutionary Computation, pp. 3245–3252 (2012)
8. Doucette, J.A., Lichodzijewski, P., Heywood, M.I.: Hierarchical task decomposition through symbiosis in reinforcement learning. In: Proceedings of the ACM Genetic and Evolutionary Computation Conference, pp. 97–104 (2012)
9. Lichodzijewski, P., Heywood, M.I.: Symbiosis, complexification and simplicity under GP. In: Proceedings of the ACM Genetic and Evolutionary Computation Conference, pp. 853–860 (2010)

10. Calabretta, R., Nolfi, S., Parisi, D., Wagner, G.P.: Duplication of modules facilitates the evolution of functional specialization. Artificial Life 6(1), 69–84 (2000)
11. Watson, R.A., Pollack, J.B.: Modular interdependency in complex dynamical systems. Artificial Life 11(4), 445–458 (2005)
12. Dempsey, I., O'Neill, M., Brabazon, A.: Survey of EC in dynamic environments. In: Foundations in Grammatical Evolution for Dynamic Environments. SCI, vol. 194, pp. 25–54. Springer, Heidelberg (2009)
13. Minku, L.L., White, A.P., Yao, X.: The impact of diversity on online ensemble learning in the presence of concept drift. IEEE Transactions on Knowledge and Data Engineering 22(5), 730–742 (2010)
14. Chong, S.Y., Tino, P., Yao, X.: Relationship between generalization and diversity in coevolutionary learning. IEEE Transactions on Computational Intelligence and AI in Games 1(3), 214–232 (2009)
15. Cuccu, G., Gomez, F.: When novelty is not enough. In: Di Chio, C., et al. (eds.) EvoApplications 2011, Part I. LNCS, vol. 6624, pp. 234–243. Springer, Heidelberg (2011)
16. Mouret, J.B., Doncieux, S.: Encouraging behavioral diversity in evolutionary robotics: an empirical study. Evolutionary Computation 20(1), 91–133 (2012)
17. Waibel, M., Keller, L., Floreano, D.: Genetic team composition and level of selection in the evolution of cooperation. IEEE Transactions on Evolutionary Computation 13(3), 648–660 (2009)
18. Jung, T., Polani, D.: Learning robocup-keepaway with kernels. In: JMLR: Workshop and Conference Proceedings – Gaussian Processes in Practice, pp. 33–57 (2007)
19. Taylor, M.E., Whiteson, S., Stone, P.: Comparing evolutionary and temporal difference methods in a reinforcement learning domain. In: Proceedings of the ACM Genetic and Evolutionary Computation Conference, pp. 1321–1328 (2006)
20. Verbancsics, P., Stanley, K.O.: Evolving static representations for task transfer. The Journal of Machine Learning Research 99, 1737–1769 (2010)
21. Gustafson, S.M., Hsu, W.H.: Layered learning in genetic programming for a cooperative robot soccer problem. In: Miller, J., Tomassini, M., Lanzi, P.L., Ryan, C., Tetamanzi, A.G.B., Langdon, W.B. (eds.) EuroGP 2001. LNCS, vol. 2038, pp. 291–301. Springer, Heidelberg (2001)
22. Hsu, W.H., Harmon, S.J., Rodriguez, E., Zhong, C.: Empirical comparison of incremental reuse strategies in genetic programming for keep-away soccer. In: Late Breaking Papers at the Genetic and Evolutionary Computation Conference (2004)
23. Brameier, M., Banzhaf, W.: Evolving teams of predictors with linear genetic programming. Genetic Programming and Evolvable Machines 2(4), 381–407 (2001)
24. Thomason, R., Soule, T.: Novel ways of improving cooperation and performance in ensemble classifiers. In: Proceedings of the ACM Genetic and Evolutionary Computation Conference, pp. 1708–1715 (2007)
25. Lichodzijewski, P., Heywood, M.I.: Pareto-coevolutionary Genetic Programming for problem decomposition in multi-class classification. In: Proceedings of the ACM Genetic and Evolutionary Computation Conference, pp. 464–471 (2007)
26. Brameier, M., Banzhaf, W.: Linear Genetic Programming. Springer (2007)
27. Okasha, S.: Multilevel selection and the major transitions in evolution. Philosophy of Science 72, 1013–1025 (2005)

Genetically Improved CUDA C++ Software

William B. Langdon and Mark Harman

CREST, Department of Computer Science,
University College London Gower Street, London WC1E 6BT, UK
W.Langdon@cs.ucl.ac.uk
http://crest.cs.ucl.ac.uk/

Abstract. Genetic Programming (GP) may dramatically increase the performance of software written by domain experts. GP and autotuning are used to optimise and refactor legacy GPGPU C code for modern parallel graphics hardware and software. Speed ups of more than six times on recent nVidia GPU cards are reported compared to the original kernel on the same hardware.

1   Introduction

Genetic Programming (GP) [1] is increasingly being used in Software Engineering [2]. We are using GP to make software more adaptable [3] and are particularly interested in GP to generate code [4,5], for bug fixing [6] and for improving existing code [7,8,9,10,11,12,13]. With increasing use of embedded and mobile devices there is a growing need to cheaply generate software which meets multiple interacting performance constraints, such as memory limits, energy consumption and real-time response [14,8]. Similarly there is increasing use of parallelism both

Fig. 1. For each pixel we calculate the sum of squared differences (SSD) between 11×11 regions centred on the pixel in the left image and the same pixel in the right hand image. The right hand 11×11 region is moved one place to the left and new SSD is calculated This is repeated 50 times. Each time a smaller SSD is found, it is saved.

M. Nicolau et al. (Eds.): EuroGP 2014, LNCS 8599, pp. 87–99, 2014.

Table 1. GPU Hardware. Year each was announced by nVidia in column 2. Third column is CUDA compute capability level. Each GPU chip contains a number of identical and more or less independent multiprocessors (column 4). Each MP contains a number of stream processors (cores, column 5) whose speed is given in column 7. Measured data rate (ECC on) between the GPU and its on board memory in last column.

Name	Capability	MP $\times$	cores	Clock GHz	Caches L1	L2	Bandwidth GB/s
Quadro NVS 290	2007 1.1	2 $\times$ 8 =	16	0.92	none		4
GeForce GTX 295	2009 1.3	30 $\times$ 8 =	240	1.24	none		92
Tesla T10	2009 1.3	30 $\times$ 8 =	240	1.30	none		72
Tesla C2050	2010 2.0	14 $\times$ 32 =	448	1.15	16/48KB	0.75 MB	101
GeForce GTX 580	2010 2.0	16 $\times$ 32 =	512	1.54	16/48KB	0.75 MB	161
Tesla K20c	2012 3.5	13 $\times$ 192 =	2496	0.71	16/32/48KB	1.25 MB	140

in conventional computing but also in mobile applications. At present the epitome of parallelism are dedicated multi-core machines based on gaming graphics cards (GPUs). Although originally devised for the consumer market, they are increasingly being used for general purpose computing on GPUs (GPGPU) [15] with several of today's fastest peta flop super computers being based on GPUs. However, although support tools are improving, programming parallel computers continues to be a challenge and simply leaving code generation to parallel compilers is often insufficient. Instead experts, e.g. [16], have advocated writing highly parametrised parallel code which can then be automatically tuned. Unfortunately this throws the load back on to the coder [17]. Here we demonstrate that genetic programming can work with an auto-tuner to adapt human written code to new circumstances and different hardware. In total we consider six types of hardware of differing ages, architectures and very different performance (Table 1). GP can give more than a six fold performance increase relative to the original system on the same hardware (Table 4).

2   Source Code: StereoCamera

The StereoCamera system was written by nVidia's stereo image processing expert Joe Stam [18] for the first version of CUDA. V1.0b is available from SourceForge but, despite Moore's Law [19], and except for my bugfix, it has not been updated since 2008.

For each pixel in the left image, GPU code stereoKernel reports the number of pixels the right image has to be shifted to get maximal local alignment (see Figure 1). It does this by minimising the sum of squares of the difference (SSD) between the left and right images in a 11×11 area around each pixel. Once SSD has been calculated, the grid in the right hand image is displaced one pixel to the left and the calculation is repeated. SSD is calculated for 0 to 50 displacements and the one with the smallest SSD is reported.

Considerable savings can be made by reducing the total number of calculations by sharing intermediate calculations [18, Fig. 3]. Each SSD calculation involves summing 11 columns (each of 11 squared discrepancy values). By saving the column sums in shared memory adjacent computational threads can calculate just their own column and then read the remaining ten column values calculated by their neighbouring threads.

After one row of pixel SSDs have been calculated, when calculating the SSD of the pixels immediately above, ten of the eleven rows of SSD values are identical. The SSD for the pixel above is then the total SSD plus the contribution for the new row *minus* the contribution from the lowest row (which is no longer included in the 11 × 11 area). The more rows which share their partial results, the more efficient is the calculation but then there is less scope for performing calculations in parallel. Ideally all the image data for both left and right images (including halos and discrepancy offsets) should fit within the GPU's texture caches. The macro ROWSperTHREAD (40) determines how many rows are calculated together in series. The macro BLOCK_W (64) determines how the image is partitioned horizontally. In practise all these factors interact in non-obvious hardware dependent ways.

3   Example Stereo Pairs from Microsoft's I2I Database

Microsoft's I2I database contains 3010 stereo images. Figure 1 (top) is a typical example. Many of these are in the form of movies taken in an office environment. Almost images all are 320×240 pixels. We took the first 200 pairs for training leaving 2810 for validation. Notice we are asking the GP to create a new version of the CUDA stereoKernel GPU code which is tuned to pairs of images of this type. As we shall see (in Section 8) the improved GPU code is indeed tuned to 320×240 images but still works well on the other I2I stereo pairs.

4   Pre- and Post- Evolution Tuning and Post Evolution Minimisation of Code Changes

In initial genetic programming runs, it became apparent that there are two parameters which have a large impact on run time but whose default settings are not suitable for the GPUs now available. It is feasible to run StereoCamera on all reasonable combinations and simply choose the best for each GPU. Hence the revised strategy is to tune ROWSperTHREAD and BLOCK_W before running the GP. (DPER, Section 5.2, is not initially enabled.) As with [6] and our GISMOE approach [10], after GP has run the best GP individual from the last generation is minimised. Finally ROWSperTHREAD, BLOCK_W and DPER are tuned again. (Often no further changes were needed.)

For each combination of parameters, the kernel is compiled and run. By recompiling rather than using run time argument passing, the nVidia nvcc C++ compiler is given the best chance of optimising the code (e.g. loop unrolling) for these parameters and the particular GPU.

BLOCK_W values were based on sizes of thread blocks used by nVidia in the examples supplied with CUDA 5.0. (They were 8, 32, 64, 128, 192, 256, 384 and 512.) All small ROWSperTHREAD values or values which divide into the image height (240) were tested. (I.e., 1, ... 18, 20, 21, 24, 26, 30, 34, 40, 48, 60, 80, 120 and 240.) Except for the NVS 290, which has only two multiprocessors, autotuning reduced ROWSperTHREAD from 40 to 5 before the GP was run. In many cases this gave a big speed up (see middle and last columns of Table 4).

The best GP individual in the last generation is minimised by starting at its beginning and progressively removing each individual mutation and comparing the performance of the new kernel with the evolved one. For simplicity this is done on the last training stereo image pair. Unless the new kernel is worse the mutation is excluded permanently. To encourage removal of mutations with little impact, those that make less than 1% difference to the kernel timing are also removed.

5   Alternative Implementations

5.1   Avoiding Reusing Threads: XHALO

Each row of pixels is extended by five pixels at both ends. The original code reused the first ten threads of each block to calculate these ten halo values. Much of the kernel code is duplicated to deal with the horizontal halo. GPUs use SIMD parallel architectures, which means many identical operations can be run in parallel but if the code branches in different directions part of the hardware becomes idle. Thus diverting ten threads to deal with the halo causes all the remaining threads to become idle. Option XHALO allows GP to use ten additional threads which are dedicated to the halo. Thus each thread only deals with one pixel. In practise the net effect of XHALO is to disable the duplicated code so that instead of each block processing vertical stripes of 64 pixels, each block only writes stripes 54 pixels wide.

5.2   Parallel of Discrepancy Offsets: DPER

The original code (Section 2) steps through sequentially 51 displacements of the right image with respect to the left. Modern GPUs allow many more threads and often it is best to use more threads as it allows greater parallelism and may improve throughput by increasing the overlap between computation and I/O. Instead of stepping sequentially one at a time through the for loop controlling the displacement, the DPER option allows SSD values for multiple (e.g. 2, 3 or 4) displacements to be calculated in parallel. So instead of increasing the for loop control variable by one, it is incremented by the same amount (e.g. 2, 3 or 4). As well as increasing the number of threads, the amount of shared memory needed is also increased by the same factor. Nevertheless only one (the smallest) SSD value need be compared with the current smallest, so saving some I/O.

6   Parameters Accessible to Evolution

The GISMOE GP system [10] was extended to allow not only code changes but also changes to C macro #defines. The GP puts the evolved values in a

Table 2. Evolvable configuration macros and constants

Name	Default	Options	Purpose
Cache preference	None	None, Shared, L1, Equal	L1 v. shared memory
-Xptxas -dlcm		' ', ca, cg, cs, cv	nvcc cache options
OUT_TYPE	float	float, int, short int, unsigned char	
STORE_Pixel	GLOBAL	GLOBAL, SHARED, LOCAL	
STORE_MinSSD	GLOBAL	GLOBAL, SHARED, LOCAL	
DPER	disabled		Section 5.2
XHALO	disabled		Section 5.1
__mul24(a,b)	__mul24	__mul24, *	fast 24-bit multiply
GPtexturereadmode	Normalized	NormalizedFloat,	Section 6.1
	Float	ElementType, no Textures	
texturefilterMode	Linear	Linear, Point	
textureaddressMode		Clamp, Mirror, Wrap	
texturenormalized		0, 1	

C #include .h file, which is complied along with the GP modified kernel code and the associated (fixed) host source code.

Table 2 shows the twelve configuration parameters. Every GP individual chromosome starts with these 12 which are then followed by zero or more changes to the code.

6.1   Fixed Configuration Parameters

OUT_TYPE. The return value should be in the range -1 to 50. Originally this is coded as a float. OUT_TYPE gives GP the option of trying other types.

STORE_disparityPixel and STORE_disparityMinSSD. disparityPixel and disparityMinSSD are major arrays in the kernel. Stam coded them to lie in the GPU's slow off chip global memory. These configuration options give evolution the possibility of trying to place them in either shared memory or in local memory. Where the compiler can resolve local array indexes, e.g. as a result of unrolling loops, it can use fast registers in place of local memory.

__mul24. For addressing purposes, older GPU's included a fast 24 bit multiply instruction, which is heavily used in the original code. It appears that in the newer GPUs __mul24 may actually be slower than ordinary (32 bit) integer multiply. Hence we give GP the option of replacing __mul24.

Textures. CUDA textures are intimately linked with the GPU's hardware and provide a wide range of data manipulation facilities (normalisation, default values, control of boundary effects and interpolation) which the original code does not need but is obliged to use. The left and right image textures are principally used because they provide caching (which was not otherwise available on early generation GPUs.) We allowed the GP to investigate other texture options. Including not using textures. Some combinations are illegal but the host code gives sensible defaults in these cases.

7   Evolvable Code

Following the standard GISMOE approach [10], a grammar describing the legal changes to the kernel source code was automatically created from the human written source code. Due to the way Stam wrote his kernel (with all variables declared at the start) no mutation moves variables out of scope. Thus almost all GP created kernels compile, link and run. The only exception being two cases where GP created legal source code which provoked bugs in the nvcc 5.0 compiler. It is believed these bugs have been fixed in 5.5.

The source code, including XHALO and DPER (Sections 5.1 and 5.2), is automatically translated line by line into a BNF grammar (see Figure 2). Notice the grammar is not generic, it represents only one program, stereoKernel, and variants of it. The grammar contains 424 rules, 277 represent fixed lines of C++ source code. There are 55 variable lines, 27 IF and 10 of each of the three parts of C for loops. There are also five CUDA specific types:

pragma allows GP to control the nvcc compiler's loop unrolling. pragma rules are automatically inserted before each **for** loop but rely on GP to enable and set their values. Using the type constraints GP can either: remove it, set it to #pragma unroll, or set it to #pragma unroll n (where n is 1 to 11).

optvolatile CUDA allows shared data types to be marked as volatile which influences the compiler's optimisation. As required by the CUDA compiler, the grammar automatically ensures all shared variables are either flagged as volatile or none are. The remaining three CUDA types apply to the kernel's header.

optconst Each of kernel's scalar inputs can be separately marked as const.

optrestrict All of the kernel's array arguments can be marked with __restrict__. This potentially helps the compiler to optimise the code. On the newest GPUs (SM 3.5) optrestrict allows the compiler to access read only arrays via a read only cache. Since both only apply if all arrays are marked __restrict__, the grammar ensures they all are or none are.

launchbounds is again a CUDA specific aid to code optimisation. By default the compiler must generate code that can be run with any numbers of threads. Since GP knows how many threads will be used, specifying it via __launch_bounds__ gives the compiler the potential of optimising the code. __launch_bounds__ takes an optional second argument. How it is used is again convoluted, but the grammar allows GP to omit it, or set it to 1, 2, 3, 4 or 5.

7.1   Initial Population

Each member of the initial population is unique. They are each created by selecting at random one of the 12 configuration constants (Table 2) and setting it at random to one of its non-default values. As the population is created it becomes harder to find unique mutations and so random code changes are included as well as the configuration change. Table 3 summarises the GP parameters.

```
<KStereo.cuh_159>   ::= "{\n"
<KStereo.cuh_160>   ::= "" <_KStereo.cuh_160> "\n"
<_KStereo.cuh_160>  ::= "init_disparityPixel(X,Y,i);"
<KStereo.cuh_161>   ::= "" <_KStereo.cuh_161> "\n"
<_KStereo.cuh_161>  ::= "init_disparityMinSSD(X,Y,i);"
```

Fig. 2. Fragments of BNF grammar used by GP. Most rules are fixed but rules starting with <_, <IF_, <for1_, <pragma_, etc. can be manipulated using rules of the same type to produce variants of stereoKernel.

7.2 Weights

Normally each line of code is equally likely to be modified. However, only as part of creating the initial population, the small number of rules in the kernel header (i.e. launchbounds, optrestrict, optconst and optvolatile) are 1000 times more likely to be changed than the other grammar rules. (Forcing each member of the GP population to be unique is only done in the initial population.)

7.3 Mutation

Half of mutations are made to the configuration parameters (Table 2). In which case one of the 12 is chosen uniformly at random and its current value is replaced by another of its possible values again chosen uniformly at random. For the code, we use the three GISMOE mutations: delete a line of code, replace a line and insert a line [10]. The additional lines of code are not random but are copied from stereoKernel itself. This is like [6] except we use the grammar.

7.4 Crossover

As in the GISMOE frame work [10], crossover creates a new GP individual from two different members of the better half of the current population. The child inherits each of the 12 fixed parameters (Table 2) at random from either parent (uniform crossover [20]). Whereas in [10] we used append crossover, which deliberately increases the size of the offspring, here, on the variable length part of the genome, we use an analogue of Koza's tree GP crossover [21]. Two crossover points are chosen uniformly at random. The part between the 2 crossover points of the first parent is replaced by the mutations between the two crossover points of the second parent to give a single child. On average, this gives no net change in length.

7.5 Fitness

To avoid over fitting and to keep run times manageable, each generation one of the two hundred training images pairs is chosen [22]. Each GP modified kernel in the population is tested on that image pair.

CUDA Memcheck and Loop Overruns. Normally each GP modified kernel is run twice. The first time it is run with CUDA memcheck and with loop over run checks enabled. If no problems are reported by CUDA memcheck and the kernel terminates normally (i.e. without exceeding the limit on loop iterations) it is run a second time without these debug aids. Both memcheck and counting loop iterations impose high overheads which make timing information unusable. Only in the second run are the timing and error information used as part of fitness. If the GP kernel fails in either run, it is given such a large penalty, that it will not be a parent for the next generation.

When loop timeouts are enabled, the GP grammar ensures that each time a C++ `for` loop iterates a per thread global counter is incremented. If the counter exceeds the limit, the loop is aborted and the kernel quickly terminates. If any thread reaches its limit, the whole kernel is treated as if it had timed out. The limit is set to 100× the maximum reasonable value for a good kernel.

Timing. Each of the Multiprocessors (MPs) within the GPU chip has its own independent clock. To get a robust timing scheme, each kernel block records both its own start and end times and the MP unit it is running on. After the kernel has finished, for each MP, the end time of the last block to use it and the start time of the first block to use it are subtracted to give the accurate duration of usage for each MP. The total duration of the kernel is the longest time taken by any of the MPs used.

Error. For each pixel in the left image the value returned by the GP modified kernel is compared with that given by the un-modified kernel. If they are different a per pixel penalty is added to the total error.

If the unmodified kernel did not return a value the value returned by the GP kernel is also ignored. Otherwise, if the GP failed to set a value for a pixel, it gets a penalty of 200. If the GP value is infinite or otherwise outside the range of expected values (0..50) it attracts a penalty of 100. Otherwise the per pixel penalty is the absolute difference between the original value and the GP's value.

7.6   Selection

As with the GISMOE framework [10] at the end of each generation we compare each mutant with the original kernel's performance on the same test case and only allow it to be a parent if it does well. In detail, it must be both faster and be, on average, not more than 6.0 per pixel different from the original code's answer. However mostly the evolved code passes both tests. At the end of each generation the population is sorted first by their error and then by their speed. The top 50% are selected to be parents of the next generation. Each selected parent creates one child by mutation (Section 7.3) and another by crossover with another selected parent (Section 7.4). The complete GP parameters are summarised in Table 3.

Table 3. Genetic programming parameters for improving stereoKernel

Representation:	Fixed list of 12 parameter values (Table 2) followed by variable list of replacements, deletions and insertions into BNF grammar
Fitness:	Run on a randomly chosen 320×240 monochrome stereo image pair. Compare answer & run time with original.
Population:	Panmictic, non-elitist, generational. 100 members.
Parameters:	Initial population of random single mutants heavily weighted towards the kernel header and shared variables. 50% truncation selection. 50% crossover, 50% mutation. No size limit. 50 generations.

Table 4. Mean speed across all 2516 I2I 320×240 stereo image pairs. ± is standard deviation. Times in microseconds. In all cases tuning leaves BLOCK_W as 64. Tuning NVS 290 *increases* ROWSperTHREAD from 40 to 120, otherwise pretuning reduces it to 5. Post GP tuning leaves ROWSperTHREAD as 5, except C2050 (14) and GTX 580 (15).

GPU name	Original	Pretuned	Ratio	GP	Speedup
Quadro NVS 290	27402±116	26019±152			1.053±0.01
GeForce GTX 295	5448± 14	1518± 4			3.589±0.01
Tesla T10	5256± 12	1436± 3	3.661±0.01	1359±38	3.861±0.11
Tesla C2050	4632± 25	3017± 15	1.535±0.01	1130± 5	4.099±0.02
GeForce GTX 580	3077± 21	1650± 6	1.865±0.01	722±29	4.248±0.17
Tesla K20c	4362± 21	1839± 18	2.373±0.03	638± 1	6.837±0.04

8 Results

Table 4 gives the speed up for six types of GPUs. By reducing ROWSperTHREAD from the original 40 to 5, pretuning (Section 4) itself gave considerable speed ups (columns 4-5 in Table 4). However for NVS 290, tuning ROWSperTHREAD increased it from 40 to 120 but only gave a modest improvement (last columns in Table 4). In all cases the original value of BLOCK_W (64) was optimal.

With CUDA 5.0 memcheck (Section 7.5), it proved impossible to keep the NVS 290 and GTX 295 operational for a complete GP run. Despite hardware monitoring, the problem remained non-reproducible. It is thought with more recent hardware, memcheck is able to catch and prevent problems caused by incorrect array indexes but on the NVS 290 and GTX 295 GPUs (with nVidia driver 310.40) incorrect program operation eventually lead to hardware lock up. This is at odds with our earlier successful use of GP on the GTX 295, where we had explicitly caught out-of-range indexes [4]. Hence it might have been better to provide our own array bounds index checking. In Table 4 the "GP" columns for the NVS 290 and GTX 295 rows are blank and the last column refers to the speed up achieved by tuning ROWSperTHREAD and BLOCK_W.

With the four more modern GPUs, the best individual from the last generation (50) was minimised to remove unneeded mutations and retuned (Section 4). This resulted in reductions in length: T10 31→14, C2050 17→10, GTX580 26→13 and K20c 29→10. The speeds of the re-tuned kernels are given in Table 4

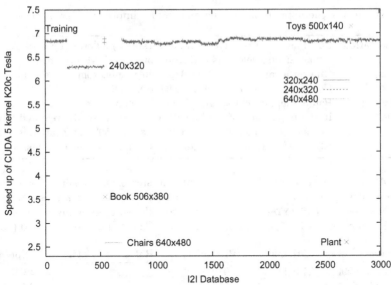

Fig. 3. Performance of GP improved K20c Tesla kernel on all 3010 stereo pairs in Microsoft's I2I database relative to original kernel on the same image pair on the same GPU. Fifty of first 200 pairs used in training. The evolved kernel is always much better, especially on images of the same size and shape as it was trained on.

under heading "GP". In each case this gave a significant speed up (last column of Table 4) compared to both the original kernel and the original kernel with the best ROWSperTHREAD setting. The speedup of the improved K20c kernel on all of the I2I stereo images is given in Figure 3. The speed up for the other five GPUs varies in a similar way to the K20c. Finally, notice typically there is very little difference in performance across the images of the same size and shape as the training data (see ± columns in Table 4).

8.1 GP Better Than Random Search

In the case of the K20c Tesla, the GP was run again for the same number of evaluations, the same population size, the same number of generations *but* with random selection of parents. The best in the whole run of 50 generations of random search is exceeded by the best in the third and subsequent GP generations.

9 Evolved Tesla K20c CUDA Code

The best of generation 50 individual changes 6 of the 12 fixed configuration parameters (Table 2) and includes 23 grammar rule changes. After removing less useful components (Section 4) four configuration parameters were changed and there were six code changes. See Figures 4 and 5.

DPER is enabled and the new kernel calculates two disparity values in parallel, Section 5.2. disparityPixel and disparityMinSSD are stored in shared memory, Section 6.1 and XHALO is enabled, Section 5.1.

Table 5. Numbers of most popular of each of the evolvable configuration macros and constants (Table 2) in the last breeding population

Fixed mutation	Tesla T10		Tesla C2050		GTX 580		Tesla K20c	
Cache	None	62	L1	52	L1	66	None	48
-Xptxas -dlcm	ca	84	not used	50	cg	42	not used	32
OUT_TYPE	`float`	100	`float`	74	`float`	76	`float`	48
STORE_Pixel	LOCAL	100	LOCAL	100	LOCAL	76	GLOBAL	70
STORE_MinSSD	SHARED	100	SHARED	100	SHARED	56	SHARED	76
DPER	disabled	100	disabled	100	used	100	used	100
XHALO	disabled	100	used	100	used	100	used	100
_mul24(a,b)	_mul24	100	*	100	*	70	_mul24	98
GPtexturereadmode	Normalized	100	Normalized	100	Normalized	100	Normalized	100
texturefilterMode	Linear	100	Linear	100	Linear	100	Linear	100
texturenormalized	default	82	default	80	default	72	default	72
textureaddressMode	Wrap	40	Clamp	66	Mirror	42	Mirror	48

The final code changes, Figure 5, are:

- disable volatile, Section 7.
- insert `#pragma unroll 11` before the `for` loop that steps through the `ROWSperTHREAD - 1` other rows (Section 2).
- insert `#pragma unroll 3` before the `for` loop that writes each of the `ROWS perTHREAD` rows of disparityPixel from shared to global memory. Its not clear why evolution chose to ask the nvcc compiler to unroll this loop (which is always executed 5 times) only 3 times. But then when nvcc decides to do loop unrolling is obscure anyway.
- Mutation `<_KStereo.cuh_161>+<_KStereo.cuh_224>` causes line 224 to be inserted before line 161. Line 224 potentially updates local variable `ssd`, however `ssd` is not used before the code which initialises it. It is possible that compiler spots that the mutated code cannot affect anything outside the kernel and simply optimises it away. During minimisation removing it gave a kernel whose run time was exactly on the removal threshold.
- Mutation `<IF_KStereo.cuh_326><IF_KStereo.cuh_154>` replaces `X < width && Y < height` by `dblockIdx==0`. This replace a complicated expression by a simpler one, which itself has no effect on the logic since both are always true. In fact, given the way `if(dblockIdx==0)` is nested inside another `if`, the compiler may optimise it away entirely.
- delete `_syncthreads()` on line 348. `_syncthreads()` forces all threads to stop and wait until all reach it. Line 348 is at the end of code which may update shared variables disparityPixel and disparityMinSSD. In effect GP has discovered it is safe to let other threads proceed since they will not use the same shared variables before meeting other `_syncthreads()`.

10 Conclusions

Correctly tuning one (originally hard coded) constant immediately gave speed ups of between 5% and a factor or 3.6 (median 2.1) (see Table 4). In all cases,

```
DPER=1 STORE_disparityMinSSD=SHARED XHALO=1 STORE_disparityPixel=SHARED
<pragma_KStereo.cuh_359><pragma_K3> <_KStereo.cuh_161>+<_KStereo.cuh_224>
<_KStereo.cuh_348> <optvolatile_KStereo.cuh_86>
<pragma_KStereo.cuh_262><pragma_K11> <IF_KStereo.cuh_326><IF_KStereo.cuh_154>
```

Fig. 4. Best GP individual in generation 50 of K20c Tesla run after minimising, Section 4, removed less useful components. (Auto-tuning made no further improvements.)

*int * __restrict__ disparityMinSSD,* //Global disparityMinSSD not kernel argument
volatile **extern __attribute__((shared)) int col_ssd[];**
volatile **int* const reduce_ssd = &col_ssd[(64)*2 -64];**
#pragma unroll 11
if(X < width && Y < height) replaced by **if(dblockIdx==0)**
__syncthreads();
#pragma unroll 3

Fig. 5. Evolved changes to K20c Tesla StereoKernel. (Produced by GP grammar changes in Figure 4). Highlighted **code** is inserted. Code in *italics* is removed. For brevity, except for the kernel's arguments, disparityPixel and disparityMinSSD changes from global to shared memory are omitted.

where genetic programming was able to run, it was able to build on this. Not only are the newer GPUs faster in themselves but the speed up achieved by GP was also larger on the newer GPUs. With final speed up varying from 5% for the oldest (which was contemporary with the original code) to a factor of more than 6.8 for the newest (median 4.0).

Future new requirements of StereoCamera might be dealing with: colour, moving images (perhaps with time skew), larger images, greater frame rates and running on mobile robots, 3D telephones, virtual reality gamesets or other low energy portable devices. We can hope our GP system could be used to automatically create new versions tailored to new demands and new hardware.

Acknowledgments. I am grateful for the assistance of njuffa, Istvan Reguly, vyas of nVidia, Ted Baker, and Allan MacKinnon. The grammar based genetic programming system is available via `ftp.cs.ucl.ac.uk` file `genetic/gp-code/StereoCamera_1_1.tar.gz`

GPUs were given by nVidia. Funded by EPSRC grant EP/I033688/1.

References

1. Poli, R., Langdon, W.B., McPhee, N.F.: A field guide to genetic programming, http://www.gp-field-guide.org.uk
2. Harman, M., Langdon, W.B., Weimer, W.: Genetic programming for reverse engineering. In: WCRE 2013, Koblenz, Germany. IEEE (2013) (Invited Keynote)
3. Harman, M., Langdon, W.B., Jia, Y., White, D.R., Arcuri, A., Clark, J.A.: The GISMOE challenge. In: ASE 2012, Essen, Germany, pp. 1–14. ACM (2012)
4. Langdon, W.B., Harman, M.: Evolving a CUDA kernel from an nVidia template. In: WCCI 2010, Barcelona, pp. 2376–2383. IEEE (2010)

5. Archanjo, G.A., Von Zuben, F.J.: Genetic programming for automating the development of data management algorithms in information technology systems. Advances in Software Engineering (2012)
6. Le Goues, C., Nguyen, T., Forrest, S., Weimer, W.: GenProg: A generic method for automatic software repair. IEEE Trans. on Soft. Eng. 38(1), 54–72 (2012)
7. Sitthi-amorn, P., Modly, N., Weimer, W., Lawrence, J.: Genetic programming for shader simplification. ACM Trans. on Graphics 30(6), article:152 (2011)
8. White, D.R., Arcuri, A., Clark, J.A.: Evolutionary improvement of programs. IEEE Trans. on EC 15(4), 515–538 (2011)
9. Orlov, M., Sipper, M.: Flight of the FINCH through the Java wilderness. IEEE Trans. on EC 15(2), 166–182 (2011)
10. Langdon, W.B., Harman, M.: Optimising existing software with genetic programming. IEEE Trans. on EC (accepted)
11. Petke, J., Harman, M., Langdon, W.B., Weimer, W.: Using genetic improvement and code transplants to specialise a C++ program to a problem class. In: Nicolau, M., Krawiec, K., Heywood, M.I., Castelli, M., García-Sánchez, P., Merelo, J.J., Santos, V.M.R., Sim, K. (eds.) EuroGP 2014. LNCS, vol. 8599, pp. 132–143. Springer, Heidelberg (2014)
12. Cotillon, A., Valencia, P., Jurdak, R.: Android genetic programming framework. In: Moraglio, A., Silva, S., Krawiec, K., Machado, P., Cotta, C. (eds.) EuroGP 2012. LNCS, vol. 7244, pp. 13–24. Springer, Heidelberg (2012)
13. Cody-Kenny, B., Barrett, S.: The emergence of useful bias in self-focusing genetic programming for software optimisation. In: Ruhe, G., Zhang, Y. (eds.) SSBSE 2013. LNCS, vol. 8084, pp. 306–311. Springer, Heidelberg (2013)
14. Tiwari, V., Malik, S., Wolfe, A.: Power analysis of embedded software: A first step towards software power minimization. IEEE Trans. on VLSI 2(4), 437–445 (1994)
15. Owens, J.D., Houston, M., Luebke, D., Green, S., Stone, J.E., Phillips, J.C.: GPU computing. Proceedings of the IEEE 96(5), 879–899 (2008) (Invited paper)
16. Merrill, D., Garland, M., Grimshaw, A.: Policy-based tuning for performance portability and library co-optimization. In: InPar. IEEE (2012)
17. Langdon, W.B.: Graphics processing units and genetic programming: An overview. Soft Computing 15, 1657–1669 (2011)
18. Stam, J.: Stereo imaging with CUDA. Technical report, nVidia (2008)
19. Moore, G.E.: Cramming more components onto integrated circuits. Electronics 38(8), 114–117 (1965)
20. Syswerda, G.: Uniform crossover in genetic algorithms. In: ICGA 1989, pp. 2–9 (1989)
21. Koza, J.R.: Genetic Programming. MIT Press (1992)
22. Langdon, W.B.: A many threaded CUDA interpreter for genetic programming. In: Esparcia-Alcázar, A.I., Ekárt, A., Silva, S., Dignum, S., Uyar, A.Ş. (eds.) EuroGP 2010. LNCS, vol. 6021, pp. 146–158. Springer, Heidelberg (2010)

Measuring Mutation Operators'
Exploration-Exploitation Behaviour
and Long-Term Biases

James McDermott[1,2]

[1] Natural Computing Research and Applications Group,
Complex and Adaptive Systems Lab, University College Dublin, Ireland
[2] Management Information Systems, Lochlann Quinn School of Business,
University College Dublin, Ireland
jmmcd@jmmcd.net

Abstract. We propose a simple method of directly measuring a mutation operator's short-term exploration-exploitation behaviour, based on its transition matrix. Higher values for this measure indicate a more exploitative operator. Since operators also differ in their degree of long-term bias towards particular areas of the search space, we propose a simple method of directly measuring this bias, based on the Markov chain stationary state. We use these measures to compare numerically the behaviours of two well-known mutation operators, the genetic algorithm per-gene bitflip mutation and the genetic programming subtree mutation.

Keywords: genetic programming, mutation, transition probability, Markov chain, stationary distribution, operator bias.

1 Introduction

In evolutionary algorithms, search is biased towards areas of high fitness. The strength of the bias is influenced by several parameters, including the selection method and mutation rate. The design of the mutation operator itself also has an effect. Some operators are more highly biased, i.e. more exploitative; others more explorative.

Although it is common to discuss the behaviour of different algorithms in these terms, a numerical measure of exploration-exploitation behaviour would be useful because it would allow research into which operators have an appropriate level of exploration for a particular search space. It would also allow direct comparison between operators.

However, exploration-exploitation behaviour is not the full story. Two operators which are equally explorative can differ in their long-term behaviour. An operator can exhibit a long-term bias towards particular areas of the search space, even without a selection pressure towards those areas. In the absence of any *a priori* assumptions on which regions are most fit, such bias might be

M. Nicolau et al. (Eds.): EuroGP 2014, LNCS 8599, pp. 100–111, 2014.

regarded as a deficiency of the operator. Although rare in many common encodings, this type of bias does arise in tree-based genetic programming (GP) [8]. Again, a numerical measure of the bias would be useful. For example, it would allow research into how strong a selection pressure is required to overcome the effect of an operator of given bias.

We propose to measure these aspects of a mutation operator using simple statistics. First, for measuring an operator's exploration-exploitation behaviour, we propose a measure based on the non-uniformity within the rows of the operator's matrix of transition probabilities. Uniform rows mean that search is unbiased by fitness, i.e. purely explorative; highly non-uniform rows mean that search is highly biased towards near neighbours of good individuals already encountered, i.e. highly exploitative.

Second, for measuring an operator's long-term bias, we use the non-uniformity of the Markov chain stationary state. An operator free of bias towards particular areas of the search space will have a uniform stationary distribution. A uniform stationary distribution does not correspond to uniform transition probabilities. Indeed, uniform transition probabilities are undesirable, since that would reduce the evolutionary search to a random search.

We demonstrate the use of these measures in very small genetic algorithm (GA) and GP spaces. The measures allow fair comparison between operators defined on these very different spaces, and a transfer of knowledge from the setting of the GA to that of GP.

1.1   Reader's Guide

Sect. 2, next, describes some related work. Definitions of the key statistical quantities are given in Sect. 3, and Sect. 4 demonstrates the use of the quantities in random-walk and hill-climbing scenarios. Sect. 5.1 gives discussion, while conclusions and future work are in Sect. 5.

2   Related Work

Our setting is the standard tree-based GP of Koza [8].

Markov chains [7] have long been used to study the behaviour of evolutionary algorithms and similar algorithms. It is worthwhile to divide this type of work into two groups: one particularly common in hill-climbing scenarios, where the Markov chain states correspond to individuals [e.g. 1]; and one where the states correspond to entire populations [e.g. 4, 15]. In our paper, states correspond to individuals.

Hu et al. [6] estimate the *visit frequency* of genotypes, effectively the same thing as the stationary distribution, using a long random walk. However, they restrict the walk to a neutral network, i.e. a set of genotypes giving the same phenotype. They find strong non-uniformity in the visit frequency in the neutral network. Because of the restriction to the neutral network, their result is not directly comparable to ours, which considers the entire space. Indeed, the description of the linear GP encoding and mutation operator they use is sufficient to show that their stationary distribution is uniform. The measures which are the focus of their work, including *accessibility, evolvability* and *robustness* of genotypes, phenotypes, and fitness values, are complementary to ours but not directly comparable.

The measures proposed by Moritz et al. [11] are not dissimilar to ours. They are based purely on sampling by random walks of varying lengths, whereas ours are based on calculation and first principles (we run random walks as demonstrations only). They require a distance function defined on the search space independent of the operator. That is, the distance function is not intended to reflect mutual accessibility of individuals via operator steps, but rather inherent or syntactic properties of the individuals. Given the distance function, short random walks are used to measure *locality*: short random walks which do not produce too much diversity (measured in terms of the distance function) indicate an operator of high locality. Long random walks are used to measure *unbiasedness*: long random walks which produce plenty of diversity indicate an operator of high unbiasedness. The motivation and experiments in this work accord with our approach to understanding search spaces. However there are two potential shortcomings. One is a requirement for a distance function defined on the search space independent of the operator. The definition of such a distance is simple in the bitstring space used in their experiments, but is not uncontroversial in some spaces, such as the space of trees. The other is the arbitrary threshold used to distinguish between short and long random walks. We claim that the theoretically-motivated stationary distribution of the Markov chain is a better approach to understanding long-term behaviour.

3   Statistics on Markov Chains

Given a vector x, we will use the notation $\mu(x)$ for the mean of x and $\sigma(x)$ for the standard deviation. Given a two-dimensional matrix p the notation $\sigma_r(p)$ will mean the vector composed of standard deviations over rows. In what follows, p will mean the operator's *transition matrix*: the matrix whose (i, j)th entry is the probability that, starting at element i of the search space, the operator will transition to element j in a single step.

An operator is fully characterised by its transition matrix. A row represents the outward transition probabilities from a single element of the search space. Highly non-uniform row vectors indicate a highly exploitative operator, while uniform row vectors indicate random search, i.e. a highly explorative operator. Therefore, we will measure short-term exploration-exploitation behaviour of an operator as $\mu(\sigma_r(p))$. Higher values mean more exploitation. Values near zero are undesirable, since that would reduce the evolutionary search to a random search. $\mu(\sigma_r(p))$ differs from other exploration-exploitation parameters, such as mutation rate, or selection tournament size, in that it is a consequence of the design of the operator, rather than a user-tunable parameter (an exception, where it is artificially controlled for a small space, is introduced in Sect. 4.1).

We will measure differences in exploration-exploitation behaviour between individuals as $\sigma(\sigma_r(p))$. Higher values mean that search is asymmetric: it tends to become more explorative when it hits some individuals, but more exploitative when it hits others.

According to Kemeny and Snell [7] (p. 218–219), "A finite Markov chain is ergodic if from any state it is possible to reach every other state. [...] Such a Markov chain has an equilibrium, i.e., a probability vector α such that $\alpha p = \alpha$. And α is strictly positive." Here p is the transition matrix. The equilibrium α is an eigenvector of the transition matrix. It expresses the probability that the chain will be in each state after it has reached equilibrium – informally, after it has "forgotten where it started".

We note in passing that ergodicity is the equivalent, in the language of Markov chains, of the *exhaustiveness* property of Moritz et al. [11]. In practice, ergodicity is easy to test from first principles rather than experiment, and it either holds (e.g. for a per-gene bit-flip operator) or fails very strongly (e.g. for single-node mutation in GP). That is, intermediate values of exhaustiveness occur only by construction of artificial operators such as the *3-fix* operator of Moritz et al. [11] which never flips the first 3 bits of a bitstring.

Any hill-climbing algorithm will use a mutation operator which gives an ergodic chain, and thus will have an equilibrium. We will call the equilibrium the *stationary distribution*, s.

The most important fact about the stationary distribution for our purposes is its uniformity or otherwise. A non-uniform stationary distribution reveals an asymmetric search. That is, it reveals a bias on the areas searched by the operator, in the long term, even in the absence of selection pressure. We will measure this bias as $\sigma(s)$. Higher values indicate greater bias.

How long a chain takes to reach equilibrium is an important research question. Various criteria have been proposed for defining the *mixing time* [9]. We will avoid this issue by making the conservative assumption that walks of 50 steps, in our small spaces, are more than enough to reach equilibrium.

In these definitions we are ignoring the effect of fitness and selection. This is deliberate, as follows. A common scenario in GP is to define a language and a set of operators, and then to use that as the representation for multiple problems. For example, we might define a language suitable for symbolic regression, and operators such as subtree crossover and subtree mutation. We might then choose a suite of datasets from some real-world source, to be regressed, or for test purposes a suite of known target functions involving logs, square roots, powers, and so on, or a suite of randomly-generated polynomials as targets. In each of these three examples, we have a single search space in which we will search for several different points in different runs. If we want to make general statements about GP, such as "mutation operator 1 is more suited to symbolic regression problems than mutation operator 2", then we must be able to study the structure of the space, and the behaviour of operators, without reference to the particular fitness function in use. This is the motivation for defining measures of exploration-exploitation behaviour and long-term bias which ignore the effect of fitness and selection.

4   Experiments

We have argued from first principles that $\mu(\sigma_r(p))$, the mean of standard deviations over rows of the transition matrix, functions as a simple measure of operator exploration-exploitation behaviour. Our first set of experiments (Sects. 4.3–4.4) aims to demonstrate this in random-walk and hill-climbing scenarios. We have also argued that $\sigma(s)$, the standard deviation of the stationary distribution, functions as a simple measure of long-term bias in the operator. Our second set of experiments (Sect. 4.5) aims to demonstrate this. We begin with experimental setup (Sect. 4.1) and statistical measures (Sect. 4.2).

4.1   Experimental Setup

Two representations are used:

- The GA-10 representation uses length-10 bitstrings, giving a search space of 1024 elements. The mutation operator is per-gene with mutation probability 0.1. When fitness is used, it is the OneMax problem, or a noisy variant. The OneMax problem has been well-studied theoretically. The expected time required to find the optimum is known to be of the order of $n \log(n)$, where n is the bitstring length [3, 5]. However, the author is unaware of a similar theoretical result giving the fitness expected to be achieved as a function of the bitstring length, mutation rate, number of generations, and degree of noise. Therefore, experimental methods rather than theoretical will be used.
- The GP-2 representation uses an alphabet of +, -, *, /, x, y, with maximum depth 2 (counting the root as depth 0), giving a search space of 1298 elements. The mutation operator is subtree mutation, where the subtree "cut" can take place at any node, including the root. Division is interpreted as the analytic quotient operator $Q(x, y) = x/\sqrt{1 + y^2}$ to avoid divide-by-zero errors [12].
  When GP fitness is used, it is defined as fitness on the Pagie-2d problem [14]. This is a symbolic regression problem with target function:

$$f(x, y) = \frac{1}{1 + x^{-4}} + \frac{1}{1 + y^{-4}}$$

which is evaluated over the space $-5 \leq x \leq 5, -5 \leq y \leq 5$ in a grid of spacing 0.4, giving 676 points of training data. There is no separate test data set.

An operator is fully characterised by its transition matrix. In order to test our measures of operator behaviour, we introduce a family of mutation operators defined by artificially altering an existing operator's transition matrix. The idea is to artificially control $\mu(\sigma_r(p))$ and study the behaviour of the resulting operator. Given an operator defined by a matrix p with generic entry $p(i,j)$, and given a positive numerical parameter a, a new mutation operator is defined by the transition matrix with generic entry $p(i,j)^a / \sum_k p(i,k)^a$. That is, each entry in the matrix is raised to the power of a. Within each row, the *ordering* of individuals from most probable outcome to least probable is unaffected by this. However, after raising to the power of a, each row does not sum to 1. Each row of the new matrix is therefore scaled so that it sums to 1, hence it is a valid transition matrix. Values of a less than 1 give new operators in which each row is more uniform than before, i.e. each individual's bias towards its neighbours is reduced. Values of a greater than 1 give new operators in which each row is less uniform than before, i.e. each individual's bias towards its neighbours is increased.

In experiments, we use values $a \in \{1/10, 1/2, 3/4, 9/10, 1, 10/9, 4/3, 2, 10\}$. The corresponding values of $\mu(\sigma_r(p))$ for GA and GP spaces can be found later as the x-values in Fig. 1.

This method of artificially controlling $\mu(\sigma_r(p))$ will fail in the case where the goal is to *reduce* an individual's bias towards its neighbours, if it has a zero probability of transitioning to some other individuals. Raising zero to any power will not change it. A possible solution is to add a small constant to all zero values before applying the above method. This is not necessary in the current work since in both the GA and GP cases, the mutation operator gives a transition matrix which is nowhere zero. In any case, this method can only work in spaces small enough to allow explicit construction of the transition matrix.

4.2   Measuring Exploration-Exploitation Behaviour

For subtree mutation in the GP space, $\mu(\sigma_r(p)) = 0.0092$, and $\sigma(\sigma_r(p)) = 0.0007$. For per-gene mutation in the GA space, $\mu(\sigma_r(p)) = 0.0115$, and $\sigma(\sigma_r(p)) = 0$.

Comparing the $\mu(\sigma_r(p))$ values shows that a GA per-gene mutation with mutation probability of 0.1 in a 10-bit space is *slightly more exploitative* than subtree mutation in depth-2 GP. This is an interesting result because it is a direct and fair comparison between operators in different spaces. Using a GA mutation probability of 1 divided by the bitstring length – here, 0.1 – gives an expectation of one bitflip per individual. This is a common value. GP subtree mutation is regarded as being quite randomising. Our results confirm that it is more explorative in its behaviour than the GA mutation operator, but the difference is not very large.

The non-zero value for $\sigma(\sigma_r(p))$ for GP shows that the outward transition probabilities are more uniform from some elements of the space than others. These more uniform elements behave as randomisers or "portals" – search becomes relatively more random when they are encountered. Mutation is *less exploitative from these elements* than from others. The quantity $\min(\sigma_r(p))$ might be used as a measure of how randomising the most randomising element is.

The zero for $\sigma(\sigma_r(p))$ for the GA illustrates the fact that a GA, with a standard per-gene mutation operator, is a *symmetric* space.

4.3   Exploration-Exploitation Behaviour and Search Space Coverage

In order to demonstrate that $\mu(\sigma_r(p))$ functions as a measure of exploration-exploitation behaviour, we define a simple measure of the exploration done by a random walk: the proportion of unique individuals encountered. This is based on the idea that highly exploitative behaviour will tend to focus search on a small area of the space, and hence to encounter the same individual more than once. Real-world EC algorithms use specific measures to avoid encountering an individual more than once. However, in this setting, no such measure is used, so the method is informative.

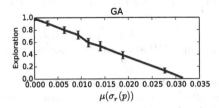 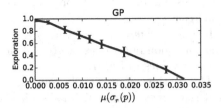

Fig. 1. Exploration behaviour versus $\mu(\sigma_r(p))$. Exploration is measured as the proportion of unique individuals visited in random walks of length 50. Errorbars indicate standard deviation of exploration value over 50 independent walks.

As shown in Fig. 1, there is a very strong $\mu(\sigma_r(p))$ effect. The "uniformified" operators, which have lower values of $\mu(\sigma_r(p))$, encounter more unique indiviuals.

4.4   Exploration-Exploitation Behaviour and Performance

In this section, we use experimental runs to study the relationship between performance, noise in the fitness landscape, and exploration-exploitation behaviour.

A difficulty in carrying out this type of study is that the effect of an operator's exploration-exploitation behaviour on performance (measured by best fitness achieved) depends not only on fitness landscape features such as ruggedness, but also on its long-term bias towards certain areas of the search space. Even if an operator has the "best" level of exploitation for a particular fitness landscape, it may also have a long-term bias away from the area of the search space where the optimum is. In this scenario, experiments to demonstrate the best value of $\mu(\sigma_r(p))$ will be misled: a more explorative version of the same operator will have a less damaging long-term bias, will perform better, and so will lead to a false conclusion concerning the "best" level of exploitation.

Therefore, to disentangle the two effects (fitness landscape, and stationary distribution), we will run a set of experiments in which there is no long-term bias towards any area of the search space. This is the case in the GA space, which by symmetry has a uniform stationary distribution, i.e. $\sigma(s) = 0$ (see Sect. 4.5, next, for results on spaces of nonzero bias). We are then free to study just the interaction of exploration-exploitation and fitness landscape features.

We start with a GA OneMax problem. Fitness is the number of on-bits in the genotype. We add a tunable amount of noise by performing k swaps between pairs of individuals' fitness values. For $k \in \{0, 1, 10, 100, 1000\}$ we achieve progressively noisier landscapes. We then use hill-climbing with each version of the GA operator to search each landscape.

Fig. 2 shows the results. For a noiseless OneMax problem, low values of $\mu(\sigma_r(p))$ (almost random search) and high values (over-exploitation) are worse than intermediate values. As noise increases, individuals effectively give no information about their neighbours, and any attempt at exploitation becomes useless. Random search (low $\mu(\sigma_r(p))$) becomes the best option.

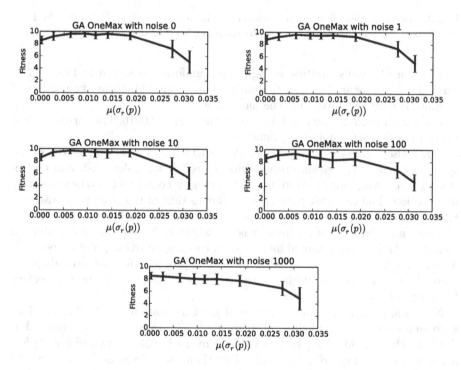

Fig. 2. Performance versus $\mu(\sigma_r(p))$. Fitness is that of the best individual found in a 50-step hill-climb on the GA space. Errorbars indicate standard deviation of fitness over 50 independent climbs.

4.5   Stationary Distributions

The ith component of the stationary distribution vector s is the probability that a random walk will be in state i (that is, a random walk will be currently at individual i) at a random time-step sometime after many steps. It can be calculated using the method of Kemeny and Snell [7].

The GA space gives a uniform stationary distribution vector, by symmetry. The stationary distribution vector for the GP space is given in Fig. 3. The 1298 trees of the space correspond to positions in the horizontal axis and are ordered in a natural way: x, y, (* x x), (* x y), (+ x x), ... (/ (/ y y) (/ y y)).

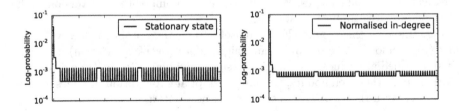

Fig. 3. Stationary distribution and normalised in-degree for the GP space. The horizontal axes contain the individuals of the space, ordered as described in the text.

The stationary distribution is highly non-uniform, as shown in Fig. 3. The vertical scale is logarithmic, so the most common individuals are two orders of magnitude more common than the most rare.

The non-uniformity can also be measured as $\sigma(s) = 0.0016$. The corresponding figure for a GA is 0, again by symmetry.

Fig. 3 also shows the normalised in-degree. That is, for each element j of the space, the sum of transition probabilities $\sum_i p(i, j)$ was calculated, and the resulting vector was normalised to sum to 1 to make it comparable to the stationary distribution. The resulting pattern is similar to that of the stationary distribution, though the non-uniformity is less pronounced. The in-degree measures the short-term probability of reaching a node, whereas the stationary distribution measures the long-term probability. In both cases, no starting-point is specified. The stationary distribution is therefore more appropriate for understanding operator bias, but cases in which the two are very different are likely rare except by construction.

Next, simulations are run to test the effect of the stationary distribution. Two individuals are chosen as being "of interest". Their statistics are summarised in Table 1. The individual x (the first element in the horizontal axis of Fig. 3) has a larger stationary distribution probability than the individual (/ (/ y y) (/ y y)) (the last element), by two orders of magnitude. The simulations confirm the expected result: the individual x is far more likely to be encountered than (/ (/ y y) (/ y y)), in a random walk. The same is true in a hill-climb, despite the much higher fitness of the individual x.

The non-uniformity of the GP stationary distribution under the subtree mutation operator has implications for search. A non-uniform stationary distribution amounts to a bias towards exploring some areas of the space more than others, even in the absence of selection pressure. The worst-case time to find the optimum occurs when the optimum is in a low-probability area of the stationary distribution. If our prior expectation of fitness is uniform over trees, then a

Table 1. Results from hill-climbs and random walks on the GP space. The probabilities of encountering two individuals of differing fitness values and stationary distribution probabilities are shown, for hill-climbs (HC) and random walks (RW).

Individual	fitness	stationary distribution	prob encounter HC	prob encounter RW
x	0.29	0.04	0.08	0.8
(/ (/ y y) (/ y y))	0.57	0.0005	0.01	0.03

non-uniform stationary distribution runs this risk. Therefore it is better to use a search operator without long-term bias.

On the other hand, a non-uniform stationary distribution could be good for search if we have a specific type of non-uniform prior. In the case of the subtree mutation operator, the stationary distribution depends only on tree shape. Fig. 3 shows that there is a bias towards the trees of a single node (values above 10^{-2}), followed by trees of three nodes (values well above 10^{-3}), followed by trees of 5 nodes (values close to 10^{-3}), with the full trees of 7 nodes (values well below 10^{-3}) being the least likely to be encountered in the stationary distribution. Although each individual tree of 7 nodes is rare in the stationary distribution, the large number of such trees means that search still spends a good deal of time among the trees of 7 nodes. If our prior expectation is that good trees are more likely to occur among the shallow trees, then the demonstrated non-uniformity of the stationary distribution may be beneficial to search. A uniform stationary distribution might give too much weight to the fuller trees, because there are so many of them: it would effectively result in a strong bias towards choosing a full tree. This point of view amounts to considering bias between tree shapes, or tree depths, rather than just between individuals.

5   Conclusions

We have proposed measures of mutation operators' short-term exploration-exploitation behaviour and long-term biases using transition probabilities and the Markov chain stationary distribution.

An appealing feature of the measures is their generality. The transition matrix abstracts all representation-specific features away, allowing comparison between operators on different spaces. Because it is relatively easy to visualise the behaviour of the GA mutation operator, this property provides a useful point of reference when reasoning about the behaviour of GP subtree mutation.

We have found that GP subtree mutation, generally regarded as a highly randomising operator, is only slightly more explorative than GA per-gene mutation with a typical mutation rate.

Using the stationary distribution of the GP space, we have found a strong bias related to program depth: shorter programs are over-sampled. This result agrees with the conclusions of Dignum and Poli [2] and other work in the operator bias literature.

The similarity in the GP space between the stationary distribution and the in-degree strongly suggests that these measures are capturing an important aspect of the structure of the space.

5.1 Limitations

Our measures are impractical in that they depend on calculations which are in-feasible for search spaces of realistic size. However, they still give useful insight. Our results with subtree mutation in a depth-2 GP space will remain qualita-tively true in a larger space. The same long-term bias will arise, differing only in degree.

It is possible to construct a counter-example to the measure of exploration-exploitation behaviour. Consider an operator with this transition matrix:

$$\begin{pmatrix} 0 & 1 & 0 \\ 0 & 0 & 1 \\ 1 & 0 & 0 \end{pmatrix}$$

This operator appears very exploitative: each row will have a high standard deviation, so $\mu(\sigma_r(p))$ will be large. However, this operator will never encounter the same individual twice, until it covers the whole space, so it might also be said to be quite explorative. The anomaly arises because of the strongly asymmetric probabilities, which destroy our intuitive concept of nearby individuals. The anomaly remains even after the forced mutation, which does not occur with real-world operators, is removed by setting all zeros to small non-zero values and normalising by row.

5.2 Future Work

Our work has considered mutation only. Integrating crossover into the Markov chain picture is possible but is postponed for future work. On the other hand, hill-climbing (a mutation-only algorithm) works surprisingly well in GP repre-sentations both old [13] and new [10].

In this context we note that with an operator like subtree mutation, there are no local optima, since there are no zero elements in the transition matrix. Hence hill-climbing might be expected to work well. However, there are many *local pseudo-optima*, i.e. individuals with vanishingly low probabilities of transitioning to anywhere better in a single step. New research measuring the strength and effect of local pseudo-optima is indicated.

All code used in this study is available for download from https://github.com/jmmcd/GPDistance .

References

[1] Bertsimas, D., Tsitsiklis, J.: Simulated annealing. Statistical Science, 10–15 (1993)

[2] Dignum, S., Poli, R.: Crossover, sampling, bloat and the harmful effects of size limits. In: O'Neill, M., Vanneschi, L., Gustafson, S., Esparcia Alcázar, A.I., De Falco, I., Della Cioppa, A., Tarantino, E. (eds.) EuroGP 2008. LNCS, vol. 4971, pp. 158–169. Springer, Heidelberg (2008)

[3] Droste, S., Jansen, T., Wegener, I.: On the analysis of the (1+1) evolutionary algorithm. Theoretical Computer Science 276(1), 51–81 (2002)

[4] Eiben, A.E., Aarts, E.H.L., Hee, K.M.V.: Global convergence of genetic algorithms: A Markov chain analysis. In: Schwefel, H.-P., Männer, R. (eds.) PPSN 1990. LNCS, vol. 496, pp. 3–12. Springer, Heidelberg (1991)

[5] Garnier, J., Kallel, L., Schoenauer, M.: Rigorous hitting times for binary mutations. Evolutionary Computation 7(2), 173–203 (1999)

[6] Hu, T., Payne, J.L., Banzhaf, W., Moore, J.H.: Evolutionary dynamics on multiple scales: a quantitative analysis of the interplay between genotype, phenotype, and fitness in linear genetic programming. Genetic Programming and Evolvable Machines 13(3), 305–337 (2012)

[7] Kemeny, J.G., Snell, J.L.: Finite Markov chains, vol. 210. Springer, New York (1976)

[8] Koza, J.R.: Genetic Programming: On the Programming of Computers by Means of Natural Selection. The MIT Press, Cambridge (1992)

[9] Levin, D.A., Peres, Y., Wilmer, E.L.: Markov chains and mixing times. AMS Bookstore (2009), http://pages.uoregon.edu/dlevin/MARKOV/

[10] Moraglio, A., Krawiec, K., Johnson, C.G.: Geometric semantic genetic programming. In: Coello, C.A.C., Cutello, V., Deb, K., Forrest, S., Nicosia, G., Pavone, M. (eds.) PPSN 2012, Part I. LNCS, vol. 7491, pp. 21–31. Springer, Heidelberg (2012)

[11] Moritz, R., Ulrich, T., Thiele, L., Buerklen, S.: Mutation operator characterization: Exhaustiveness, locality, and bias. In: Congress on Evolutionary Computation. IEEE, New Orleans (2011)

[12] Ni, J., Drieberg, R.H., Rockett, P.I.: The use of an analytic quotient operator in genetic programming. Transactions on Evolutionary Computation 17(1) (2013)

[13] O'Reilly, U.M., Oppacher, F.: Program search with a hierarchical variable length representation: Genetic programming, simulated annealing and hill climbing. In: Davidor, Y., Schwefel, H.-P., Männer, R. (eds.) PPSN 1994. LNCS, vol. 866, pp. 397–406. Springer, Heidelberg (1994), http://www.springer.de/cgi-bin/search_book.pl?isbn=3-540-58484-6

[14] Pagie, L., Hogeweg, P.: Evolutionary Consequences of Coevolving Targets. Evolutionary Computation 5, 401–418 (1997)

[15] Poli, R., McPhee, N.F., Rowe, J.E.: Exact schema theory and Markov chain models for genetic programming and variable-length genetic algorithms with homologous crossover. Genetic Programming and Evolvable Machines 5(1), 31–70 (2004)

Exploring the Search Space of Hardware / Software Embedded Systems by Means of GP

Milos Minarik and Lukáš Sekanina

Brno University of Technology, Faculty of Information Technology,
IT4Innovations Centre of Excellence
Božetěchova 2, 612 66 Brno, Czech Republic
iminarikm@fit.vutbr.cz, sekanina@fit.vutbr.cz

Abstract. This paper presents a new platform for development of small application-specific digital embedded architectures based on a data path controlled by a microprogram. Linear genetic programming is extended to evolve a program for the controller together with suitable hardware architecture. Experimental results show that the platform can automatically design general solutions as well as highly optimized specialized solutions to benchmark problems such as maximum, parity or iterative division.

1 Introduction

A general research problem, practically untouched by the genetic programming community, is whether it is possible to concurrently evolve hardware and software for a given task and whether the evolutionary system can discover general solutions to the problem (under some constraints) or highly optimized solutions to the same problem under other constraints. For example, in the case of the n-input parity problem, one evolved solution would be a general program sequentially performing the XOR operation over the intermediate result and the incoming bit (no constrains on the execution time are formulated, but the hardware size is constrained), while another solution would be an n-bit parity tree calculating the parity in parallel (no constrains on the hardware size are given, but the execution time is constrained).

This type of problems can be investigated using a platform [1] that we have developed for design and optimization of small HW/SW embedded systems, in which it is impossible to employ a general purpose processor because of its relatively high cost. The platform consists of an application specific data path controlled by a programmable logic controller which is programmed using the so-called microprograms. The overall architecture as well the microprogram are highly optimized in order to minimize area, delay and power consumption. The designer has to determine the number of registers and their bit width, the number of ALUs, the set of functions supported by each ALU, interconnection options (allowed by, for example, multiplexers), instruction set etc.

Our framework allows the designer to describe the hardware part, create a program for the logic controller, generate external stimuli and collect and analyze

M. Nicolau et al. (Eds.): EuroGP 2014, LNCS 8599, pp. 112–123, 2014.

the outputs of the system [1]. As the framework is fully programmable and configurable, a suitable search algorithm can be utilized either to optimize or even automatically design not only the program for the controller but also the hardware architecture. The goal of research, which is reported in this paper, was to remove some constrains given on the hardware modules in the original version of the framework, and demonstrate that more general problems can be solved. The proposed solution is based on extending linear genetic programming (LGP) to concurrently evolve the program for the logic controller and the hardware architecture.

The proposed approach can be classified as a combination of genetic programming and evolvable hardware. We believe that our approach is new and unique; however, some common features can be identified with conventional hardware/ software co–design based on evolutionary algorithms [2,3,4], co-evolution of programs and cellular MOVE processors [5], and genetic parallel programming (GPP) [6]. While GPP enables to automatically map a problem on parallel resources (multiple ALUs) in order to evolve efficient parallel programs, our method is more hardware oriented which allows for optimizing low-level properties of the underlying digital circuits.

In summary, the main contributions of this paper are as follows: (1) We propose an extension of our previous framework [1] in which a more general reconfigurable hardware architecture is supported. (2) We validate the proposed method of HW/SW concurrent evolution using 3 test problems. (3) We show that both general purpose solutions and application specific solutions can automatically be evolved on the proposed platform when suitable constrains are formulated.

The rest of the paper is organized as follows. Section 2 presents main features of the evolvable HW/SW platform. Section 3 is devoted to extending our platform by new features, particularly by relaxing some constraints on the organization of hardware modules. In Section 4, test problems are formulated, experimental setup is defined, and finally, obtained results are presented. Conclusions are given in Section 5.

2   Previous Work

In our previous work [1], we proposed a framework capable of concurrent evolution of HW and SW for application specific microprogrammed systems. This section will briefly summarize some basic terms so they could be used in the following sections. The framework is responsible for evolving the HW architecture and appropriate SW part as well as for providing the interconnections of the architecture with environment by providing inputs and consuming outputs.

2.1   Hardware

As can be seen in Fig. 1, the HW part is composed of a configurable datapath which is controlled by a microprogram. The components drawn in gray are responsible for instructions decoding and instruction pointer manipulation. This part is fixed and does not udergo the evolution. The parts affected by the evolution are the registers and the modules. The registers are connected to modules by a set of multiplexers composed in such way that every register can be connected to every module. The connections from module outputs to the registers are realized by a set of decoders.

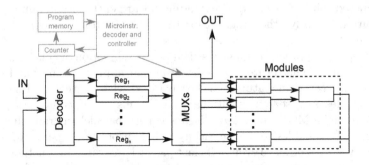

Fig. 1. HW architecture

Registers. The number of registers available in the architecture remains constant during the evolution. Their bit widths, however, can be changed by the genetic operators. Thus the width of the register can vary from 0 to a maximal value specified by the user. When the bit width of the register is set to zero, the register is considered unused, because it does not affect program execution.

Modules. Modules can be thought of as black boxes with inputs and outputs realizing an arbitrary function. Formally the module is defined as a 6–tuple

$$M = < n_i, n_o, a, p, d, f_o >, \qquad (1)$$

where n_i is the number of module inputs, n_o is the number of outputs, a is the area used by the module, p is its power consumption, $d : \mathbf{D}^{n_i} \to \mathbf{D}$ is the function specifying the processing delay and $f_o : \mathbf{D}^{n_i} \times \mathbf{Q} \to \mathbf{D}^{n_o}$ is the output function. $\mathbf{D}$ denotes a user chosen data type and $\mathbf{Q}$ is the set of module's possible internal states. The whole HW part is described by the following components:

i	the number of inputs
o	the number of outputs
$\mathbf{R} = \{r_1, r_2, ... r_r\}$	a set of registers
$\mathbf{w} : \mathbf{R} \to \mathbb{N}$	a funcion setting widths of the registers
$\mathbf{A} = \{M_1, M_2, ... M_m\}$	a set of available modules
$\mathbf{u} : \mathbf{A} \to \{0, 1\}$	a function specifying module utilization

2.2   Software

Each program is composed of instructions $i_1, i_2, ..., i_s$, where s is the program size. An instruction can be composed of several microinstructions which get executed in order in which they are specified in the instruction. The internal representation of the microinstruction is depicted in Fig. 2. The header contains an operation code specifying the type of the microinstruction and a mask defining the module usage. Then a constant may be specified, which is used by certain types of microinstructions. Finally, there are input connections $(I_{k,l})$ and output connections $(O_{k,l})$ specifications for individual modules used by the microinstruction. More detailed information can be found in the aforementioned article [1].

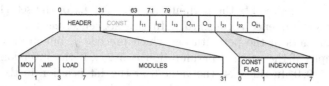

Fig. 2. Microinstruction format

3   Proposed Extensions

The architecture described in previous section had several limitations that didn't allow the evolution to create all useful compositions of modules. As the modules were arranged in parallel to each other, the only possible way of using the outputs of one module in another module was storing the results of one module in registers and passing them to another module in the following instruction. Although this method allowed the modules to use the outputs of previous modules, such connection was quite resource consuming because of the registers needed. Therefore, the need to pass the values between modules directly arose. Another issue we came across was the inability of the framework to process the inputs sequentially by one individual and in parallel by another individual. This issue has been addressed by introducing a new type of module that can be involved in instruction processing and allows the architecture to load virtually an arbitrary number of inputs inside one instruction.

3.1   Evolvable Hardware Topology Related Changes

There are several possible ways of implementing this functionality. At first, the possibility to create hardwired connection between modules was considered. However, such solution would limit the evolved architectures so that one fixed architecture would be used during the whole program execution. Therefore, the decision to let the instructions choose the interconnections between modules was made. Such a solution allows the HW architecture to vary during the program execution to fulfill current needs.

Then it was crucial to choose a suitable encoding of variable topology. The proposed solution exploits the encoding used in Cartesian Genetic Programming (CGP).

Modules Order Encoding. Similarly to CGP, the modules are organized in one row and n_c columns, where $n_c = m$. As the order of modules is not defined, it is necessary to introduce the ordering into the chromosome, in our case by permutation μ of the set $\{1, 2, ..., m\}$.

There are many ways to encode such a permutation in the chromosome (e.g. [7]). Finally the encoding proposed in [8] has been chosen due to its properties regarding genetic operators usage and fast evaluation.

This encoding represents the permutation $i_1, i_2, ..., i_m$ of the set $\{1, 2, ..., m\}$ by an inversion sequence $a_1, a_2, ..., a_m$. In this sequence, each a_j denotes the number of integers in the permutation which precede j, but are greater than j. For example, if the original permutation is $3, 2, 4, 1$, the inversion sequence would be $3, 1, 0, 0$. In this case the value 3 at the 1st position in the inversion sequence means that there are 3 values in the original permutation that precede the value 1 and are greater than the value 1. After generating the inversion sequence the genetic operators can be applied on it in common manner and then the new prescription for module ordering can be easily generated from the inversion sequence. More details can be found in [8].

Instructions Related Changes. The changes of the HW part of the architecture require some additional changes in the SW part. The changes are in allowed ranges of inputs and outputs during their initial random generation or mutations. In the previous version of the framework, the inputs were allowed to be constants or register indices. To support the interconnections between individual modules the latter one has to be changed, in order to enable the connection of the input either to a specific register or to an output of a module which precedes the current module in the module order specified by the HW part. Therefore, the parameter $n_{in} \in \mathbb{N}$ specifying the connection is generated from the interval $< 0, n_{avail})$. The number of available connections n_{avail} for an input of module M_i can be computed as

$$n_{avail} = r + \sum_{j=1}^{i} n_{oj}, \tag{2}$$

where r is the registers count and n_{oj} is the number of outputs of module M_j. This change in generating of the connections imposes also the change in instruction execution. When the instruction is executed, used modules are evaluated one by one in order specified by the chromosome. During the module execution the available inputs are limited to registers and outputs of preceding modules. If any of the preceding modules used by the instruction is disabled, the parameter specifying the input connection can be greater than the number of inputs actually available. This issue is addressed by performing the modulo operation using the actual number of available inputs. That means the instruction stays valid even after one of the modules used is disabled (e.g. by mutation). However, the connection will probably point to another module output or register. This way of instruction execution also ensures program validity when the order of modules is changed.

The last change imposed by the change of the framework is related to the outputs. In previous version of the framework, module outputs had to be connected to registers. Considering the possibility to connect the module output directly to another module input, there is no need for the output to be connected to a register. It is now possible for an output to be specified as 'no reg', which ensures the output value can be used by other modules, but will not be stored to a register.

3.2   Input Modules

As stated above, the previous version of the framework did not support the simultaneous evolution of individuals with sequential and parallel processing of the inputs. This was due to the fact that the number of inputs had to be constant. However, we came across some experiments, where this constraint imposed serious limitations. For example, when there was a possible solution, that could process four input values at once, and there were only two inputs available, the four values had to be loaded into registers before they could be processed. Increasing the number of inputs would not help in this case as e.g. a sequential solution using only two inputs would not be possible.

This issue has been addressed by introducing a new module type. According to the convention specified by formula 1, the input module is defined as

$$M_i = < 0, 1, 0, 0, d_{in}, f_o > . \tag{3}$$

As each input module represents one input, k–input system could be modeled by instantiation of k such modules.

The user can create several input modules and group them to form a specified number of input groups. Then the sequences of the input values have to be supplied for individual groups. After that the framework will set all the input modules to point to the first input value of a respective input group sequence and when the input module is executed, all modules of the same input group are updated to point to the next input value. When all the inputs from a given input group are already processed during the simulation and an input module from such an input group is executed, it returns the default value specified for this input group (e.g. 0).

3.3   Problem Encoding and Search Method

A candidate solution is represented in the chromosome as a string of integers. The first part of the chromosome is devoted to the program which is encoded in the LGP-like style [9] as a sequence of instructions, each of which consisting of several microinstructions (Fig. 2). The second part of the chromosome defines the hardware—the usage and bit widths of the registers, the usage of the modules and the μ permutation. It is ensured that the program stays valid independently of the HW architecture changes.

The initial population is generated randomly. The fitness is represented by a vector of components containing functionality, area and speed. The NSGA-II algorithm [10] is utilized because it allows for non-dominated sorting of candidate solutions and a multiobjective optimization is naturally supported. Selection is performed by a tournament method with base 2. A two-point crossover operates at the level of (micro)instructions in the software part and at the level of modules in the hardware part. Mutation modifies the specification of registers, modules or the program (microinstruction type and parameters).

4   Experimental Results

Several experiments were carried out to evaluate the proposed method. It is important to keep in mind that comparison with other methods can serve only as a rough assessment of how fast the proposed method is, because the proposed method evolves HW and SW part simultaneously and has, therefore, to explore larger search space than the methods evolving just a program. All the experiments utilize a slightly modified version of NSGA-II algorithm. When the individuals are compared, first, their functionality fitness component is compared. If the value of this fitness component is the same for both the individuals, the NSGA-II is carried out on other fitness components. Therefore the selection prefers the individuals with the highest functionality.

4.1   Newton-Raphson Division

This experiment was chosen mainly to verify the ability of the new version of framework to evolve solutions for iterative problems. We solved this task with a modified version of CGP in [11].

Problem Description. Newton-Raphson iterative division is an algorithm that finds the quotient of numbers N and D ($0.5 \leq D \leq 1.0$), iteratively. The main principle of this algorithm lies in finding the reciprocal of the divisor D and then multiplying it by N to find the desired quotient. The iterative expression for finding the reciprocal is

$$X_{i+1} = X_i + X_i(1 - DX_i) = X_i(2 - DX_i) \qquad (4)$$

This experiment was limited to finding the reciprocal of D such as in [11]. The parameters of LGP used for this experiment are listed in Table 1. The fitness function is defined as

$$f_o = \frac{1}{\sum_{i=1}^{s} \sum_{j=1}^{n_{it}} \frac{|Y_{ij} - T_{ij}|}{|Y_{ij-1} - T_{ij-1}|}}, \qquad (5)$$

where s is the number of different target reciprocals (randomly generated), n_{it} is the number of iterations, Y is an output value and T is the expected value.

Table 1. LGP parameters used for Newton-Raphson division

Parameter	Value
Population size	20
Max. generation count	100,000
Crossover probability	0.05
Mutation probability	0.7
Max. logical time	15,000
Max. program length	15
Modules used	2xADD, 2xMUL
s	10
n_{it}	10

Results. After performing 200 independent runs the results were analyzed. A solution was found in 17.5 % of runs and the computational effort needed to find a solution with 99 % probability is 2.2×10^7. That is quite an interesting result, as the computational effort of CGP was of the same magnitude, despite that CGP search space was significantly smaller. After detailed analysis of all the solutions it was found that all of them had a similar structure. The Newton–Raphson expression was always found in an expanded form $X_{i+1} = X_i + X_i - X_i D X_i$ and there was no solution which would utilize the constant 2. This result is not surprising as CGP [11] produced the same one.

4.2   Finding the Maximum

This experiment was chosen to verify the ability of the framework to find various (sequential and parallel) different solutions during one run of LGP.

Problem Description. The main goal is to find an architecture calculating the maximum out of 8 input values. There are no further constraints on the number of inputs or processing time. After providing all 8 input values, all successive values will be zeroes and the zero flag of the input module will be set, so the architecture can take appropriate action. The evolution parameters are listed in Table 2. In this experiment a new module type was involved. The comparator module (CMP) has two inputs and two outputs and when executed, it sends the smaller value to the first output and the greater one to the second output. The functionality fitness component is defined as the number of correct outputs from 16 semi–randomly generated 8–tuples.

Results. After performing 3,000 independent runs the results were analyzed. Out of the total number of 3,000 runs over 62 % have successfully found a solution, with the computational effort of 1,026,114. The evolution was able

Table 2. Evolution parameters used for the Maximum experiment

Parameter	Value
Population size	50
Max. generation count	20,000
Crossover probability	0.05
Mutation probability	0.7
Max. logical time	500
Max. program length	10
Modules used	8xIN, 8xCMP

to find various completely different solutions, including sequential and parallel solutions. We have sorted the results by their area fitness and speed fitness. The fitness values were scaled to range < 0, 100 > for better readability. The nondominated solutions are depicted in Fig. 3.

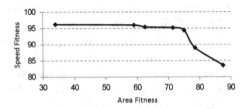

Fig. 3. The best fully–functional solutions of the maximum experiment

To show the progress of the evolution, two subsets of runs were selected. The first subset contained only the runs, which led to a minimal area solution (the rightmost ones in Fig. 3). Maximal values of the speed fitness and the area fitness were considered and the average value for each generation was computed. Fig. 4 shows that both speed fitness and area fitness grow rapidly during initial generations and then drop. This is implied by the fact that the individuals with higher functionality override other individuals even if they have higher speed and area fitness. When the functionality reaches a satisfactory level, the area fitness starts to grow, while the speed fitness still decreases. This corresponds to the expected trade-off between the area and speed.

The second subset is composed of the runs, that led to solutions with maximal speed. Fig. 5 shows that the speed fitness grows as expected, but after approximately 10,000 generations the area fitness also grows, so it appears there is no trade-off. After the investigation of the results we found out that the individuals tend to use more resources than needed at the beginning and the resources are optimized during later generations. The trade-off, however, still exists.

Another interesting fact discovered during the analysis was that some solutions were general and could process an arbitrary number of values, whereas other solutions were limited to 8 input values. The general solutions were likely

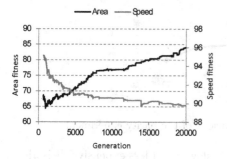

Fig. 4. Fitness progress for minimal area solutions

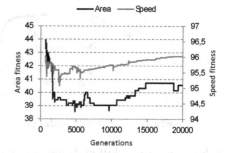

Fig. 5. Fitness progress for maximal speed solutions

to appear among the solutions with smaller area, as the evolution had to develop a loop to process all the inputs, whereas large area solutions could process all the inputs by one instruction and then output the result.

4.3 Parity

This problem was chosen because it is one of typical problems solved using various evolutionary circuit design techniques. Another reason was to find out, whether some modifications speeding up the evaluation could be used.

Problem Description. In this experiment, the goal is to find an architecture, which computes parity of the binary inputs provided. The parameters used for the experiment were the same as in the previous case, but the comparator modules were substituted by XOR modules. The functionality fitness component in this case was the number of correct outputs.

Results. After performing 3,000 independent runs of LGP we evaluated the results and found out that the computational effort is 2,358,430. That was quite interesting as this value is more than twice as large as in the previous experiment, though the problem is quite similar and XOR modules have just one output, whereas the comparator has two outputs.

After some investigation we recognized that problem is significantly influenced by the definition of the fitness function. Because the XOR function gives just two possible results for each input combination (i.e. 0 or 1), even bad solutions can get quite high fitness. For example, when the output is zero all the time during the simulation, half of the input combinations are evaluated as correct. Therefore the right solution has to have a relatively high fitness value before it is considered as better than some of the bad solutions. Despite these problems many solutions with various area/speed trade-off were found. The parameters of the best fully–functional solutions are depicted in Fig. 6.

Fig. 7 shows one of evolved solutions which is fast and resource consuming, but optimized for $n = 8$ and does not process any subsequent inputs. On the

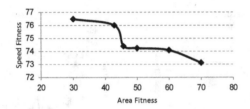

Fig. 6. The best fully–functional solutions of the parity experiment

other hand, the solution depicted in Fig. 8 is slower and less expensive. It is also a general solution, as the inputs are loaded in a loop until there are no more inputs available. The computational effort can hardly be compared with other evolutionary techniques as they usually do not use the XOR module, but try to force the evolution to compose the solution from NAND and NOR modules. Such comparison will be one of our goals in the upcoming research.

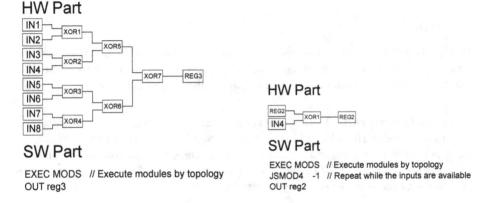

Fig. 7. Parallel solution for parity

Fig. 8. Sequential solution for parity

5   Conclusions

In this paper, we extended our platform for development of small application-specific digital embedded architectures by supporting variable module interconnections and multiple input reading mechanisms. LGP was used to evolve a program for the controller together with a suitable organization of hardware modules. The proposed extension was evaluated by evolving a simple iterative division algorithm. An important conclusion is that the platform can automatically synthesize multiple implementations, including a purely sequential solution and highly optimized parallel solutions, for a given specification

In our future research, we will deal with more complex iterative problems and their evolution on the proposed platform. However, accelerating the whole design process will be the first inevitable step.

Acknowledgments. This work was supported by the Czech science foundation project 14-04197S, Brno University of Technology project FIT-S-14-2297 and the IT4 Innovations Centre of Excellence CZ.1.05/1.1.00/02.0070.

References

1. Minarik, M., Sekanina, L.: Concurrent evolution of hardware and software for application-specific microprogrammed systems. In: International Conference on Evolvable Systems (ICES), IEEE Computational Intelligence, pp. 43–50 (April 2013)
2. Dick, R.P., Jha, N.K.: Mogac: a multiobjective genetic algorithm for hardware-software cosynthesis of distributed embedded systems. IEEE Trans. on CAD of Integrated Circuits and Systems 17(10), 920–935 (1998)
3. Shang, L., Dick, R.P., Jha, N.K.: Slopes: Hardware-software cosynthesis of low-power real-time distributed embedded systems with dynamically reconfigurable fpgas. IEEE Trans. on CAD of Integrated Circuits and Systems 26(3), 508–526 (2007)
4. Deniziak, S., Gorski, A.: Hardware/Software co-synthesis of distributed embedded systems using genetic programming. In: Hornby, G.S., Sekanina, L., Haddow, P.C. (eds.) ICES 2008. LNCS, vol. 5216, pp. 83–93. Springer, Heidelberg (2008)
5. Tempesti, G., Mudry, P.A., Zufferey, G.: Hardware/software coevolution of genome programs and cellular processors. In: First NASA/ESA Conference on Adaptive Hardware and Systems (AHS 2006), pp. 129–136. IEEE Computer Society (2006)
6. Cheang, S.M., Leung, K.S., Lee, K.H.: Genetic parallel programming: design and implementation. Evol. Comput. 14(2), 129–156 (2006)
7. Goldberg, D.E., Lingle, R.: Alleles, loci, and the traveling salesman problem. In: Proc. of the International Conference on Genetic Algorithms and Their Applications, pp. 154–159. Lawrence Erlbaum Associates, Publishers, Pittsburgh (1985)
8. Üçoluk, G.: Genetic algorithm solution of the tsp avoiding special crossover and mutation. Intelligent Automation & Soft Computing 8(3), 265–272 (2002)
9. Brameier, M., Banzhaf, W.: Linear Genetic Programming. Springer, Berlin (2007)
10. Deb, K., Pratap, A., Agarwal, S., Meyarivan, T.: A fast and elitist multiobjective genetic algorithm: NSGA-II. IEEE Trans. on Evolutionary Computation 6(2), 182–197 (2002)
11. Minarik, M., Sekanina, L.: Evolution of iterative formulas using cartesian genetic programming. In: König, A., Dengel, A., Hinkelmann, K., Kise, K., Howlett, R.J., Jain, L.C. (eds.) KES 2011, Part I. LNCS, vol. 6881, pp. 11–20. Springer, Heidelberg (2011)

Enhancing Branch-and-Bound Algorithms for Order Acceptance and Scheduling with Genetic Programming

Su Nguyen, Mengjie Zhang, and Mark Johnston

Evolutionary Computation Research Group,
Victoria University of Wellington, Wellington, New Zealand
{su.nguyen,mengjie.zhang}@ecs.vuw.ac.nz,
mark.johnston@msor.vuw.ac.nz

Abstract. Order acceptance and scheduling (OAS) is an important planning activity in make-to-order manufacturing systems. Making good acceptance and scheduling decisions allows the systems to utilise their manufacturing resources better and achieve higher total profit. Therefore, finding optimal solutions for OAS is desirable. Unfortunately, the exact optimisation approaches previously proposed for OAS are still very time consuming and usually fail to solve the problem even for small instances in a reasonable computational time. In this paper, we develop a new branch-and-bound (B&B) approach to finding optimal solutions for OAS. In order to design effective branching strategies for B&B, a new GP method has been proposed to discover good ordering rules. The results show that the B&B algorithms enhanced by GP can solve the OAS problem more effectively than the basic B&B algorithm and the CPLEX solver on the Mixed Integer Linear Programming model.

Keywords: genetic programming, scheduling, branch-and-bound.

1 Introduction

Order acceptance and scheduling (OAS) deals with two key production planning and control decisions, which are acceptance/rejection and scheduling. The goal of OAS is to optimise the use of manufacturing resources in make-to-order manufacturing systems to improve the total profit and customer satisfaction [1, 8]. This paper focuses on the OAS problem in single machine shops [1, 7–9]. Particularly, we want to determine whether to accept or reject orders from customers and how the accepted orders can be scheduled. Each order j in this case is characterised by a release time r_j, a processing time p_j, a due date d_j, a weight/penalty w_j, a maximum revenue e_j, and a deadline $\bar{d}_j$. Before an order j is processed, a (dependent) setup time $s_{i,j}$ is needed if order j is processed immediately after order i ($s_{0,j}$ is the setup time of order j when order j is processed first in the schedule). If the order is completed before the due date d_j, the profit prt_j obtained from order j is the maximum revenue e_j. Otherwise, prt_j is the remaining profit after deducting the penalty caused by the tardiness

M. Nicolau et al. (Eds.): EuroGP 2014, LNCS 8599, pp. 124–136, 2014.
© Springer-Verlag Berlin Heidelberg 2014

$T_j = \max(0, C_j - d_j)$ from e_j, where C_j is the completion time of order j. Generally, the profit obtained by an order j can be calculated by $prt_j = e_j - w_j T_j$. If orders are finished after their deadlines $\bar{d}_j$, no profit is gained and these orders are rejected. The objective of this problem is to maximise the total profit $\text{TPR} = \sum_{j \in \mathbb{A}} prt_j$ where $\mathbb{A}$ is the set of accepted orders. A Mixed Integer Linear Programming (MILP) model of this problem can be found in [8].

OAS is more challenging than the traditional scheduling problems since not only does the processing sequence of orders need to be determined, but also the combination of accepted orders must be decided. Ghosh [2] proved that OAS is NP-hard and previous works have shown that finding optimal solutions in this case is very challenging, even for small instances [1, 12, 13]. Therefore, several heuristics have been proposed to search for near optimal solutions for OAS. Rom and Slotnick [11] developed a hybrid method in which solutions found by a genetic algorithm (GA) are further improved by a local search heuristic. Oguz et al. [8] developed a simulated annealing method (ISFAN) for the OAS problem with dependent setup times in customised packing material producers and showed that their proposed method can find good solutions for large scale problem instances. Cesaret et al. [1] proposed a tabu search (TS) method to handle the same OAS problem and the experimental results showed that the proposed TS method outperformed ISFAN in most instances. Lin and Ying [4] developed a hybrid artificial bee colony (ABC) method for OAS, in which an effective iterated greedy local search heuristic is employed to enhance the quality of solutions found by ABC. Genetic programming (GP) [3] has been also applied to find reusable and effective scheduling rules to generate initial solutions for search heuristics [7]. The experimental results show that the proposed GP method can improve the effectiveness and efficiency of the search heuristics. Different representations and evaluation schemes for OAS were later investigated by Park et al. [9].

Although heuristics proposed in previous studies showed promising results, the robustness of these heuristics is still debatable because of their stochastic behaviours as well as the sensitivity of their parameters. For such critical objective functions such as the total profit, the difference between the optimal solutions and near optimal solutions can be significant. For that reason, finding optimal solutions, if possible, is desirable. Unfortunately, designing efficient exact methods to deal with OAS is very difficult. For the OAS problem in this study, solving the MILP model [1, 8] is very time consuming and can only be used to solve small instances (up to 10 orders). For larger instances, MILP usually failed to find the optimal solutions within limited computation times (3600 seconds).

1.1   Goals

Branch and Bound (B&B) is a popular optimisation approach to finding optimal solutions for scheduling problems. The efficiency of B&B depends on two main factors: (1) the upper (lower) bounds and (2) the branching strategies [10]. The upper bound (for maximisation problems) is needed in B&B in order to determine whether a node should be further explored. A tighter bound will help B&B eliminate nodes that cannot lead to optimal solutions. Meanwhile, the branching strategy is very useful to decide which branches/nodes should be explored first and indirectly improve the efficiency of B&B by quickly pruning nodes. Although the fundamental idea of B&B is quite simple, designing an efficient B&B algorithm is very challenging. This paper proposes a new genetic programming method to design branching strategies (BS) for the branch-and-bound (B&B) algorithm to deal with the OAS problem with a single machine and dependent setup times. Each individual in the proposed GP is an ordering rule for the BS to determine the order of nodes to be explored.

The specific research objectives of this paper are as follows:

- Developing a new branch-and-bound algorithm for OAS.
- Developing a new GP method to design branching strategies for B&B.
- Evaluating the performance of newly generated B&B algorithms.

1.2 Organisation

The rest of this paper is organised as follows. Section 2 describes the general B&B algorithm for OAS and the new GP method for designing branching strategies. The performance of B&B algorithms enhanced by GP is compared to that of the basic B&B and MILP in Section 3. Finally, we provide conclusions and discussions for future research in Section 4.

2   Methodology

In this section, we first provide details of the proposed B&B for OAS, including an upper bound and a basic branching strategy. Then, the description of the proposed GP method for evolving branching strategies is presented.

2.1 Branch and Bound Algorithm for OAS

This section first provides the overall procedure for B&B and an illustrative example to show how it works. Then, an upper bound and a branching strategy in B&B will be discussed.

2.1.1 Basic Algorithm

Branch-and-bound is a popular optimisation approach in scheduling [10]. Basically, there are two important steps in B&B: (1) branching and (2) bounding. The proposed B&B algorithm implicitly enumerates all candidate schedules where the branching strategy and the bounding approach are used to prune/eliminate non-optimal candidate schedules. The basic B&B algorithm proposed in this study can be described as follows:

  i. Initialise B&B with a root node containing an empty schedule; the node is marked as unexamined. Set lower bound to $-\infty$.

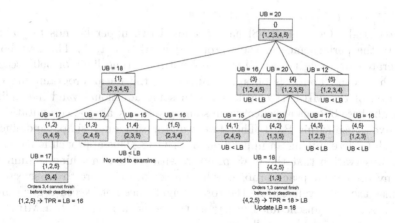

Fig. 1. Example of the proposed B&B algorithm

ii. Examine the bottom-left-most unexamined node of the search tree.
iii. Calculate the upper bound (the highest total profit that can be obtained) for the node with its current partial schedule and unscheduled orders.
iv. If the upper bound is lower than the lower bound, the node will be pruned (no longer explored).
v. If the upper bound is equal to the lower bound or there is no unscheduled order, the partial schedule from the node is a final schedule and the lower bound is updated if the total profit obtained from the considered schedule is higher than the lower bound.
vi. If the upper bound is higher than the lower bound, apply the branching strategy to generate child nodes by appending unscheduled orders into the partial schedule of the parent node.
vii. Return to step ii until there is no unexamined node.

An example of how the proposed B&B solves an instance with five orders is shown in Fig. 1. Each node is characterised by the partial solution in the upper part and the unscheduled orders in the lower part. B&B starts with the root node containing an empty schedule. The upper bound for the rooted node is 20 (see the next section to see how an upper bound can be determined). Four branches are added into the search tree (second level) by inserting an unscheduled order into the empty schedule. The branch with order 2 is not considered because it is too early to process this order (more details will be provided when we describes the branching strategy). After further exploring the bottom-left-most nodes, we obtained the first solution {1,2,5} with the total profit of 16, which is assigned to the lower bound. With this lower bound, many unexamined nodes will be discarded. After the solution {4,2,5} with the total profit 18 is found, there is no unexamined node to explore and the B&B algorithm is terminated with {4,2,5} as the optimal solution.

2.1.2. Upper Bound

In their study, Oguz et al. [8] have proposed two upper bounds for OAS to evaluate the performance of their proposed heuristics [1, 8]. The first bound is generated by using their MILP model with the time limit of 3600 seconds while the second bound is obtained by solving the linear programming (LP) relaxation of the MILP strengthened with some additional valid inequalities. Although these bounds are effective in some cases, they are too computationally expensive to use within B&B. Therefore, we proposed a new simple and efficient approach to determining an upper bound for OAS. This approach is motivated by the observation that the OAS problem with a single machine is similar to the conventional knapsack problem where a set of items are to be selected to maximise the total value while the total weight does not exceed a given limit. Given a set K of unscheduled orders at the decision moment t, a MILP of a simplified OAS model is as follows:

$$\text{maximise} \sum_{j \in L} e'_j I_j \tag{1}$$

subject to:

$$\sum_{j \in L} p'_j I_j \leq T \tag{2}$$

$$I_j \in \{0, 1\} \quad \forall j \in L \tag{3}$$

where I_j are the decision variables, which determine whether each order j is accepted ($I_j = 1$) or rejected ($I_j = 0$). All orders $j \in K$ with $C'_j < \bar{d}_j$ are included in L where $C'_j = \max\{r_j, t\} + \min_{i \in K'}\{s_{i,j}\} + p_j$ is the earliest completion time of order j ($K' = K \cup \{prev\}$ and $prev$ is the index of the previous order that has just been finished). The modified profit $e'_j = e_j - w_j \max\{0, C'_j - d_j\}$ is the highest profit that can be obtained by order j. The modified processing time $p'_j = \min_{i \in K'}\{s_{i,j}\} + p_j$ is the least time to process order j. Finally, $T = \max_{i \in K}\{\bar{d}_i\} - \min\{t, \min_{i \in K}\{r_i\}\}$ is the total time budget to process all orders.

In this MILP model, only acceptance/rejection decisions are considered and scheduling decisions are ignored. This simplified model is in the form of a knapsack problem which can be solved efficiently by some off-the-shelf optimisation approaches. In this study, dynamic programming [6] is used to solve the knapsack problem because it is effective in a wide range of problem instances. Other more sophisticated and efficient optimisation approaches such as branch-and-bound can also be used here to solve the knapsack problem. In our B&B, the upper bound is the optimal objective value obtained from the knapsack problem plus the total profit obtained from the scheduled orders in the partial solution. From our experiments, the upper bound obtained from our knapsack model is usually very close to those obtained from the LP relaxation and the MILP model of OAS [1, 8], and its computational times are much lower.

2.1.3. Branching Strategy

In order to make B&B more efficient, we need to design a good branching strategy. We apply these two rules:

i. All orders that cannot be completed before their deadline will not be considered ($C'_j < \bar{d}_j$).

ii. Only considering orders that satisfy $r_j < EC$ or $\max_{i \in K}\{s_{i,j}\} > s_{prev,j}$, where EC is the earliest completion time of all remaining orders $j \in K$.

The first rule is quite straightforward because we do not want to consider orders that cannot provide any profit. Meanwhile, the second rule tries to eliminate orders that are too early to be processed now. The first condition in this rule is similar to that used to generate active schedules [10]. However, because of the dependent setup times, the first condition becomes too strict and we need to further check if the considered order can have lower setup times if it is processed later. Therefore, we only ignore a node if the order appended to it fails to satisfy these two conditions.

Another issue that needs to be considered is the order in which generated nodes are to be visited. Unfortunately, there is currently no available approach to help us effectively explore generated nodes for the OAS problem. In the basic proposed B&B algorithm, the nodes will be explored based on their indices as shown in Fig. 1. In this case, the nodes that contain appended orders with lower indices will be examined earlier. However, this is not necessarily the most efficient approach. For example, in Fig. 1, if the node containing order 4 as the first order (the second level) is examined first, we can quickly obtain a very strong lower bound that can help to eliminate many unexamined nodes. The information of each order is very useful to decide which generated nodes in B&B should be examined first. However, finding one good approach to decide the order of nodes is not easy. In the next section, we will develop a new GP method to automatically design branching strategies through evolving ordering rules.

2.2   The New GP Method

In order to develop an effective ordering rule, this study emphasises two principles: (1) good solutions need to be found by B&B as soon as possible and (2) the nodes should be ordered in such a way that more potential nodes (leading to better solutions) can be examined earlier. The first principle aims to find a good lower bound (feasible solution) in order to prune nodes. Meanwhile, the second principle will help avoid B&B from the worst case scenarios when optimal candidate solution is at the end of the search. Previous studies [7, 9] have shown that GP can evolve scheduling rules capable of generating very good solutions for OAS. Therefore, rules evolved by GP is a promising approach to guide B&B toward good solutions. In order to make these evolved rules further cope with the second principle, the fitness function of GP will be designed to take into account the robustness of order sequence generated by the evolved rules. Our goal here is to use the solution (sequence in which orders are scheduled) found by the evolved rules as the order in which B&B will explore generated nodes. In the following sections, the representation and fitness function of the proposed GP method are described.

Table 1. Terminal and function sets for scheduling rules

Symbol	Description	Symbol	Description
R	release time r_j	P	processing time p_j
E	revenue e_j	W	penalty w_j
S	setup time $s_{prev,j}$	d	due date d_j
D	deadline $\bar{d}_j$	t	current time
#	random number from 0 to 1		
Function set		$+,-,\times,\%$ (protected division), IF	

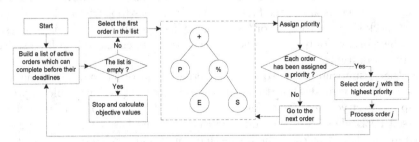

Fig. 2. Representation and evaluation of an evolved ordering rule

2.2.1. Representation

The rules evolved by GP are priority functions to calculate the priorities of orders which determine the sequence in which orders are processed. In the proposed GP method, we employ tree-based GP to evolve the ordering rules. Figure 2 shows how an example rule (P + E%S) is represented by GP and how it can be used to solve an OAS instance. The function and terminal sets used to generate scheduling rules are shown in Table 1. In this table, the protected division function % returns a value of 1 when division by 0 is attempted. Function IF includes three arguments and if the value from the first argument is greater than or equal to zero, IF will return the value from the second argument; otherwise IF will return the value from the third argument.

The procedure in Fig. 2 starts by building a list of unscheduled active orders which can be processed before their deadlines. Then, the evolved rule calculates the priority of each order in the list using the corresponding information of that order. After priorities are assigned to all orders in the list, the order with the highest priority will be processed (and certainly this order is accepted). The current time of the schedule (ready time to process the next order) is adjusted. The list of unscheduled active orders are updated and the procedure stops if no order can be completed before its deadline.

Given a set L of unscheduled orders, an order j is called active if $r_j < t(\Omega)$ where $t(\Omega) = \min_{j \in L} \left\{ \max\{r_j, t\} + s_{prev,j} + p_j \right\}$. Only active schedules are considered here in order to avoid wasting the available capacity of the machine. It should be noted that active schedules generated in this case do not necessarily contain the optimal schedule because of the dependent setup times. However, it can help us find very good (near optimal) solutions. From our experiments, evolved rules that focus on active orders are more effective than those considering all unscheduled orders [7].

2.2.2. Fitness Function

In order to measure the fitness of evolved rules, a set of training instances $\mathbb{I} = \{I_1, I_2, \ldots, I_N\}$ is used. After an evolved rule is applied to solve an instance I_k, we obtained a solution π_k containing the processing sequence of all orders (rejected orders are placed at the end of the sequence based on their indices). It is noted that π_k is also the order in which generated nodes in B&B will be sorted. The fitness of evolved rules is determined as follows:

$$fitness = \frac{1}{|\mathbb{I}|} \times \sum_{I_k \in \mathbb{I}} AR(I_k) \tag{4}$$

where

$$AR(I_k) = \frac{TPR(\pi_k)}{UB_{I_k}} + \alpha \frac{1}{|\pi_k^A| - 1} \sum_{i=1}^{|\pi_k^A| - 1} \frac{\exp(-i)TPR(\pi_k^i)}{UB_{I_k}} \tag{5}$$

In equation (5), π_k^i is used to indicate a modified solution of π_k which is generated by putting the order at position i to the start of π_k. For example, if $\pi_k = \{2, 3, 4, 5, 1\}$, the modified solution $\pi_k^2 = \{4, 2, 3, 5, 1\}$ (noted that index starts from 0). The sequence π_k^A only contains the accepted orders in π_k. If there is one order in π_k^A, $AR(I_k)$ is equal to the first term in the equation (5). $TPR(\pi_k)$ indicates the total profit obtained for the instance I_k with solution π_k and UB_{I_k} is the upper bound [1] of the instance I_k. The first term in equation (5) measures the quality of solution generated by the rule for the instance I_k. This is to ensure that evolved rules can generate good solutions. Meanwhile, the second term try to determine the effectiveness of the generated solution if it is slightly modified. The element $\exp(-i)$ is used in equation (5) to promote good solutions π_k^i with low i. Because the nodes with lower appended orders will be examined earlier, we want these nodes will lead to good solutions such that the branching strategy employing π_k can help B&B search more efficiently. The coefficient α is used to reflect the importance of modified solutions. It is noted that the second term in equation (5) is the secondary criteria for further improving the effectiveness of the ordering rule and the value of α will be set relatively low. In this case, the better evolved rules are ones with higher fitness.

2.2.3. Parameter Settings

The GP method for designing branching strategies is developed based on the ECJ20 library [5]. The parameter settings of the GP system used in the rest of this study are shown in Table 2 and are commonly employed in the GP literature [3]. The initial GP population is created using the ramped-half-and-half method [3]. Tournament selection of size 7 is used to select individuals for genetic operators and subtree mutation/crossover are used as the genetic operators. The value of α in equation (5) is set to 0.001 based on our pilot experiments.

Table 2. Parameters of the proposed GP systems

Population Size	1000	Crossover rate	90%	Mutation rate	5%
Reproduction rate	5%	Generations	50	Max-depth	8

3   Computational Results

To measure the effectiveness of the new GP method, 30 independent runs of GP are perform. This section presents the results of our experiments and analyses the performance of the proposed B&B algorithms against MILP [1].

3.1   Datasets

The effectiveness of B&B is assessed by using the benchmark instances from Casaret et al. [1]. These instances are generated based on tardiness factor τ and due date range R (refer to Casaret et al. [1] for more details). The datasets [1] contain different subsets (each has 10 instances) generated from different combinations of τ and R and the number of orders n. For training, we use the first five instances from each subset with 10 orders, $\tau \in \{0.1, 0.3, 0.5, 0.7, 0.9\}$ and $R \in \{0.1, 0.3, 0.5, 0.7, 0.9\}$ to evaluate the fitness of evolved rules (125 instances are used for training). Because both B&B and MILP are very time-consuming, we only show the results for the sets with $n = 10, 15$ and 20. The time limit for B&B algorithms to solve an instance is 300 seconds. The proposed B&B algorithm is coded in Java and run on Intel i5, 3.10 GHz CPUs, 4 GB of RAM. MILP is solved by using ILOG CPLEX 11.2 with the time limit of 3600 seconds on a work station with a 3.00 GHz Intel Xeon processor and 4GB of RAM [1].

3.2   Results

Tables 3–5 show the results of B&B algorithms and MILP [1] for each subset (with 10 instances). B&B-Basic indicates the B&B algorithm in which ordering of nodes is simply based on the indices of orders as described in Section 2.1 and illustrated in Fig. 1. B&B-GP-Best is the B&B algorithm with the branching strategy obtained by GP that results in the highest number of optimal solutions (the number of instances solved to optimality). B&B-GP-Avg shows the average performance of B&B algorithms using different branching strategies obtained from 30 runs of GP. The columns avg and max show the average and maximum deviation from the upper bound ($\%dev = 100 \times (Obj - UB)/UB$) across all instances in the subset, where Obj is the best objective value found by an opti-misation method and UB is the upper bound determined by LP relaxation and MILP [1]. For the B&B algorithms, #opt and #node respectively show the num-ber of optimal solutions found in the considered subset (maximum is 10) and the average number of generated nodes in B&B until the optimal solutions are found or the time limit is reached. The column time shows the average computational time (in seconds) to solve an instance.

Table 3. Performance of B&B algorithms on OAS datasets with $n = 10$

τ	R	B&B-GP-Avg					B&B-GP-Best					B&B-Basic					MILP		
		avg	max	#opt	#node	time	avg	max	#opt	#node	time	avg	max	#opt	#node	time	avg	max	time
0.1	0.1	0	0	10	1020	1	0	0	10	942	1	0	0	10	2430	1	0	0	1124
	0.3	0	0	10	3172	1	0	0	10	3011	1	0	0	10	6281	1	0	0	1120
	0.5	1	6	10	8211	1	1	6	10	9095	1	1	6	10	11537	1	1	6	1037
	0.7	0	0	10	9739	1	0	0	10	9422	1	0	0	10	10703	1	0	0	435
	0.9	0	0	10	5996	1	0	0	10	4540	1	0	0	10	5657	1	0	0	290
0.3	0.1	0	0	10	1061	1	0	0	10	1227	1	0	0	10	2123	1	0	0	466
	0.3	0	0	10	1166	1	0	0	10	1029	1	0	0	10	2461	1	0	0	372
	0.5	0	0	10	2260	1	0	0	10	2364	1	0	0	10	3036	1	0	0	257
	0.7	0	0	10	5719	1	0	0	10	5639	1	0	0	10	6416	1	0	0	310
	0.9	0	0	10	1764	1	0	0	10	1892	1	0	0	10	2115	1	0	0	118
0.5	0.1	0	0	10	362	1	0	0	10	327	1	0	0	10	711	1	0	0	22
	0.3	0	0	10	987	1	0	0	10	991	1	0	0	10	1339	1	0	0	53
	0.5	0	0	10	465	1	0	0	10	475	1	0	0	10	732	1	0	0	14
	0.7	0	0	10	732	1	0	0	10	729	1	0	0	10	891	1	0	0	24
	0.9	0	0	10	908	1	0	0	10	926	1	0	0	10	1126	1	0	0	27
0.7	0.1	0	0	10	111	1	0	0	10	109	1	0	0	10	174	1	0	0	1
	0.3	0	0	10	107	1	0	0	10	103	1	0	0	10	200	1	0	0	2
	0.5	0	0	10	234	1	0	0	10	239	1	0	0	10	339	1	0	0	2
	0.7	0	0	10	183	1	0	0	10	188	1	0	0	10	263	1	0	1	2
	0.9	0	0	10	202	1	0	0	10	195	1	0	0	10	372	1	0	0	2
0.9	0.1	0	0	10	60	1	0	0	10	60	1	0	0	10	82	1	0	0	1
	0.3	0	0	10	67	1	0	0	10	67	1	0	0	10	89	1	0	0	1
	0.5	0	0	10	103	1	0	0	10	103	1	0	0	10	134	1	0	0	1
	0.7	0	0	10	111	1	0	0	10	116	1	0	0	10	175	1	0	0	1
	0.9	0	0	10	151	1	0	0	10	154	1	0	0	10	213	1	0	0	1

Table 4. Performance of B&B algorithms on OAS datasets with $n = 15$

τ	R	B&B-GP-Avg					B&B-GP-Best					B&B-Basic					MILP		
		avg	max	#opt	#node	time	avg	max	#opt	#node	time	avg	max	#opt	#node	time	avg	max	time
0.1	0.1	2	3	10	108405	1	2	3	10	61262	1	2	3	10	316994	1	8	13	3600
	0.3	3	6	10	4119010	11	3	6	10	3767099	9	3	6	10	4859117	14	7	17	3600
	0.5	2	5	9	15533618	42	1	4	9	16230767	42	1	4	9	15202484	45	6	10	3600
	0.7	1	4	10	10995587	35	1	4	10	7211281	22	1	4	10	15296636	51	7	21	3600
	0.9	1	6	10	4976975	16	1	6	10	4178703	13	1	6	10	5057215	17	6	15	3242
0.3	0.1	3	6	10	139713	1	3	6	10	94154	1	3	6	10	264578	1	10	13	3600
	0.3	4	11	10	607431	1	4	11	10	545395	1	4	11	10	962959	3	11	22	3600
	0.5	4	7	10	2694645	8	4	7	10	2414528	6	4	7	10	3321530	10	11	22	3600
	0.7	3	8	10	491326	1	3	8	10	583391	1	3	8	10	561581	2	11	20	3600
	0.9	3	7	10	1004672	2	3	7	10	1011575	2	3	7	10	731211	2	9	16	3445
0.5	0.1	7	13	10	33087	1	7	13	10	33776	1	7	13	10	60940	1	12	18	3600
	0.3	7	14	10	73634	1	7	14	10	75695	1	7	14	10	88676	1	11	15	3600
	0.5	9	15	10	159159	1	9	15	10	171165	1	9	15	10	192966	1	15	26	3600
	0.7	6	10	10	64091	1	6	10	10	66129	1	6	10	10	89755	1	7	13	3600
	0.9	6	18	10	45511	1	6	18	10	45735	1	6	18	10	70822	1	7	18	3370
0.7	0.1	0	0	10	3778	1	0	0	10	3663	1	0	0	10	5628	1	0	0	84
	0.3	0	0	10	6584	1	0	0	10	6472	1	0	0	10	9669	1	0	0	89
	0.5	0	0	10	3805	1	0	0	10	3622	1	0	0	10	5417	1	0	0	101
	0.7	1	8	10	6033	1	1	8	10	6042	1	1	8	10	7617	1	1	8	884
	0.9	0	0	10	6104	1	0	0	10	6226	1	0	0	10	11060	1	0	0	289
0.9	0.1	0	0	10	541	1	0	0	10	547	1	0	0	10	761	1	0	0	1
	0.3	0	0	10	600	1	0	0	10	625	1	0	0	10	953	1	0	0	1
	0.5	0	1	10	1272	1	0	0	10	1240	1	0	1	10	1752	1	0	0	6
	0.7	0	0	10	800	1	0	0	10	794	1	0	0	10	1555	1	0	0	4
	0.9	0	0	10	1641	1	0	0	10	1591	1	0	0	10	2301	1	0	0	12

It is easy to see that B&B algorithms perform much better than MILP in all cases. For $n = 10$, both B&B and MILP can find optimal solutions for all instances. However, the computational time of B&B is much lower than that of MILP. For such small instances, it takes B&B less than 1 second to find the optimal solutions. Meanwhile, MILP may take more than 1000 seconds to solve tricky instances (with low τ). When $n = 15$, MILP fails to find optimal solutions within the time limit for most instances with τ lower than 0.7. In this case, B&B still performs very well and can find optimal solutions for all instances except a

Table 5. Performance of B&B algorithms on OAS datasets with $n = 20$

τ	R	B&B-GP-Avg					B&B-GP-Best					B&B-Basic					MILP		
		avg	max	#opt	#node	time	avg	max	#opt	#node	time	avg	max	#opt	#node	time	avg	max	time
0.1	0.1	1	3	10	13658310	53	1	2	10	9440054	36	2	7	9	26147948	105	11	19	3600
	0.3	2	5	6	40558082	155	2	3	7	36188483	140	3	6	5	49206561	195	12	19	3600
	0.5	2	5	0	64866528	290	1	3	2	59510571	242	4	7	0	66940410	300	10	22	3600
	0.7	1	3	6	28051747	127	1	2	6	29553896	120	1	4	4	35049660	189	11	23	3416
	0.9	1	4	7	16409171	93	1	3	7	17127944	90	1	5	4	30429387	211	7	15	3600
0.3	0.1	3	7	10	15023559	61	3	7	10	13222654	51	3	7	9	28025809	119	18	29	3600
	0.3	4	8	4	56945685	238	3	6	5	48991975	194	5	13	2	62290211	278	14	21	3600
	0.5	4	7	3	61971354	254	4	7	3	58650362	228	7	14	1	67713644	291	16	25	3600
	0.7	2	7	1	53896214	290	2	7	1	56407825	285	3	9	0	51175478	300	12	25	3600
	0.9	1	5	9	27466800	142	1	5	9	23677164	122	2	5	8	30044757	179	10	20	3445
0.5	0.1	4	5	10	2229492	9	4	5	10	2039746	7	4	5	10	3016267	13	13	30	3600
	0.3	5	8	10	10539815	45	5	8	10	11350418	46	5	8	10	18157776	83	17	26	3600
	0.5	5	9	10	9395168	43	5	9	10	10108685	43	5	9	10	10137940	51	16	23	3600
	0.7	5	12	9	14646644	70	5	12	9	15162947	67	4	11	9	18253777	91	14	27	3600
	0.9	5	11	10	7247546	29	5	11	10	7839154	29	5	11	10	7654847	37	12	21	3600
0.7	0.1	8	14	10	67560	1	8	14	10	67838	1	8	14	10	107048	1	12	26	3600
	0.3	8	12	10	88794	1	8	12	10	90025	1	8	12	10	160970	1	10	14	3600
	0.5	9	20	10	155301	1	9	20	10	160001	1	9	20	10	314440	1	10	27	3048
	0.7	6	12	10	186287	1	6	12	10	193912	1	6	12	10	340532	1	8	20	2954
	0.9	7	12	10	477830	2	7	12	10	477300	2	7	12	10	523932	2	10	17	3243
0.9	0.1	0	0	10	3427	1	0	0	10	3423	1	0	0	10	6171	1	0	0	2
	0.3	0	1	10	8692	1	0	0	10	8592	1	0	0	10	15614	1	0	0	9
	0.5	0	0	10	15432	1	0	0	10	15605	1	0	0	10	21609	1	0	0	80
	0.7	0	0	10	35769	1	0	0	10	35988	1	0	0	10	51195	1	0	0	114
	0.9	1	13	10	55474	1	1	13	10	56139	1	1	13	10	95111	1	1	13	467

single instance with $\tau = 0.1$ and $R = 0.5$. For the instances with $n = 20$, MILP performs poorly with τ lower than 0.9. Although B&B algorithms also have trouble finding optimal solutions for instances with $n = 20$, the final solutions found by B&B are much better than that of MILP. From the results in Tables 3–5, it is noted that the upper bound obtained by LP relaxation and MILP is quite loose as the number of order n increases. For example, for instances with $\tau = 0.5$ and $n = 15$, it is easy to see that the gaps between the optimal solutions and upper bound is still quite large (see avg and max). Given that our upper bound is competitive with the upper bound from LP relaxation and MILP, we still need to find a better and more efficient upper bound in order to improve the performance of B&B.

Within the proposed B&B algorithms, the results show that the enhanced B&B algorithms with branching strategies (partly) designed by GP are more efficient than the basic B&B algorithm in most instances. For $n = 10$, the enhanced B&B algorithm normally generates fewer nodes in order to find optimal solutions. For $n = 15$ and 20, we can see that the enhanced B&B algorithms take less times to find optimal solutions. For instances with $n = 20$, the enhanced B&B algorithms can find more optimal solutions than the basic B&B algorithm. This is because more potential nodes are examined earlier, which avoids B&B from wasting time examining non-optimal candidate schedule. Comparing B&B-GP-Avg and B&B-GP-Best, we also see that the proposed GP method is quite robust because the average performance of the enhanced B&B algorithms are close to that of the best enhanced B&B algorithm. Moreover, the fact that the ordering rules trained from smaller instances ($n = 10$) can be reused effectively on larger instances ($n = 15, 20$) suggests that the evolved ordering rules have good scalability. Therefore, we believe that the proposed GP is a promising method in order to improve the efficiency of B&B.

4   Conclusions

This paper developed a new GP method to discover better branching strategies for B&B to deal with the single machine OAS problem. The key difference between this paper and previous studies on using GP for scheduling problems is that we try to improve the efficiency of an exact optimisation approach instead of trying to improve the effectiveness (accuracy) of a heuristic approach. In this case, the algorithm we try to design guarantees to provide optimal solutions if the running time is long enough. The GP method proposed in this paper will be especially useful for the cases in which finding optimal solutions are critical; therefore, making the exact methods more efficient to cope with real-size problems is desired. The results from our experiments show that GP can enhance the efficiency of the proposed B&B algorithms by designing better ordering rules in the branching strategy.

The limitation of the proposed GP method is that the evolved rules only focus on generating a predefined order used at all levels of B&B. However, if a given partial solution is different from that predefined order, applying the predefined order to sort generated nodes may not be effective. For this reason, it would be more useful to design the ordering rule operating at the node level in order to improve the effectiveness of B&B by adapting better with the partial solutions and unscheduled orders. Moreover, it would be also interesting to examine the possibility of using GP to design dominance rules [10] in B&B to further prune nodes. Finally, it is important to further improve better and more efficient upper bound of OAS in order to cope with large scale problems.

References

1. Cesaret, B., Oguz, C., Salman, F.S.: A tabu search algorithm for order acceptance and scheduling. Computers & Operations Research 39(6), 1197–1205 (2012)
2. Ghosh, J.B.: Job selection in a heavily loaded shop. Computers & Operations Research 24(2), 141–145 (1997)
3. Koza, J.R.: Genetic Programming: On the Programming of Computers by Means of Natural Selection. MIT Press (1992)
4. Lin, S.W., Ying, K.C.: Increasing the total net revenue for single machine order acceptance and scheduling problems using an artificial bee colony algorithm. Journal of the Operational Research Society 64, 293–311 (2013)
5. Luke, S.: Essentials of Metaheuristics. Lulu (2009)
6. Martello, S., Toth, P.: Knapsack problems: algorithms and computer implementations. John Wiley & Sons, Inc., New York (1990)
7. Nguyen, S., Zhang, M., Johnston, M., Tan, K.C.: Learning reusable initial solutions for multi-objective order acceptance and scheduling problems with genetic programming. In: Krawiec, K., Moraglio, A., Hu, T., Etaner-Uyar, A.Ş., Hu, B. (eds.) EuroGP 2013. LNCS, vol. 7831, pp. 157–168. Springer, Heidelberg (2013)
8. Oguz, C., Sibel Salman, F., Bilginturk Yalcin, Z.: Order acceptance and scheduling decisions in make-to-order systems. International Journal of Production Economics 125(1), 200–211 (2010)

9. Park, J., Nguyen, S., Zhang, M., Johnston, M.: Genetic programming for order acceptance and scheduling. In: Proceedings of the IEEE Congress on Evolutionary Computation, pp. 3261–3268 (2013)
10. Pinedo, M.L.: Scheduling: Theory, Algorithms, and Systems. Springer (2008)
11. Rom, W.O., Slotnick, S.A.: Order acceptance using genetic algorithms. Computers & Operations Research 36(6), 1758–1767 (2009)
12. Slotnick, S.A., Morton, T.E.: Selecting jobs for a heavily loaded shop with lateness penalties. Computers & Operations Research 23(2), 131–140 (1996)
13. Slotnick, S.A., Morton, T.E.: Order acceptance with weighted tardiness. Computers & Operations Research 34(10), 3029–3042 (2007)

Using Genetic Improvement and Code Transplants to Specialise a C++ Program to a Problem Class

Justyna Petke[1], Mark Harman[1], William B. Langdon[1], and Westley Weimer[2]

[1] University College London, London, UK
j.petke@ucl.ac.uk
[2] University of Virginia, Charlottesville, VA, USA

Abstract. Genetic Improvement (GI) is a form of Genetic Programming that improves an existing program. We use GI to evolve a faster version of a C++ program, a Boolean satisfiability (SAT) solver called MiniSAT, specialising it for a particular problem class, namely Combinatorial Interaction Testing (CIT), using automated code transplantation. Our GI-evolved solver achieves overall 17% improvement, making it comparable with average expert human performance. Additionally, this automatically evolved solver is faster than *any* of the human-improved solvers for the CIT problem.

Keywords: genetic improvement, code transplants, code specialisation, Boolean satisfiability.

1 Introduction

Genetic improvement (GI) [14], [17, 18, 19], [23], [28, 29] seeks to automatically improve an existing program using genetic programming. Typically, genetic improvement has focussed on changes using parts of the existing system. We develop the idea of software transplantation [15] and introduce the idea of GI as a means to specialise software.

To investigate and experiment with GI for a particularly challenging problem, we selected the goal of using it to improve the execution performance of the popular Boolean satisfiability (SAT) solver MiniSAT [9]. MiniSAT is a well-known open-source C++ SAT solver. It implements the core technologies of modern SAT solving, including unit propagation, conflict-driven clause learning and watched literals [26].

Improving MiniSAT is challenging because MiniSAT has been iteratively improved over many years by expert human programmers. They have addressed the demand for more efficient SAT solvers and also responded to repeated calls for competition entries to the MiniSAT-hack track of SAT competitions [1]. We use the version of the solver from the first MiniSAT-hack track competition, MiniSAT2-070721[1], as our host system to be improved by GI with transplantation. Furthermore, this competition, in which humans provide modifications to

---

[1] Solver available at: http://minisat.se/MiniSat.html

M. Nicolau et al. (Eds.): EuroGP 2014, LNCS 8599, pp. 137–149, 2014.

a baseline MiniSAT solver, provides a natural baseline for evaluation and source of evolutionary material (which we call the *code bank*).

MiniSAT has been repeatedly improved by human programmers, through three iterations of the MiniSAT-hack track of SAT solving competitions, organised biannually. Although GP has been applied to evolve particular SAT heuristics [3], [16], MiniSAT code has never previously been the subject of any *automated* attempt at improvement using genetic programming.

SAT solving has recently been successfully applied to Combinatorial Interaction Testing (CIT) [4], [21], allowing us to experiment with GI for specialisation to that problem domain. CIT is an approach to software testing that produces tests to expose faults that occur when parameters or configurations to a system are combined [22]. CIT systematically considers all combinations of parameter inputs or configuration options to produce a test suite. However, CIT must also minimise the cost of that test suite. The problem of finding such minimal test suites is NP-hard and has attracted considerable attention [7,8], [12], [20], [24].

SAT solvers have been applied to CIT problems [4], [21], but the solution requires repeated execution of the solver with trial test suite sizes, making solver execution time a paramount concern. We follow the particular formulation of CIT as a SAT problem due to Banbara *et al.* [4], since it has been shown to be efficient.

The **primary contribution of this paper** is the introduction of multi-donor software transplantation and the result of experiments demonstrating that GI can evolve human-competitive versions of a program specialised for a non-trivial problem class. We demonstrate this by improving the 2009 incarnation of MiniSAT. Section 2 introduces our approach to GI. Section 3 presents the set up of our experiments, the results of which are described in Section 4. Section 5 briefly outlines related work and Section 6 concludes.

2   Genetic Improvement with Multi-donor Transplantation and Specialisation

We introduce our approach to GI, which uses multiple authors' code for transplantation and specialises the genetically improved software for a specific application domain (in this case CIT). We use a population-based GP. Our work is based on the genetic improvement framework introduced by Langdon and Harman [17] with minor changes. Since we are using a different program, we update the fitness function. We also do not target heavily-used parts of source code, since our program is much smaller than in previous work. Finally, we modify just one C++ file which contains the main solving algorithm. However, unlike Langdon and Harman [17], we use multiple donors and focus on specialising the program to improve it for a specific application domain.

Program Representation: We modify the code (in this case MiniSAT) at the level of lines of source code. A specialised BNF grammar is used to create a template containing all the lines from which new individuals are composed. Such a template is created automatically and ensures that classes, types, functions and data structures are retained. For instance, opening and closing brackets in C++ programs are ensured to stay in the same place, but the lines between them can be modified. Moreover, initialisation lines are also left untouched. An extract of a template for MiniSAT is shown in Figure 1. The genome used in our GP is a list of mutations (see below). Header files and comments are not included in our representation.

```
<Solver_156>    ::= "{\n"
<Solver_157>    ::= "Clause* c = Clause_new(ps, false);\n"
<_Solver_158>   ::= "clauses.push(c);"
<_Solver_159>   ::= "attachClause(*c);"
<Solver_160>    ::= "}\n"
```

Fig. 1. Lines 156–160 from the `Solver.C` MiniSAT file represented in our specialised BNF grammar. Lines marked with _Solver can be modified.

Code Transplants: We propose to evolve one program by transplanting and modifying lines of code from other programs [15]. Thus our GP has access to both the *host* program being evolved, as well as the *donor* program(s). We call all the lines of code to which GP has access the *code bank*. The donor code statements are then available for mutations of the *host* instance, but need not be used in the same order. For example, our search may combine the first half of an optimisation from one version of MiniSAT with the second half of an optimisation from another and then specialise the resulting code to CIT problems. This re-use and improvement of existing developer expertise is critical to the success of our technique.

Mutation Operator: A new version of a program (i.e. a new *individual*) is created by making multiple changes to the original program. Each such *mutation* is either a DELETE, REPLACE or COPY operation. The changes are made at the level of lines of source code, with a special case for conditional statements. A DELETE operation simply deletes a line of code, a REPLACE operation replaces a line of code with another line of code from the code bank and COPY operation inserts a line of code from the code bank into the program. In the case of conditional statements, we focus on and modify their predicate expressions.[2] For instance, the second part of a FOR loop (e.g., i<0) can only be replaced by the second part of another FOR loop (e.g., i<10) and any IF condition can be replaced with any other IF condition. Examples of the three mutation types are shown in Figure 2.

Crossover Operator: We choose to represent each individual as a list of mutations with respect to the original, which we call the *edit list*. This representation allows our technique to apply to programs of significant size [13], since we do not keep the whole of each version of the program in memory — just a list of changes. When creating individuals for the next generation, a *crossover* operation simply concatenates two individuals from the current population by appending one

---

[2] In the case of a DELETE operation we replace the predicate expression with '0' to prevent compilation errors.

```
<_Solver_159>                          # Delete line 159
<for3_Solver_533><for3_Solver_772>     # Replace the 3rd part of the 'for'
                                       # loop (i.e., loop variable increment)
                                       # in line 533 with the 3rd part of
                                       # the 'for' loop in line 772
<_Solver_806>+<_Solver_949>            # Add line 949 in front of line 806
```

Fig. 2. Examples of the three types of mutations allowed

list to another. The first parent is chosen based on its fitness value while the other is chosen uniformly among those individuals that compiled, as in previous work [17].

Fitness Function: We evaluate the fitness of an individual in terms of a combination of functional properties (those related to software correctness) and nonfunctional properties (those related to performance, quality of service, etc.) by observing its performance on SAT instances. Before the GP starts, the training set of SAT instances is divided into five groups by difficulty, which we meassure in required solving time. In each generation one test case is sampled uniformly from each group (or 'bin' following other terminology [17]) and all individuals are run on the selected test cases. This sampling helps to avoid overfitting. To evaluate an individual, the corresponding list of changes is applied to the original and the resulting source code is compiled, producing a new SAT solver that can then be executed (individuals that fail to compile are never selected).

To guide the GP search toward a more efficient version of the program, our fitness function takes into account both solution quality and program speed. For internal fitness calculations, efficiency is measured in terms of lines of code executed based on simple counter-based program instrumentation. The use of line counts (instead of CPU or wall-clock times) avoids environmental bias and provides a deterministic fitness signal. For the final presentation of our empirical results, timing measurements in seconds are also presented (see Section 4).

Selection: The GP process is run for a fixed number of generations (in our case 20) with a fixed population size (in our case 100). In the initial population each individual consists of a single mutation applied to the original program. After the fitness of each of the individuals is calculated, the fittest half of the population is chosen, filtered to include only those individuals that exceed a threshold fitness value. We focus on exploiting high-quality solutions, and thus our fitness threshold is set to select those individuals that either (1) return the correct answer in all cases, or (2) return the correct answer in all but one case and take no more than twice as long as the original solver.

Next, a set of offspring individuals is created using crossover on those selected from the current population. Also a new mutation is added to each of the parent individuals selected to create offspring. Both crossover and mutation are applied with 50% probability. If mutation is chosen, one of the three operations (i.e. REPLACE, COPY and DELETE) is selected with equal probability. If mutation and crossover do not create a sufficient number of individuals for the next generation, new individuals are created consisting of one mutation (in practice, this occurs 38% of the time). Finally, the fitness of the newly-created individuals is calculated, as described previously, and the process continues until the generation limit is reached.

Filtering: We have observed that many program optimisations are independent and synergistic. As a result, we propose a final step that combines all mutations from the fittest individuals evolved and retains all synergistic edits. This post-processing step is simplified by our edit list representation and helps to ensure that our final output benefits from more of the search space exploration conducted by the GP. Exploring all subsets of edits is infeasible. Our prototype implementation uses a greedy algorithm. Each mutation from the best individuals from all of our experiments is considered separately. We apply each operation to the original program and evaluate its fitness. Next, we order the mutations by their fitness value[3] and iteratively consider these adding only those edits that do not decrease fitness. Other efficient techniques, such as constructing a 1-minimal subset of edits [30], are possible.

3 Experimental Setup

The main hypothesis investigated in this paper is:

> *Genetic improvement with transplantation finds faster CIT-specialised MiniSAT versions than any developed by expert human programmers.*

Host & Donor Programs: We evolve MiniSAT2-070721, in particular the C++ file containing its main solving algorithm. This version was used as a reference solver in the first MiniSAT-hack competition, organised in 2009. Unless otherwise noted, we use MiniSAT and MiniSAT2-070721 interchangeably. The main solver algorithm involves 478 of the 2419 lines in MiniSAT. For our experiments we use two donor programs, which altogether provide 104 new lines of source code. The first donor is the winner of the MiniSAT-hack competition from 2009, called "MiniSAT 09z". We refer to this solver as MiniSAT-best09. The second donor program is the "MiniSat2hack" solver, the best performing solver from the competition when run on our CIT-specific benchmarks. Thus we refer to this solver as MiniSAT-bestCIT. We also added all the donor code to MiniSAT and ran this hybrid solver for comparison. We refer to this solver as MiniSAT-best09+bestCIT.

Test Cases: Real-world SAT instances from the combinatorial interaction testing area can take hours or even days to run. Thus we evaluate MiniSAT performance on a set of synthetic CIT benchmarks. Using the encoding of Banbara *et al.* [4], we translated 130 CIT benchmarks into SAT instances[4]. We kept the

---

[3] Note that since each individual is represented by a list of edits (or mutations) and at the filtering stage we consider one mutation in turn, we use the word 'mutation' and 'individual' interchangeably.

[4] Benchmarks as well as the different MiniSAT versions are available by e-mail from Justyna Petke at j.petke@ucl.ac.uk.

number of values for each of the parameters the same in every instance. This allows us to verify observed results against public catalogues of best known results [8]. We use one-third of these CIT benchmarks in the training set (which is divided into five groups, as discussed in Section 2[5]) and the rest in the verification set. We use execution time to define instance difficulty and divide the training set into five groups based on that measure. The largest instances contain over 1 million SAT clauses and MiniSAT is able to produce an answer for each of these within 30 seconds.

Code Transplants: In our experiments the seeds of high-level human optimisations targeting a generic benchmark set serve as donor code and are selected and recombined with novel changes to produce a specialised host SAT solver.[6] We conduct three sets of experiments, varying the code bank while holding the rest of the GI process constant. The donor code is selected in turn from:

1. MiniSAT-best09;
2. MiniSAT-bestCIT;
3. MiniSAT-best09 and MiniSAT-bestCIT.

We compare our evolved solver with both the host and donor programs in each of the experiments. We call our evolved solver MiniSAT-gp. Finally, we refer to the solver that results from our postprocessing filtering step (see Section 2) as MINISAT-gp-combined.

4   Results

To evaluate the efficacy of our technique, we evolve improved and specialised versions of MiniSAT and compare them to human-improved SAT solvers in terms of both runtime cost and solution quality. While internal fitness calculations are measured in terms of lines of code executed, all final results are presented in terms of CPU time data based on runs on a 1.6GHZ Lenovo 3000 N200 laptop with an Intel Core 2 Duo processor and 2GB of RAM. The GP was run with a population size of 100 and 20 generations.

In all experiments the compilation rate (using MiniSAT's provided Makefile) was high, between 79% and 81%. This high compilation rate results from our use of a specialised BNF grammar for edits, preventing most syntax errors. Runtime data reported in Table 1 is an average of 20 runs of each solver. The number of lines of code executed in each of the runs stayed the same, while time variation was less than 3%.

---

[5] The first two groups contain the fastest running instances, while those that require the longest time are in group five. Additionally, the second and fourth group contain unsatisfiable instances only, while the first and third only satisfiable ones.

[6] Adding a donor statement X to the code bank is equivalent, in terms of the search space explored, to adding IF (0) X to the input program in a preprocessing step.

Table 1. Normalized runtime comparison of MiniSAT versions, based on averages over 20 runs. The first four solvers are human written, the last four were evolved by our technique. The "Donor" column indicates the source of the donor code available in the code bank. "Lines" indicates lines of code executed, "Time" indicates CPU time executed (lower is better, all measurements normalized to original MiniSAT).

Solver	Donor	Lines	Time
MiniSAT (original)	—	1.00	1.00
MiniSAT-best09	—	1.46	1.76
MiniSAT-bestCIT	—	0.72	0.87
MiniSAT-best09+bestCIT	—	1.26	1.63
MiniSAT-gp	best09	0.93	0.95
MiniSAT-gp	bestCIT	0.72	0.87
MiniSAT-gp	best09+bestCIT	0.94	0.96
MiniSAT-gp-combined	best09+bestCIT	**0.54**	**0.83**

4.1 Transplanting from MiniSAT-best09

When the code bank included lines from the original as well as the overall best version of the solver from the MiniSAT-hack competition, GP produced a mutated version of MiniSAT that was, on average, over 5% faster than the original solver on CIT instances (see Table 1). None of the new code from MiniSAT-best09 was selected by GP in the improved individual. We observe that the best solver from the competition — which evaluated on a general, non-CIT benchmark suite — was not the most efficient one on the instances from the CIT domain. In fact, the original MiniSAT without modifications was even faster than the winner of the 2009 competition in this domain. It is thus not surprising that using donor code from MiniSAT-best09 did not admit the evolution of efficient solvers specialised to the CIT domain.

Evolution achieved runtime improvement by switching off IF and FOR loop conditions. Also, execution times of certain FOR loops were decreased using RE-PLACE operations. Table 2 shows all the mutations made in the fastest evolved version of MiniSAT.

Table 2. Mutations in the genetically improved solver (with best09 as donor)

mutation	mutated code	changes
DELETE	IF statement condition	5
DELETE	line of code	8
REPLACE	FOR loop condition	7
REPLACE	IF statement condition	2
COPY	line of code	1
total		23

Among the evolved changes, an addition operation on a variable used solely for statistical purposes was deleted, as were three assertions. The evolved changes specialised MiniSAT to the CIT instances tested, but did not retain functionality for instances from other domains. For example, one deletion removed a memory optimisation function, potentially increasing solver's chance of running into an out-of-memory error for larger instances.

4.2   Transplanting from MiniSAT-bestCIT

In the next experiment the GP code bank contained source code both from the original MiniSAT solver as well as MiniSAT-bestCIT. The evolved version of MiniSAT is, on average, 13% faster than the original solver (see Table 1). Given that it usually takes hours or even days to run a SAT solver on real-world CIT instances, such a performance improvement could have a noticeable impact.

The human-written MiniSAT-bestCIT solver also provides similar runtime results — in fact, the performance of our evolved version and the human-written version are not different in a statistically significant sense. The similarities can be explained by the changes made by the GP process, shown in Table 3.

Table 3. Mutations occurring in the genetically improved solver

mutation	mutated code	changes
DELETE	line of code	1
REPLACE	IF statement condition	1
total		2

By replacing the IF statement condition, the GP enabled a function that contained 95% of the 'new' human-written lines from MiniSAT-bestCIT. The other one-line deletion simply removed an assertion.

4.3   Transplanting from MiniSAT-best09 and MiniSAT-bestCIT

Finally, we allowed evolution to inject code from both MiniSAT-best09 and MiniSAT-bestCIT. Runtime results are presented in Table 1: the best evolved program achieved 4% runtime improvement over the original solver.

Table 4 shows the set of changes produced by genetic improvement. Lines involved in about half of the mutations were never executed in the fastest genetically modified program. Thus, GP essentially removed dead code. Moreover, five assertions were removed as well as three updates to statistical variables. In four cases parts of code were replaced with semantically-equivalent (but not necessarily equally expensive) computations.

4.4   Combining Results

In the previous experiment the GP identified a 'good change': a one-line modification that allowed 95% of the donor code to be executed. Even though the GP process produced individuals containing such a change, other mutations within all such individuals caused slower runtime or compilation errors. Our approach based on filtering holds out the promise of combining the best parts of all variants discovered.

We started with the individual composed of one mutation (see Section 2) with the best runtime performance, and iteratively added mutations from the next performant individual. Only changes that do not reduce performance or correctness are retained. The resulting 'combined' solver performs 17% faster than the original MiniSAT and outperforms all other human-written solvers considered by at least 4% (this difference is statistically significant, see Table 1).

In total, this version involved 56 evolved mutations. Eight among these were one-line assertion removals. Details of all the mutations selected are presented in Table 5.

By combining the synergistic optimisations found in the three best evolved individuals, our approach produced the fastest specialised SAT solver for CIT among all solvers developed by expert human programmers that were entered into the 2009 MiniSAT-hack competition. On the 130 benchmark instances this automatically-constructed solver performed better in 128 instances (in terms of lines of code executed). In the other two cases it was only slightly worse.

However, since small benchmarks were chosen for the training set, the evolved individual might not scale to larger problems. Manual inspection suggests that optimisations relevant to large instances may not be retained, but a systematic evaluation on separate instances is left to future work. However, we note that the evolved individual retained required functionality on the two-thirds of the instances that were held out for verification, even though it was only exposed to the other third for testing.

5 Summary of Related Work

Genetic improvement has been successfully used to automate the process of bug fixing [19]. GI has also been used to improve non-functional properties of relatively small laboratory programs [23], [27,28,29], as well as larger real world systems [17]. It has also been used to automatically migrate a system from one platform to another [18].

In this previous work on genetic improvement, GP was concerned with a single program; the program to be improved. Code is extracted, perhaps modified

Table 4. Mutations occurring in the genetically improved solver

mutation	mutated code	changes
DELETE	IF statement condition	10
DELETE	line of code	30
DELETE	FOR loop condition	10
REPLACE	FOR loop condition	10
REPLACE	IF statement condition	4
REPLACE	line of code	6
COPY	line of code	5
total		75

Table 5. Mutations occurring in the combination of the fastest genetically improved solvers

mutation	mutated code	number of changes
DELETE	IF statement condition	9
DELETE	line of code	22
DELETE	FOR loop condition	6
REPLACE	FOR loop condition	8
REPLACE	IF statement condition	3
REPLACE	line of code	4
COPY	line of code	4
total		56

and then reinserted back into the program at a different location. The focus of the present paper on transplantation from multiple programs therefore denotes an important departure from this previous literature. As a result of multiple transplantation, GP is no longer concerned with a single program to be improved, but multiple donor programs, from which code can be extracted to help guide genetic improvement.

The idea of code transplantation using GP was proposed by Harman et al. [15], but it has not hitherto been implemented, nor has it previously been demonstrated to be useful in practice. We are the first to use GP to implement and evaluate transplantation for genetic improvement.

The goal of improvement adopted by the present paper also differs from that of previous work on genetic improvement, which focused on improving non-functional properties, such as execution time [17], [23] and power consumption [28]. It has also been used to migrate code [18] and to improve functional properties (by fixing bugs) [2], [10], [13], [19]. In all of these scenarios, the full functionality of the original program is to be retained; part of the fitness function specifically checks for the absence of regression faults.

Instead we aim to *specialise* a program using genetic improvement; the full functionality of the original program therefore need not be retained. In this way, this specialisation-oriented genetic improvement is reminiscent of partial evaluation [5,6], [11], which also seeks to achieve automated program specialisation. However, whereas partial evaluation uses meaning-preserving transformation to 'hard wire' parameter choices into code (thereby specialising it to those parameter choices), we use genetic programming to search for transplants that specialise a program to a class of inputs.

In preliminary experiments with MiniSAT [25] a varied set of instances from SAT competitions were used. However, this approach led to only very modest runtime improvements (up to 2%). We have significantly improved on this preliminary work using multi-donor transplantation to achieve a human-competitive 17% improvement.

6 Conclusions

We evolved a specialised version of a C++ program using genetic improvement with transplants. Previously, genetic programming has successfully been applied to improve software behaviour of various systems leading to significant speed-ups. We investigated whether this could be achieved on a well-known software system that has been engineered by many expert human programmers. We specialised this program for a particular hard problem class and used a novel idea of code transplantation.

For our experiments we chose MiniSAT, a very popular Boolean satisfiability (SAT) solver that has been thoroughly studied. The MiniSAT-hack track of SAT competitions is specifically designed to encourage humans to make minor changes to MiniSAT code that could lead to significant runtime improvements, and hence lead to new insights into SAT solving technology. Thus this competition provides a natural source of genetic material for code transplants, as well as a natural baseline for assessing human-competitive results. We evaluated how our automated approach applies to a particular application domain, namely Combinatorial Interaction Testing.

Our fastest evolved MiniSAT version achieved 13% runtime improvement over the original solver, similar to the best version of MiniSAT for CIT. By combining the synergistic optimisations from our individuals we achieved a 17% runtime improvement. For the CIT domain our evolved solver outperforms *all* of the human-written solvers entered into that competition.

References

1. MiniSAT-hack track of SAT competition. In 2009 this was part of the 12th International Conference on Theory and Applications of Satisfiability Testing (2009), http://www.satcompetition.org/2009/
2. Arcuri, A., Yao, X.: A Novel Co-evolutionary Approach to Automatic Software Bug Fixing. In: Proceedings of the IEEE Congress on Evolutionary Computation (CEC 2008), June 1-6, pp. 162–168. IEEE Computer Society, Hong Kong (2008)
3. Bader-El-Den, M., Poli, R.: Generating SAT local-search heuristics using a GP hyper-heuristic framework. In: Monmarché, N., Talbi, E.-G., Collet, P., Schoenauer, M., Lutton, E. (eds.) EA 2007. LNCS, vol. 4926, pp. 37–49. Springer, Heidelberg (2008)
4. Banbara, M., Matsunaka, H., Tamura, N., Inoue, K.: Generating combinatorial test cases by efficient SAT encodings suitable for CDCL SAT solvers. In: Fermüller, C.G., Voronkov, A. (eds.) LPAR-17. LNCS, vol. 6397, pp. 112–126. Springer, Heidelberg (2010)
5. Beckman, L., Haraldson, A., Oskarsson, O., Sandewall, E.: A partial evaluator, and its use as a programming tool. Artificial Intelligence 7(4), 319–357 (1976)
6. Binkley, D., Danicic, S., Harman, M., Howroyd, J., Ouarbya, L.: A formal relationship between program slicing and partial evaluation. Formal Aspects of Computing 18(2), 103–119 (2006)
7. Cohen, D.M., Dalal, S.R., Fredman, M.L., Patton, G.C.: The AETG system: an approach to testing based on combinatorial design. IEEE Transactions on Software Engineering 23(7), 437–444 (1997)
8. Colbourn, C.: Covering Array Tables (2013), http://www.public.asu.edu/~ccolbou/src/tabby/catable.html
9. Eén, N., Sörensson, N.: An extensible SAT-solver. In: Giunchiglia, E., Tacchella, A. (eds.) SAT 2003. LNCS, vol. 2919, pp. 502–518. Springer, Heidelberg (2004)

10. Fry, Z.P., Landau, B., Weimer, W.: A human study of patch maintainability. In: International Symposium on Software Testing and Analysis (ISSTA 2012), Minneapolis, Minnesota, USA (July 2012)
11. Futamura, Y.: Partial evaluation of computation process – an approach to a compiler-compiler. Systems, Computers, Controls 2(5), 721–728 (1971)
12. Garvin, B.J., Cohen, M.B., Dwyer, M.B.: Evaluating improvements to a metaheuristic search for constrained interaction testing. Empirical Software Engineering 16(1), 61–102 (2011)
13. Goues, C.L., Dewey-Vogt, M., Forrest, S., Weimer, W.: A systematic study of automated program repair: Fixing 55 out of 105 bugs for $8 each. In: International Conference on Software Engineering (ICSE 2012), Zurich, Switzerland (2012)
14. Harman, M., Langdon, W.B., Jia, Y., White, D.R., Arcuri, A., Clark, J.A.: The GISMOE challenge: Constructing the Pareto program surface using genetic programming to find better programs (keynote paper). In: 27th IEEE/ACM International Conference on Automated Software Engineering (ASE 2012), Essen, Germany (September 2012)
15. Harman, M., Langdon, W.B., Weimer, W.: Genetic programming for reverse engineering. In: Oliveto, R., Robbes, R. (eds.) 20th Working Conference on Reverse Engineering (WCRE 2013), October 14-17. IEEE, Koblenz (2013)
16. Kibria, R.H., Li, Y.: Optimizing the initialization of dynamic decision heuristics in DPLL SAT solvers using genetic programming. In: Collet, P., Tomassini, M., Ebner, M., Gustafson, S., Ekárt, A. (eds.) EuroGP 2006. LNCS, vol. 3905, pp. 331–340. Springer, Heidelberg (2006)
17. Langdon, W.B., Harman, M.: Optimising existing software with genetic programming. IEEE Transactions on Evolutionary Computation (to appear)
18. Langdon, W.B., Harman, M.: Evolving a CUDA kernel from an nVidia template. In: IEEE Congress on Evolutionary Computation, pp. 1–8. IEEE (2010)
19. Le Goues, C., Forrest, S., Weimer, W.: Current challenges in automatic software repair. Software Quality Journal 21(3), 421–443 (2013)
20. Lei, Y., Kacker, R., Kuhn, D.R., Okun, V., Lawrence, J.: IPOG/IPOG-D: efficient test generation for multi-way combinatorial testing. Softw. Test., Verif. Reliab. 18(3), 125–148 (2008)
21. Nanba, T., Tsuchiya, T., Kikuno, T.: Constructing test sets for pairwise testing: A SAT-based approach. In: ICNC, pp. 271–274. IEEE Computer Society (2011)
22. Nie, C., Leung, H.: A survey of combinatorial testing. ACM Computing Surveys 43(2), 11:1–11:29 (2011)
23. Orlov, M., Sipper, M.: Flight of the FINCH through the Java wilderness. IEEE Transactions on Evolutionary Computation 15(2), 166–182 (2011)
24. Petke, J., Cohen, M.B., Harman, M., Yoo, S.: Efficiency and early fault detection with lower and higher strength combinatorial interaction testing. In: European Software Engineering Conference and the ACM SIGSOFT Symposium on the Foundations of Software Engineering, ESEC/FSE 2013, pp. 26–36. ACM, Saint Petersburg (2013)
25. Petke, J., Langdon, W.B., Harman, M.: Applying genetic improvement to MiniSAT. In: Ruhe, G., Zhang, Y. (eds.) SSBSE 2013. LNCS, vol. 8084, pp. 257–262. Springer, Heidelberg (2013)
26. Silva, J.P.M., Lynce, I., Malik, S.: Conflict-driven clause learning SAT solvers. In: Biere, A., Heule, M., van Maaren, H., Walsh, T. (eds.) Handbook of Satisfiability, Frontiers in Artificial Intelligence and Applications, vol. 185, pp. 131–153. IOS Press (2009)

27. Sitthi-amorn, P., Modly, N., Weimer, W., Lawrence, J.: Genetic programming for shader simplification. ACM Trans. Graph. 30(6), 152 (2011)
28. White, D.R., Clark, J., Jacob, J., Poulding, S.: Searching for resource-efficient programs: Low-power pseudorandom number generators. In: 2008 Genetic and Evolutionary Computation Conference (GECCO 2008), pp. 1775–1782. ACM Press, Atlanta (2008)
29. White, D.R., Arcuri, A., Clark, J.A.: Evolutionary improvement of programs. IEEE Transactions on Evolutionary Computation 15(4), 515–538 (2011)
30. Zeller, A.: Yesterday, my program worked. Today, it does not. Why? In: Wang, J., Lemoine, M. (eds.) ESEC 1999 and ESEC-FSE 1999. LNCS, vol. 1687, pp. 253–267. Springer, Heidelberg (1999)

ESAGP – A Semantic GP Framework
Based on Alignment in the Error Space

Stefano Ruberto[1,2], Leonardo Vanneschi[3], Mauro Castelli[3], and Sara Silva[2,4,5]

[1] GSSI, Gran Sasso Science Institute, INFN, 67100 L'Aquila, Italy
[2] INESC-ID, IST, University of Lisbon, 1000-029 Lisbon, Portugal
[3] ISEGI, Universidade Nova de Lisboa, 1070-312 Lisbon, Portugal
[4] LabMAg, FCUL, University of Lisbon, 1749-016 Lisbon, Portugal
[5] CISUC, Universidade de Coimbra, 3030-290 Coimbra, Portugal

Abstract. This paper introduces the concepts of error vector and error space, directly bound to semantics, one of the hottest topics in genetic programming. Based on these concepts, we introduce the notions of optimally aligned individuals and optimally coplanar individuals. We show that, given optimally aligned, or optimally coplanar, individuals, it is possible to construct a globally optimal solution analytically. Thus, we introduce a genetic programming framework for symbolic regression called Error Space Alignment GP (ESAGP) and two of its instances: ESAGP-1, whose objective is to find optimally aligned individuals, and ESAGP-2, whose objective is to find optimally coplanar individuals. We also discuss how to generalize the approach to any number of dimensions. Using two complex real-life applications, we provide experimental evidence that ESAGP-2 outperforms ESAGP-1, which in turn outperforms both standard GP and geometric semantic GP. This suggests that "adding dimensions" is beneficial and encourages us to pursue the study in many different directions, that we summarize in the final part of the manuscript.

1 Introduction

In the last few years, researchers have dedicated substantial efforts to the integration of semantic awareness in Genetic Programming (GP) [1]. For a review of the state of the art in the field, the interested reader is referred to Chapter 3 of [2]. Very succinctly, among the different studies that have been made, several are aimed at incrementing semantic diversity in the evolving population (like for instance [3]). In some cases, studies are "indirect": standard GP genetic operators are used to produce new individuals, that are only accepted and inserted into the new population if some semantic criterion is satisfied (see for instance [4,5,6]). Also, new genetic operators have been defined that act "directly" on the semantics of programs. For instance, [7] defines geometric semantic operators, showing that they induce a unimodal fitness landscape for any problem consisting in matching input data into known target values (like regression and classification). An efficient implementation of those operators is presented in [8]. Using this implementation, several different applications have been tackled [9], suggesting a clear advantage in incorporating semantic awareness directly in the GP search.

The work presented in this paper is strongly related to these last contributions, since it directly incorporates semantic awareness in GP. Nevertheless, it does so from a different perspective. Considering the definition of semantics as the vector of output values

M. Nicolau et al. (Eds.): EuroGP 2014, LNCS 8599, pp. 150–161, 2014.
© Springer-Verlag Berlin Heidelberg 2014

of an individual on the training cases (as for instance in [4,5,7]), we first introduce the concept of *error vector* of an individual. It simply consists in a translation of its semantics by subtracting the vector of target values. In this way, we are able to define an *error space*, where GP individuals are represented by their error vectors and the target is represented by the origin of the Cartesian system. Then we introduce the concept of *optimally aligned individuals*, i.e. a pair of individuals whose error vectors lie on the same straight line intersecting the origin in the error space. Afterwards, we show that this concept can be extended by, informally, "adding one dimension", and this allows us to introduce the concept of *optimally coplanar individuals*, i.e. a triple of individuals whose error vectors lie on the same bi-dimensional plane intersecting the origin in the error space. We show that given a pair (respectively a triple) of optimally aligned (respectively optimally coplanar) individuals, it is possible to construct a globally optimal solution analytically. With this result in mind, and with the goal of discovering whether looking for optimally aligned or coplanar individuals is easier than directly looking for an optimum, we present two new GP systems. We call the general framework Error Space Alignment GP (ESAGP) and we present ESAGP-1, whose objective is to find two optimally aligned individuals, and ESAGP-2, whose objective is to find three optimally coplanar individuals. We also discuss how to generalize the approach to any number of dimensions. Finally, we present an experimental study in which ESAGP-1 and ESAGP-2 are compared with standard GP [1] (ST-GP from now on) and with geometric semantic GP as implemented in [8] (GS-GP from now on), on two complex real-life applications in the field of drug discovery.

The paper is structured as follows: in Section 2 we introduce the concepts of error vector and error space, presenting the definition of optimally aligned individuals. Section 3 presents ESAGP-1. In Section 4 we extend the notion of optimally aligned individuals, introducing the concept of optimally coplanar individuals. We present ESAGP-2 and then we discuss how to generalize the idea to any number of dimensions. Section 5 contains our experimental study. The test problems are presented, the experimental settings are specified and the results are shown and discussed. Finally, Section 6 concludes the paper and suggests several possible directions for future work.

2   Alignment in the Error Space

Let $\mathbf{X} = \{\vec{x_1}, \vec{x_2}, ..., \vec{x_n}\}$ be the set of input data, or fitness cases, of a symbolic regression problem, and $\vec{t} = [t_1, t_2, ..., t_n]$ the vector of the respective expected output or target values (in other words, for each $i = 1, 2, ..., n$, t_i is the expected output corresponding to input $\vec{x_i}$). A GP individual (or program) P can be seen as a function that, for each input vector $\vec{x_i}$ returns the scalar value $P(\vec{x_i})$. Following [7], we call *semantics* of P to the vector $\vec{sp} = [P(\vec{x_1}), P(\vec{x_2}), ..., P(\vec{x_n})]$. This vector can be represented as a point in a n-dimensional space, that we call *semantic space*. Remark that the target vector $\vec{t}$ itself is a point in the semantic space and, in general, it does *not* correspond to the origin of the Cartesian system (except for the very particular and rare case in which the expected output is equal to zero for each fitness case).

We now introduce a new notion, clearly related to the one of semantics, that we call *error vector*. The error vector of a GP individual P is the vector $\vec{ep} = \vec{sp} - \vec{t}$. It can be represented as a point in a n-dimensional space, that we call *error space* (even though used for different purposes, a similar idea can be found in [10]). Each vector in the semantic space is translated in the error space by subtracting $\overrightarrow{t}$. So, the target is translated in the error space into the origin of the Cartesian system. It is worth noticing that, once we have the error vector of an individual P, it is immediate, for instance, to calculate the root mean square error (RMSE) of P on training data (RMSE $= \sqrt{\sum_{i=1}^{n} e_i^2}$, where e_i is the ith coordinate of $\overrightarrow{e_P}$), a measure that is often used as fitness by standard GP in symbolic regression problems (see for instance [1]). We now define a new concept, whose importance will later become clear.

Definition 1. (Optimally Aligned Individuals). *Two GP individuals A and B are* optimally aligned *if it exists a scalar constant k such that:* $\overrightarrow{e_A} = k \cdot \overrightarrow{e_B}$

In other words, two individuals A and B are said to be optimally aligned if their respective error vectors are directly proportional, with a proportionality constant k. The reason why we use the term "aligned" for such individuals becomes clear by looking at Figure 1(a), where a simple bi-dimensional error space is represented. In this figure, A and B are two optimally aligned individuals: the points that represent their respective error vectors are aligned with each other and with the origin of the Cartesian system.

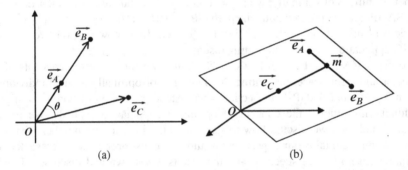

(a)   (b)

Fig. 1. Part (a): Representation of a simple bi-dimensional error space. Individuals A and B are optimally aligned, i.e. their respective error vectors are directly proportional. The angle between the error vector of A (as well as B) and the one of C is θ. Part (b): A simple tri-dimensional error space. We point out that it is possible to find a point m that is aligned with the error vectors of any pair of individuals A and B and optimally aligned with a third individual C.

The concept of optimally aligned individuals is important in the context of this paper because, given any two optimally aligned individuals, we can obtain a globally optimal solution in a very simple way. Let A and B be two optimally aligned individuals. Then, directly applying Definition 1, we have $\overrightarrow{e_A} = k \cdot \overrightarrow{e_B}$. Applying the definition of error vector, the previous equation can be rewritten as $\overrightarrow{s_A} - \overrightarrow{t} = k \cdot (\overrightarrow{s_B} - \overrightarrow{t})$, from which it follows that $\overrightarrow{t} = \frac{1}{1-k} \cdot \overrightarrow{s_A} - \frac{k}{1-k} \cdot \overrightarrow{s_B}$. This implies that, if we find two optimally aligned individuals, whose syntactic structure we represent with A and B, and if we know the proportionality factor k between their respective error vectors, then individual whose syntactic structure is:

$$P_{opt} = \frac{1}{1-k} \cdot A - \frac{k}{1-k} \cdot B \qquad (1)$$

has a semantic vector that perfectly corresponds to target $\vec{t}$, and thus it is a globally optimal solution. Interestingly, this property holds independently from the quality (for instance measured by means of the RMSE) of A and B: even two extremely "bad" individuals (in terms of RMSE), if they are optimally aligned, can be used to produce a globally optimal solution. As a direct consequence, the new objective of GP can now be to find two optimally aligned individuals, instead of directly finding a globally optimal solution.

This raises at least the following two questions: (1) How can we use GP to look for a pair of optimally aligned individuals? (2) Is searching for two optimally aligned individuals easier for GP than directly searching for a globally optimal solution? The answer to question (1) is that several different strategies can be adopted. In this paper, which to the best of our knowledge represents the first effort of using GP to look for two optimally aligned individuals, we propose the ESAGP framework introduced in the following sections. Section 6 contains a discussion of possible alternative strategies. In order to answer question (2), we perform experiments where an instance of ESAGP, whose goal is to find a pair of optimally aligned individuals, is compared with ST-GP [1] and with GS-GP [8].

3   One Step Error Space Alignment GP: ESAGP-1

ESAGP-1 is based on the idea that GP should work with the objective of minimizing the *angle* between the error vectors of pairs of individuals (looking for a pair for which this angle is equal to zero). Figure 1(a) graphically represents the angle θ between the error vectors of individuals A (as well as B) and C. Remembering that $\theta = \arccos((\vec{e_A} \times \vec{e_C})/(||\vec{e_A}|| \cdot ||\vec{e_C}||))$ (where $\times$ represents the scalar product between two vectors and $||\vec{v}||$ is the Euclidean norm of vector $\vec{v}$) the angle between the error vectors of two individuals is easy to calculate once we have their semantics. It is worth emphasizing that the objective of ESAGP-1 is to find optimally aligned individuals, regardless of their individual quality (for instance, as measured by the RMSE). To achieve this goal, we follow two ideas: (1) all the individuals found during the evolution, and not only the ones in the population at each generation, can be potential members of an optimally aligned pair; (2) the search cannot be driven by a measure of distance to the target in the semantic space (like the RMSE), but instead by a different fitness function that promotes the discovery of optimally aligned individuals.

To implement idea (1), ESAGP-1 maintains an archive of all the "semantically new" individuals that have been found during the GP run. Every time a new individual P is generated, the algorithm checks whether it is optimally aligned with any of the individuals already in the archive. If it is not, P is added to the archive, unless the archive already contains an individual with the same semantics, and the algorithm continues. Otherwise, the algorithm terminates returning the newly found pair of optimally aligned individuals. In Section 5 we present experimental results, reporting an RMSE value at each generation for the ESAGP framework. That error is obtained like this: at each generation, we consider the pair of individuals (A, B) such that A belongs to the population and B belongs to the archive, and such that the angle between $\vec{e_A}$ and $\vec{e_B}$ is minimum. Then, we construct the individual that approximates an optimal solution by applying

Equation (1). In order to do that, we need a value for the scalar constant k. Given that A and B are not optimally aligned, $\vec{e_A}$ and $\vec{e_B}$ are not perfectly proportional, so k can only be approximated. Let $a_1, a_2, ..., a_n$ be the coordinates of $\vec{e_A}$ and $b_1, b_2, ..., b_n$ the coordinates of $\vec{e_B}$. In this work, we use as k the median of the values $a_1/b_1, a_2/b_2, ..., a_n/b_n$. We remark that this RMSE value is only calculated for comparing the results returned by the ESAGP framework with ST-GP and GS-GP. It is never used for selection or in any other way during the evolution.

To implement idea (2), ESAGP-1 uses a fitness function that has no relationship with the distance to the target in the semantic space. To define this new fitness function, ESAGP-1 calculates a particular point in the error space, that we call *center of attraction*, or simply *attractor*. The fitness of an individual is the angle between its error vector and the attractor, and it has to be minimized (in other words, small angles are better than large ones). The attractor must be chosen in such a way to promote the evolution of optimally aligned individuals. Our idea is to choose a point that, informally, represents the majority of the individuals in a population, standing "in the middle of" an area where most of the error vectors of the individuals in the population are found. Therefore, the objective of the algorithm becomes driving the population towards this central point. We use as attractor the following vector: $\vec{a} = \sum_{P \in Pop} \vec{e_P}/||\vec{e_P}||$ where Pop is the current population and $||\vec{v}||$ is the Euclidean norm of vector $\vec{v}$. In principle, the attractor could be calculated only once in the beginning of the run, using the initial population, or it could change dynamically during the run, for instance recalculating it at each generation (or at prefixed intervals). We have evaluated both alternatives in a set of preliminary experiments. The results suggested that modifying the attractor during the run does not significantly affect the performance of the algorithm. For this reason, in this paper we report the results obtained by fixing the attractor in the beginning of the run, using the individuals in the initial population.

Besides the novel fitness function, another interesting characteristic that distinguishes ESAGP-1 from standard GP is the procedure that forms the pairs of individuals for mating. ESAGP-1 uses a strategy that encourages semantic diversity, that we call *orthogonal coupling*. Let d be the dimension of (i.e. the number of individuals belonging to) the population. Orthogonal coupling works by performing d independent tournaments (using the standard tournament selection algorithm), allowing us to generate a repository of d parents. Subsequently, an iterative process is performed where, at each iteration, one parent A is picked at random and its partner B is chosen as the individual currently in the repository such that the angle between $\vec{e_A}$ and $\vec{e_B}$ is the closest to $90°$. A and B are then removed from the repository and the process iterated until the repository is empty. Preliminary tests (not shown) have revealed that orthogonal coupling does not help the performance of standard GP on the real-life problems tackled here. However, when used with a preliminary implementation of ESAGP-1, it allowed significant improvements. Thus we decided to use orthogonal coupling.

4 Two Steps Error Space Alignment GP: ESAGP-2

The main information we gathered from the experiments performed with ESAGP-1 (whose results are discussed in Section 5) is that searching for two optimally aligned individuals is an easier task than directly searching for a globally optimal individual (at least for the studied problems). This opens an array of new and promising ways of easing the task of GP, and a question naturally arises: given two individuals whose error vectors are *not* aligned with the origin of the Cartesian system, can we still use them to build an optimal solution? Answering positively to this question is the main objective of ESAGP-2. The idea is shown in Figure 1(b). Let us assume that we have two individuals, like A and B in the figure, for which the straight line joining the error vectors is not aligned with the origin of the Cartesian system. It is possible to find a point $\vec{m}$ that lies on the straight line joining $\vec{e_A}$ and $\vec{e_B}$ and that is aligned with the error vector of another individual C and the origin. This property holds for any three points that lie on a bi-dimensional plane intersecting the origin. This allows us to extend Definition 1 to the bi-dimensional case.

Definition 2. (Optimally Coplanar Individuals). *Three GP individuals A, B and C are optimally coplanar if the bi-dimensional plane on which $\vec{e_A}$, $\vec{e_B}$ and $\vec{e_C}$ lie also intersects the origin of the Cartesian system in the error space.*

Given three optimally coplanar individuals A, B and C, we can obtain an equation to express target $\vec{t}$, and consequently we can find a globally optimal solution analytically. In fact, given that $\vec{e_A}$ and $\vec{e_B}$ are aligned with each other and with $\vec{m}$, applying the same reasoning as in Section 2, we can write: $\vec{s_A} - \vec{n} = w \cdot (\vec{s_B} - \vec{n})$, where $\vec{n}$ is the vector that corresponds to $\vec{m}$ in the semantic space (i.e. $\vec{m} = \vec{n} - \vec{t}$) and w is a scalar constant. Analogously, the following relationship holds between $\vec{n}$ and the semantics of C: $\vec{n} - \vec{t} = k \cdot (\vec{s_C} - \vec{t})$, where k is a scalar constant. Now we can obtain $\vec{n}$ from the first equation, replace it in the second one and solve it to obtain $\vec{t}$. In this way, we find:

$$\vec{t} = \frac{1}{(1-k)(1-w)} \cdot \vec{s_A} - \frac{w}{(1-k)(1-w)} \cdot \vec{s_B} - \frac{k}{1-k} \cdot \vec{s_C} \qquad (2)$$

Equation (2) can also be written in the following implicit form:

$$w \cdot \vec{s_B} - w \cdot k \cdot \vec{s_C} + w \cdot k \cdot \vec{t} - w \cdot \vec{t} + k \cdot \vec{s_C} - k \cdot \vec{t} + \vec{t} - \vec{s_A} = 0 \qquad (3)$$

Equation (3) can be used to find the scalar values k and w. In particular, let a_1 and a_2 be two different coordinates of vector $\vec{s_A}$. Analogously, let b_1 and b_2 be the corresponding coordinates of vector $\vec{s_B}$ and c_1 and c_2 the corresponding ones in vector $\vec{s_C}$. We can write the following system of equations:

$$\begin{cases} w \cdot b1 - w \cdot k \cdot c1 + w \cdot k \cdot t1 - w \cdot t1 + k \cdot c1 - k \cdot t1 + t1 - a1 = 0 \\ w \cdot b2 - w \cdot k \cdot c2 + w \cdot k \cdot t2 - w \cdot t2 + k \cdot c2 - k \cdot t2 + t2 - a2 = 0 \end{cases} \qquad (4)$$

Considering k and w as unknown values, we can solve the system in Equation (4), obtaining:

$$k = \frac{a1 \cdot b2 - a2 \cdot b1 - a1 \cdot t2 + a2 \cdot t1 + b1 \cdot t2 - b2 \cdot t1}{a1 \cdot c2 - a2 \cdot c1 - b1 \cdot c2 + b2 \cdot c1 - a1 \cdot t2 + a2 \cdot t1 + b1 \cdot t2 - b2 \cdot t1} \qquad (5)$$

$$w = \frac{a1 \cdot c2 - a2 \cdot c1 - a1 \cdot t2 + a2 \cdot t1 + c1 \cdot t2 - c2 \cdot t1}{b1 \cdot c2 - b2 \cdot c1 - b1 \cdot t2 + b2 \cdot t1 + c1 \cdot t2 - c2 \cdot t1} \qquad (6)$$

At this point, the values of k and w obtained in Equations (5) and (6) can be replaced in Equation (2), and this allows us to obtain a globally optimal solution (i.e. an individual whose semantics is exactly equivalent to the target).

In order to write the system in Equation (4), we have to choose two particular coordinates of $\vec{s_A}$, $\vec{s_B}$ and $\vec{s_C}$. It is worth pointing out that, if A, B and C are optimally coplanar, the obtained k and w are the same independently on the chosen pair of coordinates. But given that this event is quite rare, and more often this situation is only approximated, the choice of the coordinates may be important. Extending the approach used by ESAGP-1, we exhaustively consider all the possible pairs of coordinates; for each one of these pairs, we calculate the values of k and w as in Equations (5) and (6) and the values used in Equation (2) to approximate a globally optimal solution are the medians of these calculated values.

Basically, ESAGP-2 works as ESAGP-1 with the following two major differences: (1) the attractor, this time, is not a straight line, but a bi-dimensional plane; (2) every time a new individual P is generated, it is compared with all the possible *pairs* of individuals in the archive, looking for a pair of individuals that are optimally coplanar with P.

To define the attractor (point (1)), ESAGP-2 calculates a plane that informally lies "in the middle" of the error vectors of the individuals in the population. To do this, we use a k-means clustering method [11] to partition the error vectors of the initial population into two groups. Then we use the centroids of these two clusters to calculate the attractor. In particular, the attractor is the (unique) bi-dimensional plane that intersects these two centroids and the origin of the Cartesian system in the error space. The implementation of the k-means algorithm we have used is the one provided by the MATLAB environment [12], in which we have used angles, instead of Euclidean distance or other types of distances, for calculating the similarity between the vectors (this is an option that MATLAB provides). All the other parameters of the k-means algorithm were set to the default values of MATLAB. Once the attractor is defined, ESAGP-2 uses as fitness the angle between the error vector of the individual and the attractor. In order to calculate an angle between a vector and a plane, we use the SVD (Singular Value Decomposition) method, exactly as presented in [13].

To control whether three optimally coplanar individuals have been found (point (2)), every time a new individual P is generated, all the possible pairs of error vectors in the archive are exhaustively analyzed and the bi-dimensional plane intersecting those vectors and the origin of the Cartesian system is generated. Then we check whether $\vec{e_P}$ also belongs to that plane. Analogously to ESAGP-1, ESAGP-2 terminates if three optimally coplanar individuals are found. Otherwise, if the semantics of P is unique, P is added to the archive and the algorithm continues.

Besides the previously mentioned differences between ESAGP-2 and ESAGP-1, a third one exists: with ESAGP-2 it may happen that the size of the archive grows considerably during the evolution, and the exhaustive analysis of all the pairs may slow down the process excessively (a circumstance that we have never observed for ESAGP-1 in our experiments). Thus, in ESAGP-2 we have limited the maximum size of the archive using a predefined parameter M. When the number of individuals in the archive reaches M, every time an individual must be added to the archive another one is removed. The version we present in this paper removes the individual that has the largest angle with the attractor. In our experiments, we have empirically observed that a good compromise between computational speed and effectiveness of the method could be obtained by setting $M = 80$. Thus, we have used this value here. However, the influence of the archive size in the overall performance of the system has to be investigated more deeply in the future.

Generalizing to μ Dimensions. If we compare the idea that inspired ESAGP-1 (graphically represented in Figure 1(a)) with the one of ESAGP-2 (represented in Figure 1(b)), we can informally say that the transition from ESAGP-1 to ESAGP-2 consisted in "adding one dimension": in ESAGP-1 we look for two points that must be aligned on (i.e. must belong to) a straight line intersecting the origin of the Cartesian system; in ESAGP-2 we look for three points that must belong to a bi-dimensional plane intersecting the origin. Interestingly, this last property can also be seen as a composition of the elementary property (alignment) that has to be respected on a straight line in ESAGP-1: $\vec{e_A}$, $\vec{e_B}$ and $\vec{m}$ have to be aligned; $\vec{m}$, $\vec{e_C}$ and the origin must be aligned, too. It is not hard to convince oneself that this process can be iterated (maintaining the same informal terminology, we could say that "more dimensions can be added"), up to a point in which the number of used dimensions is equal to the number of fitness cases of the regression problem we want to solve. In other words, for any μ between 1 and the number of fitness cases, it is possible to define a GP system whose objective is to find $\mu + 1$ individuals that belong to the same μ-dimensional hyperplane intersecting the origin (a property that can also be seen as the composition of μ alignments), which we hypothetically call ESAGP-μ. Although in this paper we focus on ESAGP-1 and ESAGP-2, as a first step in this research path, the definition of a general strategy allowing us to obtain an ESAGP-μ for any possible number of dimensions μ is an important part of our current research (see Section 6). In that study, the issue of computational complexity has to be carefully considered: both the complexity of the system of equations needed to find the expression of the global optimum and the growth of the archive may become serious problems as μ increases. Thus, while ESAGP-1 has a computational complexity comparable to ST-GP and the one of ESAGP-2 can be easily controlled by limiting the size of the archive, ESAGP-μ, for large values of μ, may turn out to have a large computational cost, and implementation strategies to reduce it may be necessary.

5   Experimental Study

Test Problems. We have chosen two hard regression problems in the field of drug discovery to test both ESAGP variants. The objective of these problems is the prediction of two important pharmacokinetic parameters: human oral bioavailability (%F) and median lethal dose (LD50), also called toxicity, of medical drugs. Both problems have already been tackled by GP in published literature and for a discussion of them the reader is referred to [14]. The %F (respectively LD50) dataset consists in a matrix of 260 (respectively 234) rows (instances) and 242 (respectively 627) columns (features). Each row is a vector of molecular descriptor values identifying a drug; each column represents a molecular descriptor, except the last one, that contains the known target values of the considered pharmacokinetic parameter. Both these datasets are freely available from the GP benchmarks website, gpbenchmarks.org.

Experimental Settings. For each of the four GP variants (ST-GP, GS-GP, ESAGP-1, ESAGP-2), 30 independent runs were performed, each using one of 30 different random partitions of the dataset in training (70%) and test (30%) sets. In each run, for each generation we record the RMSE of the best individual on the training set, and the RMSE of the same individual on the test set (and also the number of nodes of that individual). The results we report are the median values of the 30 runs. All the runs used populations of 100 individuals. Tree initialization was performed with the Ramped Half-and-Half method [1] with a maximum initial depth of 6. The function set contained the four binary arithmetic operators $+$, $-$, $*$, and $/$ protected as in [1]. The terminal set contained as many variables as the number of features of each dataset. Tournaments of size 4 were used to select the parents of the new generation. To create new individuals, ST-GP, ESAGP-1 and ESAGP-2 used standard (subtree swapping) crossover [1] and (subtree) mutation [1] with probabilities 0.9 and 0.1, respectively. GS-GP used geometric semantic crossover [7] and geometric semantic mutation [7], each with probability 0.5 (the best setting according to [8]). Survival was elitist, as it always copied the best individual into the next generation. ESAGP-1 and ESAGP-2 both used orthogonal coupling as described in Section 3. For ESAGP-2 a maximum archive size $M = 80$ has been used, while for ESAGP-1 no size limit was imposed for the archive.

Experimental Results. The results we have obtained are reported in Figure 2. For all the experiments, tests of statistical significance were performed. In particular, the Kolmogorov-Smirnov test has shown that, for all our experiments, the data were not normally distributed and hence a rank-based statistic has been used. The Wilcoxon rank-sum test for pairwise data comparison with Bonferroni correction has been used under the alternative hypothesis that the samples do not have equal medians. Plots (a) and (b) report the results obtained on the %F problem, respectively on the training and test set. In both cases, the small inset in the upper right corner portrays the results of the evolution during the first 50 generations. On these small plots we can see that ESAGP-2 outperforms ESAGP-1, which outperforms ST-GP and GS-GP on both training and test sets. According to the Wilcoxon test, the differences at generation 50 are statistically significant. However, as shown in [8,9], GS-GP is a powerful but slow method: geometric semantic operators induce a unimodal fitness landscape, but also explore it with small steps. Thus, for a fair comparison, the execution of GS-GP has to be continued for a number of generations larger than 50. The large plot (a) shows that on the training set ST-GP and GS-GP at generation 350 find solutions of comparable quality to the ones found by the ESAGP variants at generation 50 (these differences are not statistically significant). The large plot (b) shows that on the test set the ESAGP variants in 50 generations find results that are comparable with the ones found by GS-GP in 350 generations (the differences are not statistically significant) and even better (with statistical significance) than the ones found by ST-GP in 350 generations. Interestingly, even if we allow GS-GP to run for 2000 generations (not shown), the results obtained on the test set are not statistically different from the ones obtained by the ESAGP variants in 50 generations. Summarizing, the ESAGP variants are able to find results of comparable quality to GS-GP, but much faster. Furthermore, ESAGP-2 outperforms ESAGP-1. As plots (c) and (d) show, similar conclusions can be drawn also for the LD50 problem. More in particular, on the training set (plot (c)) the results found by the ESAGP variants in 50 generations are comparable

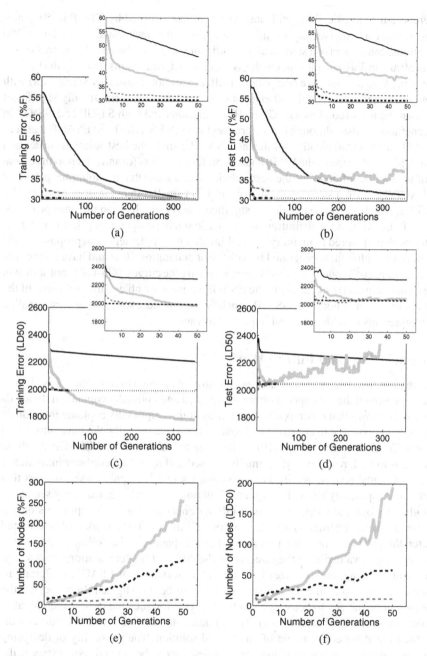

Fig. 2. Plot (a) (respectively plot (b)) shows the evolution of the (median) best fitness on the training (respectively test) set for the %F problem. The insets show an enlargement of the plots for the first 50 generations. Plots (c) and (d) are analogous to plots (a) and (b), but for the LD50 problem. Plot (e) (respectively plot (f)) shows the evolution of the (median) number of nodes of the best individual for the %F (respectively LD50) problem. The legend for all the plots is: - - - ESAGP-1 - - - ESAGP-2 —— GS-GP —— ST-GP.

(differences not statistically significant) with the ones returned by ST-GP in 50 generations, worse (in a statistically significant way) than the ones found by ST-GP in 350 generations, and better (in a statistically significant way) than the ones found by GS-GP both in 50 and in 350 generations. On the test set (plot (d)) the results found by the ESAGP variants in 50 generations are comparable (differences not statistically significant) with the ones returned by ST-GP in 50 generations, and better (in a statistically significant way) than the ones found by GS-GP in 50 generations and both ST-GP and GS-GP in 350 generations. Also, although the differences between ESAGP-1 and ESAGP-2 at generation 50 are not statistically significant, ESAGP-2 finds the best solutions faster and thus it is, also in the case of the LD50 dataset, preferable. Plots (e) and (f) report the evolution of the number of nodes of the best individual and show that the solutions produced by ESAGP-1 are (in a statistically significant way) smaller than the ones produced by ESAGP-2, which are (in a statistically significant way) smaller than the ones produced by ST-GP. Looking at the definition of geometric semantic operators [7], it is not difficult to see that, if stored in memory (something that the implementation proposed in [8] does not), the individuals generated by GS-GP at generation 50 would have a length of approximately 10^{16} nodes (and this is the reason why the curve of GS-GP is not shown in these plots). Summarizing, not only the ESAGP variants are able to find solutions of the same quality as, or better than, GS-GP, much faster, but these solutions are also smaller, which represents an additional and important advantage.

6   Conclusions and Future Work

We have introduced the notion of error vector, strongly related to semantics. Based on it, we have presented the concepts of optimally aligned and optimally coplanar individuals and we have shown that if two optimally aligned or three optimally coplanar individuals are found, it is possible to construct a global optimum analytically. We have introduced two new Genetic Programming (GP) variants, called ESAGP-1 and ESAGP-2, whose objective is to find, respectively, optimally aligned and optimally coplanar individuals. The experimental results, obtained on two complex real-life applications, suggest that searching for optimally aligned or coplanar individuals is easier than directly searching for a globally optimal solution, as most GP systems do. This work represents only a first step in a research track that looks very promising and future work will be directed to extend/improve the presented methods. Several paths can be followed, beginning with a thorough evaluation of the effects that the different implementation options (e.g. orthogonal coupling, archive size) have on the performance of ESAGP. Different alternative methods to define the attractor should also be investigated. In particular, the attractor can be the error vector of an individual (for instance the closest individual to the point currently used as attractor). Thus, finding an alignment with the attractor allows the immediate construction of an optimal solution. The possibility of designing a variant that does not use any attractor also deserves to be studied. For instance, the fitness of an individual could be the minimum angle between its error vector and the ones of the individuals stored in the archive. We are currently designing a completely different framework in which an individual is represented by a pair of expressions and the fitness is equal to the angle between the error vectors of these two expressions. This new framework can be more general and versatile than the one presented here, since evolution is given complete freedom to produce aligned individuals in any area of the error space, instead of focusing in the area of the attractor. Furthermore, this framework is easily extendable to more than two dimensions, simply by using multi-dimensional vectors of expressions as individuals. The results presented here seem to indicate that "adding dimensions" is beneficial, therefore a general framework should allow the final user to perform the evolutionary search in any desired number of dimensions. Even better, the system could automatically search in the most promising number of dimensions.

Acknowledgments. The authors acknowledge projects EnviGP (PTDC/EIA-CCO/103363/ 2008), MassGP (PTDC/EEI-CTP/2975/2012) and InteleGen (PTDC/DTP-FTO/1747/2012), FCT, Portugal.

References

1. Koza, J.R.: Genetic Programming: On the Programming of Computers by Means of Natural Selection. MIT Press, Cambridge (1992)
2. Nguyen, Q.U.: Examining Semantic Diversity and Semantic Locality of Operators in Genetic Programming. PhD thesis, University College Dublin, Ireland (July 18, 2011)
3. Beadle, L., Johnson, C.G.: Semantic analysis of program initialisation in genetic programming. Genetic Programming and Evolvable Machines 10(3), 307–337 (2009)
4. McPhee, N.F., Ohs, B., Hutchison, T.: Semantic building blocks in genetic programming. In: O'Neill, M., Vanneschi, L., Gustafson, S., Esparcia Alcázar, A.I., De Falco, I., Della Cioppa, A., Tarantino, E. (eds.) EuroGP 2008. LNCS, vol. 4971, pp. 134–145. Springer, Heidelberg (2008)
5. Nguyen, Q.U., Nguyen, X.H., O'Neill, M., McKay, R.I., Galvan-Lopez, E.: Semantically-based crossover in genetic programming: application to real-valued symbolic regression. Genetic Programming and Evolvable Machines 12(2), 91–119 (2011)
6. Nguyen, Q.U., Nguyen, X.H., O'Neill, M.: Semantics based mutation in genetic programming: The case for real-valued symbolic regression. In: Matousek, R., Nolle, L. (eds.) 15th International Conference on Soft Computing, Mendel 2009, pp. 73–91 (2009)
7. Moraglio, A., Krawiec, K., Johnson, C.G.: Geometric semantic genetic programming. In: Coello Coello, C.A., Cutello, V., Deb, K., Forrest, S., Nicosia, G., Pavone, M. (eds.) PPSN 2012, Part I. LNCS, vol. 7491, pp. 21–31. Springer, Heidelberg (2012)
8. Vanneschi, L., Castelli, M., Manzoni, L., Silva, S.: A new implementation of geometric semantic GP and its application to problems in pharmacokinetics. In: Krawiec, K., Moraglio, A., Hu, T., Şima Etaner-Uyar, A., Hu, B. (eds.) EuroGP 2013. LNCS, vol. 7831, pp. 205–216. Springer, Heidelberg (2013)
9. Vanneschi, L., Silva, S., Castelli, M., Manzoni, L.: Geometric semantic genetic programming for real life applications. In: GP Theory and Practice. Springer (2013)
10. Martinez, Y., Naredo, E., Trujillo, L., Galvan-Lopez, E.: Searching for novel regression functions. In: 2013 IEEE Congress on Evolutionary Computation (CEC), pp. 16–23 (2013)
11. Mitchell, T.M.: Machine Learning. McGraw-Hill (1997)
12. MATLAB: version 7.10.0 (R2010a). The MathWorks Inc., Natick, Massachusetts (2010)
13. Wedin, P.: On angles between subspaces of a finite dimensional inner product space. In: Kagstrom, B., Ruhe, A., (eds.): Matrix Pencils. Lecture Notes in Mathematics, 263–285. Springer (1983)
14. Archetti, F., Lanzeni, S., Messina, E., Vanneschi, L.: Genetic programming for computational pharmacokinetics in drug discovery and development. Genetic Programming and Evolvable Machines 8, 413–432 (2007)

Building a Stage 1 Computer Aided Detector for Breast Cancer Using Genetic Programming

Conor Ryan[1], Krzysztof Krawiec[2], Una-May O'Reilly[2],
Jeannie Fitzgerald[1], and David Medernach[1]

[1] University of Limerick, Ireland
{Conor.Ryan,Jeannie.Fitzgerald,David.Medernach}@ul.ie
[2] CSAIL, MIT, Cambridge, MA, USA
{KKrawiec,UnaMay}@csail.mit.edu

Abstract. We describe a fully automated workflow for performing stage 1 breast cancer detection with GP as its cornerstone. Mammograms are by far the most widely used method for detecting breast cancer in women, and its use in national screening can have a dramatic impact on early detection and survival rates. With the increased availability of digital mammography, it is becoming increasingly more feasible to use automated methods to help with detection.

A stage 1 detector examines mammograms and highlights *suspicious* areas that require further investigation. A too conservative approach degenerates to marking every mammogram (or *segment* of) as suspicious, while missing a cancerous area can be disastrous.

Our workflow positions us right at the data collection phase such that we generate textural features ourselves. These are fed through our system, which performs PCA on them before passing the most salient ones to GP to generate classifiers. The classifiers give results of 100% accuracy on true positives and a false positive per image rating of just 1.5, which is better than prior work. Not only this, but our system can use GP as part of a feedback loop, to both select and help generate further features.

Keywords: Genetic Programming, Classification, Mammography.

1 Introduction

In national mammography screening, radiologists quickly examine the mammograms of thousands of women to determine if there are early signs of a cancerous growth, or a lesion that requires more attention. It is essential to discover signs early, as survival is directly correlated with early detection [1]. In the event that a closer inspection is required, the woman must be re-called. This is very stressful to patients, and an overly conservative approach to screening can result in disillusionment with the process, with women becoming less inclined to participate. This work aims to improve the early detection of true positives by evolving detectors which, although accurate, are not overly conservative.

M. Nicolau et al. (Eds.): EuroGP 2014, LNCS 8599, pp. 162–173, 2014.

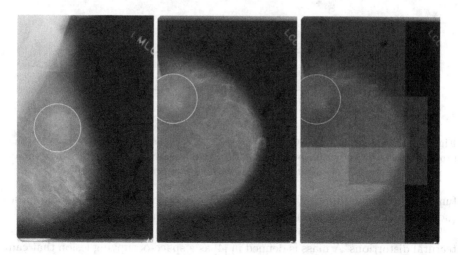

Fig. 1. Mammograms. On the left is the *MLO* view, with benign microcalcifications magnified, while in the middle is the *CC* view, with a cancerous mass magnified. Notice the extra information in the background of the image, such as view labels. On the right is the same CC view divided into segments; each segment is examined separately for suspicious areas by the method proposed in this paper.

In general, most automated approaches to mammography divide the images into segments [2] upon which their analysis is performed. Each segment is examined in turn for signs indicative of suspicious growths. This work takes a radically different approach by considering textural asymmetry *across* the breasts as a potential indicator for suspicious areas. This is a reasonable approach because, although breasts are generally physically (in terms of size) *asymmetrical*, their *parenchymal* patterns (i.e., their mammographic appearance) and, importantly, the texture of their mammograms, are typically relatively uniform [3].

The following section describes mammography and related work, while Section 3 shows how we go from raw mammograms to GP classifiers. The specifics of the GP experiments are detailed in section 4 and the results are in section 5. We finish with the conclusions and future work in section 6.

2   Mammography

Routine mammographic screening, particularly at a national level, is by far the most effective tool for the early detection and subsequent successful treatment of breast cancer [3] [1]. Screening is usually performed on asymptomatic women over a certain age (e.g. over 60 in most European countries) at regular periods, typically every two or three years.

Two views of each breast are recorded. The craniocaudal (CC) view, which is a top down view, and the mediolateral oblique (MLO) view, which is a side view taken at an angle. See Figure 1 for examples of each view. The white areas in the mammograms are made up of the parenchyma, which is essentially the

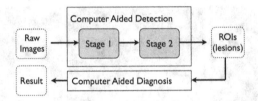

Fig. 2. A typical flowchart for Computer Aided Detection and Diagnosis. Stage 1 of the process tries to detect suspicious areas with a high sensitivity, while Stage 2 attempts to reduce the number of suspicious lesions without compromising the sensitivity.

functional tissue within the breast, while the black areas are made up of adipose (non-functioning fatty) tissue which is transparent under X-rays.

The images are then examined by radiologists who look for masses and architectural distortions. A mass is defined in [4] as a space-occupying lesion that can be seen in at least two views. Mammograms often contain calcifications, which are tiny deposits of calcium (typically, but not always, benign) that show up as bright spots in the images.

2.1   Computer-Aided Detection of Mammographic Abnormalities

Various levels of automation exist in mammography, which can generally be divided into Computer-Aided *Detection* (CAD) and Computer-Aided *Diagnosis* (CADx) [2]. In this work we concentrate exclusively on CAD. In particular, what is known as *Stage 1* detection.

A typical workflow for a computer-aided system is shown in Figure 2. The first stage of CAD is to detect suspicious regions, which are then examined by more specialised routines in the second stage. The output of this stage is a set of *Regions of Interest* (ROIs) which are passed either to a radiologist or to a CADx system which outputs the likelihood of malignancy. The involvement of radiologists and/or later stages obviates the need for a perfectly understandable system, as any diagnostic action is determined by them.

As with many medical applications, mammography demands near-perfection, particularly in the identification of True Positives (TPs) which is measured as the percentage of test cases containing cancerous areas identified. In general, Stage 1 detectors are quite conservative [2] and often return a relatively high False Positives per Image (FPI) rate, that is, the number of areas from an image that are incorrectly identified as having cancerous masses.

The FPI rate is subsequently reduced by the stage 2 detectors. However, the rate of FPI can have an impact on the speed and quality of stage 2 detectors, as a too-conservative approach will degenerate to returning virtually every image. Although this would return a perfect TP rate, the FPI rate would render the system virtually useless.

2.2   Feature Extraction

Mammograms are large (the images in this work are of the order 3600 × 5600 pixels) grey-scale images, so detection relies on the existence of *features*, which describe various properties of the image. Features are typically extracted using either area- or pixel-based measures. We focus exclusively on area-based features in this paper as they are better suited to the identification of ROIs (because the images are so large) than their pixel-based counterparts, which are best suited for highly localized search. Section 3 below describes the features extracted.

2.3   Related Work

Although several CAD systems already exist, most are Stage 2 detectors [2] and focus on particular kinds of masses, e.g. spiculated masses. Of the more general systems, the best reported appears to be that of Li et al [5] with 97.3% TP and 14.81 FPI. Similar work by Polakowski [6] had a lower TP rate (92%) but with a much lower FPI rate (8.39). Given the very low incidence of TPs, it isn't clear how statistically significantly better (if at all) the Li results are.

More recent work in mammography has been concerned with a combination of feature selection and classification [7]. The most successful of these reports a result of 96.3% accuracy, which, although impressive, does not give the break-down between TPs and FPI. The standard method of reporting results is the TP/FPI breakdown, which is what we will present.

GP has been used a handful of times in this area, most notably by [8] who designed a Stage 2 cancer detector for the well known Wisconsin Breast Cancer dataset, in which they used the features extracted from a series of Fine Needle Aspirations (FNAs) and an evolved neural network. Ludwig and Roos [9] used GP to estimate the prognosis of breast cancer patients from the same data set, initially using GP to reduce the number of features, before evolving predictors. Langdon and Harrison [10] took a different approach, using biopsy gene chip data, but their system approached a similar level of automation.

Smaller scale work was conducted by [11] who examined a database of 57 images, each of which already had 22 features detected, and who used GP in combination with various feature selection methods to reduce the dimensionality of the problem. Microcalcifications were targeted by [12], in a CADx application, where they took 128 × 128 pixel segments, each of which contained at least one microcalcification and predicted the probability of it being malignant.

Most systems operate only at the *Classification* stage, although more recent work also considers *Feature Selection*. As we generate our own features, we can modify and parameterize them based on the analysis of our classifiers. While the focus of this paper is on the classification system, because we extract the features from the images ourselves, GP will eventually form part of a feedback loop, instructing the system about what sorts of features are required. See section 6 for more details on this.

Most previous work relies upon previously extracted features, and all the previous work mentioned above deals with a single breast in isolation (although using segmentation and multiple views). Our work leverages the research by Tabar [3] which indicates that, in general, both breasts from the same patient have the same textural characteristics. Our hypothesis is that breasts that differ texturally may contain suspicious areas.

3   Workflow

Part of the challenge in a project like this is to choose how to represent the data. A typical mammogram used in this study is 3575×5532 pixels and 16 bit gray-scale, which is a challenging size of data to deal with. The following workflow was created. Steps 1–5 are concerned with the raw images, while steps 6 and 7 use GP to build and test classifiers.

1. Separation (of breast from background)
2. Suppression of background
3. Segment breast
4. Feature extraction
5. Construct training data
6. Build classifier
7. Test classifiers

3.1   Separation

Figure 1 shows that much of the images consist of background, and clearly, this must first be removed before calculating segments and extracting features. Removing the background is a non-trivial task, partly because the non-uniformity of breast size across patients, but also because of the difficulty in taking consistent mammograms. Due to the pliable nature of the breasts and the manner in which the mammograms are photographed (by squeezing the breast between plates), even the same breast photographed twice on the same machine (after a reset) is likely to look different.

3.2   Suppression of the Background

The background of the image is never perfectly homogeneous, and it includes at least one tag letter indicating if the image is either a right or left breast. This is often augmented by a string of characters indicating which view (CC or MLO) was taken. These backgrounds need to be replaced with homogeneous ones to correctly process the image in a later stage.

We used local thresholding with threshold defined as an average of mean and median, calculated from each pixels circular neighborhood of radius 20. We empirically determined that initializing the process by considering each horizontal line, the 3 consecutive "above average" pixels (with $x < 500$) were part of the breast (and pixels with the same coordinates and lower abscissa) is an efficient method to detect the breast and suppress any possible problems linked to glitches between the breast and the left border of the mammogram.

3.3 Segmentation

Our approach is to divide each image into three segments, and to examine each segment separately. As there can be more than one suspicious area in an image, we return *true* for as many segments as the systems finds suspicious, meaning that an image can have several positives returned. With Stage 1 detectors such as ours, this is described by the FPI of an image, as discussed in section 2.3.

Of course, the maximum FPI is capped by the number of segments that the breast is divided into. Using fewer segments means that the FPI will be lower, but the cost is the detection of the TPs is substantially more difficult because the area is larger.

We wanted to segment the breast into three parts of roughly similar size. One is based around the nipple and one each for of the top and bottom of the rest of the breast. Three segments is quite a small number, and this essentially makes the task more difficult, as the closer the segment size is to the masses being detected, the more different the segments will be from the rest of the breast. However, for this paper, we do not experiment with smaller segment sizes.

The three segments intersect, to help reduce the possibility of a mass going unnoticed. To realize the splitting, we first needed to have an idea of the position of the nipple. In this case, we considered the furthest right non-background pixel that was neither on the top 15% and not in the bottom 15% of the image and its coordinate (n_x, n_y). We then used the line of the coordinate $x = n_x * 6/7$ to find the top non-background pixel $(n_x * 6/7, t_y)$ and the bottommost non background pixel $(n_x * 6/7, b_y)$ on this line. The three parts are then defined as **Nipple:** $x > n_x/2$, $y < t_y$ and $y > b_y$; **Top:** $x > n_x * 6/7$ and $y > (b_y + t_y)/2$ and **Bottom:** $x < n_x * 6/7$ and $y > (b_y + t_y)/2$.

Figure 1 gives an example of segments extracted using this technique.

3.4 Textural Features

To quantitatively describe the textural charactersitics of breast tissue, we calculate a Grey Level Co-occurrence Matrix (CM) for each segment and for each breast. Given a neighborhood relationship r, an element $c(i,j)$ of a CM of image f is the probability that a pixels p and its neighbor pixel q have brightness values i and j respectively, i.e., $\Pr(r(p,q) \wedge f(p) = i \wedge f(q) = j)$. To keep the CM size manageable, we first reduce the number of gray levels to 256 (from 65535 in the original images) via linear scaling. Because textures in mammograms are often anisotropic (directionally dependent), we independently calculate CMs for four orientations corresponding to two adjacent and two diagonal neighbors. Next, we calculate the 13 Haralick features [13], which reflect (among others) contrast, entropy, variance, and correlation of pixel values. By doing this for each orientation, we obtain 52 features per segment, which are subsequently passed to the classifier. This part of processing is realized in Matlab [14].

Segments are rectangular and often extend beyond the breast, thus containing some background. A CM calcuated from such a segment in a conventional way would register very high values for black pixels $(f(p) = 0$ or $f(q) = 0)$ and so distort the values of Haralick features. One cannot simply ignore black pixels, as many images contain large sections of adipose tissue, which appears as black in mammograms and, which is in its own right useful information. Therefore, prior to calculating the CM, we increase by one the intensity of every pixel within the breast, using the information resulting from the segmentation stage (see previous subsection). The pixels that already had the maximal value retain it (this causes certain information loss, albeit negligible one, as there are typically very few such pixels). Then, once the CM has been calculated, we simply "hoist" the CM up and to the left to remove the impact of the unmodified background pixels.

Feature Selection The *neighbourhood* of the CM can be varied, such that the calculation is conducted on pixels further away from each other, but, each extra neighbourhood examined results in another 52 features per segment. Here, we only examine a neighbourhood of 1. A preliminary analysis using PCA revealed that virtually all variance resides in the Haralick entropy features, so we discarded the remaining ones and let GP focus on entropy features.

4   Experimental Setup

This work employs University of South Florida Digital Database for Screening Mammography (DDSM) [15] which is a collection of 43 "volumes" of mammogram cases. A volume is a collection of mammogram cases (typically about 80-100 different patients) and can be classified as either *normal, positive, benign* or *benign without callback*. All patients in a particular volume have the same classification.

The incidence of positives within mammograms is roughly 5 in 1000 [1], giving a massively imbalanced data set. To ensure that our training data maintains a more realistic balance, we deliberately select only a single volume. We use cases from the **cancer_01** and three of the **normal** volumes (volumes 1 to 3). We do not use any images from either the **benign** or **benign without callback** volumes in this instance, although if this work were to be extended, one would expect cases from those volumes to be classified as positives as they contain something that is at least *suspicious*.

This results in a total of 370 cases, 80 of which contain cancerous growths (which we call *positive* in the following). However, if one were to consider these as individual breasts, which is reasonable, given that each is examined independently (i.e. most, but not all, patients with cancerous growths do not have them in both breasts), then the number of non-cancerous images increases by a factor of around 3 – two for each non-cancerous case and one for most cancerous growths. Thus, we obtain two different distributions, one for the non-segmented views (80 positives (P), and 690 negatives, (N)), and and one for the segmented ones (81 Ps and 2272 Ns). The number of Ps increases because in one case the cancerous growth appeared in two segments of a breast; because the segments overlap, both were tagged as P.

---

[1] The actual incidence over a patient's lifetime is closer to 1 in 7 [16].

Table 1. The setups employed. Each was generated from the *same* data set.

Name	Ps	Ns	Description
B1S1V1	80	690	One breast, 1 segment, 1 view; uses CC view only
B1S2V2	80	690	One breast, 2 segments, 2 vies; uses both CC and MLO views
B1S3V1	81	2272	One breast, 3 segments, 1 view; as B1S2V1, but with three segments
B2S4V1	81	2272	Two breasts, 4 segments, 1 view; both CC views, two segments each

There are a total of four segments for each image: one for the entire image (A), and one for each of the three segments (A_t, A_b, A_n). However, when it comes to processing the data, we wish to be able to exploit the differences between the segment and the rest of the breast (i.e. between A and A_x) but also between the opposite breast and the corresponding segment, say B and B_x. Thus, each training instance becomes A, A_x, B, B_x, R, where R is the diagnosis **for that segment**. Notice that this means in a breast that contains one suspicious area, we generate two non-suspicious areas, as well as generating three times as many Ns as we initially had. Note that changing the perspective from mammograms to segments changes the distribution of decision classes, as each negative mammogram contributes three negative segments, but also, each positive mammogram contributes two negative segments (typically, only one segment contains cancerous growth). The imbalance in the data was handled in all cases by using Proportional Individualised Random Sampling [17].

Based on this dataset, we consider several setups by varying the number of breasts, views and segments taken into account (see Table 1). The following terminology is used: $BXSYVZ$, where X is the number of breasts, Y the number of segments and Z the number of views. In the cases where there is just one view (B1S1V1, B2S2V1) we use the CC views, while in the cases where the breast has been segmented, the system attempts to classify whether or not the *segment* has a suspicious area or not. In particular, **B2S2V1** is a special setup which investigates the use of asymmetry. It uses solely on the CC view; the segment chosen from the opposing breast (i.e. not the one being investigated) is the same corresponding segment to the one chosen in the breast under investigation.

4.1 GP Setup

All experiments used a population 200 individuals, running for 100 generations, with a crossover rate of 0.8 and mutation rate of 0.2. The minimum initial depth was 4, while the maximum depth was 17. The instruction set was small, consisting of just $+, -, *, \%$. The tree terminals (leaves) fetch the PCA features as defined in Section 3.4, with four available per segment. All runs were repeated 30 times.

To transform a continuous output of a GP tree into a nominal decision (Positive, Negative), we binarize it using the method described in [18], which optimizes the binarization threshold individually for each GP classifier.

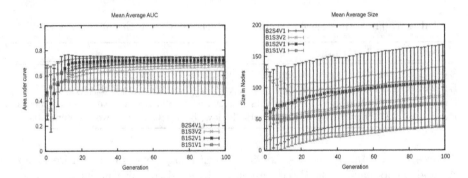

Fig. 3. (Left) AUC for population mean, averaged over three cross validation folds. Not shown are the best-of-generation results, which show that all but B1S1V1 are not statistically significantly different. (Right) Average size of individuals. Notice that the most feature-rich set up (B2S4V1) produces the smallest individuals.

We employed NSGA-II [19] as the selection and replacement strategy, with the *MuLambda* ratio set to 0.5 (i.e., all parents and offspring are merged into one mating pool before running Pareto-based selection). We balanced **three** fitness objectives, where AUC is a the area under ROC, calculated using the Mann-Whitney [20] test:

– Objective 1: FP Rate;
– Objective 2: 1−TP Rate;
– Objective 3: 1−AUC.

5   Results

We performed three-fold cross-validation (CV, [21]) for all setups and show the changes of AUC over generations in Figure 3, averaged over CV folds. The left inset plots the AUC of best-of-generation individual, and the right the AUC objective averaged over the entire population. The results suggest that simply increasing the number of views or segments gives a huge boost to performance. In fact, in B1S1V1, even the best individual returned Positive on virtually all cases, except, rather ironically as shown in Table 2, some of the Negatives. This shows that simply returning P for any input is not a reasonable strategy.

The best AUC plots appear to show that there is little evolution in terms of the best individual, and indeed, there is a quite gentle slope, but there is improvement. Furthermore, there is considerable exploration of the Pareto front, which exists in three dimensions. Finally, the crucial figures, of course, are the TP and FPI counts for the *test set*, which we report in Table 2. Two of our setups yielded individuals that correctly classified 100% of the cancerous cases. The best of these was the individual trained to view breast asymmetry, and it returned just 1.5 FPI. Although not a perfect comparison as the same image data isn not available, contrast this with the results reported in section 2.3 with scores

Table 2. TP and FPI rates obtained by best-of-run classifiers when applied to test data (average and maximum (best) over cross validation folds)

Dataset	Avg. TP	Avg FPI	Best TP	Best FPI
B1S1V1	100%	0.92	89%	3
B1S2V2	94%	0.65	97%	1.75
B1S3V1	95%	0.65	100%	1.75
B2S4V1	95%	0.60	100%	1.5

of 97% TP and FPIs of 4-15. The individuals produced by GP are actually quite small and were surprisingly understandable, although their content is beyond the scope of this paper. On average, the smallest individuals were produced by B2S4V1, even though this set up had the highest number of terminals.

6 Conclusions and Future Work

We have presented an entire workflow for automated mammogram analysis with GP at its core. Our system operates with raw images, extracts the features and presents them to GP, which then evolves classifiers. The result is a Stage 1 cancer detector that achieves 100% accuracy on unseen test data from the USF mammogram libary, with only 1.5 FPI.

The experimental set up that had the lowest FPI was the one that compared both entire breasts, the segment under investigation and the corresponding segment from the other breast, showing that we successfully leveraged textural breast asymmetry as an potential indicator for cancerous growths. Breast asymmetry will exist in both views. Our current best results only use one view (CC); the clear next step is employ both views.

One minor limitation of this work is that all the cancers examined came from the same volume. However, it is reasonable to assume that for any automated system, a classifier will be generated for a specific type of X-ray machine used by a screening agency. Digital mammograms come in the DICOM [22] format which contains much meta-data, including the specific machine and location where the mammogram was taken. This means that it is feasible to produce machine-specific classifiers which are trained to deal with the particular idiosyncracies of various machines. However, our next step will be to train the system across multiple volumes to test the impact on the TP/FPI scores.

Most prior work examines just a single step in the typical workflow, i.e. the *classification* step, assuming the existence of previously selected features and concentrating on extracting the best possible results from those features. We are, however, positioned to leverage the ability of GP to produce solutions that are in some way human-readable, and treat GP as *part* of the workflow, rather than the entire focus of the work. This means that, as the work progresses, we can create a feedback loop which examines the GP individuals to ascertain which terminals (features) are most useful, and extract more information related to those from the data. This is possible because data acquisition is also part of our workflow; this is a system that accepts raw mammograms and outputs marked ROIs.

GP is the essential element of the workflow, as it is responsible for synthesizing the classifier by processing the previously selected and transformed image features. For this paper, feature selection was conducted through PCA, which dramatically reduced the number of features, and pointed to entropy as the key feature. However, one major advantage we have over most researchers is that, because we control the entire workflow, we can easily generate new CMs with larger neighbourhoods. Current work is examining the ways in which GP is combining them and initial results are very positive; these results will then be compared with other machine learning systems, specifically SVMs and C4.5, to investigate the specific impact that GP has, particularly as the number of features increase.

Our segments are relatively large. While we were still able to maintain a 100% TP rate with them, there is a case to be made for examining smaller segments, as the smaller these are, the better it is for the later stage.

Finally, although the Haralick textural measures are powerful, they are not the only features that have been used in image analysis. Our system also extracts Hu invariants [23] and Local Binary Patterns [24]; we will use GP to combine these with the Haralick features to further decrease the FPI.

Acknowledgments. C. Ryan acknowledges support from the Science Foundation of Ireland and the Irish-U.S. Fulbright Comission. K. Krawiec acknowledges financial support from the Polish-U.S. Fulbright Commission and from grants no. DEC-2011/01/B/ST6/07318 and 91507.

References

1. Tabar, L., et al.: A new era in the diagnosis of breast cancer. Surgical Oncology Clinics of North America 9(2), 233–277 (2000)
2. Sampat, M., Markey, M., Bovik, A.C.: Computer-aided detection and diagnosis in mammography. In Bovik, A.C., (ed.): Handbook of Image and Video Processing. Elsevier Academic Press (2010)
3. Tot, T., Tabar, L., Dean, P.B.: The pressing need for better histologic-mammographic correlation of the many variations in normal breast anatomy. Virchows Archiv 437(4), 338–344 (2000)
4. American College of Radiology: ACR BIRADS Mammography, Ultrasound & MRI, 4th edn. American College of Radiology, Reston (2003)
5. Li, H., et al.: Computerized radiographic mass detection part i: Lesion site selection by morphological enhancement and contextual segmentation. IEEE Trans. Med. Imag. 20, 289–301 (2001)
6. Polakowski, W.E., Cournoyer, D.A., Rogers, S.K.: Computer-aided breast cancer detection and diagnosis of masses using difference of gaussians and derivative-based feature saliency. IEEE Trans. Med. Imag. 16, 811–819 (1997)
7. Ganesan, K., et al.: Decision support system for breast cancer detection using mammograms. Proceedings of the Institution of Mechanical Engineers, Part H: Journal of Engineering in Medicine 227(7), 721–732 (2013)

8. Ahmad, A.M., Khan, G.M., Mahmud, S.A., Miller, J.F.: Breast cancer detection using cartesian genetic programming evolved artificial neural networks. In: Soule, T., et al. (eds.) GECCO 2012: Proceedings of the Fourteenth International Conference on Genetic and Evolutionary Computation Conference, Philadelphia, Pennsylvania, USA, July 7-11, pp. 1031–1038. ACM (2012)
9. Ludwig, S.A., Roos, S.: Prognosis of breast cancer using genetic programming. In: Setchi, R., Jordanov, I., Howlett, R.J., Jain, L.C. (eds.) KES 2010, Part IV. LNCS, vol. 6279, pp. 536–545. Springer, Heidelberg (2010)
10. Langdon, W., Harrison, A.: Gp on spmd parallel graphics hardware for mega bioinformatics data mining. Soft Computing 12(12), 1169–1183 (2008)
11. Nandi, R.J., Nandi, A.K., Rangayyan, R., Scutt, D.: Genetic programming and feature selection for classification of breast masses in mammograms. In: 28th Annual International Conference of the IEEE Engineering in Medicine and Biology Society, EMBS 2006, New York, USA, pp. 3021–3024. IEEE (August 2006)
12. Völk, K., Miller, J.F., Smith, S.L.: Multiple network CGP for the classification of mammograms. In: Giacobini, M., et al. (eds.) EvoWorkshops 2009. LNCS, vol. 5484, pp. 405–413. Springer, Heidelberg (2009)
13. Haralick, R., et al.: Texture features for image classification. IEEE Transactions on Systems, Man, and Cybernetics 3(6) (1973)
14. MATLAB: version 8.2 (R2012a). MathWorks Inc., Natick, MA (2013)
15. Heath, M., Bowyer, K., Kopans, D., Moore, R., Kegelmeyer, W.P.: The digital database for screening mammography. In: Yaffe, M. (ed.) Proceedings of the Fifth International Workshop on Digital Mammography, pp. 212–218. Medical Physics Publishing (2001)
16. Kerlikowske, K., Grady, D., Barclay, J., Sickles, E.A., Eaton, A., Ernster, V.: Positive predictive value of screening mammography by age and family history of breast cancer. Journal of the American Medical Association 270, 2444–2450 (1993)
17. Fitzgerald, J., Ryan, C.: A hybrid approach to the problem of class imbalance. In: International Conference on Soft Computing, Brno, Czech Republic (June 2013)
18. Fitzgerald, J., Ryan, C.: Exploring boundaries: optimising individual class boundaries for binary classification problem. In: Proceedings of the Fourteenth International Conference on Genetic and Evolutionary Computation Conference, GECCO 2012, pp. 743–750. ACM, New York (2012)
19. Deb, K., Pratap, A., Agarwal, S., Meyarivan, T.: A fast and elitist multiobjective genetic algorithm: Nsga-ii. IEEE Transactions on Evolutionary Computation 6(2), 182–197 (2002)
20. Stober, P., Yeh, S.T.: An explicit functional form specification approach to estimate the area under a receiver operating characteristic (roc) curve, vol. 7 (2007), http://www2.sas.com/proceedings/sugi27/p226--227.pdf7
21. Geisser, S.: Predictive Inference. Chapman and Hall, New York (1993)
22. Whitcher, B., Schmid, V.J., Thornton, A.: Working with the DICOM and NIfTI data standards in R. Journal of Statistical Software 44(6), 1–28 (2011)
23. Hu, M.: Visual pattern recognition by moment invariants. Trans. Info. Theory IT-8, 179–187 (1962)
24. Ojala, T., Pietikäinen, M., Harwood, D.: Performance evaluation of texture measures with classification based on kullback discrimination of distributions. In: Proceedings of the 12th IAPR International Conference on Pattern Recognition (ICPR 1994), pp. 582–585. IEEE (1994)

NEAT, There's No Bloat

Leonardo Trujillo, Luis Muñoz, Enrique Naredo, and Yuliana Martínez

Tree-Lab, Doctorado en Ciencias de la Ingeniería, Departamento de Ingeniería
Eléctrica y Electrónica, Instituto Tecnológico de Tijuana, Blvd. Industrial y Av. ITR
Tijuana S/N, Mesa Otay C.P. 22500, Tijuana B.C., México
{leonardo.trujillo,lmunoz}@tectijuana.edu.mx,
{enriquenaredo,ysaraimr}@gmail.com
www.tree-lab.org

Abstract. The Operator Equalization (OE) family of bloat control
methods have achieved promising results in many domains. In particular, the Flat-OE method, that promotes a flat distribution of program
sizes, is one of the simplest OE methods and achieves some of the best
results. However, Flat-OE, like all OE variants, can be computationally expensive. This work proposes a simplified strategy for bloat control
based on Flat-OE. In particular, bloat is studied in the NeuroEvolution
of Augmenting Topologies (NEAT) algorithm. NEAT includes a very
simple diversity preservation technique based on speciation and fitness
sharing, and it is hypothesized that with some minor tuning, speciation
in NEAT can promote a flat distribution of program size. Results indicate that this is the case in two benchmark problems, in accordance with
results for Flat-OE. In conclusion, NEAT provides a worthwhile strategy
that could be extrapolated to other GP systems, for effective and simple
bloat control.

Keywords: NEAT, Bloat, Operator Equalization.

1 Introduction

Situating genetic programming (GP) within the larger machine learning community, it is evident that GP still suffers from some theoretical and practical
issues that have limited its acceptance as a general problem solving tool [1].
Concretely, GP is seen as an inefficient search method, since it has a large computational overhead and produces highly complex or uninterpretable solutions.
These inefficiencies are mostly related to two underlying problems in standard
GP algorithms. Firstly, most GP systems search directly within the space of syntactic expressions, making it difficult to explicitly analyze the fitness landscape
or search gradient. To address this, some researchers are now considering other
spaces that are concurrently sampled during a GP search, such as semantic space
[2] and behavioral space [3–5]. Secondly, given that GP employs a variable length
representation, it is severely hampered by the effects of the bloat phenomenon.
Indeed, bloat can be seen as the main cause of the high computational costs and
unnecessary complexity of evolved solutions. Because of this, bloat has been the

M. Nicolau et al. (Eds.): EuroGP 2014, LNCS 8599, pp. 174–185, 2014.

topic of much research, that ranges from theoretical analysis to heuristic bloat control [6].

Recently, the bloat control method called Operator Equalisation (OE) has shown promise [7], given its theoretically sound foundation and outstanding results, summarized in the recent paper by Silva et al. [8]. OE is reviewed in the following section, for now let us state that the main idea behind OE methods is that of explicitly enforcing a specific distribution of program size at each generation. Early works on OE focused on determining the best distribution that would allow the GP search to find nearly optimal solutions without incurring bloat. However, while different size distributions have been used, a recent paper by Silva [9] suggested that the best distribution might also be the simplest, a flat distribution of program size.

Building on these insights, this paper studies bloat from a different but related view point. This work considers a GP-like system designed to evolve neural networks (NNets), called NeuroEvolution of Augmenting Topologies (NEAT) [10]. While NEAT is a popular algorithm within the evolutionary computation (EC) community, it is normally not considered as a GP algorithm. However, the differences between what might be considered a standard GP and NEAT are slight. Moreover, while the differences are small, their effects can be substantial. In particular, NEAT indirectly enforces restraints on the program size distribution by employing speciation and fitness sharing during the search. While the original intent was to protect structural innovations and promote an incremental evolution of solution complexity, this work hypothesizes that an indirect consequence is that it generates a (nearly) flat distribution of program size. Therefore, based on the results from Silva [9], it follows that NEAT should also perform a bloat-free search.

Therefore, the experimental work presented here is aimed at illustrating that NEAT does not bloat, in accordance with the conclusions of [9]. Moreover, as it will be described below, this is achieved by very simple and widely known methods within the EC community, speciation and fitness sharing. Finally, while previous papers have speculated or assumed that NEAT might actually have some intrinsic bloat control properties, this paper is the first (to the authors knowledge) that explicitly studies bloat in NEAT and attempts to determine under what circumstances can NEAT evolve without bloat.

The rest of the paper proceeds as follows. Section 2 reviews bloat related research and the OE family of methods. Afterwards, NEAT is presented in Section 3 and the hypothesis of this work is outlined. Section 4 presents the experimental work and summarizes the main results. Finally, concluding comments and future work are outlined in Section 5.

2   Bloat

Bloat is normally defined as the increase in average program size without a proportional increase in fitness. This definition is quite fuzzy, but in general we can state that bloat occurs when the best fitness stagnates while the average program size continues to grow. In what follows, we provide a brief overview of related research; for a more detailed survey see [6, 8].

2.1   Causes of Bloat and Bloat Control Methods

As stated before, bloat has been one of the main areas of GP research, and also represents one of its most intriguing open challenges [1]. The most well established explanation regarding the causes of bloat is the fitness-causes-bloat theory (FCBT), developed by Langdon and Poli [11]. The FCBT is based on the fact that: a) there is a many-to-one mapping from syntactic space to semantic or fitness space; and b) there are exponentially more large programs with a given fitness than small ones. Hence, if a particular fitness value is desired, there is a tendency towards larger, or bloated, programs during a GP search, simply because there are more large programs than small ones. Indeed, stating that the search for fitness is the main cause of bloat is by now uncontroversial, since it is basically the underlying factor in all major theories of bloat [6]. Moreover, recent work suggests that a GP search that does not consider fitness explicitly can in fact avoid bloat by promoting solution novelty [12, 5].

Currently, one of the most useful theories that describe the bloating process is the crossover bias theory (CBT), developed by Dignum and Poli [13]. Focusing on standard Koza style GP, the CBT states that bloat is produced by the effect that subtree mutation has on the tree size distribution. While the average size of trees is not affected by crossover, the size distribution is. Subtree crossover produces a large number of small trees, which for most problems achieve very low fitness. Therefore, selection will favor larger trees, causing an increase in the average tree size within the population, effectively bootstrapping the bloating effect. Given the insights provided by the CBT, Dignum and Poli [7] proposed the Operator Equalisation bloat control method, that focuses on explicitly controlling the distribution of program sizes at each generation. OE has produced impressive results in several benchmark and real-world problems, and the original proposal has lead to a family of related methods [8]. Despite the success of OE, there are several concerns with the method. For instance, it relies on a computationally expensive process of generating, evaluating and in many cases rejecting program trees that do not fit the target distribution. Moreover, recent results suggest that some of the underlying assumptions in OE may not be justified, as discussed below.

2.2   The Secret Behind Operator Equalization

Silva attempted to develop a stripped down OE method, that would be simpler, with a lower computational cost, while also preserving the main properties of OE [9]. However, the proposed simplified approximation failed at controlling bloat. The reason for this appears to lie in a contradiction of OE with the CBT. Since the CBT suggests that small individuals are harmful to the evolutionary process, OE methods tend to promote target size distributions that exclude such individuals. However, while the methods are designed to promote such distributions, in practice OE does not actually fit them. In fact, [9] shows that OE tends to produce uniform or flat distributions, with a roughly similar proportion of trees of different sizes, from small to large trees. This lead Silva to propose the Flat-OE variant, where a flat target is sought, and experimental results suggest that Flat-OE can control bloat while not compromising the quality of the evolved solutions.

The original strategy by Silva in [9] seems quite reasonable: determine the underlying properties of OE and develop an approximate algorithm that satisfies these properties. The proposal was to use Brood recombination [14] and dynamic limits [6] as the general *ingredients* underlying OE. While this combination failed, it did so because the underlying assumptions behind what OE was actually doing were wrong. However, the general strategy merits further attention; i.e., develop an approximate version of OE that is based on computationally simpler methods. In this paper, the same strategy is adopted, but instead of attempting to reproduce the original OE algorithms, the goal is to focus on Flat-OE. To do so, our proposal is to step out of the traditional GP framework, and study an algorithm that is widely used in other EC areas.

3 NeuroEvolution of Augmenting Topologies

The main contribution of this work is to study bloat in a GP algorithm that approximates the basic functionality of Flat-OE by inducing a flat distribution of program size. The algorithm studied here is NeuroEvolution of Augmenting Topologies (NEAT), developed by Stanley and Miikkulainen [10]. While NEAT was originally proposed as an algorithm to automatically generate neural networks (NNets), it should in fact be considered as a GP variant. Moreover, NEAT is constructed in such a way that it is able to promote a size distribution that approximates that of Flat-OE, something that is shown in the experimental section of this paper. Moreover, NEAT accomplishes this using simple and well-known EC methods. In what follows, NEAT is presented and its most relevant details are discussed. Additionally, care is taken to convince the reader that the general approach followed by NEAT fits in nicely within the GP paradigm, and that as such, it is a relevant object of study from the GP point of view.

3.1 NEAT Features

In their original paper, Stanley and Miikkulainen present NEAT as a variable length genetic algorithm that explicitly encodes the topology and set of connection weights of a NNet [10]. The basic NEAT algorithm can be broken down into the following main features or components.

The first main ingredient of NEAT is its reliance on a special variable length representation. The genome is conceptually divided in two segments: the first contains node genes that specify the set of input, output and hidden nodes of the network; while the second segment contains the set of connection or synaptic genes, that specify the input and output node of each connection and its respective weight. To allow search operations that are coherent between NNets of different sizes, NEAT includes historical markings for each synaptic connection. In this way, when crossover is performed between two parent NNets, that can have different network topologies, the connection genes are first aligned based on these historical markings, identifying the shared structure between both parents (nodes and connections). Matching genes between two parents are randomly inherited from either parent, but any disjoint or excess genes are inherited from the most fit parent. Moreover, the connection weights are also inherited after a crossover operation. One thing that NEAT does not evolve is the activation functions, these are set a priori for all hidden and output nodes.

Second, since NEAT is designed to search for NNets, the variable length representation encodes graph structures. Other search operators include a parameter (weight) mutation, and structural mutations that can either add nodes or add connections. This set of search operators is unusual, in the sense that they always produce offspring of equal or larger size than the parents, a configuration that promotes code growth.

Third, NEAT encourages an incremental evolution of solution complexity (size). The initial population only contains NNets that share the same minimal topology, in most cases this is a fully connected feedforward NNet with no hidden neurons and random connection weights. NEAT assumes that the best way to perform the search is to start with the simplest NNets, and progressively build complexity through the search operators. In this way, if the problem can be solved by a parsimonious NNet the search might be able to find it early on, and only if it fails will the search progress to larger topologies.

Finally, NEAT incorporates a scheme that protects topological innovation. At the beginning of the run all of the individuals share the same initial structure, and the search focuses on improving the connection weights of the networks. The search operators progressively add structural elements (node or connection) to the base topology, and each time a new node and/or connection is generated its weight is instantiated randomly. This causes a problem, because a randomly generated connection with a randomly set weight will, with high probability, have a destructive effect on fitness. However, it is reasonable to assume that an increase in structural complexity might be required to solve difficult problems; therefore, there is a need to protect these structural innovations so they are not discarded by selection. NEAT accomplishes this by using speciation based on topological similarities and fitness sharing [15], where the fitness of each individual is penalized based on its similarity with other individuals. The key element in the NEAT proposal is the use of a problem specific distance measure δ, based on the topological similarities between two NNets expressed by the number of disjoint genes D and excess genes G between them, given by

$$\delta = \frac{c_1 \cdot G + c_2 \cdot D}{N} + c_3 \cdot \overline{W} \, , \tag{1}$$

where $\overline{W}$ is the average weight difference of matching genes, N is the number of genes in the larger genome, and c_x are linear parameters.

3.2 NEAT, GP and Bloat

The last point of the preceding section is key to the bloat discussion and how NEAT relates to Flat-OE. It can be argued that grouping NNets based on topology is not the best way to promote a diverse set of functional behaviors [16]. Nevertheless, speciation based on topological similarities can promote a diverse population of network topologies; i.e. a diverse population of network shapes and, most importantly, sizes. Therefore, NEAT provides a promising algorithmic approximation to the main strategy underlying Flat-OE. If the previous observation is correct then we should expect NEAT to evolve bloat free. This is the focus of the experimental work in this paper, evaluate if NEAT bloats on standard benchmark problems. Before turning to the experimental setup and results, lets first contextualize NEAT within the broader GP paradigm.

GP can be defined as a variable length evolutionary algorithm that evolves syntactic expressions that are interpreted as simple computer programs, functions, operators or models. On the other hand, NEAT is a variable length evolutionary algorithm that evolves graph structures which represent NNets. From this general perspective, we can state that NEAT is a special form of GP, where evolved solutions express instances from a narrow class of functions, those that can be represented as NNets. However, the results obtained with NEAT can provide useful insights to the GP paradigm as a whole, just as any other experimental work done with other common GP variants.

Additionally, it is important to mention that it has been previously hypothesized that NEAT might intrinsically control bloat[1]. For instance, it was speculated that the crossover operator might in some way discourage bloat; however this is probably incorrect, since in every case crossover will produce offspring that are at least as large as their parents, while also incurring a decrease in fitness due to the structural modifications which tend to be highly destructive. Speciation has also been identified as a possible bloat control mechanism, however, as will be shown in the experimental work, the original NEAT implementation does present bloat, and care must be taken in adequately parameterizing NEAT. Therefore, this work is the first to identify a proper bloat-free NEAT configuration, and the first to extensively and explicitly evaluate NEAT from the perspective of the bloat phenomenon.

4 Experiments

The goal of the experimental work is to determine if NEAT can evolve without bloating. Since NEAT is a fairly complex and intricate algorithm, we employ the freely available Java implementation[2] which closely follows the original NEAT

---

[1] To the authors knowledge, the only explicit discussion of this issue is given in the official NEAT website http://www.cs.ucf.edu/~kstanley/neat.html

[2] http://nn.cs.utexas.edu/?jneat

Table 1. Parameter settings used in the experimental setup for NEAT and Bloat-Free NEAT (BF-NEAT)

Parameters	NEAT	BF-NEAT
Weight mutation power	2.5	9.0
Recurrent probability	1.0	0.1
Disjoint parameter c_1	1.0	0.5
Excess coefficient c_2	1.0	1.0
Weight coefficient c_3	0.4	0.0
Compatibility threshold δ_{min}	3.0	9.0
Age significance	1.0	9.0
Survival threshold	0.2	0.8
Population size	200	200
Drop-off age	50	1000

algorithm published in [10] [3]. To evaluate the algorithm, two standard benchmark problems are used, the XOR problem and 3-bit parity problem, which are both distributed as part of the Java library. NEAT performance is analyzed using fitness, and the total size of the solutions, given by the number of nodes in each solution. To visually analyze NEAT behavior, the results are presented using three types of plots. Firstly, plots that show how the actual distribution (histogram) of program size evolves over time, considering the number of individuals and the number of species of a certain size that are present within the population at each generation; in the case of species size, this is determined by the average of all individuals that belong to a species. Secondly, classic convergence plots of best solution fitness and best solution size w.r.t. generations, to compare different algorithm configurations. Finally, all of the results presented below are averages of thirty independent runs.

One of the main limitations with NEAT is that it uses a large set of parameters. Therefore, NEAT is tested using the parameter values suggested in [10]; see second column of Table 1[4]. Figure 1 presents plots that summarize the performance on the XOR problem, considering the size distribution at each generation. Figure 1a shows the distribution of individuals based on the number of nodes and 1b shows the distribution of species. First, it is clear that the size distribution of NEAT is biased toward larger programs at each generation, as small programs are quickly replaced by larger ones, this leads to an evident bloating effect during the run. Similarly, Figure 2 presents the same analysis for the Parity problem, exhibiting similar trends.

---

[3] While there are many open implementations of NEAT available, many of them are modified or simplified variants of the original algorithm, and it is not straightforward to determine what consequences these modifications, no matter how slight, can have on the search dynamics.

[4] Some parameters were omitted due to size limitations, these are kept with their default values.

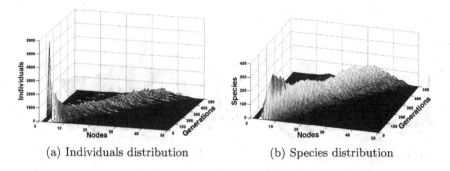

(a) Individuals distribution   (b) Species distribution

Fig. 1. Evolution of Size for NEAT on the XOR problem: a) Size distribution of individuals based on number of nodes; b) Size distribution of species based on number of nodes

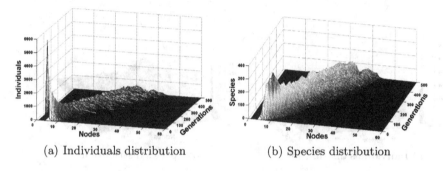

(a) Individuals distribution   (b) Species distribution

Fig. 2. Evolution of Size for NEAT on the Parity problem: a) Size distribution of individuals based on number of nodes; b) Size distribution of species based on number of nodes

At first, these results suggest that NEAT cannot promote a flat distribution of program size; i.e. does not run bloat-free. Therefore, NEAT is reparametrized as shown in the third column of Table 1, this NEAT configuration is called bloat-free neat or BF-NEAT. The main changes are justified as follows.

- First, $c_3 = 0$ because $\overline{W}$ is not relevant to a speciation process that needs to promote size diversity.
- Second, $c_1 = 0.5$ and $c_2 = 1$, focusing the speciation condition on the number of excess genes, which are the most relevant when considering code growth.
- Third, the parameter *mutation power* controls the range of possible values for connection weights; this is increased to 9, allowing the search to thoroughly explore each NNet topology.
- Fourth, the *age significance* parameter is increased w.r.t the original implementation, which protects new individuals and species. Note that doing so slightly encourages program growth, since the search operators will always produce larger NNets.

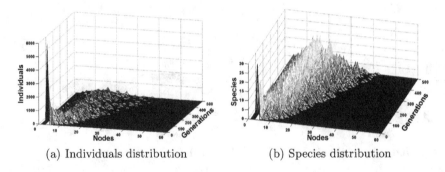

(a) Individuals distribution   (b) Species distribution

Fig. 3. Evolution of Size for BF-NEAT on the XOR problem: a) Size distribution of individuals based on number of nodes; b) Size distribution of species based on number of nodes

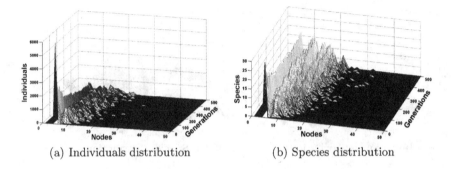

(a) Individuals distribution   (b) Species distribution

Fig. 4. Evolution of Size for BF-NEAT on the Parity problem: a) Size distribution of individuals based on number of nodes; b) Size distribution of species based on number of nodes

- Fifth, *survival threshold* defines the percentage of the best individuals that can reproduce, using a small value makes the search process more greedy, potentially biasing the search in other ways.
- Sixth, the parameter *dropoff age* eliminates under-performing species every certain number of generations; however according with FlatOE size diversity should not be lost during the run.

With these modifications, the same experiments are repeated for BF-NEAT, evaluating its performance on XOR and Parity, the results are shown in Figures 3 and 4. In this case, the effects of the new parameters are clear, a flatter distribution of program sizes is exhibited, and the bloating effect is substantially curtailed. Additionally, Figures 5 and 6 compare the performance of NEAT and BF-NEAT, on the XOR and Parity problems respectively. Figures 5b and 6b show how solution size evolves, and Figures 5c and 6c show how the best fitness evolves. From these figures it is possible to state that solution size is greatly reduced in BF-NEAT, without compromising solution quality.

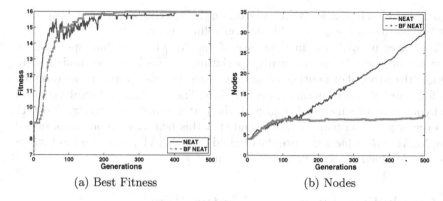

(a) Best Fitness   (b) Nodes

Fig. 5. Performance on the XOR problem: a)Best Fitness and b)Number of Nodes

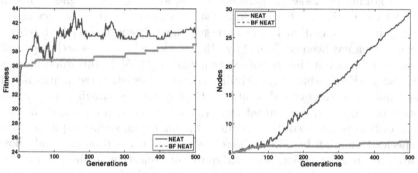

(a) Parity NEAT vs. BF NEAT Fintness (b) Parity NEAT vs. BF NEAT Nodes

Fig. 6. Performance on the Parity problem: a)Best Fitness and b)Number of Nodes

4.1 Discussion

In general, the initial results are encouraging, suggesting that the hypothesis of this work is correct, NEAT can be executed without bloat by promoting a close to uniform distribution of program size. Let us now analyze what might be the main causes for these results. To do so, we consider each of the NEAT features, and analyze what, if any, might be their influence.

First, NEAT uses a graph representation, which by itself has no intrinsic bloat controlling properties. Second, maybe the search operators are designed to discourage code growth. However, the original NEAT algorithm only used search operators that promoted an increase in size, which is highly unusual in GP. Nonetheless, NEAT can be configured to run bloat free.

Third, NEAT starts off evolution with the smallest possible topology that considers all of the input elements or terminals. According to the CBT, this can encourage bloat, since small solutions will normally exhibit below average fitness. Moreover, by starting with the smallest possible size of individuals, populations can only increase in size for NEAT to explore the search space. Hence, it appears that this feature is not responsible for controlling bloat.

This leaves us with the final feature of the NEAT algorithm, specification based on topology or size. Basically, speciation in NEAT can be configured to promote the survival of solutions of different sizes. In other words, it can promote a uniform, or flat, distribution of program sizes. The experimental results confirm this hypothesis, which are coherent with the performance exhibited by Flat-OE. However, it is also crucial to understand that this behavior cannot be obtained using NEAT *out-of-the-box*, since the original set of NEAT parameters and values were not designed to explicitly control bloat.

5   Concluding Remarks and Future Work

This paper studies the bloat phenomenon in GP, following the insights provided by the Flat-OE method. What previous results suggest is that by preserving diversity within the population, bloat can be substantially controlled [9]. Moreover, this general idea has been confirmed by other works, where the search is guided based on solution novelty instead of solution quality [12, 5]. In this work, bloat is studied using NEAT, which explicitly incorporates speciation techniques based on the topology of the evolved solutions. Results are encouraging, the simple speciation process controls bloat effectively, when an adequate parametrization of the algorithm is provided. In particular, the algorithm should explicitly promote species formation based on differences related to solution size and allow the search to promote exploration, without easily rejecting smaller, and older, individuals. Future work will focus on extrapolating the lessons learned in this study to a more common GP system, such as tree-based GP or linear GP. In these cases, care will need to be taken to define a proper similarity measure, and an extensive evaluation in diverse domains should be carried out. Nevertheless, it appears that bloat control might be simple to implement and promote using the insights provided by NEAT.

Acknowledgments. Funding provided by CONACYT (Mexico) Basic Science Research Project No. 178323, DGEST (Mexico) Research Projects No.5149.13-P and TIJ-ING-2012-110 and IRSES project ACoBSEC from the European Commission. Second, third and fourth authors are supported by CONACYT (Mexico) scholarships, respectively No. 302526, No. 232288 and No. 226981.

References

1. O'Neill, M., Vanneschi, L., Gustafson, S., Banzhaf, W.: Open issues in genetic programming. Genetic Programming and Evolvable Machines 11(3-4), 339–363 (2010)
2. Moraglio, A., Krawiec, K., Johnson, C.G.: Geometric semantic genetic programming. In: Coello Coello, C.A., Cutello, V., Deb, K., Forrest, S., Nicosia, G., Pavone, M. (eds.) PPSN 2012, Part I. LNCS, vol. 7491, pp. 21–31. Springer, Heidelberg (2012)

3. Naredo, E., Trujillo, L., Martínez, Y.: Searching for novel classifiers. In: Krawiec, K., Moraglio, A., Hu, T., Etaner-Uyar, A.Ş., Hu, B. (eds.) EuroGP 2013. LNCS, vol. 7831, pp. 145–156. Springer, Heidelberg (2013)

4. Naredo, E., Trujillo, L.: Searching for novel clustering programs. In: Proceeding of the Fifteenth Annual Conference on Genetic and Evolutionary Computation Conference, GECCO 2013, pp. 1093–1100. ACM, New York (2013)

5. Trujillo, L., Naredo, E., Martínez, Y.: Preliminary study of bloat in genetic programming with behavior-based search. In: Emmerich, M., et al. (eds.) EVOLVE - A Bridge between Probability, Set Oriented Numerics, and Evolutionary Computation IV. AISC, vol. 227, pp. 293–305. Springer, Heidelberg (2013)

6. Silva, S., Costa, E.: Dynamic limits for bloat control in genetic programming and a review of past and current bloat theories. Genetic Programming and Evolvable Machines 10(2), 141–179 (2009)

7. Dignum, S., Poli, R.: Operator equalisation and bloat free gp. In: O'Neill, M., Vanneschi, L., Gustafson, S., Esparcia Alcázar, A.I., De Falco, I., Della Cioppa, A., Tarantino, E. (eds.) EuroGP 2008. LNCS, vol. 4971, pp. 110–121. Springer, Heidelberg (2008)

8. Silva, S., Dignum, S., Vanneschi, L.: Operator equalisation for bloat free genetic programming and a survey of bloat control methods. Genetic Programming and Evolvable Machines 13(2), 197–238 (2012)

9. Silva, S.: Reassembling operator equalisation: a secret revealed. In: Proceedings of the 13th Annual Conference on Genetic and Evolutionary Computation, GECCO 2011, pp. 1395–1402. ACM, New York (2011)

10. Stanley, K.O., Miikkulainen, R.: Evolving neural networks through augmenting topologies. Evol. Comput. 10(2), 99–127 (2002)

11. Langdon, W.B., Poli, R.: Fitness causes bloat. In: Proceedings of the Second On-line World Conference on Soft Computing in Engineering Design and Manufacturing, pp. 13–22. Springer (1997)

12. Lehman, J., Stanley, K.O.: Abandoning objectives: Evolution through the search for novelty alone. Evol. Comput. 19(2), 189–223 (2011)

13. Poli, R., Langdon, W.B., Dignum, S.: On the limiting distribution of program sizes in tree-based genetic programming. In: Ebner, M., O'Neill, M., Ekárt, A., Vanneschi, L., Esparcia-Alcázar, A.I. (eds.) EuroGP 2007. LNCS, vol. 4445, pp. 193–204. Springer, Heidelberg (2007)

14. Altenberg, L.: The evolution of evolvability in genetic programming. In: Kinnear Jr., K.E. (ed.) Advances in Genetic Programming, pp. 47–74. MIT Press, Cambridge (1994)

15. Goldberg, D.E., Richardson, J.: Genetic algorithms with sharing for multimodal function optimization. In: Proceedings of the Second International Conference on Genetic Algorithms and their Application, pp. 41–49. Erlbaum Associates Inc., Hillsdale (1987)

16. Trujillo, L., Olague, G., Lutton, E., Fernández de Vega, F., Dozal, L., Clemente, E.: Speciation in behavioral space for evolutionary robotics. Journal of Intelligent & Robotic Systems 64(3-4), 323–351 (2011)

The Best Things Don't Always Come in Small Packages: Constant Creation in Grammatical Evolution

R. Muhammad Atif Azad and Conor Ryan

CSIS Department, University of Limerick, Ireland
{atif.azad,conor.ryan}@ul.ie
http://bds.ul.ie

Abstract. This paper evaluates the performance of various methods to constant creation in Grammatical Evolution (GE), and validates the results against those from Genetic Programming (GP). Constant creation in GE is an important issue due to the disruptive nature of *ripple crossover*, which can radically remap multiple terminals in an individual, and we investigate if more compact methods, which are more similar to the GP style of constant creation (*Ephemeral Random Constants* (ERCs), perform better.

The results are surprising. The GE methods all perform significantly better than GP on unseen test data, and we demonstrate that the standard GE approach of *digit concatenation* does not produce individuals that are any larger than those from methods which are designed to use less genetic material.

Keywords: Grammatical Evolution, Constants, Symbolic Regression, Genetic Programming, Digit Concatenation.

1 Introduction

Typically, symbolic regression finds a function to explain a given data set. In traditional Machine Learning [1] this involves optimising the parameters of a pre-defined *objective* function using an Artificial Neural Network (ANN), Support Vector Machine (SVM) or some other numerical method. These methods work efficiently partly because, with a known target function, they only explore the parameter space to minimise the error between expected and predicted outputs.

Genetic Programming (GP) takes symbolic regression to another level: it explores both the space of functions and the associated parameters (constants) simultaneously. Therefore, finding suitable numeric constants is essential to how GP performs. However, GP typically does not involve specialised mechanisms for optimising numeric constants. Instead, GP uses *ephemeral random constants (ERCs)* [2], that randomly initialise numeric terminal nodes in a GP population. Thereafter, genetic operators recombine and filter out (possibly erroneously) these ERCs. The combined tasks of optimising structure and constants can be very difficult: for example Keijzer [3] noted that given a target function of $100+x^2$

M. Nicolau et al. (Eds.): EuroGP 2014, LNCS 8599, pp. 186–197, 2014.

such that $x \in [-1, 1]$, GP approximated the numeric constant 100 but lost the genetic material to encode x^2. To combat this, Keijzer proposed *linear scaling*, a form of linear regression to optimise the slope and intercept of evolving GP functions to assist GP. Other proposals include numerical methods [4][5] as well as specialised mutation operators [6][7].

This paper investigates methods for evolving constants in Grammatical Evolution (GE) [8] on a number of problems from the symbolic regression domain. GE is a genetic programming system that maps a genotype, a linear string of 8 bit integers termed *codons*, to a functional expression from a language of choice, which is defined by a context free grammar (CFG). Usually, GE uses *digit concatenation* [9] to evolve constants. In this method, a string of GE codons select the constant defining rules from a grammar to yield the desired constant.

Since digit concatenation uses several codons to produce a number, that number can change when passed onto offspring, unlike a number encoded in a more compact way, i.e. as in GP. This is due to the so-called *ripple effect* of GE crossover, [10] which propagates changes to genetic material from left to right. We compare digit concatenation to two other *compact* methods that do not require several codons to encode a constant: these are, a GE version of ERCs called *persistent random constants (PRCs)* [9] and a *codon injection* method that directly converts a GE codon into a floating point value.

This work goes further than previous studies which focused on evolving solutions which were a single constant [11–13], because, as [6] notes, optimising constants alongside mathematical functions is a different challenge and, we believe, more relevant to the GP community. One early related work [9] showed the utility of digit concatenation to a few instances of *Binomial-3* problem [14]; here we *also* consider other problems. Moreover, we compare different methods both with and without linear scaling and also compare against the benchmark results from GP because GP is commonly used for symbolic regression. Finally, previous work solely compared **training** results; instead, we also consider unseen **test** data as well as genome lengths of the individuals to ascertain if the compact methods breed relatively more predictive and compact genomes.

The results show that GP consistently outperforms GE on training data; however, on the test data, GE, regardless of the constant creating method, does better. However, among themselves, the various GE methods perform equally well on all the criteria. Notably, the genome lengths with digit concatenation are no greater than those with the compact methods. Moreover, using GP-like PRCs does not bridge the gap in training results of GP and GE, which suggests that the key difference between GP and GE is how the respective genetic operators behave. We also conclude that the compact methods are not *effectively* compact, give our reasons for that and give directions for further work.

The rest of the paper is organised as follows: section 2 gives a background to constant creating methods in GE and builds a motivation to this study; section 3 describes the experimental setup, presents the results and discusses the lessons we can learn from these results; finally, section 4 concludes the paper.

2   Background

Digit concatenation with GE [11] [9] requires a CFG with appropriate rules for generating numeric constants. For example, with the grammars below and a rule `<expr> ::= <const> | -<const>`, cat-UnLtd can, in theory, encode any real constant, whereas cat-0-to-5 limits the values to the domain $(-5, 5)$.

cat-UnLtd: cat-0-to-5:

```
<const> ::= <cat>.<cat>            <const>::= <fdig>.<cat>
<cat>   ::= <cat><digit>|<digit>   <cat>   ::= <cat><digit> | <digit>
<digit>::= 0 | 1 | 2 | 3 | 4       <fdig>  ::= 0 | 1 | 2 | 3 | 4
        | 5 | 6 | 7 | 8 | 9        <digit> ::= 0 | 1 | 2 | ... | 9
```

This approach has some side effects. First, the number of codons GE takes to encode a constant is equal to the number of digits in it. Later, crossover can break the constant so that it does not pass on to the offspring intact. This is unlike as in GP, where an ERC is atomic. Thus, a stronger *causality* exists in GP, where offspring are likelier to resemble their parents. In fact, as noted in [6], a small number of ERCs quickly dominate the population, with many appearing multiple times in later generations. This is what initially motivated us to ask if GE can benefit from a more GP-like approach, as it appears as though GP first settles on the constants and then builds structure (functions) around them. Second, GE is free to encode a greater number of digits than that allowed by the underlying machine architecture, and as the machine ignores these additional digits, they provide a bloating opportunity. Thus, the next question is: does digit concatenation produce longer genomes than those with an ERC type approach?

To answer these questions we consider two *compact* representations for GE constants. The first, termed *persistent random constants* (PRCs) [11] embeds randomly generated constants (from a given range) inside the grammar as alternative choices. A single codon can pick a constant by selecting the corresponding rule. Previously digit concatenation outperformed PRCs when the objective was to evolve a single constant [11]. As the second method, we consider a *codon injection* method [15], whereby when the non-terminal `<const>` is read, the following 8 bit codon value is converted into a floating point value in a given range. As in [12, 13], only a single codon produces a numeric constant.

While previous work investigated evolving a fixed constant, this paper concerns the more traditional symbolic regression. We check if compact representations are *effectively* more compact: that is, whether these methods produce higher fitness *and* smaller genomes. We also note results on unseen data to see if any method produces better predictive models.

3   Experiments

For the *best fit* individual we note: score on training data (best fitness); score on unseen (test) data; and genome length. We record genome lengths to compare which method requires more genetic material. Digit concatenation takes multiple codons to create a single constant (unless the constant has just a single digit); likewise, multiple PRCs may combine to create a constant. We record these statistics every generation and present their mean values over 100 independent runs. Moreover, we also record all the statistics with linear scaling.

Also, we use results for GP as a benchmark. Clearly, GP differs from GE in many ways: the genetic representation and genetic operators differ; consequently, we expect some difference in performance. However, since GP is more widely used for symbolic regression, we consider its results to validate the performance of GE. We want to see if the difference in performance is consistent (GP is always better or worse than GE), and whether using a relatively more GP-like approach with PRCs bridges the gap in performances of GP and GE.

We consider five different constant creating methods for GE. These are (legends in brackets): digit concatenation with constants from an infinite real domain (`cat-UnLtd`); digit concatenation with *absolute values* of constants limited to $(0, 5)$ (`cat-0-to-5`); 50 and 25 persistent random constants embedded in the grammar (`50-PRC-0-to-5` and `25-PRC-0-to-5`) also derived from $(0, 5)$; and the codon injection method that directly decodes a GE codon into a numeric value (`codon-0-to-5`). All these methods can also generate negative numbers.

The respective grammars incorporate problem specific input variables and arithmetic operators in a prefix notation.

3.1   Problem Suite and Evolutionary Parameters

All experiments use a population size of 500, roulette wheel selection, steady state replacement and crossover with a probability of 0.9. For GE, we use the conventional [8][16] bit wise mutation with a probability of 0.01, while for GP, we use point mutation with a standard probability value of 0.1 [2]. We use ramped half and half initialisation for GP with an initial maximum tree depth of 4; for GE we use the grammatical counterpart of this initialisation termed *sensible initialisation* [16]. Sensible initialisation uses a context free grammar to generate derivation trees for GE using a ramped half and half approach. We use a maximum initial depth of derivation trees of 10 (which is larger than 4 for GP) since a big derivation tree can still yield a small abstract syntax tree and GE grows trees at a slower rate than with standard GP [9].

Although we do not constrain tree sizes or maximum depth for GP (and GE), in the experiments reported here the average tree size for GP never exceeds 250; this is well below the maximum size allowed by a commonly used maximum tree depth of 17 for binary trees. Another side effect of a maximum tree depth is that it can prohibit extremely deep *skinny* trees. Deep skinny trees can encode a particularly non-linear behaviour which may promote overfitting the training data if the functions set contains unary transcendental functions [17]; however, we only use binary arithmetic functions in this study.

We use six different problems from the symbolic regression domain here. As Keijzer [3] notes, choosing a good set of problems for testing symbolic regression is difficult in the absence of an established set of benchmarks. Like Keijzer, we use the following problems from previous work on symbolic regression.

$$f(x) = 0.3x\sin(2\pi x) \tag{1}$$
$$f(x) = 1 + 3x + 3x^2 + x^3 \tag{2}$$
$$f(x,y) = 8/(2 + x^2 + y^2) \tag{3}$$
$$f(x,y) = x^4 - x^3 + y^2/2 - y \tag{4}$$
$$f(x,y) = x^3/5 + y^3/2 - y - x \tag{5}$$
$$f(x_1, \cdots, x_{10}) = 10.59x_1x_2 + 100.5967x_3x_4 - 50.59x_5x_6 + 20x_1x_7x_9 + 5x_3x_6x_{10} \tag{6}$$

(1) comes from [18]; (2), also termed as *Binomial-3*, is a scalably difficult problem for GP [14] and has been investigated with GE [9]; (3), (4) and (5) come from [4]; and (6), referred to as *Poly-10* in the figures in this paper, is a version of a difficult problem described in [19]. The dimensionality of these problems varies between 1 and 10 and their difficulty to GP type approaches also varies as is visible from the scales of the best fitness plotted in Fig. 1.

We use a variant of the standard one point crossover for GE termed *effective crossover* [15]. Since the entire lengths of GE chromosomes may not be used for mapping, the non-mapping regions in GE chromosomes can grow larger and larger; this transforms crossover into a duplication operator as crossing over in the non-mapping regions does not innovate in the phenotype space. Therefore, the effective crossover restricts the crossover point to within the mapping regions.

As noted in [3], protected division (and protected operators in general) can lead GP to producing models that do not generalise well to unseen data; therefore, we do not use protected division. Instead, in the case of a division by zero, we penalise the offending individual by assigning it the worst fitness value of 0.0.

All the GE experiments use libGE [15], while the GP experiments use TinyGP[1]. Evolutionary runs terminate after completing 50 generations. GP uses 50 constants from the domain $(-5, 5)$ and like GE, only uses arithmetic operators.

For each problem, we randomly initialise input variables between -1.5 and 1.5 and generate 100 data points. We randomly choose 50 data points for training and an equal number of data points for testing on unseen data (test data).

3.2   Results

Figures 1-4 plot the results of the experiments. The x-axis consistently corresponds to 50 generations. The training and test scores are sums of squared errors (SSE) normalised between 0.0 and 1.0 (1.0 being the ideal score) as follows: $score = \frac{1}{1+SSE}$. Each sampled point in the plots depicts an average over 100 independent runs. As in [20], the 95% confidence limits of the error bars at each point are computed as follows: $\overline{X} \pm 1.96\frac{\sigma}{\sqrt{n}}$, where $\overline{X}$ and σ are the mean and standard deviation of n observations; $n = 100$ represents the number of runs in this case. We can be 95% confident that the statistical population lies within these limits, and that a lack of overlap with another error bar means that the corresponding populations are different.

---

[1] http://cswww.essex.ac.uk/staff/rpoli/TinyGP/

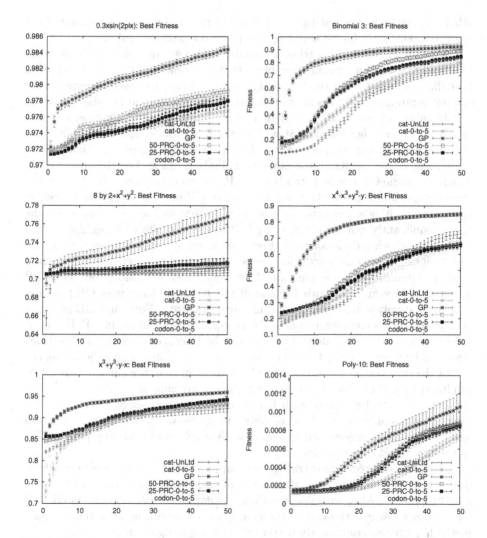

Fig. 1. This figure plots mean of best fitness achieved per generation for all the problems. No GE setup wins or loses consistently. On four problems, GP is significantly better than any GE method.

Figures 1-3 plot the results for experiments without using linear scaling. Fig. 1 plots the best fitness on *training* data and shows that none of the GE constant creating setups stands out consistently. In fact, various GE methods do quite similarly. Moreover, GP does at least as well as GE (and usually better). Also, using the PRCs does not bring GE any closer to GP.

Of particular interest is `cat-UnLtd`: unlike all other methods, GE chooses from an infinite domain of constants. Except for problem (6), a domain of [-5,5] is suitable and even advantageous. However, `cat_UnLtd` does no worse than the other GE methods, suggesting that the larger range of constants available (and the correspondingly larger search space) poses no extra difficulty.

For problem (6) we also tried a domain of [-49,49] to assist methods other than `cat-UnLtd` in approximating important constants of 100 and 50 but even that did not change the relative performances; owing to space constraints we can not reproduce those results in this paper. Results also do not show that the brittle nature of constants with digit concatenation when facing crossover is a disadvantage any more than that with compact methods: both `cat_UnLtd` and `cat-0-to-5` perform competitively with respect to the compact methods.

Fig. 2 plots the results for the same individuals as in Fig. 1 on the unseen data. Again, no single GE method stands out. GP, however, changes behaviour on the unseen data: unlike on the training data where GP performed at *least* as well as GE methods, it now performs only at *most* as well as GE methods, and some times significantly worse. Again, using PRCs does not affect GE significantly.

Next, we check if digit concatenation costs more by requiring longer genomes. Fig. 3 plots the genome lengths for the best fit individuals and shows that again digit concatenation is no worse than the compact methods. Moreover, while GP genomes clearly grow towards the end of the runs, the lengths of GE genomes remain relatively stable after an initial growth or drop. Note that GE genomes encode derivation trees instead of abstract syntax trees (ASTs) in GP. However, the set of leaves of a GE derivation tree can be interpreted as an AST and this AST can be much smaller than the corresponding derivation tree; hence, at the end of the runs the ASTs encoded by GE derivation trees are smaller than those produced by GP even when the genome lengths are similar.

Next, we consider results with linear scaling. Due to space restrictions, we present results only on test data; we only summarise the results on training data and omit those on genome lengths because their relative trends are quite similar to those without linear scaling.

While, as expected, linear scaling helps improve best fitness for all the setups during training, the relative performances of various GE methods remain mutually competitive. Also, with linear scaling, the gap in the performance of GP and GE narrows towards the end of the run; however, again, none of the compact methods performs consistently better or worse than digit concatenation.

The scores on test data in Fig. 4 are also similar to those without linear scaling: again, all of the various GE setups perform competitively; similarly, GP performs at most as well as GE on the unseen data.

3.3 Discussion

The results from section 3.2 show that with the given evolutionary parameters and data sets, GE performs equally well with a variety of constant creating methods; however, GE differs significantly from GP. We only compared with GP to check if there is enough reason to improve GE so it can match the more widely prevalent method, that is, GP. The best fitness results, particularly without linear scaling, show that GP *trains* better than GE; however, it does so at the cost of degrading test set results. This is not altogether surprising given the growing

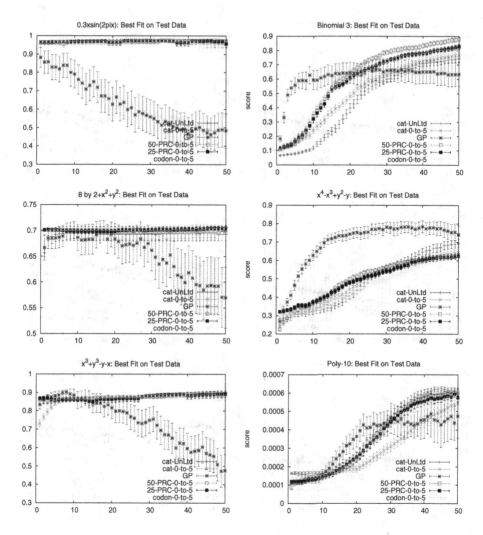

Fig. 2. This figure plots mean of Test Score per generation corresponding to Best-Fit individuals reported in Figure 1. No GE setup wins or loses consistently. On three problems, performance consistently degrades for GP.

GP literature which aims to improve performance on unseen data [17] [18]. What is surprising, however, is that GE does so much better, at least on these problems.

The real focus of this work, however, is on comparing various constant creating methods with GE. Digit concatenation is natural and easy to implement with GE; however, it can take many codons to encode a single constant. As a result, GE has to find a right sequence of codons and then ensure that crossover does not break that sequence. Moreover, with the ripple crossover [10] in GE, constants can not always transfer intact from the parent to offspring. However, the results

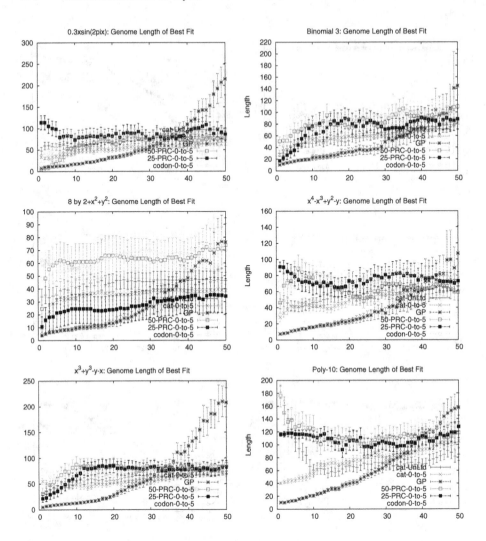

Fig. 3. This figure plots the mean genome lengths of the best fit individuals reported in Figure 1. No GE setup maintains significantly different lengths.

here show that the compact methods (PRCs and codon injection) do not *train* better than digit concatenation; this agrees with results in [9] [11]. However, on a greater set of problems, we additionally find that compact methods produce neither smaller genomes (surprisingly) nor better test set results.

The question then is: why does digit concatenation work as well as the other methods? There can be two reasons. First, even with the compact methods if the desired constant is not available, evolution combines various constants to get the right one. Thus, PRCs, or ERCs in GP, are not always less *breakable* with crossover. Secondly, [21, pp151-153] showed for a symbolic regression problem

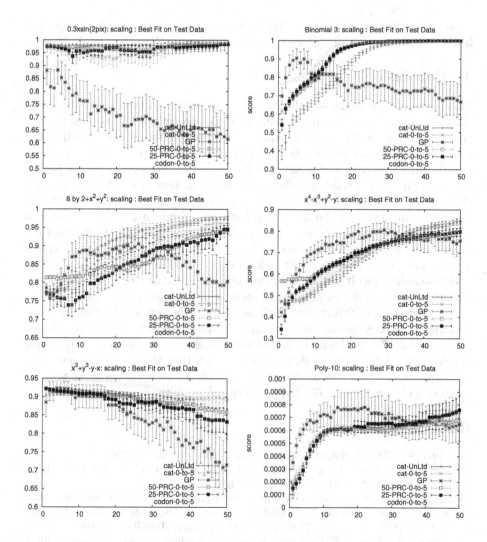

Fig. 4. (With Linear Scaling): this figure plots mean of Test Score per generation for the Best-Fit individuals. No GE setup wins or loses consistently.

that crossover mostly produces offspring with significantly worse fitness values. Also, [6] showed that even with a careful numeric mutation that only slightly changes the constants in a GP tree, crossover does no better than with random mutation that uniformly replaces a constant from within a given range. Despite that GP trains well in this paper. This suggests that passing constants from the parents to offspring is not crucial to GP: after all, even a constant ideal for a parent may be totally unsuitable for the offspring.

Therefore, to improve the performance of GE on symbolic regression there are two ways forward. First, find a crossover operator that recombines individuals in a more favourable way, although this issue is not unique to just GE. The second is to assist the genetic operators with numerical methods such as in [3] [4] [5].

4   Conclusions

This paper compares the so-called digit concatenation method of creating constants in Grammatical Evolution with what this paper calls the compact methods to creating constants. The paper raises two questions: first, whether the constants with digit concatenation are so brittle against crossover that taking a more GP-like approach to constants with compact methods improves the performance of GE; and second, whether digit concatenation breeds longer genomes than those with compact methods. The results from the problems considered in this paper suggest that the answer to both the aforementioned questions is a resounding no. Because compact representations may also have to *synthesise* a constant when a suitable one is not available, we hypothesise that these constants are also not robust enough to outperform digit concatenation.

A fascinating result is that, although GP outperforms GE on training data, GE actually does substantially better on unseen test data.

The next steps in this research will be to do further critical evaluation of the performance of GE on test data, as well as its ability to generalise. In particular, work such as [17] [18] should be added to GE to ascertain if GE enjoys the same benefits that GP does from them. Finally, given that the desruptive nature of GE's crossover appears to be extremely valuable for generalisation, we propose creating a GP equivalent, *GPRipple*, which will have the same operation.

References

1. Mitchell, T.M.: Machine learning. McGraw Hill, New York (1996)
2. Koza, J.R.: Genetic Programming: On the Programming of Computers by Means of Natural Selection. MIT Press, Cambridge (1992)
3. Keijzer, M.: Improving symbolic regression with interval arithmetic and linear scaling. In: Ryan, C., Soule, T., Keijzer, M., Tsang, E.P.K., Poli, R., Costa, E. (eds.) EuroGP 2003. LNCS, vol. 2610, pp. 70–82. Springer, Heidelberg (2003)
4. Topchy, A., Punch, W.F.: Faster genetic programming based on local gradient search of numeric leaf values. In: Spector, et al. (eds.) Proceedings of the Genetic and Evolutionary Computation Conference (GECCO 2001), July 7-11, pp. 155–162. Morgan Kaufmann, San Francisco (2001)
5. McKay, B., Willis, M., Searson, D., Montague, G.: Non-linear continuum regression using genetic programming. In: Banzhaf, et al. (eds.) Proceedings of GECCO 1999, Orlando, Florida, USA, July 13-17, vol. 2, pp. 1106–1111. Morgan Kaufmann (1999)
6. Ryan, C., Keijzer, M.: An analysis of diversity of constants of genetic programming. In: Ryan, C., Soule, T., Keijzer, M., Tsang, E.P.K., Poli, R., Costa, E. (eds.) EuroGP 2003. LNCS, vol. 2610, pp. 404–413. Springer, Heidelberg (2003)
7. Evett, M., Fernandez, T.: Numeric mutation improves the discovery of numeric constants in genetic programming. In: Koza, et al. (eds.) Genetic Programming 1998: Proceedings of the Third Annual Conference, University of Wisconsin, Madison, Wisconsin, July 22-25, pp. 66–71. Morgan Kaufmann (1998)

8. O'Neill, M., Ryan, C.: Grammatical Evolution: Evolutionary Automatic Programming in a Arbitrary Language. Genetic programming, vol. 4. Kluwer Academic Publishers (2003)

9. Byrne, J., O'Neill, M., Hemberg, E., Brabazon, A.: Analysis of constant creation techniques on the binomial-3 problem with grammatical evolution. In: Tyrrell, et al. (eds.) 2009 IEEE Congress on Evolutionary Computation, Trondheim, Norway, May 18-21, pp. 568–573. IEEE Computational Intelligence Society, IEEE Press (2009)

10. O'Neill, M., Ryan, C., Keijzer, M., Cattolico, M.: Crossover in grammatical evolution. Genetic Programming and Evolvable Machines 4(1), 67–93 (2003)

11. Dempsey, I., O'Neill, M., Brabazon, A.: Constant creation in grammatical evolution. International Journal of Innovative Comput. and Applic. 1(1), 23–38 (2007)

12. Augusto, D.A., Barbosa, H.J.C., Barreto, A.M.S., Bernardino, H.S.: Evolving numerical constants in grammatical evolution with the ephemeral constant method. In: Antunes, L., Pinto, H.S. (eds.) EPIA 2011. LNCS, vol. 7026, pp. 110–124. Springer, Heidelberg (2011)

13. Augusto, D.A., Barbosa, H.J.C., Barreto, A.M.S., Bernardino, H.S.: A new approach for generating numerical constants in grammatical evolution. In: Krasnogor, et al. (eds.) GECCO 2011: Proceedings of the 13th Annual Conference Companion on GECCO, Dublin, Ireland, July 12-16, pp. 193–194. ACM (2011)

14. Daida, J.M., Bertram, R.R., Stanhope, S.A., Khoo, J.C., Chaudhary, S.A., Chaudhri, O.A., Polito II, J.A.: What makes a problem GP-hard? Analysis of a tunably difficult problem in genetic programming. Genetic Programming and Evolvable Machines 2(2), 165–191 (2001)

15. Nicolau, M., Slattery, D.: libGE - Grammatical Evolution Library (2006)

16. Ryan, C., Azad, R.M.A.: Sensible initialisation in grammatical evolution. In: Barry, A.M. (ed.) GECCO 2003: Proceedings of the Bird of a Feather Workshops, Genetic and Evolutionary Computation Conference, Chigaco, pp. 142–145. AAAI (July 2003)

17. Vladislavleva, E.J., Smits, G.F., den Hertog, D.: Order of nonlinearity as a complexity measure for models generated by symbolic regression via pareto genetic programming. IEEE Trans. on Evolutionary Computation 13(2), 333–349 (2009)

18. Keijzer, M., Babovic, V.: Genetic programming, ensemble methods and the bias/variance tradeoff - introductory investigations. In: Poli, R., Banzhaf, W., Langdon, W.B., Miller, J., Nordin, P., Fogarty, T.C. (eds.) EuroGP 2000. LNCS, vol. 1802, pp. 76–90. Springer, Heidelberg (2000)

19. Poli, R.: A simple but theoretically-motivated method to control bloat in genetic programming. In: Ryan, C., Soule, T., Keijzer, M., Tsang, E.P.K., Poli, R., Costa, E. (eds.) EuroGP 2003. LNCS, vol. 2610, pp. 204–217. Springer, Heidelberg (2003)

20. Costelloe, D., Ryan, C.: On improving generalisation in genetic programming. In: Vanneschi, L., Gustafson, S., Moraglio, A., De Falco, I., Ebner, M. (eds.) EuroGP 2009. LNCS, vol. 5481, pp. 61–72. Springer, Heidelberg (2009)

21. Banzhaf, W., Nordin, P., Keller, R.E., Francone, F.D.: Genetic Programming – An Introduction; On the Automatic Evolution of Computer Programs and its Applications. Morgan Kaufmann, San Francisco (1998)

Asynchronous Evolution
by Reference-Based Evaluation:
Tertiary Parent Selection and Its Archive

Tomohiro Harada[1,2] and Keiki Takadama[1]

[1] The University of Electro-Communications,
1-5-1 Chofugaoka, Chofu, Tokyo, Japan
[2] Research Fellow of the Japan Society for the Promotion of Science DC, Japan
harada@cas.hc.uec.ac.jp, keiki@inf.uec.ac.jp
http://cas.hc.uec.ac.jp

Abstract. This paper proposes a novel *asynchronous reference-based evaluation* (named as ARE) for an asynchronous EA that evolves individuals independently unlike general EAs that evolve all individuals at the same time. ARE is designed for an asynchronous evolution by tertiary parent selection and its archive. In particular, ARE asynchronously evolves individuals through a comparison with only three of individuals (i.e., two parents and one *reference* individual as the tertiary parent). In addition, ARE builds an archive of good *reference* individuals. This differ from synchronous evolution in EAs in which selection involves comparison with all population members. In this paper, we investigate the effectiveness of ARE, by applying it to some standard problems used in Linear GP that aim being to minimize the execution step of machine-code programs. We compare GP using ARE (ARE-GP) with steady state (synchronous) GP (SSGP) and our previous asynchronous GP (Tierra-based Asynchronous GP: TAGP). The experimental results have revealed that ARE-GP not only asynchronously evolves the machine-code programs, but also outperforms SSGP and TAGP in all test problems.

Keywords: Genetic programming, asynchronous evolution, machine-code program.

1 Introduction

In general Evolutionary Algorithms (EAs) typified as Genetic Algorithm (GA) [1] and Genetic Programming (GP) [2] evolve individuals (solutions) by repeating a *generation* step. This approach waits for evaluations of all individuals and generates a next population through the parent selection and the individual deletion. This requires that all individuals are evaluated at the same time, i.e., it requires to wait for the slowest evaluation of a certain individual when the evaluation time of individuals differ from each other, which consumes a heavy computational time. To tackle this problem, *asynchronous* approaches have recently been proposed [3][4], that evolves individuals independently, i.e., individuals do not have to wait for the

M. Nicolau et al. (Eds.): EuroGP 2014, LNCS 8599, pp. 198–209, 2014.

evaluations of other individuals. As GP employing the asynchronous approach, we have proposed TAGP (Tierra-based Asynchronous Genetic Programming) [5] as one kind of machine-code GP based on the idea of a biological simulator, Tierra [6]. The advantages employing the asynchronous approach for machine-code GP are summarized as follows: (1) it can continue to evolve individuals (programs) even if individuals cannot complete their evaluation (e.g., due to an infinite loop), because it is not required to wait for the evaluation of all individuals, and (2) it increases the chance of selecting quickly evaluated individuals by evolving them immediately after completing their evaluations.

Our previous research [5] reported that TAGP can asynchronously evolve the machine-code programs even if they include loop structure. However, TAGP has the following two essential problems: (1) Unlike general EAs, TAGP cannot guarantee to select good individuals as the parents from a population, which prevents performance improvements, (2) since TAGP selects individuals as the parents or deletes them depending on a threshold based on an absolute evaluation, it is difficult to properly evolve individuals in the case that a proper threshold cannot be determined.

To overcome these problems, this paper proposes a novel asynchronous reference-based evaluation (named as ARE) for an asynchronous EA by *tertiary* parent selection and its *archive*, which not only inherits the advantage of TAGP but also overcomes its weak points.

In particular, in ARE, an *archive* mechanism employed which preserves good individuals to improve the performance. Parent are selected and individuals are deleted asynchronously through a comparison of the two parents with the *tertiary* parent that is randomly selected from an archive of good individuals. This step checks whether two parents are bad individuals. This is called a *reference-based evaluation*, a relative evaluation, which does not require a threshold as an absolute evaluation like TAGP. To investigate the effectiveness of ARE, this paper applies it to the Linear GP problems and compares GP using ARE (ARE-GP) with steady-state GP (SSGP) [7] as the synchronous GP and with TAGP as the asynchronous GP.

This paper is organized as follows. Section 2 introduces TAGP that we proposed and explains its problems. Section 3 proposes the novel asynchronous reference-based evaluation for an asynchronous EAs. Section 4 conducts the experiments for comparing the results of ARE-GP with those of SSGP and TAGP, and discuss their results. Finally, our conclusion is given in Section 5.

2   Tierra-Based Asynchronous Genetic Programming

2.1   Overview

TAGP (Tierra-based Asynchronous Genetic Programming) [5] is a kind of machine-code GP employing the asynchronous approach. TAGP is based on the idea of a biological simulator, Tierra [6]. It uses a system like Tierra to evolve programs that solves given tasks. Unlike Tierra, TAGP introduces fitness and executes parent selection and mechanisms that delete individuals based on fitness.

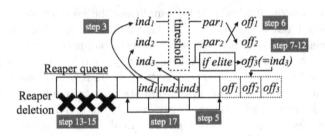

Fig. 1. An illustration of TAGP

2.2   Algorithm

Fig 1 shows an illustration of TAGP, while Algorithm 1 explains it further. In Algorithm 1, ind indicates an individual just after evaluation, $ind.f$ and $ind.f_{acc}$ respectively indicate the fitness and a fitness accumulated through a repeated evaluation process of ind, and MAX_POP indicates the maximum population size. All individuals are stored in a queue named as *reaper queue*. Firstly, each individual is evaluated in (pseudo-)parallel (step 1), and it accumulates its fitness to $ind.f_{acc}$, when its evaluation completes (step 2). If its accumulated fitness exceeds a certain threshold (e.g., the maximum fitness in Algorithm 1), the threshold is subtracted from the accumulated fitness and it generates offspring(step 3-6). For example, if the accumulated fitness of ind_1 and ind_3 exceed the threshold (the maximum fitness), they generate offspring in the genetic operators as shown in Fig. 1. And if ind has the maximum fitness and it is better than the individual that previously has the maximum fitness, ind is replicated as an *elite* individual without any genetic operations in order to preserve the good individuals in the population (step 7-12). For example, if ind_3 has the maximum fitness, it is replicated as the elite individual as shown in Fig. 1. The position of each individual in the queue changes depending on whether an individual can generate offspring or not. If an individual generate offspring, its position in the queue shifts toward lower (step 5), otherwise its position shifts toward upper (step 17). For example, in Fig. 1, since ind_1 and ind_3 generate their offspring, their positions in the queue shift toward lower, while since ind_2 cannot generate offspring, its position shifts toward upper. If the population size exceeds the maximum population size, the reaper queue mechanism removes the individual located at the top in the reaper queue (step 13-14). For example, when three offspring are added as shown in Fig 1, three individuals at the top of the reaper queue is removed.

The main feature of TAGP is summarized as follows: (1) Each individual in TAGP can be asynchronously evolved without waiting for other evaluation because the parents are selected to evolve their offspring only depending on their accumulated fitness, i.e., such parent selection is executed when the accumulated fitness of an individual exceeds a certain threshold, and (2) the reaper queue mechanism in TAGP can remove an individual that requires huge evaluation

---

Algorithm 1. An algorithm of TAGP

---

1. Evaluating fitness of ind $(ind.f)$
2. $ind.f_{acc} \leftarrow ind.f_{acc} + ind.f$
3. **if** $ind.f_{acc} \geq f_{max}$ **then**
4. $ind.f_{acc} \leftarrow ind.f_{acc} - f_{max}$
5.   Shifting the position of ind toward lower
6.   Generating offspring of ind
7.   **if** $ind.f = f_{max}$ **then**
8.   **if** $ind.f$ is better than $ind_{elite}.f$ **then**
9.   Replicate ind without genetic operations
10.   **end if**
11. $ind_{elite} \leftarrow ind$
12.   **end if**
13.   **if** Population size>MAX_POP **then**
14.   Removing the individual at the top of the queue
15.   **end if**
16. **else**
17.   Shifting the position of ind toward upper
18. **end if**

---

time or does not complete its evaluation (e.g., because of an infinite loop) *before* completing its evaluation.

3   Asynchronous Reference-Based Evaluation

This paper proposes a novel *asynchronous reference-based evaluation* (named as ARE) for an asynchronous EA, which not only inherits the advantages of TAGP but also overcomes the problems of TAGP. In this section, we firstly explain the main concept of ARE, and then its algorithm.

3.1   Concept

The main concept of ARE is based on (1) the preservation of good individuals (i.e., *archive*) and (2) the deletion of bad individuals with quick evaluation with the *relative* evaluation which does not require a threshold as an *absolute* evaluation like in TAGP. Regarding the first issue (i.e., the good individuals preservation), it is generally difficult to guarantee to preserve the good individual in a population due to an asynchronous manner, which means that good individuals are not always to be selected as parents for an evolution. To keep good individuals, the *archive* is employed to preserve good individuals in ARE while deleting the individuals that (a) have low fitness or (b) require a huge evaluation time (or do not complete their evaluation). From the viewpoint of the low fitness, if the individuals are worse than the reference individual (described in the next paragraph), they become candidates for the deletion. From the viewpoint of the huge evaluation time, on the other hand, the reaper queue

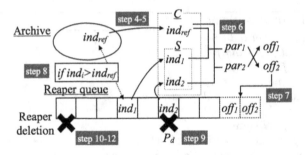

Fig. 2. An illustration of ARE

is employed to determine the individual that should be deleted using the same mechanism as TAGP.

Regarding the second issue (i.e., the deletion of bad individuals with quick evaluation with the *relative* evaluation), what should be noted here is that, in the asynchronous evaluation, the individuals that have high fitness are regarded as good like the general EAs, while individuals that complete their evaluation are also regarded as good. However, the individuals that quickly complete their evaluation do not always have good fitness. Due to such a feature, the individuals with quick evaluation are preferentially selected as parents regardless of its fitness. This results in the population being filled with offspring generated by such parent, and it is easy to fall into local optima through this kind of an evolution. To avoid such a situation, all individuals are compared with a high fitness individual that has already completed its evaluation. This is called the *tertiary* or *reference* individual. If they are worse than the reference individual, they are not selected as parents. This contributes to selecting the good individuals by excluding bad individuals whose evaluation time is short. In ARE, an evaluation based on a comparison with a reference individual is called as *relative* evaluation, which does not require a threshold as an *absolute* evaluation. Concretely, the parent selection and the individual deletion are asynchronously executed to evolve individuals through a comparison of the offspring with the *reference* individual.

Finally, the main difference between ARE and TAGP is summarized as follows: (1) TAGP requires the accumulated fitness and the selection threshold f_{max}, while ARE does not require these conditions, i.e., any fitness function in ARE can be employed like general EAs. This means that ARE can be applied to the problems where an optimal solution is unknown, and (2) TAGP does not have the archive mechanism, while ARE has it to guarantee to maintain the good individuals in the archive. This mechanism increases the selection pressure for better individuals by excluding bad individuals.

3.2 Algorithm

Fig. 2 shows an illustration of ARE, while Algorithm 2 explains it further. In Algorithm 2, *ind* indicates an individual just after evaluation. All individuals

---

Algorithm 2. An algorithm of ARE

1. Evaluating fitness of ind $(ind.f)$
2. $S \leftarrow ind$
3. **if** $|S| = 2$ **then**
4.   Randomly selecting ind_{ref} from archive
5. $C \leftarrow S \cup \{ind_{ref}\}$
6.   Selecting two individuals from C and generating offspring
7.   Adding offspring into the bottom of the reaper queue
8.   Replacing ind_{ref} with an individual in S that is better than ind_{ref}
9.   Removing individuals in S that is worse than ind_{ref} in the probability P_d
10.   **if** Population size>MAX_POP **then**
11.   Removing individuals depending on the reaper queue
12.   **end if**
13. $S \leftarrow \phi$
14. **end if**

---

are stored in either the reaper queue or the archive. Like TAGP, in ARE, the individuals are evaluated in (pseudo-)parallel (step 1), and the parent individuals are selected when two individuals complete their evaluations (here we call them *temporally-selected individuals*). One of the unique aspects of ARE, is that parent selection is done by the tournament selection from the temporally-selected individuals (S in Algorithm 2) and the reference individual (ind_{ref} in Algorithm 2) that is randomly selected from the archive (step 4-6) (Note that two individuals (not three) are selected in TAGP). This mechanism guarantees that individuals with high fitness will be mated with. After the parent selection, the two offspring generated from the two selected parents are added into the bottom of the reaper queue (step 7).

Other unique aspects of ARE are the use of an archive mechanism that preserves good individuals and the deletion mechanism limit the archive size. In order to determine the individuals that should be archived or should be deleted, the temporally-selected individuals are compared with the reference individual. If one of the temporally-selected individuals is better than the reference individual, it is archived and the reference individual change its position to the bottom of the reaper queue alternatively (step 8). To maintain the diversity of the individuals in the archive, if the better temporally-selected individual already exists in the archive and the reference individual is unique in the archive, they are not replaced each other. For example, if ind_1 is better than ind_{ref}, ind_1 is archived and ind_{ref} is added to the bottom of the reaper queue as shown in Fig. 2. This mechanism guarantees to preserve the good individuals in the archive. On the other hand, if the temporally-selected individuals are worse than the reference individual, they are removed from the reaper queue with a certain probability P_d (step 9) (This deletion is called *fitness deletion*, and the probability P_d is called *fitness deletion probability*). For example, if ind_2 is worse than ind_{ref}, ind_2 is removed from the reaper queue with the probability P_d with the fitness deletion as shown in Fig 2.

If the temporally-selected individuals are not removed and the population size exceeds the maximum population size, the reaper queue mechanism removes the individual located at the top of the reaper queue (step 10-11) (Afterward this deletion is called *reaper deletion*). For example, when two offspring are added but only one individual (ind_2) is removed as shown in Fig. 2, one individual at the top of the reaper queue is additionally removed with the reaper deletion.

What should be noted here is that the fitness deletion probability P_d determines the ratio between the fitness deletion and the reaper deletion. In particular, when P_d is higher, the fitness deletion is increasingly executed, while the reaper deletion is decreasingly executed. On the other hand, when P_d is lower, the fitness deletion is decreasingly executed, while the reaper deletion is increasingly executed. Since a lot of individuals are removed before their evaluations completes if the reaper deletion increases, P_d can control how long the reaper deletion waits for the individuals that require long evaluation time.

4   Experiment

4.1   Settings

To investigate the effectiveness of ARE, we apply ARE to Linear GP (LGP) [8][9] using the machine code which we used in our previous research, and conduct experiments to compare GP using ARE (ARE-GP) with steady-state GP (SSGP) [7] as the asynchronous GP and TAGP as the asynchronous GP. The reason why we employ LGP is that an individual (program) in LGP has variable length chromosome and evaluation time of each individual generally differ from each other. Furthermore, since a machine-code program has probability to include the loop structure, individuals that include the infinite loop and do not complete their evaluation can be generated.

Our machine-code programs use the instruction set of the PIC10 [10] embedded processor developed by Microchip Technology Inc. It has 33, 12 bit instructions. These include addition, subtraction, Boolean logic, bitwise, and branch instructions. It does not include multiplication. For this reason, multiplication has to be achieved by repeating addition and bitwise operations in loop structures. A program can use any of 16 general purpose registers and one register (named working register). Each register consists of 32bits.

Test problems in this experiment are shown in Table 1. The problems are classified two types, one is Arithmetic problems that requires numeric calculations, and another is Boolean problem that requires logical calculation. In particular since Arithmetic problems require multiplication that is achieved with loop structures, they has high probability to generate programs that include infinite loops. In this experiment, the aim is to evolve program that minimize the time taken by the execution step by starting from an initial program that completely accomplishes the given task.

Table 1. Test problems in this experiment

Arithmetic		#data	Boolean		#data
A1	$f(x) = x^4 + x^3 + x^2 + x$	16	B1-2	{5,8}bit-Parity	{32,256}
A2	$f(x) = x^5 - 2x^3 + x$	16	B3-4	{5,7}bit-DigitalAdder	{32,128}
A3	$f(x) = x^6 - 2x^4 + x^2$	16	B5	6bit-Multiplexer	64
A4	$f(x,y) = x^y$	25	B6	7bit-Majority	128

Table 2. Parameters

Parameter	value	Parameter	value
#evaluations	10^6	Crossover rate	0.7
Max. program size	256	Mutation rate	0.1
Pop. size	100	Insertion rate	0.1
f_{max}	100	Deletion rate	0.1

The following fitness functions are respectively employed for Arithmetic and for Boolean:

$$f_{arith} = f_{max} - \frac{1}{n}\sum_{i=1}^{n}|\hat{y}_i - y_i^*| \tag{1}$$

$$f_{bool} = f_{max} - \frac{2}{n}\sum_{i=1}^{n}\delta(\hat{y}_i, y_i^*), \delta(x,y) = \begin{cases} 1 & x = y \\ 0 & x \neq y \end{cases}, \tag{2}$$

where $\hat{y}_i$ indicates the ith output value of a program, while y_i^* indicates the ith target value. Note that the reason why the sum of difference is subtracted from f_{max} is that TAGP employs the parent selection depending on the accumulated fitness. Although ARE-GP and SSGP do not require such transformation, this experiment uses same fitness function. Individuals are compared in order of (1) fitness, (2) execution step, and (3) program size.

Common parameters in all GPs are shown in Table 2. The crossover combines two programs at two different crossover point, while the mutation randomly changes one random instruction in a program. The instruction insertion inserts one random instruction into random point, while the instruction deletion remove one random instruction from a program. In SSGP, the maximum execution step is set to 50,000, and if a program does not complete in this limit, its fitness is evaluated as $-\infty$.

All experiments start from filling the population with an initial program. Each experiment is conducted 30 independent trials, and we evaluate GPs regarding the average execution step after the maximum number of evaluations.

4.2 Results

Table 3 shows the average execution step of the best program in the population after the maximum number of evaluations. In Table 3, all results are normalized by the average execution step of TAGP, i.e., the result of TAGP is 1 in

Table 3. Averages of the minimum execution step after the maximum evaluations (normalized by the result of TAGP). ARE-GP changes the archive size as {5, 10, 20, 30}.

Problem	SSGP	ARE-GP archive size			
		5	10	20	30
A1	1.415	**0.852**	0.860	0.960	1.018
A2	1.429	**0.881**	0.883	0.964	1.120
A3	1.463	**0.863**	0.934	1.026	1.173
A4	0.976	0.881	**0.872**	0.919	0.903
B1	**0.954**	0.974	0.956	0.993	1.019
B2	1.007	0.991	**0.979**	0.986	1.023
B3	1.055	0.972	**0.967**	0.985	0.986
B4	1.024	0.965	**0.953**	0.965	0.968
B5	1.582	**0.864**	0.901	0.924	0.918
B6	1.174	0.891	0.909	**0.820**	0.990

Table 4. Averages of the minimum execution step after the maximum evaluations (normalized by the result of TAGP). ARE-GP changes the fitness deletion probability P_d as {0.1, 0.3, 0.5, 0.7, 0.9}, and the archive size is 5 ($P_d = 0.5$ is the same as Table. 3).

Problem	ARE-GP fitness deletion probability P_d				
	0.1	0.3	0.5	0.7	0.9
A1	2.273	0.880	0.852	**0.817**	0.868
A2	2.401	0.881	0.881	0.863	**0.836**
A3	2.607	0.886	0.863	**0.862**	0.880
A4	3.615	3.615	**0.881**	0.931	1.132
B1	0.974	0.976	0.974	0.954	**0.942**
B2	1.018	0.973	0.991	**0.956**	0.982
B3	0.977	0.973	**0.972**	0.988	0.979
B4	0.965	0.958	0.965	0.963	**0.955**
B5	**0.857**	0.883	0.864	0.887	0.891
B6	**0.890**	1.025	0.891	0.965	0.917

all problems, and the best result (the shortest execution step) in each problem is indicated as **bold** style. In ARE-GP, we confirm different archive sizes $5, 10, 20$, and 30. From these results, it is easily confirmed that ARE-GP can asynchronously evolve programs using only relative evaluation and without the thresholds required in TAGP. Furthermore, it is revealed that ARE-GP outperforms TAGP in all problems. In particular small archive size such as 5 and 10 reliably gives better performance. The reason why large archive size such as 30 is not good is that since ARE avoids overlap of programs in the archive, low fitness programs remain in the archive and the selection pressure depending on the reference program decreases. From this fact, it is indicated that the archive size should be set as small size.

To verify the effect of the difference of the fitness deletion probability P_d, we confirm different probability $0.1, 0.3, 0.5, 0.7$, and 0.9. Here the archive size is set as 5, and $P_d = 0.5$ results the same as the previous one. The results are shown in Table 4, where all results are also normalized by the result of TAGP, and the best result in each problem is indicated as **bold** style.

From these results, it is revealed that high fitness deletion probability such as $P_d \geq 0.5$ is effective in most problems, while, in all Arithmetic problems,

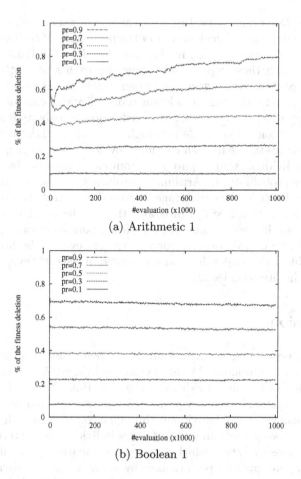

(a) Arithmetic 1

(b) Boolean 1

Fig. 3. Percentage of the fitness deletion, where the archive size is 5, and $P_d = 0.5$

small probability $P_d = 0.1$ is worse than the results of TAGP. Actually, these cases hardly evolve programs from the initial program. Arithmetic problems requires loop structures to achieve multiplication, in particular Arithmetic 2 include double loops to calculate x^y. If the loop structures are broken with the genetic operation, offspring lose the loops and they quickly complete their evaluation. Such programs succumb to reaper deletion so most programs that include loops are removed before their evaluation. To wait loop calculation and to remove programs that are evaluated to quickly, we have found a high fitness deletion probability to be effective.

As mentioned above, the fitness deletion probability P_d determines the ratio between the fitness deletion and the reaper deletion. Fig. 3 shows the change of the ratio of the fitness deletion that is calculated as $\%_{cp} = \#del_{cp}/(\#del_{cp} + \#del_{rp})$, where p_{cp} indicates the percentage of the fitness deletion, while $\#del_{cp}$ and $\#del_{rp}$ respectively indicate the number of the fitness deletion and the reaper deletion in a certain evaluations. In Fig. 3, the horizontal axes show the number of evaluations, while the vertical axes show the percentage of the fitness deletion. Each line shows the average $\%_{cp}$ in the case that $P_d = \{0.1, 0.3, 0.5, 0.7, 0.9\}$. Note that although these figures only show the results of Arithmetic 1 and Boolean 1, we confirm same trend in all other problems in each problem type.

From these results, the fitness deletion probability can controls the ratio of two deletions. In particular, when the fitness deletion probability is low, the ratio of the fitness deletion is low, while it is high, the ratio of the fitness deletion is high. This indicates that ARE can consider how long the reaper queue deletion waits for the individuals that require huge computational time by changing the fitness deletion probability. In Arithmetic problems, the percentage of the fitness deletion is lower in the early stage of evolution even if the fitness deletion probability is high. At this stage, programs that are better than the archive is easily evolved, so the replacement between a temporally-selected program and an archived program often occurs. For this reason, even if the fitness deletion probability is high, the reaper deletion is executed in the early evolution because of decreasing the fitness deletion.

5   Conclusion

This paper proposed a novel *asynchronous reference-based evaluation* (named as ARE) for an asynchronous EA that evolves individuals independently unlike general EAs that evolve all individuals at the same time. ARE is designed for an asynchronous evolution by tertiary parent selection and its archive. In particular, ARE asynchronously evolve individuals through a comparison with only three of individuals (i.e., two parents and one *reference* individual as the tertiary parent) unlike synchronous evolution which involves a comparison with all population members. ARE improves its performance by archiving good individuals as the *reference* individual. To investigate the effectiveness of ARE, this paper applies it to the Linear GP (LGP) problems. We have conducted experiments that aim to minimize the execution step of machine-code programs. An experiment comparison of ARE-GP with steady-state GP (SSGP) as the synchronous GP and our previous GP (Tierra-based asynchronous GP: TAGP) as the asynchronous GP, produced the following implications: (1) ARE-GP asynchronously successfully evolved machine-code programs, showing that ARE-GP does not require the thresholds of TAGP, (2) ARE-GP outperformed TAGP in all test problems, in particular, smaller archive size in ARE-GP reliably gives better performance

What should be noticed here is that these results have only been obtained from one type of problem, i.e., Linear GP. Therefore, further careful qualifications and justification, such as an analysis of results using other general LGP problems such as symbolic regression or classification problem, are needed to extend the range of application of ARE to other EA domain. Such important directions must be pursued in the near future in addition to the following future research: (1) the parallelization under the ARE framework because the asynchronous approach is suitable for the parallelization; and (2) an adaptation of the fitness deletion rate

P_d and the archive size depending on the evolution degree or the diversity of the population because these parameters gives a big influence to the performance of ARE.

Acknowledgments. This work was supported by Grant-in-Aid for JSPS Fellows Grant Number 249376.

References

1. Goldberg, D.E.: Genetic Algorithms in Search, Optimization and Machine Learning, 1st edn. Addison-Wesley Longman Publishing Co., Inc., Boston (1989)
2. Koza, J.: Genetic Programming On the Programming of Computers by Means of Natural Selection. MIT Press (1992)
3. Lewis, A., Mostaghim, S., Scriven, I.: Asynchronous multi-objective optimisation in unreliable distributed environments. In: Lewis, A., Mostaghim, S., Randall, M. (eds.) Biologically-Inspired Optimisation Methods. SCI, vol. 210, pp. 51–78. Springer, Heidelberg (2009)
4. Glasmachers, T.: A natural evolution strategy with asynchronous strategy updates. In: Proceeding of the Fifteenth Annual Conference on Genetic and Evolutionary Computation Conference, GECCO 2013, pp. 431–438. ACM, New York (2013)
5. Harada, T., Takadama, K.: Asynchronous evaluation based genetic programming: Comparison of asynchronous and synchronous evaluation and its analysis. In: Krawiec, K., Moraglio, A., Hu, T., Etaner-Uyar, A.Ş., Hu, B. (eds.) EuroGP 2013. LNCS, vol. 7831, pp. 241–252. Springer, Heidelberg (2013)
6. Ray, T.S.: An approach to the synthesis of life. Artificial Life II XI, 371–408 (1991)
7. Reynolds, C.W.: An evolved, vision-based behavioral model of coordinated group motion. In: Proc. 2nd International Conf. on Simulation of Adaptive Behavior, pp. 384–392. MIT Press (1993)
8. Banzhaf, W., Francone, F.D., Keller, R.E., Nordin, P.: Genetic programming: an introduction: on the automatic evolution of computer programs and its applications. Morgan Kaufmann Publishers Inc., San Francisco (1998)
9. Brameier, M.F., Banzhaf, W.: Linear Genetic Programming, vol. 117. Springer (2007)
10. Microchip Technology Inc.: PIC10F200/202/204/206 Data Sheet 6-Pin, 8-bit Flash Microcontrollers. Microchip Technology Inc. (2007)

Behavioral Search Drivers
for Genetic Programing

Krzysztof Krawiec[1,*] and Una-May O'Reilly[2]

[1] Poznan University of Technology, 60-965 Poznań, Poland
[2] Computer Science and Artificial Intelligence Laboratory,
MIT, Cambridge, MA, USA

Abstract. Synthesizing a program with the desired input-output behavior by means of genetic programming is an iterative process that needs appropriate guidance. That guidance is conventionally provided by a fitness function that measures the conformance of program output with the desired output. Contrary to widely adopted stance, there is no evidence that this quality measure is the best choice; alternative *search drivers* may exist that make search more effective. This study proposes and investigates a new family of *behavioral search drivers*, which inspect not only final program output, but also program behavior meant as the partial results it arrives at while executed.

1 Introduction

A typical optimization problem can be formalized as $p^* = \arg\min_{p \in P} f(p)$, where f is the *objective function* being optimized (minimized for the sake of this paper), and P is the space of candidate solutions (programs in the case of genetic programming, GP). When searching the entire space P is computationally infeasible, a heuristic search algorithm is used to find a solution $\hat{p}$ that brings $f(\hat{p}) - f(p^*)$ as low as possible. The heuristic employs f to drive the search process; in particular, in evolutionary computation it is common to use f as the fitness function.

Employing the objective function in its original form as such *search driver* appears natural, as it clearly defines the search goal. However, finding an optimal solution is the *ultimate* goal of the algorithm, the reaching of which depends on the decisions made in particular iterations of the search process. To succeed, a search algorithm should make the right decisions in possibly all iterations. Putting that into evolutionary terms, it should promote solutions that are *evolvable*, i.e. likely to turn into better solutions in subsequent iterations. However, evolvable solutions are not necessarily preferred by the objective function, as it typically has no insight into the *prospective* quality of a candidate solution.

We argue that using objective function as a search driver is not always desirable and that better alternatives exist. In GP, additional information can be gathered from program behavior, meant as partial outcomes it arrives at during execution, and used to promote evolvable programs. In [1] we proposed a specific

---

* Work conducted as a visiting scientist at CSAIL, MIT.

M. Nicolau et al. (Eds.): EuroGP 2014, LNCS 8599, pp. 210–221, 2014.

variant of such *behavioral evaluation*, termed Pattern-Guided Genetic Programming (PANGEA), and demonstrated its strengths on a set of benchmarks. Here, we present a rationale for and detailed analysis of behavioral evaluation.

2   Background

A GP task is a set T of *tests* (fitness cases). A test is a pair (x, y), where x is the input to be fed into a program, and y is the desired output. In general, xs and ys can be arbitrary objects, however we limit our interest here to synthesis of Boolean functions, so x is a vector of values of Boolean input variables, and y is a Boolean desired output.

The fitness of a program p is a measure of the conformance of its output with the desired outputs. For each test $(x, y) \in T$, p is provided with input x and executed, returning output which we denote as $p(x)$. We say that p *solves test* (x, y) if $p(x) = y$. The fitness of a program is simply the number of tests it does not solve, i.e.:

$$f(p) = |\{(x, y) \in T : p(x) \neq y\}|. \tag{1}$$

For Boolean problems we will prefer a more concise vector formulation. The desired outputs of tests in T can be gathered into a vector called *target* t, and the outputs produced by p for tests from T into its *semantics* $s(p)$. Then, fitness is the Hamming distance between program semantics and target:

$$f(p) = |s(p) - t|. \tag{2}$$

The fitness defined in this way is obviously minimized fitness, and a program p solves a task if $f(p) = 0$.

3   Motivation

A good search algorithm should be able to find an optimal solution (or a decent suboptimal solution) given limited computational resources. To this aim, the objective function it employs should convey the information about (e.g., be proportional to) the number of steps required to reach the goal (an optimal solution). By 'step' we will mean in the following a single application of a search operator (here: mutation).

Unfortunately, conventional fitness functions used in GP (Eq. 2) do not meet this expectation. To illustrate this, consider the example shown in Table 1. Column t defines the target of a 3-argument Boolean function synthesis task. The next column presents the outputs (semantics) of a program $p_0 = (x_1$ and $(x_2$ or $x_3))$ which happens to be an optimal solution to this problem. By mutating p_0 (replacing the *and* instruction with the *or* instruction, as underlined) we obtain program p_1, which commits error 4 on this task (according to Hamming distance). By mutating p_1 again, we obtain p_2, whose error amounts to 2.

Let us now revert this process and assume that p_0 has not been found yet, and p_1 and p_2 are two candidate solutions (e.g., individuals in a population in an evolutionary run). Because p_2 commits smaller error than p_1, a conventional based

Table 1. An exemplary sequence of two mutants p_1, p_2 obtained from program p_0 via one-point mutations (marked in bold)

x_1 x_2 x_3	t	p_0 $(x_1$ and $(x_2$ or $x_3))$	p_1 $(x_1$ **or** $(x_2$ or $x_3))$	p_2 $(x_1$ or $(x_2$ **and** $x_3))$
0 0 0	0	0	0	0
0 0 1	0	0	1	0
0 1 0	0	0	1	0
0 1 1	0	0	1	1
1 0 0	0	0	1	1
1 0 1	1	1	1	1
1 1 0	1	1	1	1
1 1 1	1	1	1	1
Objective function f:		0	4	2

fitness function will favor it over p_1. This is unfortunate, because p_2 requires two mutations to reach p_0, while for p_1 one mutation is sufficient[1].

The example illustrates the problem signaled in the Introduction. The objective function is by definition the right yardstick for assessing program *quality*. However, in general it does not correlate well with the number of search steps to the optimum, and so it is not necessarily the best means to predict the 'prospective' quality of a candidate solution and drive the search process. In the following we demonstrate that, at least for domains like GP, alternative search drivers can be defined that prove better in that respect.

4   Behavioral Evaluation of Programs in GP

Behavioral evaluation can be explained by starting with conventional fitness, which is the discrepancy between program output (the value returned by the root node in case of tree-based GP) and the desired output, aggregated over the tests (Eq. 2). Behavioral evaluation, in contrast, takes into account not only the final program output, but also program behavior meant as the intermediate values returned by program subexpressions. In this paper we consider tree-based GP[2], so we collect the values calculated by the k topmost nodes of program tree, i.e., the k first nodes when traversing the program tree in breadth-first order (if the tree happens to be smaller, we use all tree nodes). These values, collected for all tests in T, form a $|T| \times k$ table. The ith table column corresponds to the ith node in the tree and thus forms a *feature* that describes program behavior at that point of its execution. In particular, the first feature corresponds to the root node and thus captures the output of entire program $p(x)$.

We then extend this table by an extra column, which holds the search target t. The extended table forms a training set that defines a task of supervised machine learning from examples, with t serving as a decision attribute. A classifier v is induced from this set and the properties of that classifier are used to define the

---

[1] In general, another optimal solution $p^* \neq p_0$, $s(p^*) = t$ may exist that can be reached from p_2 through a single mutation. This however does not invalidate this argument. We will return to this issue when explaining our sampling procedure.

[2] In [1], we employed an analogous procedure to gather behavioral features from linear programs written in the Push language.

behavioral fitness of the evaluated program p. We then define behavioral fitness as an aggregate of three components:

1. The conventional objective, i.e., the error committed by the program, $f(p)$,
2. The complexity $c(v(p))$ of the classifier $v(p)$ induced from the training set,
3. The error $e(v(p))$ the classifier v commits on the training set.

The rationale behind taking into account the latter two components is as follows. The trained classifier maps (perfectly or not) the program behavior (captured in the features) onto the desired program output. In an ideal case, its predictions perfectly match the desired output and thus $e(v) = 0$. The closer that error is to zero, the more we can claim that the features (and indirectly program behavior) *relate* to the desired output.

However, classifier error does not tell the whole story about the relatedness between program behavior and the desired output, because the classifier can itself be more or less complex. Consider two programs for which the induced classifiers commit the same error. If one of them is simpler than the other, then we can claim that the behavior of the corresponding program is closer related to the desired output. In the case of decision trees used in [1] and here, complexity can be conveniently expressed as the number of decision tree nodes.

The key motivation for behavioral evaluation is that relatedness may convey information about the *prospective* quality of a program. Low error and/or low complexity indicate that program arrives at intermediate results (captured in features) that can be mapped onto the desired output, and thus a small number of transformations (e.g, mutations) can turn it into an optimal program. Conventional fitness function is insensitive to this aspect of program characteristics, as it observes only the final program outcome and measures only its direct match with the desired output.

5   The Experiment

In following we examine several behavioral search drivers by considering the particular measures defined in the previous section (f, c, e) separately and in aggregation. We are primarily interested in how well a search driver correlates with the expected number of search steps that a program p needs to undergo to reach the search target t, i.e., to arrive at the descendant p' such that $s(p') = t$.

To avoid bias towards a specific set of GP tasks (e.g., commonly used benchmarks), we consider a large sample of tasks. For Boolean tasks with tests enumerating all combinations of input variables, there is one-to-one correspondence between tasks and targets, so we will use these terms interchangeably.

Sampling Procedure. To carry out the analysis, we would ideally consider a sample of programs with known distances from a given target, where by distance we mean the *minimal* number of mutations required to reach the optimum. Obtaining such data is however computationally challenging, as distance is the length of the shortest sequence of mutations, and the number of such sequences grows exponentially with program size. Moreover, as we intend to consider many targets, relying on distance becomes technically infeasible.

Algorithm 1. The pseudocode of the function generating a single random walk in the space of programs. The result is a list of programs of length $n + 1$, where each program is a mutant of its predecessor.

```
1: function RANDOMWALK(n)
2:     p_0 ← RANDOMPROGRAM( )
3:     walk ← (p_0)
4:     for i ← 1 . . . n do
5:         repeat
6:             p_i ← MUTATE(p_{i-1})
7:         until p_i ≠ p_0
8:         walk ← append(walk, p_i)
9:     return walk
10: end function
```

Due to this limitation, we abandon the use of minimal number of steps in favor of the *expected* number of steps. We generate a random program, assume that it defines a target (GP task), and run a random walk from that program using single-point mutation as a search operator. We chose this search operator as it introduces minimal change possible (compared to, e.g., subtree-replacing mutation). Such a random walk can be seen as a search process in reverse (albeit not explicitly driven by any search driver).

The sampling procedure is shown in Algorithm 1. RANDOMWALK generates a starting program p_0 by calling the RANDOMPROGRAM function (which is guaranteed to return a program with non-trivial, i.e., non-constant, semantics). The program defines a target $t = s(p_0)$. p_0 is then mutated n times, and the ordered list of mutants representing the walk is returned by the function upon its completion. However, mutants are not allowed to be syntactically identical with the starting program of the walk (i.e., a walk is not allowed to turn into a cycle; see line 7 of the algorithm). Without this constraint, some walks would return to the starting point, and regularities in the results would be harder to notice.[3]

RANDOMWALK does not guarantee that i is the *smallest* number of mutations required to transform the starting program p_0 into the ith program of the walk, p_i (and vice versa); a shorter sequence of mutations connecting p_0 and p_i may exist. Also, RANDOMWALK does not ensure that i is the smallest number of mutations that have to be applied to p_i in order to reach the *target* t. A shorter sequence of mutations may exist that transforms p_i into a yet another program $p' ≠ p_0$ such that $s(p') = s(p_0) = t$.

By relying on random walks (and thus on the expected rather than the minimal number of mutations), in the following experiment we are able to consider large programs composed of up to 255 tree nodes (tree depth limit 7), which with four instructions leads to search space cardinality of the order of 4^{255}.

---

[3] Note however that we allow a walk to revisit any other search point except for the target. This is our deliberate design choice to make the walks behave analogously to a search process, which may cycle, however it terminates when it reaches the target.

Table 2. The parameters of experimental setup

Instruction set: nonterminals:	and, or, nand, nor
Instruction set: terminals:	up to 12 input variables
Program generation (RANDOMPROGRAM)	ramped half-and-half
Minimal tree size	23 (minimal binary tree using 12 variables)
Maximal tree size	255 (full binary tree of depth 7)
Mutation operator (MUTATE)	single point mutation
Walk length	16

Experimental Setup. We compare the characteristics of different search drivers on the domain of Boolean function synthesis (Table 2). The search operator used to generate our random walks is single point mutation, which selects a random node in a program tree and replaces it with another instruction of the same arity. We chose this operator as it introduces a minimal change in program code and thus may be likened to single bitflip mutation in genetic algorithms. The instruction set thus does not contain the 'not' instruction, because it cannot be modified using single point mutation. Terminals are not mutated, so the set of active variables and the target t remain unchanged in a given random walk.

The RANDOMWALK procedure (Algorithm 1) used to generate programs is ramped half-and-half (RHH) with ramp set to depth 7. As all instructions are binary, half of the programs in the sample (those generated by the 'full' part of RHH) are full binary trees of depth 7, with 127 leaves, which makes them likely to use all or almost all input variables. For the programs generated using the 'grow' case of RHH, we impose a lower size limit of $2 * 12 - 1 = 23$ nodes, so that even the smallest programs have the chance to use all 12 input variables. This limit is also essential for generating sufficiently long random walks (for small trees, a walk generated using single point mutation is doomed to return to the starting point quickly, when it exhausts all combinations of instructions).

The behavioral search drivers (Section 4) gather 15 features from program execution and use J4.8 decision tree inducer to build a classifier [2][3] (an unpruned tree is used, i.e., option -U). Note that this learning method is insensitive to the ordering of attributes, so for instance swapping the arguments of a commutative instruction in a program does not affect its behavioral evaluation.

A random walk's starting program may happen to use all input variables, but is not guaranteed to do so. The input variables that are absent in the starting program become irrelevant for a walk. Thus, although the total number of variables is 12, even a one-variable task may occur in the sample (the zero-variable trivial tasks are rejected at the spot). For every task we determine the number of effective variables, and in the following we factor the results for tasks with variable number varying from 6 to 12 (we assume that tasks with five or fewer variables are too trivial to reveal the kind of regularities we search for). In this way, we avoid aggregation over tasks with different numbers of variables, which would make interpretation of results more difficult.

Absolute (raw) Values of Search Drivers. In this experiment we observe how the search drivers vary along random walks. We compare the search drivers

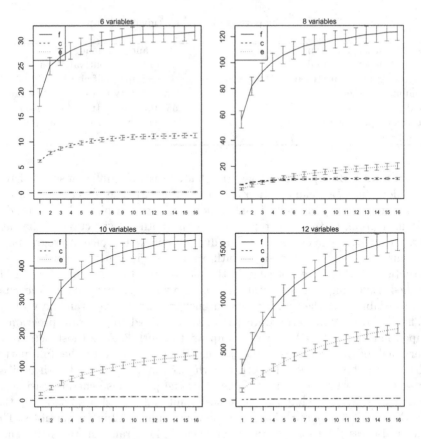

Fig. 1. Search drivers as a function of the number of mutations, for tasks with 6, 8, 10, and 12 relevant variables. f: program error, c: classifier complexity, e: classifier error. Whiskers mark 10% of standard deviation.

presented in Section 4: program error (f), and the behavioral measures: the complexity of the classifier induced from program behavior (c), and the classifier error (e). We first build a sample of random walks by calling RANDOMWALK 100,000 times. For every walk, we iterate over its elements (mutated programs), and apply every search driver to them, assuming that the target is defined by the first program in the walk $(t = s(p_0))$. We factor the results by the number of relevant variables in a problem.

Figure 1 presents the search drivers as functions of the number of mutations, averaged over the walks in the sample. Let us emphasize that, while these averaged curves are clearly monotonic, the search drivers for *individual* walks most often are not: a subsequent mutation is likely to decrease the value of the driver (as illustrated in the example in Section 3). Thus, the variance of the raw data is very high: the whiskers show only 10% of standard deviation. Presenting individual walks would make the figures completely illegible.

As mutations accumulate, the features gathered from the behavior of a program become less related to the target, so the classifier has to be more complex (increasing c) to correctly predict the desired output, and it tends to commit more errors (increasing e). Depending on problem size, the behavioral search drivers grow simultaneously (which happens here for problems with 8 and 10 variables[4]), or individually: for the small problems (6 variables) the classifier is often perfect ($e = 0$), while for the difficult ones (12 variables) building a well-performing classifier becomes impossible so c levels-off. However, at least one of them keeps rising with the subsequent mutations, and in this sense they complement each other. This suggests that c and e can be aggregated to form a compound search driver that would monotonically increase with the number of mutations and avoid stagnation. Given the relative comparison of standard deviations, there is a chance that such compound driver could be less prone to leveling-off than the conventional fitness function f, but this analysis cannot be deemed conclusive in this respect.

The decision tree classifiers are very small on average (search driver c), even for tasks that involve more input variables. This can be explained by strong inter-dependencies between features collected from GP subexpressions. For instance, consider a program that contains a compound expression (p_1 *and* p_2), and that this expression and its subexpressions p_1, p_2, are behavioral features used by our approach. If a given decision tree node uses the compound expression, the features p_1 and p_2 will be always *true* in the 'positive' branch of that node, and the tree induction algorithm will not use them in that part of the tree.

Correlation Analysis. Above we analyzed the *absolute* values of search drivers. However, what matters in practice is often only whether a search driver increases or decreases with the expected number of mutations to target, particularly when the search is driven by *relative* comparisons of candidate solutions (e.g., tournament selection). Thus, here we analyze how search drivers *qualitatively correlate* with the number of accumulated mutations.

We use the sample of walks generated in the previous experiment. First, we factor it with respect to the number of relevant variables. Next, we plot the Spearman correlation coefficient between a search driver and the number of mutations from all data points with up to l mutations, where $l = 1..16$. We choose the Spearman coefficient as it relies on ranks and thus cares only about the qualitative differences between values (as argued above). Effectively then, a point with abscissa l in the graphs shows correlation coefficient for random walks trimmed to length l.

The results, shown in Fig. 2, are partially consistent with the absolute values shown in Fig. 1. As mutations accumulate, the correlation coefficients for f and c deteriorate, as these search drivers tended to levels-off the most in Fig. 1 (except for c for 6 variables). The classifier error e however maintains relatively stable correlation along the walk, though it is rather low compared to the remaining drivers (so low that for 6 variables the plot is out of plotting range). Overall, the behavioral drivers start becoming competitive and often provide better correlation than f, Interestingly, they frequently do so for long random walks, which

---

[4] The growth of c is barely visible due to the range of vertical axis.

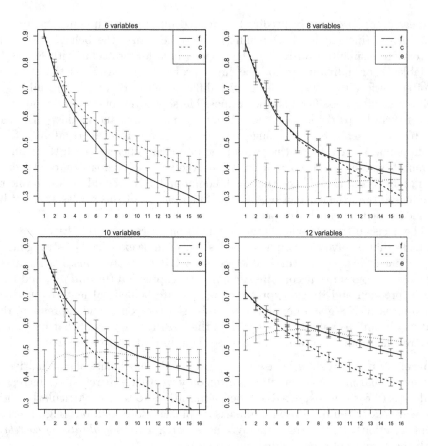

Fig. 2. Spearman coefficient between the number of mutations in a walk and search drivers, for walks of different total length (horizontal axis). Whiskers mark 0.99-confidence intervals.

looks particularly attractive, as it suggest that they may provide better search gradient far from the target.

The new result in comparison to Fig. 1 is that c and e are largely uncorrelated (if they were, their plots would have to be similar). This suggests, even more than Fig. 1, that c and e may complement each other in a nontrivial way.

Correlation Analysis for Compound Search Drivers. As the individual search drivers saturate after a number of mutations (Fig. 1), we do not expect any of them alone to be a useful search driver, so here we try to aggregate them.

Direct additive aggregation of our search drivers would be unjustified, as c is the number of tree nodes, while f and e are expressed in tests (and c is typically much smaller, see Fig. 1). To provide a common platform for these quantities, we resort to information theory and attempt to estimate the amount of information conveyed by these components. For simplicity, rather than calculating the *exact* number of bits required to encode f, e, and c, we simply pass each of them

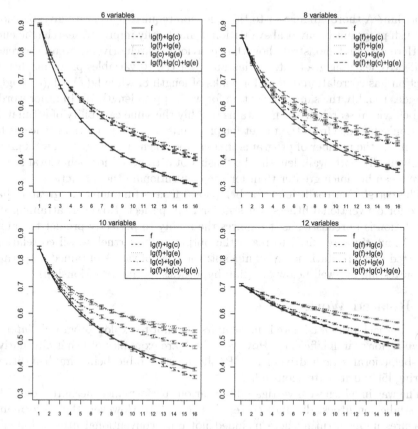

Fig. 3. Spearman correlation between the number of mutations in a walk and **aggregates** of search drivers, for walks of different total length (horizontal axis). Whiskers mark 0.99-confidence intervals.

through a logarithm, meant as a rough measure of information content (see, e.g., [4] for considerations on exact formulas).

We consider compound measures constructed from all combinations of f, c, and e, and show them in Fig. 3, with the plot for f repeated after Fig. 2 for reference[5]. Comparison of these plots to individual search drivers in Fig. 2 clearly suggests that fusing the behavioral search drivers is beneficial. For all combinations of components, correlation is not worse, and often better, than that for conventional fitness f. In particular, the aggregate that consistently (i.e., for all considered numbers of variables) provides the highest or close to the highest correlation involves all components $(\lg(f) + \lg(c) + \lg(e))$, which corroborates the outcomes we obtained with PANGEA [1].

The 0.99-confidence intervals clearly indicate that the compound search drivers are in most cases significantly better than the conventional fitness function f. However, what can be the potential implications for the efficiency of a search

---

[5] We skip the logarithmic transform for f, as it is monotonic so it cannot affect ranking, and thus has no effect on Spearman correlation.

algorithm? A thorough answer to this question requires a separate investigation; for Push programs behavioral evaluation dramatically improved search efficiency [1]. Here we can demonstrate how the behavioral search drivers extend the reach of effective learning gradient. For instance, for the 10-variables problems, fitness function has correlation of 0.51 for walks of length 8, while $\lg(f) + \lg(c) + \lg(e)$ provides roughly the same correlation for walks up to length 16. In other words, the behavioral search driver maintains roughly the same capability of estimating solution's distance from the target for programs that are more than twice as far from it. As the number of programs that can be reached by a random walk grows exponentially with walk length, the 'basins of attraction' for behavioral search drivers can be much greater than for the conventional fitness function.

The correlation coefficients for behavioral fitness functions are greater than those for conventional fitness, yet still far from perfect. However, attaining full correlation is unrealistic, as it requires the ability to perfectly predict the number of mutations required to reach the optimum. Nevertheless, all correlations reported here are statistically significant: the control values obtained by permutation testing are well below 0.1 (null hypothesis: no interrelationship).

6   Related Work

The approach presented here is novel in its attempt to exploit program's *internal behavior* for search efficiency. However, there are examples of using alternative, non-behavioral search drivers in GP, the most notable being implicit fitness sharing [5] and its extensions [6].

The way in which we investigated the various performance measures resembles the studies on fitness-distance correlation (e.g., [7]). However, the performance measures under scrutiny here included not only conventional fitness, but also the behavioral drivers. Also, we relied on the expected number of search steps, rather than a distance, as a measure of anticipated computational effort.

The MDL principle has been used in GP means of controlling the trade-off between model complexity and accuracy. For instance, Iba *et al.* [8] used it to prevent bloat in GP by taking into account the error committed by an individual as well as the size of the program. A few later studies followed this research direction (see, e.g. [9]).

By focusing mostly on the effects of program execution (the partial outcomes reflected in trace features) rather than on syntax, behavioral evaluation can be seen as following the recent trend of semantic GP, initiated in [10]. Interestingly, it also resembles evolutionary synthesis of features for machine learning and pattern/image analysis tasks [11]. However, here the classifier serves only as a scaffolding for evolution; it is supposed to provide 'gradient' when the program output alone is unable to do so.

7   Conclusion

We demonstrated that behavioral search drivers provide more reliable information about the expected number of mutations needed to reach the optimum.

Given two candidate solutions, behavioral evaluation is more likely to predict correctly which of them requires fewer modifications to reach the search target, which has obvious implications for search efficiency. Also, by providing a more comprehensive information of program's *prospective* quality, it extends the effective learning gradient further from the target, and promotes evolvability.

The presented results characterize the domain of Boolean functions, and abstract from any specific task in that domain. Given the analogous results obtained with with a different program representation and for non-Boolean problems [1], we hypothesize that behavioral evaluation can be potentially leveraged in different genres of GP.

Acknowledgments. The authors thank the reviewers for rich feedback and constructive suggestions. Both authors acknowledge support from the Li Ka Shing Foundation, and K. Krawiec acknowledges support from the Polish-U.S. Fulbright Commission and from grants no. DEC-2011/01/B/ST6/07318 and 91507.

References

1. Krawiec, K., Swan, J.: Pattern-guided genetic programming. In: Blem, C., et al. (eds.) GECCO 2013: Proceeding of the Fifteenth Annual Conference on Genetic and Evolutionary Computation Conference, Amsterdam, The Netherlands, pp. 949–956. ACM (2013)
2. Quinlan, J.: C4.5: Programs for machine learning. Morgan Kaufmann (1992)
3. Hall, M., Frank, E., Holmes, G., Pfahringer, B., Reutemann, P., Witten, I.H.: The weka data mining software: an update. SIGKDD Explor. Newsl. 11(1), 10–18 (2009)
4. Quinlan, J.R., Rivest, R.L.: Inferring decision trees using the minimum description length principle. Inf. Comput. 80(3), 227–248 (1989)
5. Smith, R., Forrest, S., Perelson, A.: Searching for diverse, cooperative populations with genetic algorithms. Evolutionary Computation 1(2) (1993)
6. Krawiec, K., Lichocki, P.: Using co-solvability to model and exploit synergetic effects in evolution. In: Schaefer, R., Cotta, C., Kołodziej, J., Rudolph, G. (eds.) PPSN XI. LNCS, vol. 6239, pp. 492–501. Springer, Heidelberg (2010)
7. Tomassini, M., Vanneschi, L., Collard, P., Clergue, M.: A study of fitness distance correlation as a difficulty measure in genetic programming. Evolutionary Computation 13(2), 213–239 (2005)
8. Iba, H., Sato, T., de Garis, H.: System identification approach to genetic programming. In: Proceedings of the 1994 IEEE World Congress on Computational Intelligence, Orlando, Florida, USA, vol. 1, pp. 401–406. IEEE Press (1994)
9. Zhang, B.T., Mühlenbein, H.: Balancing accuracy and parsimony in genetic programming. Evolutionary Computation 3(1), 17–38 (1995)
10. McPhee, N.F., Ohs, B., Hutchison, T.: Semantic building blocks in genetic programming. In: O'Neill, M., Vanneschi, L., Gustafson, S., Esparcia Alcázar, A.I., De Falco, I., Della Cioppa, A., Tarantino, E. (eds.) EuroGP 2008. LNCS, vol. 4971, pp. 134–145. Springer, Heidelberg (2008)
11. Krawiec, K., Bhanu, B.: Visual learning by evolutionary and coevolutionary feature synthesis. IEEE Transactions on Evolutionary Computation 11(5), 635–650 (2007)

Cartesian Genetic Programming: Why No Bloat?

Andrew James Turner and Julian Francis Miller

Electronics Department, University of York
Heslington, York, YO10 5DD, UK
{andrew.turner,julian.miller}@york.ac.uk

Abstract. For many years now it has been known that Cartesian Genetic Programming (CGP) does not exhibit program bloat. Two possible explanations have been proposed in the literature: neutral genetic drift and length bias. This paper empirically disproves both of these and thus, reopens the question as to why CGP does not suffer from bloat. It has also been shown for CGP that using a very large number of nodes considerably increases the effectiveness of the search. This paper also proposes a new explanation as to why this may be the case.

1 Introduction

Bloat, the uncontrolled growth in program size, is a serious issue for Genetic Programming (GP) that has received much study [1] [2]. However, bloat does not appear in Cartesian Genetic Programming (CGP) [3]. In the literature there are two possible theories as to why CGP does not exhibit bloat; Neutral Genetic Drift (NGD) [3] and length bias [4]. This paper introduces both of these theories and then proceeds to empirically disprove them by removing the underlying assumptions each of them make. This leaves us with no explanation for the lack of bloat in CGP and opens the topic for further investigation.

The investigations also show that there is an evolutionary pressure to increase the program size when the current program size is insufficient[1] to solve a given task. Conversely we find empirically that there is no evolutionary pressure to decrease the program size if the current program size is much larger than required to solve a given task. It therefore appears that using large program sizes is not detrimental to CGP, in keeping with previous results [5] which show it is actually beneficial. A new hypothesis is presented as to why this is the case. When subject to a mutation operator, using a large number of nodes causes, on average, the fitness of an individual to vary by a lesser degree than when using a smaller number of nodes. Using a large number of nodes has smoothed out the fitness landscape making it easier to navigate. This accords with the desirability of synonymous redundancy in representations introduced by Goldberg and Rothlauf who propose that genotype representations should have the property that mutational neighbours represent similar phenotypes [6].

---

[1] This is compatible with the length bias theory [4] as is discussed later.

M. Nicolau et al. (Eds.): EuroGP 2014, LNCS 8599, pp. 222–233, 2014.

The remainder of the paper is as follows: Section 2 describes CGP, Section 3 discusses bloat and past theoretical work surrounding bloat and CGP, Section 4 describes a series of experiments which empirically investigate the described theories with the results given in Section 5 and finally Sections 6 and 7 provide a discussion and closing conclusions.

2 Cartesian Genetic Programming

CGP [7] [8] is a form of GP which represents computational structures as directed, usually acyclic graphs indexed by their Cartesian coordinates. Each node may take its inputs from any previous node or program input. The program outputs are taken from the output of any internal node or program inputs. This structure leads to many of the nodes described by the CGP chromosome not contributing to the final operation of the phenotype, these inactive, or "junk", nodes have been shown to greatly aid the evolutionary search [5] [9] [10].

The nodes described by CGP chromosomes are arranged in a rectangular $r \times c$ grid of nodes, where r and c respectively denote the user-defined number of rows and columns. In CGP, nodes in the same column are not allowed to be connected together. It is important to note that any architecture (limited by the number of nodes) can be constructed by arranging the nodes in a $1 \times n$ format where the n represents the maximum number of nodes (columns). Using this representation the user does not need to specify the topology, which is then automatically evolved along with the program.

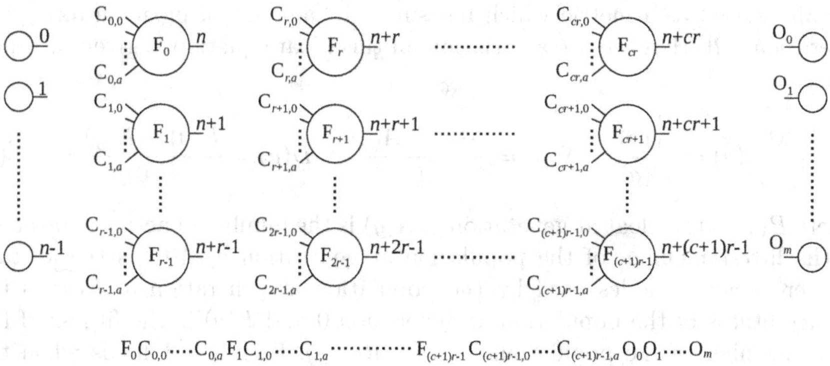

$$F_0 C_{0,0} \cdots C_{0,a} F_1 C_{1,0} \cdots C_{1,a} \cdots\cdots\cdots\cdots F_{(c+1)r-1} C_{(c+1)r-1,0} \cdots\cdot C_{(c+1)r-1,a} O_0 O_1 \cdots O_m$$

Fig. 1: Depiction of a Cartesian Genetic Programs structure with chromosome encoding below, taken from [8]

Figure 1 gives the general form of a CGP showing that a CGP chromosome can describe multiple input multiple output programs with a range of node transfer functions and arities. In the chromosome string, also given in Figure 1, F_i denote the function operation at each node, C_i index where the node gathers its inputs and each O_i denote which nodes provide the outputs of the program. It should be noted that CGP is not limited to only one data type, it may be used for Boolean values, floats, images, audio files, videos etc. CGP generally uses the Evolutionary Strategy (ES) algorithm $(1 + \lambda)$-ES. In this algorithm each generation contains $1 + \lambda$ candidates and the fittest is chosen as the parent. The next generation is formed by this parent and λ offspring obtained through mutation of the parent. It is important to note that if no offspring are fitter than the parent, but at least one has the same fitness as the parent, then the offspring is chosen as the new parent. In CGP, the λ value is commonly set as four. The connection genes in the chromosomes are initialised with random values that obey the constraints imposed by the CGP structural parameters r and c. The function genes are randomly chosen from the allowed values in the function lookup table. The output genes O_i are randomly initialised to refer to any node or input in the graph. The standard mutation operator used in CGP works by randomly choosing valid alleles at a randomly chosen gene locations. The reason why both a simple operator and a simple evolutionary algorithm are so effective is related to the presence of non-coding genes. Simple mutations can connect or disconnect whole sub-programs. For a more detailed description of CGP see [8].

3   Bloat and CGP

Bloat can be defined as "program growth without (significant) return in terms of fitness" [11], that is, if program length is increasing disproportionately to fitness improvements then bloat is said to be occurring. This definition has been formally stated as a metric which measures the amount of bloat on any given generation [12]. Here we use a variation on this bloat equation is given in Equation 1:

$$B(g) = \frac{N(g)}{D(g)}, \quad N(g) = \frac{\hat{A}(g) - \bar{A}(0)}{\bar{A}(0)}, \quad D(g) = \frac{\bar{F}(0) - \hat{F}(g)}{\bar{F}(0)} \quad (1)$$

Where $B(g)$ is the bloat at generation g, $\hat{A}(g)$ is the number of active nodes used by the fittest member of the population at generation g, $\bar{A}(0)$ is the average number of active nodes used by the population at generation 0, $\bar{F}(0)$ is the average fitness of the population at generation 0 and $\hat{F}(g)$ is the fitness of the fittest member of the population at generation g. Equation 1 holds when the target is to minimise the fitness to zero. When the fitness is to be maximised the fitness values can be amended by subtracting the current fitness from the target fitness; thus transforming the problem into a minimisation task. The equation effectively gives the ratio of increase in program size to improvement in fitness. If the program size is increasing disproportionately to fitness then the bloat value will also increase, thus indicating bloat.

The bloat equation given in [12] was adapted here to show the amount of bloat exhibited by the fittest member of the population; as opposed to the average bloat of the population. There are two reasons for this alteration: 1) CGP uses a $(1 + \lambda)$-ES without crossover, and so the only solution of interest is the current fittest. 2) The small population sizes typically used by CGP leads to very noisy average active nodes and fitness values which are hard to analyse graphically.

Figure 2 gives three examples of the unaltered bloat metric when used by the original authors; see [12] for further details of their experiments. As can be seen in Figure 2, bloat is easily detected by a high continuous increase in the bloat metric.

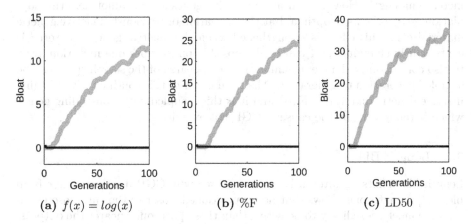

Fig. 2: The bloat metric comparing standard GP (light gray) and DynOpEq GP (black) on (a) symbolic regression and (b)(c) two real world classification tasks. Images taken from [12].

Although CGP uses fixed size genotypes, each genotype can encode phenotypes (programs) of different lengths. This is because many of the genes in the genotypes are typically inactive or "junk" and are therefore not decoded into the phenotype. If bloat occurred in CGP it would via a disproportionate increase in active nodes with respect to fitness. The following subsections introduce two theories found in the literature which have been proposed to explain why CGP does not bloat.

3.1   Neutral Genetic Drift

One of the many theories surrounding why GP in general suffers from bloat is the drift hypothesis [13]. The drift hypothesis goes as follows. When a population is trapped in a local optimum many of the parents children will have the same or very similar fitness. A method often used by GP is to replace parents with their children if their fitness is equal or very similar; with the aim to improve genetic diversity and to escape local optima with future mutations. If adding or removing a small number of nodes does not lessen the fitness of the child then the child may be larger or smaller respectively. Additionally it has been shown that for a given chromosome size there exist more solutions with the same fitness which are larger than smaller [14]. Therefore there exists an evolutionary pressure to increase the size of the program when trapped in local optima.

It is argued in [3] that CGP does not suffer from bloat due to the inactive genes causing NGD [15]. Their argument is that when a population is trapped in a local optimum the majority of the mutations which do not cause a reduction in fitness will be mutations affecting inactive genes; as opposed to active genes. Mutating inactive genes cannot alter the program size, therefore CGP does not increase in length. However mutating inactive genes alone cannot help the population escape the local optima, but the activation of previously inactive genetic material can. This effect is strengthened when the inactive genetic material is continuously changing as it causes the possible phenotypes one mutation away to also continuously change; meaning that a wide area of the search space can be sampled generation to generation. The term given to this continuously changing inactive genetic material is NGD and it is this, coupled with non-coding genes, which is thought to be the cause of CGP not exhibiting bloat.

3.2   Length Bias

Length bias offers an alternative argument for why CGP does not suffer from bloat [4]. Length bias shows that nodes positioned closer to the chromosome inputs are much more likely to be active than those positioned nearer the outputs. This is because when CGP encodes feed-forward (acyclic) networks each node can only gather its inputs from previous nodes i.e. those closer to the inputs. This means that nodes closer to the inputs have a higher probability of being active; as the probability of any given node being an active node is directly proportional to the number of nodes which can connect to that node. This results in a higher concentration of active nodes towards the inputs. This bias towards small networks is why CGP does not suffer from bloat.

4   Experiments

The aim of the experiments presented is to identify if NGD, length bias or another factor is responsible for the lack of bloat in CGP. This is achieved by removing the main assumption behind each theory as to why CGP does not suffer from bloat. For the NGD theory this is achieved by preventing NGD from occurring and for the length bias theory this is achieved by removing the length bias. The results obtained on each task are also compared to a neutral search, to ensure that the fitness functions used are not producing a pressure to create small programs.

All of the experiments are investigated using the six bit parity and the Pagie1 [16] symbolic regression tasks. The parity task uses AND NAND OR and NOR node functions[2] and the fitness is calculated as the number of incorrect outputs produced when all possible inputs are swept. The Pagie1 task, Equation 2, uses $+ - \times \%\ e^n$ and $\ln(|n|)$ node functions and the fitness is calculated as the sum of the absolute differences between the correct and actual outputs when both inputs are swept from -5 to 5 in 0.4 increments. In all cases, unless otherwise stated, the following parameters are used: $(1+4)$-ES, three percent probabilistic mutation[3], one hundred columns, one row and allowed ten thousand generations before terminating the search. Each experiment is repeated fifty times in order to produce reliable averages.

$$y(x_1, x_2) = \frac{1}{1 + x_1^{-4}} + \frac{1}{1 + x_2^{-4}} \tag{2}$$

4.1   Regular CGP

The first experiment is to apply regular unaltered feed-forward CGP to the two tasks. This is to confirm the result that CGP does not exhibit bloat [3] and provide results to which the other experiments can be compared against.

4.2   No Neutral Genetic Drift

The NGD theory as to why CGP does not suffer from bloat is reliant upon CGP actually exhibiting NGD. NGD can be prevented in CGP by only allowing *active* genes to be mutated. This causes the inactive genetic material to become static and thus cannot drift. Inactive nodes can still become active however if an active node connects to them when mutated. By only allowing active genes to be mutated, CGP is functionally equivalent but without NGD.

If CGP without NGD is shown not to exhibit bloat then NGD cannot be the cause of CGP not bloating. Conversely if CGP without NGD is shown to exhibit bloat then NGD must be the cause of CGP not bloating.

Interestingly the method of only allowing active genes to be mutated has the opposite goal of accumulating mutation [17], a CGP mutation method designed to heighten NGD.

4.3   Recurrent CGP

The length bias theory as to why CGP does not suffer from bloat is reliant upon CGP exhibiting a length bias. Length bias occurs as nodes can only connect to previous nodes in the network. However, if this restraint is removed then length bias no longer applies. This restraint can be removed by placing no restrictions on where each node can gather its inputs i.e. by allowing recurrent as well as feed forward connections. This form of CGP is referred to as recurrent CGP as it allows for recurrent connections. Allowing recurrent connections means that

---

[2] The XOR gate is omitted to increase the difficulty of the tasks.

[3] Where each gene is mutated with a given probability.

the probability of a given node being active is no longer a function of its position within the genotype. Therefore length bias has been removed.

The implementation of recurrent CGP is identical to that of feed-forward CGP except that no restraints are placed on where each node can connect its inputs. Under these conditions it is possible for a node to be used as an input to another node before it has calculated its own output value. Therefore, before each fitness evaluation all of the active nodes are initialised to output zero. During the fitness functions the outputs are read from the program in the same way as for regular feed-forward CGP: 1) apply a set of inputs 2) update every active node once from inputs to outputs (allowing the clocked feedback) 3) the program results are read from the output nodes.

If recurrent CGP does not suffer from bloat then the cause of feed-forward CGP not exhibiting bloat cannot be due to length bias. However if recurrent CGP does suffer from bloat then the cause of feed-forward CGP not exhibiting bloat must be due to length bias.

4.4   Neutral Search

It is possible that the fitness functions used to investigate bloat may themselves produce a pressure to create small program sizes; for instance if they require small program sizes to solve the given task. Although this is unlikely, it should be investigated and found to be untrue in order for the results of the other experiments to be valid.

This is achieved by comparing the percentage of active nodes used by the six bit parity and Pagie1 tasks with the percentage used by a neutral search. A neutral search is where the fitness is set to zero regardless of the programs functionality i.e. it is a neutral fitness landscape. If it is shown that the six bit parity and Pagie1 tasks use a lower percentage of active nodes than that used by a neutral search then it would indicate that these tasks are applying an evolutionary pressure to produce small program sizes which could be responsible for CGP not bloating.

In order to make a fair comparison between the percentage of active nodes used by neutral search and the six bit parity and Pagie1 tasks, the number of inputs and outputs of the evolved programs must be consistent. That is, when comparing neutral search to the six bit parity task the neutral search must also evolve solutions with six inputs and one output; and equivalently for the Pagie1 task. This is because the number of inputs and outputs is likely to influence the percentage of active nodes.

The experiment is investigated for 1, 5, 10, 50, 100, 500 and 1000 nodes (columns with rows set to one), to identify if the results vary over a range of topology limits.

5   Results

The results of the described experiments are now presented. In all but the neutral search experiments, the results are given graphically showing the fitness, number of active nodes and bloat values of the best member of the population at each generation averaged over the fifty runs. The bloat value is calculated using Equation 1. The technique is identified as bloating if the bloat value rises continuously throughout evolutionary time.

5.1   Regular CGP

The results of applying regular feed-forward CGP to the six bit parity and Pagie1 tasks are given in Figure 3. Here it can be seen that CGP is not exhibiting bloat during evolution with the bloat value actually falling in the six bit parity case. Although it can be seen that the number of active nodes does increase over evolutionary time, it does so only when the fitness also improves and is therefore not bloat as defined in Section 3.

The initial high values of bloat seen in Figure 3 for the six bit parity task is thought to be because of the high increase in active nodes during the beginning of the search. It appears that the initial randomly generated chromosomes have too few active nodes to solve the task. This causes a sharp increase in the number of active nodes during the first few generations. This appears in the bloat value until these additional active nodes causes a significant increase in fitness at which point the bloat value starts to fall.

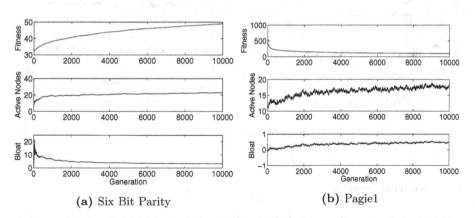

(a) Six Bit Parity   (b) Pagie1

Fig. 3: Regular feed-forward CGP

5.2   No Neutral Genetic Drift

The results of applying CGP without NGD are given in Figure 4 for both the six bit parity and Pagie1 tasks. Here it can be seen that CGP without NGD is still not exhibiting bloat and so NGD cannot be the cause of CGPs lack of bloat.

5.3   Recurrent CGP

The results of applying recurrent CGP are given in Figure 5 for both the six bit parity and Pagie1 tasks. Here it can be seen that recurrent CGP is still not exhibiting bloat and so length bias cannot be the cause of CGPs lack of bloat.

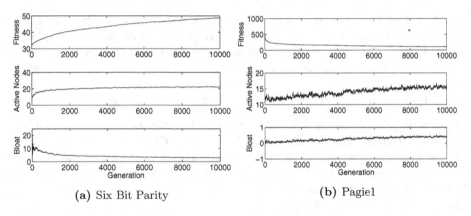

(a) Six Bit Parity   (b) Pagie1

Fig. 4: Feed-forward CGP without NGD

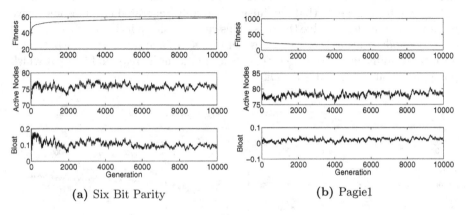

(a) Six Bit Parity   (b) Pagie1

Fig. 5: Recurrent CGP

5.4   Neutral Search

Figure 6 gives a comparison between the percentage of active nodes, over a range of available nodes[4], for the neutral and guided search problems[5]. The figure clearly shows that for small numbers of available nodes the percentage of active nodes used by the guided searches far exceeds the percentage used by the neutral searches. However, for higher numbers of available nodes the percentage of active nodes used by the guided searches approach that used by the neutral searches. Therefore it can be concluded that the six bit parity and Pagie1 tasks are not producing an evolutionary pressure to create small program sizes and are therefore not responsible for the observed lack of bloat in the previous results.

---

[4] Where available nodes refers to the product of the rows and columns. As rows was always set as one however available nodes and columns are equivalent.

[5] Where a guided search is the opposite to a neutral search i.e. toward a real task.

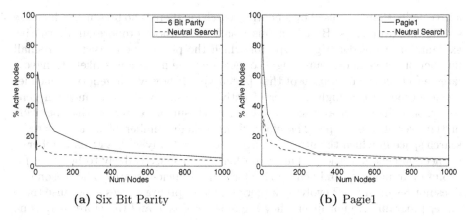

(a) Six Bit Parity   **(b)** Pagie1

Fig. 6: Regular feed-forward CGP applied to the two tasks and equivalent neutral searches

6 Discussion

As is seen in Section 5.2, CGP without NGD does not exhibit bloat and so NGD is unlikely to be the cause of CGP not exhibiting bloat. However it is important to note that this result does not suggest that the presence of inactive genes themselves are not responsible. It was shown in Section 5.3 that recurrent CGP also does not suffer from bloat, and as length bias only applies to feed-forward CGP it therefore cannot be the cause of CGP not exhibiting bloat. It was also shown in Section 5.4 that the tasks used to study CGP and bloat did not themselves produce a bias towards small program lengths; strengthening the conclusions.

Interestingly it is reported in [4] that CGP struggles to increase the number of active nodes during evolution even when a given task requires it; due to length bias. In Section 5.4 however it can be seen that CGP consistently used more active nodes on both tasks than for the neutral searches when given a low number of available nodes. This indicates that CGP is increasing the number of active nodes when the task requires it. This effect is also seen in the increasing number of active nodes during evolution in Sections 5.1 and 5.2. This however is in keeping with the results found in [4] which investigated the effect of length bias in extreme cases where it was required that CGP used a very high percentage of active nodes; here the experiments were for real tasks typical of the applications of CGP.

It has been shown previously for CGP that using a large number of available nodes aids the search considerably [5]. This was thought to be because large numbers of available nodes produced a high percentage of inactive nodes aiding the search through NGD. However it was later shown in [4] that length bias causes very few inactive nodes to be present among the active nodes, weakening the effect. Interestingly, the results given in Section 6 show that when CGP is allowed a very large number of nodes there is no evolutionary pressure to use less active nodes than that used by a neutral search i.e. there is no pressure to increase smaller program sizes. Based on this result the authors propose an alternative explanation. Consider a genotype for which the phenotype consists of a small number of active nodes, any single connection gene mutation is likely to have a large effect on the operation of that phenotype. If however a genotype encodes a phenotype with a high number of active nodes, any single connection gene mutation is likely, on average, to have a much smaller effect on the operation of the overall phenotype. Therefore, using a high number of nodes creates a search space in which the fitness changes more gradually with a given number of connection gene mutations. This smoother search space is likely to be easier for evolution to navigate and hence make for a more efficient search. The reason this does not result in CGP evolving larger and larger program sizes is because these larger programs are not fitter, they are more *evolvable* and therefore there is no direct pressure to increase the program size. However, this hypothesis currently has no empirical evidence and is left for future investigation.

Another interesting result is that recurrent CGP outperformed feed-forward CGP on the six bit parity task[6]; a task which does not require recurrent connections. This is due to the fixed order of inputs applied to each circuit when evaluating the fitness function. Recurrent CGP was producing the correct outputs based on the current inputs *and* previous inputs, not on the current inputs alone. Although these evolved circuits would therefore not operate correctly as parity generators, it does show the ingenuity of evolution and how using recurrent programs for feed-forward tasks can provide an unexpected, albeit unfair, advantage.

7   Conclusion

Although this paper does not give a possible cause of CGP not exhibiting bloat, it does help disprove two previous explanations found in the literature; namely NGD and length bias. Additionally it has been shown that CGP increases the number of active nodes when a given task requires it; although this effect has limitations as shown in [4]. A new hypothesis has also been presented as to why using large numbers of available nodes is beneficial for CGP. That is, using large program sizes could help smooth out the search space making for easier navigation.

References

1. Luke, S., Panait, L.: A comparison of bloat control methods for genetic programming. Evolutionary Computation 14(3), 309–344 (2006)
2. Silva, S., Costa, E.: Dynamic limits for bloat control in genetic programming and a review of past and current bloat theories. Genetic Programming and Evolvable Machines 10(2), 141–179 (2009)

---

[6] After ten thousand generations feed-forward CGP scored an average fitness of 49.22 whereas recurrent CGP scored an average fitness of 58.62.

3. Miller, J.: What bloat? Cartesian genetic programming on Boolean problems. In: 2001 Genetic and Evolutionary Computation Conference Late Breaking Papers, pp. 295–302 (2001)
4. Goldman, B.W., Punch, W.F.: Length bias and search limitations in Cartesian genetic programming. In: Proceeding of the Fifteenth Annual Conference on Genetic and Evolutionary Computation Conference, pp. 933–940. ACM (2013)
5. Miller, J., Smith, S.: Redundancy and computational efficiency in Cartesian genetic programming. IEEE Transactions on Evolutionary Computation 10(2), 167–174 (2006)
6. Rothlauf, F., Goldberg, D.E.: Representations for Genetic and Evolutionary Algorithms. Physica-Verlag (2002)
7. Miller, J.F., Thomson, P.: Cartesian genetic programming. In: Poli, R., Banzhaf, W., Langdon, W.B., Miller, J., Nordin, P., Fogarty, T.C. (eds.) EuroGP 2000. LNCS, vol. 1802, pp. 121–132. Springer, Heidelberg (2000)
8. Miller, D.J.F. (ed.): Cartesian Genetic Programming. Springer (2011)
9. Vassilev, V.K., Miller, J.F.: The Advantages of Landscape Neutrality in Digital Circuit Evolution. In: Miller, J.F., Thompson, A., Thompson, P., Fogarty, T.C. (eds.) ICES 2000. LNCS, vol. 1801, pp. 252–263. Springer, Heidelberg (2000)
10. Yu, T., Miller, J.F.: Neutrality and the evolvability of boolean function landscape. In: Miller, J., Tomassini, M., Lanzi, P.L., Ryan, C., Tetamanzi, A.G.B., Langdon, W.B. (eds.) EuroGP 2001. LNCS, vol. 2038, pp. 204–217. Springer, Heidelberg (2001)
11. Poli, R., Langdon, W.W.B., McPhee, N.F., Koza, J.R.: A field guide to genetic programming (2008), Published via, http://lulu.com and freely available at http://www.gp-field-guide.org.uk
12. Vanneschi, L., Castelli, M., Silva, S.: Measuring bloat, overfitting and functional complexity in genetic programming. In: Proceedings of the 12th Annual Conference on Genetic and Evolutionary Computation, pp. 877–884. ACM (2010)
13. Soule, T., Heckendorn, R.B.: An analysis of the causes of code growth in genetic programming. Genetic Programming and Evolvable Machines 3(3), 283–309 (2002)
14. Langdon, W., Soule, T., Poli, R., Foster, J.: The evolution of size and shape. Advances in Genetic Programming 3, 163 (1999)
15. Kimura, M.: The neutral theory of molecular evolution. Cambridge University Press (1984)
16. McDermott, J., White, D.R., Luke, S., Manzoni, L., Castelli, M., Vanneschi, L., Jaskowski, W., Krawiec, K., Harper, R., De Jong, K., et al.: Genetic programming needs better benchmarks. In: Proceedings of the Fourteenth International Conference on Genetic and Evolutionary Computation Conference, pp. 791–798. ACM (2012)
17. Goldman, B.W., Punch, W.F.: Reducing wasted evaluations in cartesian genetic programming. In: Krawiec, K., Moraglio, A., Hu, T., Etaner-Uyar, A.Ş., Hu, B. (eds.) EuroGP 2013. LNCS, vol. 7831, pp. 61–72. Springer, Heidelberg (2013)

On Evolution of Multi-category Pattern Classifiers Suitable for Embedded Systems

Zdenek Vasicek and Michal Bidlo

Brno University of Technology,
Faculty of Information Technology,
IT4Innovations Centre of Excellence
Brno, Czech Republic
{vasicek,bidlom}@fit.vutbr.cz

Abstract. This paper addresses the problem of evolutionary design of classifiers for the recognition of handwritten digit symbols by means of Cartesian Genetic Programming. Two different design scenarios are investigated – the design of multiple-output classifier, and design of multiple binary classifiers. The goal is to evolve classification algorithms that employ substantially smaller amount of operations in contrast with conventional approaches such as Support Vector Machines. Even if the evolved classifiers do not reach the accuracy of the tuned SVM classifier, it will be shown that the accuracy is higher than 93% and the number of required operations is a magnitude lower.

1 Introduction

Classification represents one of the important problems related to the applications of pattern recognition. In general, multi-category pattern classification problem relates to the classification of a given feature vector presented on the classifier's input to one of the finite number of classes. The common approach is to reduce this problem into multiple binary (i.e. two-class) classification problems [1]. The classifier then consists of several binary classifiers identifying the presence of a specific property in the feature vector. The binary classifiers can distinguish between (i) one of the labels and the rest or (ii) between every pair of classes. The first method is known as one-versus-all approach and the classification of new instances is performed by a winner-takes-all strategy, in which the classifier with the highest output function assigns the class. The second method is denoted as one-versus-one approach. The classification is done by a max-wins voting strategy, in which every classifier assigns the instance to one of the two classes, then the vote for the assigned class is increased by one, and finally the class with the most votes determines the instance classification.

To learn a classifier, supervised machine learning is usually applied in practice. This approach involves a set of samples of annotated data; e.g. a set of images with known content. Among others, Neural Networks and Support Vector Machines (SVM) represent the most popular approaches nowadays [2].

M. Nicolau et al. (Eds.): EuroGP 2014, LNCS 8599, pp. 234–245, 2014.

There are two design objectives in practice. Typically, the goal is to optimize the reliability of the classification process, i.e. maximize the probability indicating how sure the result can be considered to be put in the (correct) class. This is done via accuracy. Another important objective is complexity of a resulting classifier which can include the number of features needed to be supplied to the classifier, the size of the classifier model, or the average number of operations required to classify a given input. This objective is important especially for mid-performance or low-performance embedded systems where the classification time plays a significant role.

Various, usually application-specific, methods for performing the classification task were published in literature. Apart from the traditional approaches, bio-inspired algorithms were applied to solve various pattern recognition problems. For example, Multiple Network Cartesian Genetic Programming was applied to the classification of mammogram images [3]. The authors demonstrated that theirs method is able to correctly classify patterns as being malignant or benign despite the fact that no pre-processing was applied. While the paper focuses on a common design objective, i.e. maximization of the classifier's accuracy, Kowaliw et al. proposed to apply Cartesian Genetic Programming (CGP) to the automated discovery of features for an image classification problem [4]. In particular, the recognition of nuclear inclusions was investigated.

Recognition of handwritten digits is a typical multi-category pattern classification problem. The feature vector can be represented by the sub-sampled digitized image of a digit to be classified, however, to improve the precision of the classifier the image is usually preprocessed (e.g. normalized, descaled, etc.). As the variety of handwriting styles represents the main challenge of the character classification, the preprocessing mitigating the variability of the input symbols is believed to be an essential part of the successful systems. However, it was shown that there can be developed methods requiring minimal amount of pre-processing before performing the recognition itself. For example, Convolutional Neural Network was introduced to cope with the variability of handwritten characters [5].

The drawback of the popular pattern recognition systems is the high amount of nontrivial, mostly floating-point, operations that have to be performed to accomplish the recognition. This disadvantage forces the designers to make a compromise and utilize simpler recognition algorithm exhibiting lower precision. The evolvable hardware community demonstrated that very efficient and sometimes also patentable implementations of physical designs can be obtained using evolutionary computation. For example, evolutionary design of non-linear image filters is a typical application in which the evolutionary approaches have a great potential to produce solutions that can compete with conventional designs or even produce significantly better results [6]. It was shown that the evolved filters exhibit better quality in terms of detail preservation, noise suppression as well as implementation cost in FPGA.

If we analyze the published evolutionary designed classifiers dealing with recognition of handwritten characters, we can identify that (i) simplified input in form of binary images is utilized, and (ii) the obtained accuracy is, unfortunately, far from accuracy of the conventional approaches. Jin applied CGP at the gate-level to the recognition of letters encoded using 5x6 bits [7]. Rehman and Khan developed a hardware system for fast recognition of handwritten characters [8]. In this case, CGP was utilized to evolve a circuit consisting of 1-bit morphological multiplexers.

The goal of this paper is to introduce a method for the evolutionary design of classifiers suitable for software as well as hardware implementation on the systems with a limited amount of available resources. The aim is to provide an approach that allows designers to construct classifiers exhibiting the trade-off between accuracy and complexity of the computation. Design of multi-category classifiers of handwritten digit symbols was chosen as a case study. This classifier represents a basic component of our target application. The evolutionary design is conducted using CGP, similarly to the aforementioned approaches. However, functional level CGP operating with 8-bit operands is applied in this paper.

The paper is organized as follows. Section 2 briefly introduces CGP. Section 3 describes the proposed method. Section 4 summarizes the experimental setup. Section 5 presents and discusses the obtained results. Concluding remarks are given in Section 6.

2   Cartesian Genetic Programming

In this work we will apply Cartesian Genetic Programming which represents a variant of genetic programming having the ability to encode arbitrary cyclic as well as acyclic graph structure using a linear string of integers [9].

2.1   Representation

To represent a candidate solution having n_i primary inputs (input variables) and n_o primary outputs, the CGP utilizes a set of nodes arranged in n_c columns and n_r rows. Each node can perform one function taken from an a priori given finite set of functions Γ. A specific interconnection of the elements gives rise to a functional circuit.

A candidate solution is encoded using a sequence of integers specifying (i) functions of the nodes, (ii) interconnection of the nodes, and (iii) connection of the primary outputs. The primary inputs as well as the output of each node in the grid have assigned a unique integer (index) . The functions of the nodes are also identified by integer values. Then, the CGP encoding consists of $n_c \cdot n_r$ triplets (i_1, i_2, f) followed by a single tuple $(o_1, o_2, \ldots, o_{n_o})$ consisting of n_o integers. Each triplet encodes the connection of one CGP node and contains: (1) input index i_1, (2) input index i_2, and (3) index of the performed function f. The input indices determine which nodes's outputs (or primary inputs) are connected to this node. The n_o-tuple at the end specifies the indices of nodes where the primary outputs are connected to. Usually, the following restriction to the interconnection is applied. Each node can be connected either to the output of a node placed in previous l columns or to one of the primary inputs.

2.2   Search Algorithm

The search in the search space is conducted using evolutionary strategy [9]. The population consists of a finite number of $\lambda + 1$ chromosomes. Usually λ is set to 4. Each chromosome encodes single candidate solution. The first population is generated randomly at the beginning of evolution. In order to create a new population, the fittest individual is selected as a new parent and by applying a point mutation operator λ offspring are generated. The steps of the evolution loop are repeated until either a satisfactory solution is found or a maximal number of generation is reached.

3   Evolutionary Design of Classifiers

Let us consider a classification problem consisting of c different categories. A single classification network that produces a single output determining index of the class the input instance belongs to (i.e. that produces a number in range 0 to $c - 1$) can be utilized. However, the classification network having c binary or c real-valued outputs is utilized in practice. In this case, each output produces a likelihood that a given input data belongs to the corresponding class. Alternatively, the problem of multi-category classification can be decomposed to several binary classifiers working in parallel respecting the aforementioned one-versus-all or one-versus-one approach.

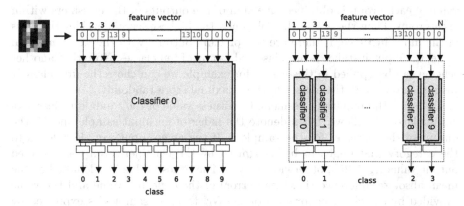

Fig. 1. Recognition of handwritten digits using (i) classifier network with ten outputs (left), and (ii) set of binary classifiers (right)

Both approaches will be evaluated in this paper. In particular we will be interested in (i) the direct evolution of a classifier circuit with c outputs, and (ii) the evolution of c binary classifiers distinguishing between one of the c classes and the rest. In both cases, the goal of the EA is to find a graph structure (circuit) that inputs a feature vector and produces single or multiple values determining the membership of an input instance to a given class. To minimize the complexity of software as well as hardware implementation of resulting classifier, we restrict the data types to 8-bit integer values only. Then, the 8-bit output value calculated by the evolved classifiers is interpreted as follows. Zero value indicates that it is definite that the input instance does not belong to a given class, while the maximum value (i.e. 255) informs that it is definite that the processed instance belongs to a given class.

Let us look in more detail at the problem of evolutionary design of handwritten digits recognizer. Let W be width and H be height of the input image. Then, the first design scenario (denoted as C10) involves a design for a single circuit with $W \times H$ inputs and ten outputs. The structure of the corresponding classifier is depicted in Figure 1. Each of the outputs provides 8-bit value. The output with the highest value determines the class.

The second design scenario (C1) consists of the following steps. Firstly, a set of binary classifiers needs to be created. This step involves to evolve single output circuits with $W \times H$ inputs. Then, the fittest solution for each class is determined. Finally, the chosen solutions form ten groups that are utilized in the resulting classifier. The structure of the classifier is shown in Figure 1.

It is supposed that a single evolutionary designed classifier will not be able to provide the required accuracy. Hence to increase the overall performance, we can combine more evolved solutions together. This principle is applicable to both design scenarios. The advantage of the evolutionary design is that each evolutionary run usually produces a solution that works on a different principle.

The class the input image belongs to is determined as follows. The output value of each group is obtained as a sum of the outputs of the classifiers within each group. Then the group that obtained the highest score identifies the class of the input instance. If there are two or more outputs with the same maximal score, the input instance is not classified to any of ten classes. Note that another scheme can be applied in this case – for example we can chose the first class or we can chose one of the classes having maximal score randomly.

To design the required classifiers, the fitness value of the candidate classifiers is calculated as follows. Let s denote the index of an input sample and C_s the output of the classifier for the sample s. If the given input sample belongs to the category that ought to be recognized by the classifier, then the expected output value $E_s = 255$, otherwise $E_s = 0$. The fitness value is calculated as the mean absolute difference (i.e. mean error) of the expected value and the value provided by the classifier for each of the N_{tr} training samples as expressed by the following equation.

$$f = \frac{1}{N_{tr}} \sum_{s=1}^{N_{tr}} |E_s - C_s|$$

The goal of the evolutionary algorithm (EA) is to minimize f. Note that the absolute value corresponds to the sum of separately calculated differences for each output for C10.

4 Experimental Setup

The classification problem is defined as follows. There are ten classes corresponding with ten handwritten digits 0–9 represented using a feature vector consisting
of 196 attributes encoded as 8-bit integers. The feature vector is obtained from
a down-sampled gray-scale image ($W = 14$, $H = 14$).

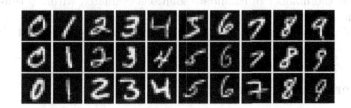

Fig. 2. Randomly picked samples from the training set of MNIST database

In order to evolve the classifiers, the MNIST database consisting of 70 000
isolated and labeled handwritten digits is utilized [10]. This database is divided
into a training set of 60 000 and a test set of 10 000 digits. The digits are
normalized to gray-scale images with 28×28 pixels. An example of some training
samples is shown in Figure 2.

Table 1. The list of functions that can be implemented in each CGP node

index	function	description	index	function	description
F0	255	constant	F6	$x \gg 2$	division by 4
F1	x	identity	F7	$x + y$	addition
F2	$255 - x$	inversion	F8	$x +^S y$	addition with saturation
F3	$max(x, y)$	maximum	F9	$(x + y) \gg 1$	average
F4	$min(x, y)$	minimum	F10	$(x > 127) ? y : x$	conditional assignment
F5	$x \gg 1$	division by 2	F11	$|x - y|$	absolute difference

The parameters of the evolutionary system were chosen as follows. The CGP
array consists of 100 (200, for first design scenario, i.e. C10) nodes arranged as a
single row. The maximal value of the l-back parameter is used. Each node can be
configured to one of the functions whose list is shown in Table 1. The functions
operate over 8-bit integers. The goal of the EA is to find a program that processes
196 8-bit input attributes and produces a single (or ten for scenario C10) 8-bit
output(s).

The evolutionary strategy utilized to search through the search space works
with the population consisting of 5 individuals. The mutation operator modifies

up to 5 randomly selected genes. For the scenario C10, 100 independent evolutionary runs were performed. For the scenario C1, 100 independent evolutionary runs were performed for each class. The evolution was stopped if the maximal number of generations ($25 \cdot 10^6$) was reached.

In order to speedup the evolution, we implemented an approach that was proposed in [11]. The experiments were carried out on a cluster of computers consisting of Intel Xeon X5670 2.4 GHz processors. The preliminary experiments showed that the number of candidate solutions evaluated within a time period increased more than 25 times. Approximate 150 candidate solutions can be evaluated within one second. The 8-bit training data occupies approx. 10 Mbytes of memory.

5   Experimental Results

Firstly, let us consider the scenario C10. The results of the evolutionary design of the classifiers are summarized in Table 2. Table contains average fitness value (i.e. the mean error per training sample as defined in Section 3), its standard deviation, and the worst and best fitness value. In order to evaluate the convergence of evolutionary design process, the parameters are shown also during the evolutionary process – i.e. at multiples of $5 \cdot 10^6$ evaluated generations. All the values are calculated from 100 independent evolutionary runs. It can be determined, that there is an exponential dependency between the number of evaluated generations and the average fitness value. The improvement in the fitness value decreases with the increasing number of evaluated generations.

Table 2. The average (f_{av}), best (f_{bst}) and worst (f_{wst}) fitness value with standard deviation (f_{std}) after a certain number of evaluated generations for C10

generations	parameter			
	f_{av}	f_{std}	f_{bst}	f_{wst}
$5.0 \cdot 10^6$	143.8	12.2	113.7	166.3
$10.0 \cdot 10^6$	132.1	13.3	96.6	156.8
$15.0 \cdot 10^6$	127.8	12.6	95.2	154.1
$20.0 \cdot 10^6$	125.2	12.7	94.4	154.1
$25.0 \cdot 10^6$	123.2	12.3	93.7	153.7

The results for the second scenario, in which the goal was to design ten binary classifiers, are summarized in Table 3 which contains average mean error and its standard deviation for each of ten classes. The average values are calculated from 100 independent evolutionary runs performed independently for each class. Similarly to the previous design scenario, we can identify the exponentially dependency between average fitness value and number of generations. We can also identify that the difficulty of the evolutionary design of a classifier depends

Table 3. The average fitness value and standard deviation (emphasized) after a certain number of evaluated generations for C1

generations	digit									
	0	1	2	3	4	5	6	7	8	9
$5.0 \cdot 10^6$	2.07	2.47	5.56	6.68	5.84	6.90	2.75	6.39	8.64	8.28
	1.29	*4.72*	*1.74*	*1.91*	*1.31*	*2.39*	*0.81*	*2.50*	*1.83*	*4.21*
$10.0 \cdot 10^6$	1.32	1.09	4.44	5.48	4.97	5.66	2.25	5.16	7.34	6.50
	0.80	*0.39*	*1.37*	*1.25*	*0.99*	*1.83*	*0.46*	*2.43*	*1.59*	*3.37*
$15.0 \cdot 10^6$	1.00	0.89	4.02	4.96	4.62	5.17	2.06	4.50	6.71	5.57
	0.77	*0.33*	*1.23*	*0.96*	*0.94*	*1.67*	*0.45*	*2.22*	*1.41*	*2.44*
$20.0 \cdot 10^6$	0.86	0.77	3.83	4.69	4.35	4.90	1.95	4.13	6.45	5.18
	0.76	*0.30*	*1.17*	*0.97*	*0.88*	*1.47*	*0.43*	*2.12*	*1.31*	*2.31*
$25.0 \cdot 10^6$	0.74	0.74	3.79	4.60	4.31	4.74	1.91	3.96	6.41	5.10
	0.51	*0.29*	*1.18*	*0.95*	*0.88*	*1.41*	*0.43*	*2.03*	*1.31*	*2.32*

on a target object whose presence should be identified. The programs evolved for classification of digits 0, 1 and 6 exhibit significantly lower mean error than those for rest of the classes.

If we compare the parameters of the evolved programs, we can identify, that the binary classifiers exhibit approx. four times lower mean error. While the average mean error per a single output is 12.5 ($f_{av}/10$) for C10, the average mean error per a single output is 3.63 (average from values in the last but one row of Table 3) for C1.

The parameters of three best evolved solutions are given in Table 4. For each evolved solution, three parameters are given: (i) fitness value calculated using

Table 4. Fitness value (f_{bst}), number of utilized operations (n_{ops}) and number of utilized attributes of feature vector (n_{fea}) of three fittest solutions

parameter	digit									
	0	1	2	3	4	5	6	7	8	9
f_{bst1}	0.10	0.17	1.47	2.10	2.30	1.91	0.54	1.27	3.44	2.81
n_{ops1}	58	72	75	67	77	61	68	78	81	76
n_{fea1}	37	43	41	43	54	41	42	49	51	48
f_{bst2}	0.10	0.20	1.86	2.18	2.81	2.32	0.84	1.40	3.93	2.90
n_{ops2}	38	58	85	76	69	82	58	83	77	75
n_{fea2}	25	36	54	49	44	40	36	52	53	48
f_{bst3}	0.10	0.26	2.07	2.82	2.88	2.42	0.90	1.49	4.18	3.01
n_{ops3}	48	47	76	79	65	69	76	76	70	81
n_{fea3}	33	32	50	49	45	44	50	45	41	47

the training set, (ii) the number of operations, i.e. utilized nodes employed in the computation, and (iii) the number of features that are involved in computation. The number of the employed features corresponds with the number of primary inputs utilized by CGP nodes. If we compare the evolved solutions for a certain class (i.e. the same digit), we can identify that different programs consisting of various number of operations and utilizing different number of features are employed. It confirms the well-known feature of evolutionary design that each evolutionary run has the ability to produce different solution. In our case it represents a benefit, as this could be beneficial when an ensemble of classifiers is assembled.

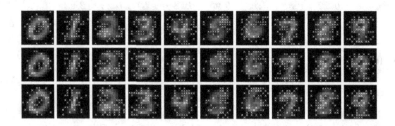

Fig. 3. Utilization of feature vector's attributes by the best evolved binary classifiers detecting the presence of one class. The attributes that contribute to the classifier's output are marked using crosses. The digits on the background were obtained by averaging all the training data for a given digit.

Figure 3 shows which features are utilized by the best evolved classifiers whose parameters are summarized in Table 4. To obtain the coverage we evaluated the best evolved solutions. It can be seen that the arrangement of the features follows the shape of the digits except of digit 5. The evolution probably determined that the attributes situated in upper right part of the image sufficiently determine

```
def digit0_bst2(f):
    v0 = F11(f124, f82); v1 = F3(f116, f115); v2 = F3(v0, f157); v3 = F4(f101, f120)
    v4 = F8(f81, v1); v5 = F5(f145); v6 = F8(f144, v2); v7 = F3(v5, v6)
    v8 = F8(f105, f170); v9 = F10(v7, v4); v10 = F11(f101, v3); v11 = F3(f119, f91)
    v12 = F9(v10, f89); v13 = F4(v11, v9); v14 = F3(f19, v8); v15 = F9(f127, v20)
    v16 = F8(v15, v14); v17 = F4(v12, v16); v18 = F11(v9, v13); v19 = F11(v17, v12)
    v20 = F3(f36, f108); v21 = F4(v18, v19); v22 = F8(v21, v21); v23 = F4(f95, v22)
    v24 = F4(v20, f93); v25 = F10(v22, v9); v26 = F4(v25, v24); v27 = F7(v26, v26)
    v28 = F8(f72, f67); v29 = F3(v27, v23); v30 = F3(v28, f65); v31 = F0()
    v32 = F4(v30, v29); v33 = F8(v32, v32); v34 = F8(v33, v33); v35 = F8(v34, v34)
    v36 = F8(v35, v35); v37 = F10(v36, v31)
    return v37
```

Fig. 4. One of the best evolved classifiers for classification of digit 0

Table 5. Parameters of C10 classifiers constructed using the fittest N evolved classifiers

classifier	N	n_{ops}	n_{fea}	n_{hit}	n_{miss}	n_{uncls}	precision	recall
C10-1	1	171	78	7 709	1 481	810	0.842	0.771
C10-3	3	514	128	8 410	1 537	53	0.855	0.841
C10-5	5	874	152	8 484	1 476	40	0.861	0.848
C10-7	7	1 244	161	8 740	1 238	22	0.881	0.874
C10-9	9	1 619	167	8 727	1 258	15	0.880	0.873
C10-15	15	2 716	170	8 885	1 111	4	0.892	0.888

this digit. The rest of the attributes probably helps to improve the precision. One should expect that digit 0 could be identified using a few attributes situated near the center of the image detecting the presence of hole. Evolutionary designed classifiers, however, somehow follow the shape of the digit.

Figure 4 shows structure of the evolved classifier for the classification of digit 0 exhibiting the fitness value f_{bst2}. The discovered program consists of 38 operations. It means that 38 CGP nodes were active while the rest of the nodes (i.e. 62) were not involved in computation of the output value. As it can be determined from code or image in second row and first column of Figure 3, the evolved classifier utilizes the knowledge of 25 attributes. The attributes of the feature vector are denoted as f_i, where $0 \leq i \leq 195$. Functions F3 (maximum), F4 (minimum) and F8 (saturated addition) represent the most frequent operations involved in the computation.

5.1 Evaluation of the Evolved Classifiers

In order to evaluate quality of the evolved classifiers and compare the proposed design scenarios, the discovered solutions were executed on test part of MNIST database consisting of 10 000 samples. The results obtained for the first design scenario - design of a classifier with 10 outputs - are summarized in Table 5. The first row includes parameters of the best evolved solution, the rest of the rows contains parameters of classifiers constructed as combination of N best evolved classifiers. The output of each utilized classifier is combined according to the description given in Section 3. Note that a relative strict approach was chosen; if two or more outputs exhibit the same highest output value, the sample is categorized as unclassifiable.

Table 5 includes the number of operations (n_{ops}) and utilized attributes of a feature vector (n_{fea}) involved in the computation, the number of correctly and incorrectly classified samples (n_{hits}, n_{miss}), the number of unclassifiable samples (n_{uncls}), precision and recall. Note that the precision is the ability of the classifier not to label as positive a sample that is negative, while the recall is the ability of the classifier to find all the positive samples. The accuracy (hit rate) of the best evolved C10 classifier denoted as C10-1 is 77.1%. The average accuracy calculated from all of 100 evolutionary runs is 65.99%. Unfortunately,

Table 6. Parameters of C1 classifiers constructed using the fittest N evolved classifiers

classifier	N	n_{ops}	n_{fea}	n_{hit}	n_{miss}	n_{uncls}	precision	recall
C1-1	10	688	149	8 606	490	904	0.946	0.861
C1-3	30	2 126	173	9 190	581	229	0.940	0.919
C1-5	50	3 511	180	9 289	589	122	0.940	0.929
C1-7	70	4 944	186	9 343	587	70	0.941	0.934
C1-9	90	6 337	188	9 358	583	59	0.941	0.936
C1-15	150	10 489	191	9 359	618	23	0.938	0.936

the accuracy increases only slightly with the increasing number of the utilized classifiers N. If $N = 15$, the accuracy is about 4.7% higher than accuracy of single evolved classifier; the number of operations increases approx. five times.

Table 6 summarizes the parameters for the second design scenario - design of binary classifiers. Note that the number of utilized classifiers N is in multiples of 10, because 10 evolved binary classifiers must be combined together to obtain a complete multi-class classifier network. Comparing to the parameters given in Table 5, the number of employed operations increased substantially. Single C1-1 classifier requires approx. the same amount of operations as C10-15 consisting of 15 instances. However, the classifiers constructed as a combination of binary classifiers exhibit significantly better accuracy. The classifier C1-5 combining 50 binary classifiers provides the accuracy of 92.9%. This accuracy is achievable as the evolved binary classifiers exhibit near 98% hit rate in average.

To compare the results with conventional approach, SVM with RBF kernel was applied to the same training data. The obtained accuracy was 98.21%. The parameters of SVM was chosen as follows $C = 2^3$, $\gamma = 2^{-5}$. The model of SMV was obtained using libSVM. The values of the attributes were normalized to the range (0,1). The best SVM parameters C and γ were obtained using Cross-validation and Grid-search approach. Even if it is hard to compare the number of operations directly, we can make an estimate based on the number of utilized SVs and number of nonzero coefficients. The trained SVM model uses 7 477 SVs, and contains 441 907 coefficients in total. From this point of view, the proposed classifiers require only a fraction of operations to determine result. Moreover, they do not need to normalize the input data to produce a result.

6   Conclusion

We presented an evolutionary method for the design of multi-category classifiers by means of CGP. Two different design scenarios were investigated: the evolutionary design of (i) a classifier with 10 outputs and (ii) set of binary classifiers. The goal was to evolve programs for the recognition of handwritten digit symbols that require reasonable amount of computation resources. To improve the accuracy, the possibility of combination of more classifiers was investigated.

Even if the evolved classifiers do not reach the accuracy of the tuned SVM classifier, it was shown that the accuracy is higher than 93%. However, the number of required operations and their complexity represents one of the main advantage of the designed classifiers. While the SVM classifier utilizes hundreds thousands of floating point operations, our classifiers use a few thousands of simple 8-bit operations. It means that the evolved classifiers are more advantageous for software as well as hardware realization.

In overall, the proposed method can be considered as successful. As we didn't investigate multiple criteria during the selection of the best evolved solutions, we believe that the accuracy should be even better. This represents potential objective for the future research.

Acknowledgments. This work was supported by the Czech science foundation project 14-04197S.

References

1. Duan, K.-B., Keerthi, S.S.: Which is the best multiclass SVM method? An empirical study. In: Oza, N.C., Polikar, R., Kittler, J., Roli, F. (eds.) MCS 2005. LNCS, vol. 3541, pp. 278–285. Springer, Heidelberg (2005)
2. Cortes, C., Vapnik, V.: Support-vector networks. Machine Learning 20(3), 273–297 (1995)
3. Völk, K., Miller, J.F., Smith, S.L.: Multiple network CGP for the classification of mammograms. In: Giacobini, M., et al. (eds.) EvoWorkshops 2009. LNCS, vol. 5484, pp. 405–413. Springer, Heidelberg (2009)
4. Sekanina, L., Harding, L.S., Banzhaf, W., Kowaliw, T.: Image Processing and CGP. Natural Computing Series, pp. 181–215. Springer (2011)
5. LeCun, Y., Bottou, L., Bengio, Y., Haffner, P.: Gradient-based learning applied to document recognition. Proc. of the IEEE 86(11), 2278–2324 (1998)
6. Vasicek, Z., Bidlo, M., Sekanina, L., Glette, K.: Evolutionary design of efficient and robust switching image filters. In: Proc. of the 2011 NASA/ESA Conference on Adaptive Hardware and Systems, pp. 192–199. IEEE Computer Society (2011)
7. Jin, W., Bin-bin, T., Chang-hao, P., Gai-hui, L.: Statistical method-based evolvable character recognition system. In: IEEE International Symposium on Industrial Electronics, pp. 804–808 (2009)
8. Rehman, A., Khan, G.M.: Polymorphic circuit design for speedy handwritten character recognition using cartesian genetic programming. In: Proc. of the 2011 Frontiers of Information Technology, pp. 79–84. IEEE Computer Society, Washington, DC (2011)
9. Miller, J.F.: Cartesian Genetic Programming. Springer (2011)
10. LeCun, Y., Cortes, C., Burges, C.J.C.: The MNIST database, http://yann.lecun.com/exdb/mnist
11. Vašíček, Z., Slaný, K.: Efficient phenotype evaluation in cartesian genetic programming. In: Moraglio, A., Silva, S., Krawiec, K., Machado, P., Cotta, C. (eds.) EuroGP 2012. LNCS, vol. 7244, pp. 266–278. Springer, Heidelberg (2012)

Author Index